The Sure Line

BERYL NEW

DEDICATION

This collection of thirty-one stories set in a small coastal community is dedicated to everyone who has ever survived one of life's storms and lived to celebrate the victory.

***

Navigating inherent racial issues, spirituality, and life's episodes is like skirting the ocean current that hits the coastal shore thousands of times every day.

Shore lines change based on many factors: wind, sun, moon, impending storms, and daily weather patterns. More powerful than the elements which impact a shore line is the Word of God, The <u>Sure</u> Line.   It never changes. The Book of Wisdom contains affirmations, directives, and warnings that have ageless applications.

"Trust in the Lord with all thine heart; and lean not unto thine own understanding. In all thy ways acknowledge Him, and He shall direct thy paths." Proverbs 3:5 & 6, KJV

CONTENTS

BERYL NEW

ACKNOWLEDGMENTS

I honor God for the gifts He has entrusted to me. I pray that these gifts will inspire and bless others.

I thank God for the people He has placed in my life, for each of them has inspired and blessed me.

I encourage you to read a chapter a day. It may take you about a month. Let these stories minister to you. And, always remember that the surest knowledge in the world is the Word of God. Every line discloses His unconditional love for us. He gave us His everything, His Son. When we accept Him, we receive everything -- everlasting, abundant life. To truly know this is Wisdom, and he who has Wisdom has everything!

I'm Gonna Lay Down My Burdens

"The fear of the Lord is the beginning of knowledge: but fools despise wisdom and instruction." Proverbs 1:7

*

"God! I hate this traffic!" Florence hit the steering wheel hard with her right fist. "I don't know why I have to go to this stupid meeting anyway! This is <u>his</u> job, not mine!" Reaching around to grab the back of her head, she knocked her designer sunglasses off. "Oooh, there goes that headache again!" The glasses landed on the floor of the passenger side. She bent down to pick them up. A car horn blared. "What?" she screamed, frowning as she sat back up. In her rearview mirror, her eyes made contact with the driver behind her. His hands were up in the air. "What?" she screamed at him, frustrated. The cars in front of her started to move. "Dang, is he in a hurry!" He honked at her again

"It's not my fault!" She screamed at him in the mirror. Anger flooded her. "Everybody's mad at me! My husband's mad at me! Those old church ladies are mad at me! Now, some guy in a beat up old car is mad at me. Even <u>I'm</u> mad at me! I'm so sick of it all!" Traffic began to move. Florence felt defeated, ready to collapse in tears. How much her life had changed in the past year! She never thought she would marry after what happened to her.

Growing up in church, she knew what it meant to be "taught right". Grandma was the church mother, so Florence and her sister were at every "womens'" meeting. Refreshments were usually chips and dip, cookies, and watery cherry Kool-Aid. It was usually warm. Sometimes, it made you want to throw up, especially if it was hot in the church dining room. If one of the mothers felt like baking that day, or had some leftover because no one at their house wanted to eat it, there would be some cake. Usually, it was that kind with the homemade meringue frosting that was half melted by the time it was served.

They were sure to talk about everything from skirt lengths to "that Jezebel spirit". Before they started, Florence knew everything they were going to say. By the time the meeting ended, she would feel guilty and repent for things she had never done, but maybe thought about doing. She wanted to get married after they talked about what a wife should do, but she was afraid that no man would want her to be the kind of woman they were saying she, and all of the other teenage girls, had to be. Before the meeting was over, all were repenting and vowing to never kiss a boy...again.

Her sister, Rosemary, had been the first of the teens to officially date. Brady was a Marine, originally from California. He was stationed at the base located a half-hour from Tisdale Beach. Brady was really his last name, but that's what everybody called him. He was really good-looking, but he was also sincerely saved. He spent Sunday afternoons with the pastor. All they did was eat and talk about the Bible. Then, he would come to the Sunday evening service and preach a message in the testimony service. All of the girls were in love with him; all except Rosemary. Rosemary was in college. She wasn't interested in boys, or at least that's what she said. What church members didn't know, though, was that Brady and Rosemary were writing letters to each other all throughout the week, but then acting like they didn't know each other on Sundays.

All of that changed when Brady got orders to deploy to fight in the Gulf War. Brady was afraid he might not make it back. So, they talked to Pastor. He married them the next weekend. When Brady left, Rosemary stayed in town to finish school. Florence and Rosemary would read Brady's letters when they arrived. Rosemary would read Florence the letters she was sending back to him. Florence soon became an intimate member of their relationship. Sometimes when she would tell Rosemary what to write, it seemed like she was really the one writing to Brady and he was responding to her. When he would describe how intensely hot it was in the desert, or the pranks he and his buddies would play on each other, she felt like she was right there watching it all, suffering and laughing along with him.

She admired Brady for his courage and his ability to be strong when he was afraid. His vivid details about narrowly escaping IEDs were exciting. She felt pride when he bashfully shared the compliments that his sergeant gave him in front of the squadron when they awarded his citations and medals. He was collecting quite a few!

Whenever anyone talked about the war or she saw pictures of the fighting on television, she thought about Brady and about how glad she would be when she could finally see him with her own eyes and know that he was home safely.

One morning, they received the word. Brady was going to be sent back to the states in thirty days! Rosemary was so excited! She and Florence began to plan for his return. They started apartment shopping and found a nice little one-bedroom near the advertising office where Rosemary was now working. It was a really cute little neighborhood in the southwest part of town, close to the beach and some of the Old Town tourist spots. Brady would love it, even if they had to furnish it with second-hand things. But, as long as her man was back, they would make it work!

Truth be told, Florence was just as excited as Rosemary to see Brady again! He was her brother-in-law, but he was more. During the two years he was gone, she had been pretending more and more that Brady was <u>her</u> husband. Every day, she slipped deeper and deeper into an imaginary world where she and Brady were married, sharing exciting, loving times throughout the day and night. He was totally committed to her happiness: protecting her, parading her, loving her. And, Rosemary was nowhere in the picture!

Pastor's nephew had come down from Boston. He had always felt a call to the ministry. So, he moved to Tisdale Beach to be mentored by his uncle. James Patterson was a solid young man and the church mothers loved him! He wasn't all that handsome; but he wasn't ugly, either. A couple of the teenage girls would giggle whenever he would say something to them, but he never dated anyone or even acted like he was interested in any of them. He was the kind of young man that girls felt safe around, like a big brother. Tall, dark brown skinned, just a little on the plump side with a funny personality, he seemed like a man who would be a great pastor, father, and husband.

The blare of a car horn shook her from her reverie. "Oh no! I missed my exit! Now they'll really talk about me, late as I'm going to be!" Florence began to sweat, even though cool conditioned air blasted through the car vents. She looked anxiously for an exit ramp. "Shoot! This is going to take all day!"

Suddenly, a car in the right lane sped up and got in front of her. "That's just the break I need," thought Florence as she moved swiftly over into the right lane and quickly joined the flow of traffic exiting the freeway onto Forest Street. Going down two blocks, she took another right. In her mirror, she saw the man who had honked and motioned his exasperation at her on the freeway still behind her. His eyes connected with hers in her rearview mirror. They were dark, but somewhat familiar. "What is up with him?" she thought. "Yeah, this is all I need today, some crazy nut with road rage following me to the church mothers' tea." A wave of hysteria began to roll upward in a desperate laugh. "Lord, I did not sign up for all of this! What happened to working out my <u>own</u> soul's salvation? Why would You pick me, of all people, to be a pastor's wife?"

Metropolitan Community Church was a nice, friendly group of saints. They had been a church family for more than forty years. When Grandma was a middle-aged mother in the church, the man Florence grew to know as "Pastor" retired from the Marines as the base chaplain. Not long after that, the former pastor died suddenly. Pastor had been coming to the church from time to time when he wasn't ministering on the base and developed a good relationship with the former pastor. He had even preached for him a few times. When the former pastor died, his wife asked Pastor to give the eulogy. The church members fell in love with him and asked him to become their new pastor. Timing was perfect. Within two weeks, he and his family moved into the parsonage, beginning his long career as pastor of Metropolitan.

Florence and Rosemary had come to live with their Grandma that same summer. Supposedly, that arrangement was for the summer only. But, their parents split up while they were gone. Their dad moved back to North Carolina, and their mother got a job working long hours in a town close to the one where they grew up. Grandma said she would keep them so they wouldn't have to raise themselves. Pastor was the only pastor Florence ever really knew until she married one herself.

Pastor didn't bug Rosemary too much. It was like he already knew that she wouldn't get herself into any trouble. But it seemed like he stayed on Florence! He was always talking to her, always preaching at her, always telling her about how much God loved her and had a plan for her life, but she was going to have to "sell out to the flesh" and accept the fact that Christ loved her and there was nothing she could do about it!

"What is it?" she asked herself in exasperation. "Do I have a sign on my back that says – 'Caution: Sinner on Board'?" Florence turned into the church parking lot. "Well, I guess the Bible does say that you will know them by their fruit. I probably look like a crabapple tree." She secured the gear shift into "Park" and turned off the ignition. "They gotta keep working on me! Oh, Lord," she said as she looked at the cars in the lot, "they're all here, and I am totally late. Well, this will just give them something else to talk about."

Florence reached over the console to the back seat and grabbed her purse. Out of the corner of her right eye, she saw that the beat-up car that had been following her was now parking on the other side of the street. The driver had pulled in under the shade of a tall oak tree, so it was hard to see from her car window who he was or what he looked like. She got nervous. "What is this guy up to?"

Tugging her purse between the seats, her right arm flew back into her face, knocking her sunglasses off again. "Lord, are you trying to tell me something about these glasses?" she asked loudly. Leaving them on the floor of the backseat where they had fallen, she picked up the store-bought peach pie that she had repackaged under aluminum foil to look like she had baked it. When she lifted it from the front passenger seat, she noticed that the pan had sweated and left a round, pie pan-shaped wet spot on her upholstery. "Oh no! Now I'm messing up my car fooling with these people! Lord, help me!"

With her hands full and her frustration level at the boiling point, she balanced her stuff and her attitude and adroitly slid her slender body under the steering wheel and out of the car. Placing the sweaty pie pan on the hood of her baby blue BMW, she power-locked the doors and dropped her keys in her purse. Suddenly, she sensed someone behind her. "I shouldn't have locked my doors!" she thought, beginning to panic.

Florence swiftly turned around. "Who are you? Why are you following me?" She locked eyes with the strange man. Glaring at him, he glared right back.

"Do you know what you did back there?" he demanded.

"What are you talking about? I was driving down the freeway and you honked at <u>me</u>! I didn't do anything to you! You're the one who harassed me and followed me!" She poked her long, impeccably-manicured pink polished right index fingernail toward his quivering, sweat-dripping nose. He did not appear the least bit intimidated

Stepping toward her he said, "Lady, you cut me off when you got on the freeway! I had been trying to get over and you came up on my left side and squeezed in, almost making me wreck into you! You acted like you didn't even see me, you were so busy talking to yourself. Looking like you were in a trance. What's the matter with you? Are you on some drugs or something? Good thing you're going to a church. You need some help." Even though he was delivering an angry rant, he was talking in a clipped and controlled manner, with his voice down low.

"Well, I didn't wreck into you, did I? Though I'm not sure how you would be able to tell, looking at your car!" Her voice grew louder and more shrill with each sentence.

Florence noticed that his face did not register any emotion, just his voice. "What is up with this guy?" she thought. "Maybe I need to just walk away and go on into the church. He might be a psycho!" Florence began to walk toward the church. Her hands were full and she was beginning to get more nervous. She tried to walk straight and with purpose to throw him off, but her legs kept wobbling and the tiny heel tips on her stilettos kept slipping inward on the hot pavement.

He moved quickly to catch up with her. Before she knew it, he was right in her left ear, talking quietly and evenly as he walked right alongside her. She could feel his hot breath on her left earlobe. It felt like the tip of his sweaty nose was touching her hair. "You don't even care, do you?" he said in a serious, nasally tone. "Do you know where I was going? Do you understand that I was under a time crunch? Now, it's too late. Because of you. How are you going to make this right? I can't get that time back!" He gripped her left arm firmly with his right hand, stopping her in her tracks.

"Get your hands off of me!" she hissed, snatching her arm out of his grasp. She turned toward him, angry. "Who are you? What do you think you can do to me about something that happened thirty minutes ago?" She began to breathe heavily. "Okay, I'm sorry! I should not have been rushing to get to this stupid church tea. I should not have been talking to myself. I should have seen you in my right mirror. I should have stopped and let you on the freeway in front of me. I should have let you hit my BMW even though you wouldn't have been able to pay to repair it. I shouldn't have gotten out of bed today. I should have died a long time ago so that I couldn't hurt anyone else in my life ever again. And, I should have made my own peach pie so that I would have felt worse for what I'm about to do!"

Turning quickly, Florence smashed the pie in his face and then ran as fast as she could to the side door of the church. She began to beat on the heavy wooden door with both fists, kicking it with her right foot, hoping someone would hear and hurry to open up the door. "Open the door, open the door!" she hollered as loudly as she could. She was afraid to turn around to see where the man was, scared that he may have cleared his eyes and was on his way to attack her. For the first time in her life, she felt like she was about to get in trouble for something she didn't intend to do. Usually, she agreed she should be in trouble for something she knew she had done when she hadn't cared about the consequences she was sure to face. This time, though, something was definitely different.

When her sister found out she had seduced her husband to sleep with her when he returned from the Gulf War, she knew that she had done wrong and her sister had a reason to be hurt and mad at her. It wasn't about both her and Brady knowing better. It wasn't even about the fact that she waited until he was drunk to start messing with him. It was all her plan and Brady shouldn't have been blamed at all. Shoot, he really didn't even remember much about what happened. It was about her, once again, cooking up a whole new pot of mess in her all-too-easy-to-slip-into emotional fantasy kitchen where what she wanted life to be was how it was – no matter what her reality looked like and how negatively her fantasies affected others, especially those who really loved her.

So, Rosemary and Brady had moved to California to get a new start on their relationship, and she lost yet another leg on the stool that she had grown accustomed to holding her up. Mama had died ten years back from alcohol poisoning. She wasn't sure where her Daddy was, somewhere in North Carolina. He had stopped writing when she was about eight years old. Grandma died two months before she got married. Pastor died during the winter that same year that Grandma died. Talk about a motherless child! She often wondered why God left her here to keep messing up. "Don't You need me up there too?" she had prayed when Grandma was being lowered into the ground.

It was unseasonably cold that April morning. Standing out at the cemetery with the wind blowing pale new leaves off of the trees onto the brown, frost-glazed ground, she remembered noticing how everything just looked gray and crystallized. What an odd combination, she had thought.

A color so plain and awful combined with a prismatic feature so sparkly with the potential to be so beautiful! Kind of like death and life. Only, she wasn't used to seeing the life anymore.

She hadn't realized that she was still kicking the door. Her big toe throbbed, but she could barely feel the pain. A sob rose from her stomach. Her knees began to feel weak. "What if no one hears me," she thought. Panic swept up her neck and her ears started to tingle with heat. Suddenly, the door swung open. Florence collapsed into the arms of a mother.

"Sister Patterson! What is wrong with you?"

"That man back there! He's chasing me!"

"What man?"

"That man!" Florence spun around, pointing desperately. She saw nothing but the remnants of a peach pie splattered across the parking lot in front of her car. A piece of aluminum foil was covered by an upside-down pie pan, one corner waving at her in the wind. The man was gone.

"Sister Patterson, are you feeling all right?" The mother looked her deep in the eyes. Her compassion and concern were evident, her eyebrows raised as she spoke very slowly.

"Yes, I'm okay!" Florence screamed. "Look, there was a strange man who followed me from the freeway all the way over here. He kept honking and honking at me, and when I got here he parked that junk car over there..." Florence pointed across the street. There was no car under the tree. A yellow cat with an extremely long tail walked with leisurely aloofness toward the curb and sat down in the grass swishing its tail, almost exactly where the car had been parked.

"He was there," Florence said weakly, as if she was trying to convince herself. "He was right there!" Her pink polished right index finger pointed emphatically at the cat, punctuating the last two words with frenzied emphasis. The cat looked at her with lazy hazel eyes and continued to swish its tail back and forth, back and forth.

Florence slid into the door, her knees giving way to the emotional weakness that was now enveloping her like the fog used to do on the beach when she would slip away when reality was becoming too uncomfortable. She loved the ocean. She loved the smell of the salty water and the rank fishy odor that was an odd combination of comfort and repulsion. The water was nonjudgmental. It always seemed to welcome her, especially when people were mad at her. It blanketed her in its warm, thick, comforting fog. It hid her from the people she figured would want to hurt her in the same ways she had hurt them.

She could hear voices and laughter. She could smell the sweet, warm scent of fresh baked goods. She could feel the inviting coolness of the deep, inner recesses of the building. As the mother's arm slid around her waist, she suppressed the urge to bury her nose into a warm shoulder and cry and cry. Cry away the fear and the shame. Cry herself back to a time when everything was all right; when her mother wasn't drinking and her father wasn't staying away for days; when she and Rosemary hid because they were playing hide-and-seek and not because they didn't want their Daddy to beat them like they could hear him beating their mother. Then, they could let him find them when he was done and he and Mama were kissing so that the girls would know that everything was all right. But, it wasn't. And she wasn't. What was worse, she couldn't remember when things were ever all right.

"That's why Pastor told James to marry me," she thought, as she felt consciousness slipping. "Pastor promised he wouldn't leave until he knew I was all right. But, I never got all right. So, he told James to marry me so that he could look out for me. Take care of the poor and needy. And I'm so needy!"

"What you say, Sister Patterson?" The mother's voice sounded fuzzy and far away. It sounded like the old telephone did when there was rain and lightning and thunder and Grandma told her not to use the phone but she did anyway because she <u>wanted</u> to get struck by lightning and she thought the static in the line would come through that thick black cloth-covered cord and go through her ear and down her body and around to her heart and just kill her quick.

"Y'all, come quick! Help me! Oh Lord, God help us! Somebody call an ambulance! Y'all come help me! We need to pray! Hurry up! Sister Patterson just fainted! She needs some help!"

Like a Tree Planted By the Waters, I Shall Not Be Moved!

"He keepeth the paths of judgment, and preserveth the way of the saints." Proverbs 2:8

*

This cove that had become his favorite. Even though there were close to one hundred of these coves, he had seen nearly a quarter of them and this one was the most impressive of all. The trees were what made it special, he thought. They were tall trees with trunks that were bare two-thirds of the way up and topped with rich green leaves and strong sturdy branches. They reminded him of tall men with full heads of hair.

Men who looked like that had raised him and taught him what it meant to be Godly, loving, responsible heads of their households. They were preachers, all of them. Their greatest messages, though, were preached more in their daily walks of faith than with their powerful oratorical skills. Make no mistake, these men could preach! They would preach under a strong anointing until sinners would cry out to be saved and saints would shout, "Lord, help me!" Then, they would love so genuinely that children would laugh as they played "ring-around-the-rosy" while clinging to their long black pant legs, circling around them until they became dizzy and fell out, tangled at their feet.

Even as a child growing up in Massachusetts, he had enjoyed the outdoors. No matter the season, his mother knew she could always find him in the woods near their house when she could find him nowhere else. There he would be, kneeling on the thick, mossy underbrush in front of a large round tree stump, lips moving silently as he was lost in ethereal communion with the Creator. Creatures near him seemed to join in the worship. In their sanctuary with James as their leader, when he bowed, every squirrel became still. When he stood and lifted his hands in worship, the trees began to sway, their arms joining in the praise. When he raised his large bass voice to sing the hymns of the old church, the birds too broke forth in their ritualistic tunes.

He knew as a small child that he had received the same call as his patriarchs. He was a preacher, a pastor. He was to bear the cross of ministry, to care for God's flock, to preach the Word and be instant, in season and out of season, to give an account to anyone who asked about the hope that he possessed. He often told his father, "I heard God call my name. I will never forget that day. He said, 'James, will you work for Me?' I thought about the story of Samuel when he was at Eli's house. I said, 'Yes, Lord, I will work for You.' I don't have to decide what I want to be when I grow up. I know I want to be a preacher."

Tonight, he sat on the fallen limb of driftwood that was his chosen place to meditate and thought about the last time he talked with his mother. She was a strong .woman who birthed seven sons, but he was the only one who survived to young adulthood. Three of his brothers died at birth. Actually, one lived for about half of the birth day and then died. The doctors said they all had congenital heart disorder. The brother who was ten months older than him died in his sleep at three months of age. That death had taken a great toll on his mother, yet she decided to try right away to have another baby. James was born, and she claimed him as her gift from God, sent to comfort her heart.

He remembered that she described him as "strapping". He always chuckled at that word, and she always used it when she told his life story. He never got a whipping in his life, but she used the word "strap" to describe him. He wondered if she thought he might die if he ever got a whipping. She probably did not want to risk that. Yet, he knew that he had never been a child to give her or his father a minute's trouble. He recalled wanting to disobey a couple of times. But, on each occasion he thought he heard a soft voice saying, "No." It could have been his grandmother. She was half Cherokee, a very stoic woman who never said much, but she always watched. Yet, it sounded more like a man's voice. He later realized that it was the Holy Spirit guiding him even at a young age.

The last brother died when he was fifteen. That was the worst memory of his life. He was two years younger than James. They had grown up as best friends along with being close brothers. They were their parents pride and joy, and people often thought they were twins. John was as tall as James and they looked nearly identical. Their father called them his "Sons of Zebedee". They were invited to preach together at many churches in the Boston area, beginning when John was twelve and James was fourteen. For two years, they were introduced as the "Preaching Sons of Zebedee" and the offerings they received for their dual ministry were placed in a special savings account so that they would one day be able to go to Bible college, something their preaching predecessors had never been able to do.

One summer afternoon, their father came home with some exciting news. One of his fellow pastors was also a teacher at a Bible college in New Jersey. They were having a summer camp meeting and offering scholarships for up-and-coming young ministers to attend. There would be plenty of church, preaching, fellowship, and training. He wanted to offer two of the scholarships to James and John.

James recalled the camp as one of the most inspiring experiences of his lifetime. The sound of the choir in the midst of the powerful organ-playing, the congregation clapping, and the feet stomping roused his spirit in ways he had never felt before. This is what it felt like to be moved by the Spirit! After service, the young people would fellowship on the camp grounds. One of the young brothers and his family sold hamburgers and ice cold soda, which went very fast as soon as the last "Amen" was sung! Children chased one another across the grounds with ice cream in cones melting and running down between their fingers. This attracted dirt even faster on their faces and hands, so they took pleasure in hugging and kissing everyone they could on their way to be scrubbed in the rickety outdoor bathrooms.

Somehow, he and John were selected out of all of the young preachers to bring the message on Friday night. They prayed and fasted, and God sent a great Word. The altar was full of young people who prayed and cried as they gave their hearts to God. Both he and John, along with many of the other young ministers, prayed with all of those who had come forward. The feeling of exhilaration he felt after that service was one that he had never known. Truly, this camp meeting had been designed by God to confirm their calling and propel them into a ministry of evangelism in partnership. As he went to sleep that night, praying and thanking God for such a successful night of ministry, he felt like the future was open to them and God was rewarding his parents for all of the sorrow and loss they had experienced.

He was in a deep sleep. He recalled faintly hearing someone call his name while he was preaching a fiery message. As he woke up, he remembered saying the words, "And behold, I come quickly."

"James!"

"Johnny? What is wrong?"

"James, I'm having a tough time breathing. I think I might be allergic to something I ate. I don't feel good."

He sat up and turned on the light. He moved toward John's bed and looked closely. John looked very pale.

"Brother, what's wrong? How are you feeling?" He recalled how cold John felt when he touched his cheek. Immediately, he went to the hallway and hollered for help. Suddenly, John began to wheeze and gasp for air. James ran back to him and sat him up in the bed. "John! John! Take it easy! Calm down. Get some breath!"

James propped some pillows behind John's head and sat him up straight. By then, John was severely gasping. James ran to the pitcher to fill a glass of water. While he was pouring the water, he could hear John faintly cry, "James, James, James…"

"I'm coming, Brother!" He dropped the half-filled glass and ran back to his brother. Tears started to flow. Even as he recalled this experience, watching the waves gently lap the shore, coming closer and closer to the tips of his shoes, tears began to gather in the wells of his eyes. "No matter how long ago it has been, no matter how much I have thought about this, no matter how well I know that there was nothing more I could do, the pain still rises from my bowels to meet my cheeks."

By the time the counselor made it to the room, John had gone to meet his reward. God's will was complete in his life. He had dedicated himself to the Lord, to be a witness, to win souls to the Kingdom. His work was done. Now, James knew he had to work on, twice as hard, for the both of them.

So, he recalled the words his mother had spoken to him just a few days before she went on to celebrate eternal life with John and her five other sons who were at rest with the Lord. She had said, "James, you have been better to me than ten sons. I now know why God took all of your brothers and left you for me. It is because I would not have been able to stand my life had I gotten seven times the love I have gotten from you. When you meet the woman that you choose to marry, make sure that she is the one who can bear your great love."

He truly had not understood those words until recently. In fact, he had chuckled just a bit when she said this. He thought that she may have been referring to something physical. But, when he looked into her eyes, he knew that she was puzzled at his reaction. She was speaking of something deeply spiritual and had assumed that he understood. So, he decided that he did not want to disappoint her by asking her to explain. He just hid those words in his heart, as Mary had done when God spoke something unexplainably deep and spiritual to her. And now, he finally understood.

Just as Christ bore the sins of the world on his cross, James had borne Florence's sins on his. Not that he could save the world or anyone in it. But, he had been given the assignment of carrying the cross of responsibility for the woman who became his wife because his uncle willed it so. It had been his uncle's burden to carry this poor child whose spirit had been disfigured by abusive parents and a detached sister. She had not been taught to love because she had not been exposed to love. Some people only have one or two people who give love to their lives. Hardly no one can say they have never had anyone give them love. Those who knew her may have said that she had her grandmother, the church mother. But, the truth of the matter was that she had severed that relationship when she was eight years old.

One Sunday, his uncle had asked her how her grandmother was feeling. That was a day when both girls had come to church alone, which was unusual. Pastor assumed that Mother White was ill, and probably thought that he should go by and check on her if she wasn't feeling well. When he had asked Rosemary, she just shook her head nervously and walked away. Florence walked up right behind Rosemary to give him her customary hug. He turned her around and said, "Daughter, how is Mother this morning?"

Florence replied, "Pastor, ain't nothing wrong with Grandma! She said that she was sick and tired of hearing you preach about how much you love and 'preciate your wife, trying to make her feel all high and mighty cause you say it's like how Christ love the church, when everybody know she don't like none of us! So, she said she was going to stay home today cause she don't feel like hearing all that, and if anybody asks we 'sposed to say that she is sick and <u>feeling</u> tired. But, that's a lie, Pastor, and you said don't lie. So, I'm gonna tell you everything what she said, and if she wants to lie, she can do it for herself."

Rosemary told Mother White everything that Florence said, and she reportedly got whipped so bad that she had to stay in the house for a week because she was whelped and bruised so badly that Mother White didn't want anyone to know what she had done to the child in her rage.

Well, Pastor found out, and after that he took her under his wing and protected her like he would have done his own daughter. He knew he couldn't trust her care to anyone else, especially when her sister betrayed her and her grandmother punished her so severely for telling the truth. He kept that vow to himself until he died; and before he died, he passed it on to James.

But now, that weight was getting mighty heavy to bear. James loved Florence sincerely and strongly. He had always been attracted to her, even though she had seemed to not care much for him. But, his uncle had talked to her and let her know that James was going to take care of her so that no one would ever be able to hurt her again. James would never leave her. He would love her and be a good husband to her. So, when Pastor died and left the church to James, he also left Florence to James.

Florence was a kind wife, though it seemed she was just going through the motions when performing her wifely duties. She didn't ask for much, but did want the best of the things she did ask for. He bought her the BMW she wanted, though he thought it was somewhat flamboyant for the wife of a pastor of a small church. Still, he had saved money from what his parents and uncle had left him, so he figured he might as well spend some of it to make her happy. She was a beautiful woman with dark hair and dark eyes. Her skin was a reddish-brown and she was thin but well-shaped. Florence liked dressing up, so he made sure she had an allowance that would support her fashion taste. But, she really didn't like being a pastor's wife. She liked going to church, and she often told him how much she enjoyed his message, but she didn't like the people. At all. It wasn't that she was standoffish. It was more that she was insensitive and really did not want to be bothered with anyone or anything that disrupted her sheltered world. She just wanted James, his preaching, and their home. That was all, besides the car and clothes.

Sometimes, he could hear her talking to herself in the kitchen or the bathroom. When they first married, he would come from wherever he was to where she was talking. He thought perhaps someone had stopped by to visit, so he should come out and greet them. However, he would always find her just standing there talking to herself. She would look at him as if nothing unusual was going on. He learned to just smile at her and then she would smile back and go on talking to herself. He prayed many times and asked God to heal her, but he had not seen anything happen yet. Once, he heard the same voice he had heard as a child say, "My grace is sufficient for you." He knew the rest of the scripture, and began to quote that when he would hear her experiencing these episodes: "My strength is made perfect in weakness."

He knew that she had been discussed after he had left the last church business meeting. One of his deacons had called him to let him know.

"Pastor, you know I love you and Sister Patterson, so I have to let you know that some of the church members were talking about her after the meeting on Monday night. They are concerned about her mind and wonder if she is fit to be a figurehead in our church. Pastor, I told them to shut up! You are the pastor, not Sister Patterson. You love her and she wouldn't hurt anybody. I told them that before they talk about her they need to pray for her, like the Bible says. But, I just wanted you to know."

He knew, and he knew why. Florence made them uncomfortable. They weren't sure what she might do. He knew she was harmless to everyone, except herself. But, he also knew that appearances were important.

He couldn't bear the thought that he might lose the church that his uncle entrusted to him behind the woman that his uncle assigned to him. He knew that God was in control, but he also knew that this cross was testing his faith. He had a love for God that was not affected by the works of men. He had a love for his wife that would not allow him to ever separate himself from her.

Drops of rain began to fall gently on his head. The tops of the trees were joining together to protect him from the rain. He thought about the faith of his fathers, and saw them standing over him saying, "Trust your God. Follow the path that we have walked before you. There is no storm that can continue when you rebuke the wind and speak 'Peace' to the waves. Stand like the tree that is planted beside the water."

The message he had preached last Sunday began to echo in his mind. Suddenly, he could feel its roots deep in his spirit. He had entitled the message, "The Courage of the Martyr". He had talked about how God gives a special grace to those who are called to suffer for His sake. He talked about the disciple Stephen who was stoned to death for preaching the gospel and sharing the love of God, but when he died he saw Jesus standing up in Heaven, cheering him on to victory. That was the type of grace James was given right now to complete his God-given assignment and carry his wife through this valley to the victory of deliverance by the strength of God's love.

As the rain drops became heavier, the gentle ocean waves began to gain strength and rise, faster and higher, on the shore. "Iron sharpens iron," James thought. "The Kingdom of Heaven suffers violence, and the violent take it by force. As the water falls more forcefully from the heavens, the waters on the earth are strengthened to respond with added force. All right, Lord, I get the message: it's time to fight!

I Was Sinking Deep in Sin, Far From the Peaceful Shore

"My son, forget not my law; but let thine heart keep my commandments; for length of days, and long life, and peace, shall they add to thee." Proverbs 3:1,2

*

The squeaky hinge on the bedroom door woke him up. Wishing for just a few more minutes to rouse himself, he felt her hair on his left arm. It hung lifelessly over the side of the mattress. Even though he bent his elbow, half-trying to push her away, her nose snuggled his ear. "Stop, girl..." he said.

She would not be discouraged. She jumped up on his back. He rolled over quickly. "I said stop!" He pushed her off. She jumped back on the bed and began to lick his face. "Coco! Get down, girl!" He swung his legs over the side of the bed and his large chocolate Lab hopped on his lap. He ruffled her hair. "Girl, you are getting too big to do this! Okay, I know you want to go outside. Let me get my shoes on!" Big for nine months old, Lincoln sometimes wondered if she was actually a Lab/St. Bernard mix. His friend, Byron, told him that her parents were a golden Lab and a chocolate Lab when he took her off Byron's hands as a pup.

"She won't get that big," Byron promised.

Lincoln couldn't even trust Byron to tell him the truth about a dog! "What kind of friend is that?" he said to himself.

"Linc! Breakfast is ready!"

"Thanks, Pa! I'm just going to let Coco out the deck door."

"All right, man. Just wanted you to know the food's hot."

Lincoln hadn't yet figured out if he was back in town for his grandfather or for himself. "Papa does pretty good for an eighty-four year old man," Lincoln thought. As he watched Coco run around in a circle before squatting down at her favorite spot, he wondered what would happen if he went back to the college town he had lived in for the past two years.

"Why am I standing here watching a dog do her doo?" he said to himself. "Can my life be this boring? No, I guess it really isn't." Maybe it was at the house sometimes, but certainly not at work. Definitely not at work.

Coco kept running around the yard, sniffing at bushes, trees, corners on the house, and on the fence line in her usual pattern. Lincoln chuckled to himself, "Ah, she's trying to see if her boyfriend has been coming around looking for her. Is this why they call dudes 'dogs'? Leaving their marks in fifty different places? Wow! I never thought I would be one of those guys."

"Lincoln?"

"Yes, Papa."

"I'm going in to town early this morning. Do you want a ride to work?"

Good old Grandpa. He's going to make sure I get to work. On time. Old school but real cool. I love that man! "Yes sir! I'll be right in to get ready."

"Don't forget your breakfast."

"Yes sir." That bacon and coffee really smelled good and his stomach was starting to growl. Coco was ready to eat, too. Lincoln filled her food bowl with dry food and gave her fresh water from the sink. As he set the water bowl on the floor beside the washing machine, he wondered what drama would occur at work today. "Lord, those are some crazy people!"

As he walked back to his room, he could hear Coco lapping up her water. That slurppy sound made him think about that girl. She was cute, but she was strange. Something wasn't quite right about her, like her spirit was off track. She looked good, but she looked weird. She was kind of like those people who could have been a clone. You know, like something about them was not authentic. "I wonder if she has a belly button?" He laughed a little. "I'll have to check next time." Next time. There really shouldn't – couldn't be a next time. Not if he wanted to feel right.

The warm water hit his head and face with a gentle force. He wanted to just stay there, letting the water beat on him. But, he knew that he had less than an hour to get dressed and eat if he was going to be on time. "Papa will make sure of that!" Lincoln chuckled.

He pulled out his black twill pants with the hard crease in the front. "Ain't nothing wrong with looking good!" he said to himself as he slipped them off the hanger. One thing his grandmother had taught him well was how to iron. She said that if he didn't know anything else, he needed to know how to iron and cook. Nothing was worse than seeing a man in wrinkled clothes. It made him look trifling! And, if he knew how to cook at least one good thing, he wouldn't have to marry a woman just so he could eat.

Marriage. Not something he thought a lot about these days. Oh, he figured he would get married one day, when he found the right woman. He wanted that perfect family with the beachfront cottage and the little white picket fence protecting everything he owned. Surrounded and protected by whiteness. What an interesting picture. Especially now.

Lincoln checked himself in the big round mirror on the wall. He nodded his head a little while he lifted the tips of his collar so that they would set evenly on each collarbone. He splashed a palmful of a light and spicy cologne on his chin and the backs of his arms as he walked into the kitchen.

"Boy, you let your food get cold!"

"That's okay, Pa, I'll just pop it in the microwave. And, I know you are about to talk about 'back in the day when you were growing up and there wasn't no microwave'!"

"Yeah, and that's when we ate when we was called to the table, because after that it was going to be cold and there wasn't nothing you could do about it!" Papa reached over and hunched Lincoln with his elbow, which Lincoln grabbed and shook.

"Come on, Papa, you got to catch up to the times! You keep hanging with me, and I'll bring you into the 21st century! We got cell phones and everything these days! I'm thinking I need to get you one so I can keep up with you."

"What, boy, I don't need no keeping up! I keeps up with myself! Just so I know where I am, it don't matter who else knows. I ain't going to lose myself!"

Lincoln chuckled. "Pa, I'm not worried about you losing yourself. I'm worried about that girlfriend of yours kidnapping you!" He hugged Papa hard from behind as he reached around him to take his plate out of the microwave. Papa shook him off.

"What you talking about, Linc? I ain't got no girlfriend!" Papa looked irritated, but Lincoln could see a little twinkle in Papa's brown eyes. He also noticed how they looked like they were turning a light bronze color, and he could see the pronounced green speckles in each iris.

"Papa sure has some funny eyes. They change colors all the time," Lincoln thought. "Sometimes they're dark brown, sometimes light brown. I wonder if my eyes change." Lincoln thought about how his grandmother used to tell him that he looked like his grandfather had 'spit' him out of his mouth. Unfortunately, he couldn't remember what his father looked like. His mother either, for that matter. He had seen plenty of pictures, but he had never seen them.

Lincoln was born on a cold January morning. His mother wanted to have him in the good hospital the next town over. It was new and modern. Many of the doctors were residents who had recently graduated from the university's medical school. She wanted her baby to be born in the best conditions possible.

Lincoln was a healthy baby, and his mother enjoyed all of the pampering she got during the four-day hospital stay. At least, that is what his grandmother had told him every time she narrated the story of his first week of birth. She never added the part that he once heard her tell one of her friends over the phone. He was about eight and had come into the house on a hot summer day to get a cold drink of water. Grandma must not have heard him come in the door. Otherwise, he would have heard her holler, "Shut that door! Don't you be running in and out of here, letting all that hot air in! If you go outside, stay outside!" Instead, he heard her say, "Yeah, that boy's mama never did like it down here. She thought she was too good for plain people. She wanted to be like white folk. Act like she was rich or something. My son never would have died if she wasn't so hoity toity, making my baby drive all that way in the ice and snow to pick her and Lincoln up from that big city hospital. They couldda stayed right here! But, no, things had to go her way. And look what that got us! My Charles dead! And me left with his baby boy!"

The story she told Lincoln, every time he asked to hear it, was that his father had come to pick up him and his mother from the hospital and take them to the new little house he had bought for them, but the road was icy and snow-packed. When a big truck tried to pass them on the little county highway, his father Charles lost control of the car and spun off of the road. The car hit a tree and landed on its side in a ditch.

A nice couple who was driving behind them stopped their car in the middle of the road and ran down to help. They saw that Charles had been crushed by the impact between the steering wheel and the driver's door. His mother, Lorena, was lying outside of the car in the snow. Her neck was broken. But he, her precious Lincoln, was wrapped up in his blanket, lying in the passenger seat that his mother had flown from. It was as if she had carefully laid him down before she lost her life.

The couple told her that Lincoln just looked up at them with wide open eyes. He never cried while they moved him to their car to keep him warm before the police arrived. He never cried during the hours that they waited to contact Papa and Grandma. The couple said they knew he should have been hungry or wet, but he never cried.

The other part of the story that Grandma never told him was that he never cried until the police matron handed him to her and she began to hug him hard and sob her heart out at the loss of her precious son. That is when he opened his lungs and wailed out his own sorrow for two days straight. Papa told him that part of the story. He also told him that he was to never forget those two days, because he would need to know for the rest of his life that he had already taken the time to mourn his parents, and that was it.

Sipping the last of his too-sweet coffee, he mused as to how much he really was like his Papa. No nonsense, not given to much emotion. When it's done, it's done.

As he and Papa drove into town, he noticed Papa's smooth caramel-colored hands wrapped comfortably around the steering wheel. For an old man, he looked good, and could easily have passed as a man twenty years younger. Passed. That's what that white girl at college tried to convince him he could do – pass. For what? He was comfortable with his skin. Grandma used to tell him in the summer his skin looked like golden fried chicken. But in the winter, he looked like a white boy with a little tan. He knew he got that color from his mother. Grandma used to say she had a lot of white in her family and could have passed for white if she wanted to. Today, he noticed that his hand was close to the same color as Papa's. "So, why the white gotta come from my mother's side?" he murmured.

"What was that you say, son?"

"Oh, nothing, Papa. Just talking to myself." Lincoln chuckled.

"Watch out now, boy. They be looking at you like they look at pastor's wife!"

Lincoln looked at Papa, incredulous. Then, he began to laugh so hard that he doubled over. Papa kept turning his head toward Lincoln, first with a big grin and then starting to laugh harder the more Lincoln laughed. Soon, Lincoln heard Papa's signature hoarse laugh that sounded like a "hoo,hoo" with intermittent coughs. That made Lincoln laugh more, which kept Papa going, sounding like an old owl with a bad cold.

"Stop, Pa! You're killing me!" Lincoln wiped his eyes. Now, his nose was starting to run. "Ah, man!" he gasped, trying to catch his breath. "Whoooo! I will never be <u>that</u> crazy! Do you know what she did last week?"

"Hush, boy, I can't breathe, and if I can't breathe I can't drive!" Papa was still in a fit of laughter. "Stop now, 'fore you make me wreck. Stop! Whew! Ah, I'm too old for this. Shouldn't be talking about nobody no way!"

"Papa, you're the one that started all this! Look, here I am at work. Thanks for the ride." Lincoln was still laughing as Papa pulled the car beside the curb in front of the small grocery store. As he slid out of the door, he patted Papa's right shoulder. "I'll get a ride home with Byron tonight after work. You be good, now!"

Papa was still chuckling. "Looks like I better go back and wake up and start all over again if I'm gonna do that! But, I'll try!"

"You'll be all right, Papa! See you later!" Lincoln waved as he stepped on the store porch and pulled the lanyard with the door key out of his right front pocket. He stepped in the door and smelled the familiar odor of a combination of laundry detergent, almost-fresh fruit, and some kind of freezer odor. He started turning on lights, even though he loved all of the bright daylight that flooded into all of the windows every day. Sometimes, he felt like he could work in this store every day of his life and be the happiest man in the world. There was something very secure about being here. Things never changed. The routine was comforting. The only thing that ever disturbed the store was people. Especially Byron and that girl right now.

Lincoln had never been a drinker, not even in college. He didn't like the one taste of beer he had at a party when he was a freshman. The smell of hard liquor had turned his stomach, so he hadn't even tasted that. But, just to be sociable, he gave in to Byron when he begged him to go to the young peoples' bar that night.

There were only a few bars in town. Most of them had been there for decades. But, one of the guys who grew up in the town had gone away for a few years and made a little money. When he came back, he bought a rundown bar. He fixed it up so that it would attract a new, young crowd. Lots of surf boards and straw hats decorated the walls. He had a few stuffed and mounted swordfish posted around, too. It wasn't real fancy, but it looked different from the old peoples' bars. So, that is how people identified it – as the young peoples' bar. It had a name, something like Tiki Water. But, everybody just called it the young peoples' bar.

Meeting that girl made him think that maybe it hadn't been such a bad idea to go to the bar with Byron. She was fine! He'd dated white girls at college, so that wasn't such a big deal. But, he was a little confused. Byron kept telling him to talk to her, like he was trying to hook them up. But, it looked to Lincoln like her and Byron had something going on. They would always look at each other and laugh at the same time, like they had some kind of little private joke going on.

Even when Byron was around, she acted like she really wanted Lincoln to talk to her. And, Lincoln really wanted to talk to her. She was built like a swimsuit model. Her hair was long with a little bit of a natural curl. When she stood in the sunshine, you could see bronze highlights running through it. He didn't notice that until their second date.

The first date was the evening after they met at the young peoples' bar. Byron set it up, in fact. He suggested that they all go to the movies – Lincoln and Lindsay (that was her name) and Byron and Vanessa. Byron had been going out with Vanessa since the 7th grade. Whenever you thought about Byron, you automatically thought about Vanessa. Lincoln wasn't sure why they hadn't gotten married yet. They just seemed to go together. But, after that night, Lincoln thought Vanessa might know something that he didn't know, which may be why she hadn't married Byron yet.

The movie was stupid. But, none of them were watching it, anyway. Lindsay really wasn't acting like they had just met the day before. Lincoln thought she might be a little fast, almost desperate, but he wasn't caring that much right then. Vanessa was texting on her cell phone throughout most of the movie and laughing out loud when there wasn't even anything funny on the screen. People kept turning around to look at her. Byron would nudge her and she would just say, "What?" He was slouched down in the seat looking mad.

Lincoln and Byron had been best friends as long as Lincoln could remember. They went to the same church, sat in the back pew since the time they were nine or ten, and made fun of everybody to make the time go by faster. Sometimes, they would draw pictures of cars and houses and talk about what they were going to be when they grew up. Byron went to college. He flunked out and came back home after the first semester of his freshman year. Lincoln had gotten a football scholarship to the state university, but was red-shirted after an early season injury. The coach let him keep his scholarship second semester but cut him at the end of the year. Lincoln liked the town and the school, though, so he started job hunting in order to help pay his tuition for the next year.

One day, he walked into a grocery store near the campus and asked for the manager. When he met him, he asked if they needed any help. He was hired on the spot. He worked all summer and lived cheap, saving most of his money. From then on, he kept his job and paid his own way. He was really proud of his independence. Then, his grandmother died and Papa asked him to come back home to help him. Lincoln wasn't convinced, though, that Papa really needed any help. Maybe he was just lonely. Maybe Lincoln was, too.

Lincoln caught himself whistling a song he hadn't heard, let alone thought about, in a long time. It had a catchy tune, and at first he didn't recognize it. Then, he recalled how he used to like to watch Brother Green direct it as he led the church in the hymn service. "Love lifted me, love lifted me. When nothing else could help, love lifted me." Every time they would get to the end of the chorus, Brother Green would slow things way down and hold his right hand up high in the air, making it shake like the wind was blowing through his fingers. "Love......lifted......me....!" Lincoln and Byron would nudge each other and laugh at Brother Green. They thought he was a little queer anyway. So, when his hand would be flopping around and his head was tilted back with his big rheumy eyes rolling around and his fat lower lip trembling like he was getting ready to cry, they would crack up with laughter. Oh, the things you would see in church!

Lincoln finished his round of checking the store and made his way back to the front register. He was so glad that Mr. Bobby had taken his word on his grocery store management experience and let him step right into this job when he came back after Grandma's funeral. Plus, he knew that Mr. Bobby was old and tired and would be relieved for someone dependable to open up the store in the mornings so that he could make it on in when he felt like it.

He had talked Mr. Bobby into hiring Byron, and later Lindsay, to help him out. In the summer, the store was a busy spot. People bought a lot of consumables like milk, bread, meat, and produce. It was a lot for just one person to keep an eye on. Plus, things had to be stocked and shelved, along with rotated so that the old sold before the new. Some afternoons, there might be twenty or thirty people in the store at one time. Crime had never really been an issue in this town. But, drugs had become a problem in the next city over, and every now and then there would be a stranger or two stopping into the store to buy things that most of the locals didn't buy, like Zigzag rolling papers. People used to use them to roll their own cigarettes, but Lincoln knew why most young people would buy them now.

Byron had turned out to be a very dependable employee. He showed up on time every day and was very polite to all of the customers. He made new ones want to come back, and he joked around in a good-natured way with all of the town folk. From the old to the young, he had a familiar word for each one. He might ask about what they were cooking, or how much candy they had bought that week and if they were working for old Dr. Nelson, the town dentist. He would tease the little girls about the little boys. He would tease the old women about the old men. In fact, Lincoln began to wonder if business had grown since Byron had come on board.

Lindsay was another subject. She was professional at work and never acted as if she and Lincoln had anything but a working relationship. Byron would give her a ride to and from work because they lived down the street from one another. Byron's mother's house was a few blocks away from Lindsay's apartment building. But, once they got to work, they acted like strangers. They weren't even cordial. They just acted like the other one wasn't even there until it was time to go home.

Usually, Vanessa would stop by the store at lunch time and buy a bag of potato chips, a Snickers bar, and a bottle of Pepsi for lunch. You would have thought that Byron would have let her have it on the house if he was at the cash register, but he didn't. She would pay like anybody else, and then she and Byron would go out and sit on the porch while she ate her lunch. After that, she would leave when she had about ten minutes to get back to work. Sometimes, if things were slow, Lincoln and Lindsay would go out and join them on the porch. They'd all talk and laugh, and Byron and Lincoln would clown on each other while the girls laughed at them.

When Lincoln would ride home with Byron and Lindsay, he would sometimes wonder why Vanessa was so cool with the two of them being together so much without her. But then, he wondered why that didn't make him uncomfortable, too. She was supposed to be his girl, but she really wasn't acting like it. She seemed like a shell of a person that was willing to pretend to be normal in order to cover up the fact that she wasn't. For a long time, it didn't matter because he wasn't that serious about her, anyway. He knew girls could be moody. Maybe that was the problem. But, there was something going on that he couldn't put his finger on. And, that nagged him. What made him more puzzled was that he felt like Byron was somehow part of his confusion, and that made him uncomfortable.

He really didn't want the girl, but he didn't want to be played, either. He didn't care if Byron did want to go out with her; all he had to do was let him know straight up. He couldn't understand why Vanessa would still be hanging so tight with Byron if she thought he was messing around on her. And, Lindsay wasn't saying, or doing, anything but walking around like somebody in a coma.

"That's it!" Lincoln felt something cold run across his forehead and settle on his shoulders. "That chick has got to be on some kind of drugs. Something that doesn't make her look or act high. What kind of stuff could that be? And what would Byron have to do with that?"

Just then the bell jingled, signaling that someone had come in the front door. "Welcome to Bobby's!" Lincoln said. He saw a man he didn't recognize wearing a sun hat with gold fishing lures hanging from the brim. "Can I help you find something?"

The man walked toward him. Putting his hands on the counter, he said, "Yes, you can." I'm looking for a girl. A white girl." He paused. Lincoln felt drops of sweat forming between his nose and upper lip. "Her name is Lindsay. Know her?"

Lincoln was used to thinking quickly, but his brain had shifted into slow motion. Words were not coming to his mouth or his brain. He took a deep breath and cleared his throat. "There's lots of white girls around here. What does she look like?" Lincoln tried to muster a smile and look interested.

"I think you know her," the man said. "I've seen you with her. A few times."

"Oh, <u>that</u> Lindsay," Lincoln replied. He tried to switch his tone to a humorous one, but things still weren't working in his brain.

"Yes, <u>that</u> Lindsay. Do you know who I am? Did she tell you about me?"

"Why would she?" Lincoln thought. "You look old enough to be her father." Aloud, Lincoln questioned, "Sir, may I ask why you are looking for Lindsay? As her supervisor, I can't give you any information."

"I see how this is playing out. You're trying to protect her. You haven't seen the real Lindsay, yet." The man started to laugh. "I'm your guardian angel, young man. I'm trying to save your soul from the grip of a demon. She will take you down, boy. Just like an alligator, twisting and turning until she pulls you down to the bottom of a murky swamp and takes her time eating your flesh, one chunk at a time."

Lincoln began to feel fearful. Where had he seen this man before? His eyes looked familiar, but he couldn't place his face. Had he come to the store before? That's it! He was driving some old beat up car. He'd been there a couple of times in the past three weeks. Each time, he would sit out in the parking lot a long time. Just when Lincoln would be about to go outside and check things out, the man would get out of the car and come in the store and buy something small, like a pack of gum or a bottle of soda. Each time, he would keep his eyes down, like he didn't want to ever make eye contact. Once, though, Lincoln caught him looking at him as he walked into the store. There was something strange about his eyes. Then he realized – they were the same color as his eyes and Papa's.

"That's all right, don't tell me anything," the man said as he backed his way to the door of the store, "but I bet the day will come when you will wish you did. And I might not be around to tell you that I told you so. Though that won't make much difference by then." He turned to open the door with his left hand, then turned right back around and looked Lincoln dead in the eye. "If that other boy is really your friend, tell him that her candy is actually poison. Everything sweet's not good for you."

When the man closed the door, the bell rang again. Lincoln realized that his legs were shivering. He walked over to the large front window and watched the man get into his old beat up car. The motor turned over quietly and the man drove away. Before he did, he looked straight in the window at Lincoln. Reflexively, Lincoln stepped back. When he looked back again, there was nothing in the lot. Something small and shiny lying on the floor, right at his feet, caught his eye. Lincoln leaned over to pick it up. It was a gold fishing hook.

I've Already Been to the Water

"Hear, ye children, the instruction of a father, and attend to know understanding."   Proverbs 4:1

*

Candi asked Duane if they could turn off the air conditioning and just roll down the windows. Riding down the highway with the man who was soon to be her husband with the coastal air rushing in her face made her feel more free than she ever had. Someone had opened the door and let her spirit out! She loved her parents, but the prison they had kept her in for all of her life had been stifling. The fresh air felt so good.

"How you feeling, baby? Are you scared?" Duane looked at her and smiled hesitantly.

Candi thought for a moment, then moved closer to him and put her left arm through his right. "Naw, not at all! I love you, man, and I will be so glad to be your wife!"

"That's what I'm talking 'bout!" Duane put his arm around her, handling the steering wheel skillfully with his left hand. "But, we better hurry." He looked at the dashboard clock. "Girl, we got twenty minutes to make sure we are man and wife before the sun goes down!"

Candi picked up the map. "Do you know how to get to his house?"

"Sure," Duane said. "It's right off of Highway 201 Bypass. Take a right at Exit 6, go on down two blocks, take another right, two more blocks, and we're there."

"Uh oh, look at you!" Candi said, teasingly. "Sounds like you been there before! Are you sure I'm the first Mrs. Murray?"

"The first and the last!" said Duane, and kissed her on the cheek. "I knew the first time I saw you that *'you was the one'*!

"And only!" Candi finished. "Oh, baby, I hope we are talking and laughing about this on our 60th anniversary! How we ran away to get married. And, I hope we can reminisce about how everything worked out all right."

"Don't worry, Candi," Duane said, seriously. "It's going to be all right. Now, help me look for Exit 6. I think we're getting pretty close."

Even though Duane was trying to put on a brave front, he was really nervous. What was he thinking about, taking this girl down here to marry her? Had he lost his mind? No, he lost his heart.

He would never forget that day when he had stopped in to the barber shop to see if he could get his hair cut real quick. Somehow, his barber forgot his standing appointment and was overbooked. There were six people ahead of him. He was so mad he didn't know what to do. "I've been coming to this dude for over six months, and he tries to act like today isn't a Thursday and it's not 11:30!" he had said to himself! "Well, I'm not going to wait two hours. I'll just find me another barber."

He had driven downtown and spotted one of those old red and white barber poles you sometimes see in old-school sitcoms. He was worried that the barber might be an old white man who wouldn't know how to cut his hair. "Oh well," he thought, "anybody can do a military cut."

He parked his car at the meter and put in a quarter. "I might not be all that long," he thought, "especially if things don't look right." Walking in the door, he saw that he was the only one in the shop. An old white man came from the back with a few combs in his hand. They looked at each other. For a moment, it seemed like time had frozen. Duane cleared his throat as the man was asking, "Can I help you?"

Duane smiled nervously. "Yes sir! How are you doing today? I wondered if I could get a haircut?"

The old man paused for a moment, looking at Duane's head. "I guess I can do that," he said.

"All right!" Duane walked over to the chair and sat down. "What's your name, sir? Thanks for getting me in."

The old man just shook out a blue cape and attached its Velcro tabs around Duane's neck. He lifted the chair with the foot pump until the back of Duane's head was level with his eyes. Then, he took it down about three inches.

"What type of cut are you wanting?"

"Do you know anything about a *quo vadis*?" Duane asked.

"I'm a barber, son. Tell me what you want."

"Take some off of the top, please, and edge me up real good," Duane said. "And, if you can, fade me down a little on the sides."

"You from around her, son?" The old man started up the clippers. Duane hoped he knew what he was doing. Sometimes, his temper got the best of him. It led him to make impulsive decisions that hadn't always worked out in his favor.

"Yes, sir. I have been stationed at the base for about four years. I'm trying to decide if I should re-up or come on out with my benefits and go to college. Haven't made up my mind yet."

"Military is good. Teaches you good habits. Steady work. They can't fire you unless you mess up real bad." The old man gave a quick laugh. "I'm an ex-military man. Did me real good. You ought to think about that." He turned the chair to the left. Duane caught a sideways glance of his head.

"That doesn't look too bad," he thought. "Maybe this old guy knows what he's doing."

"So, you stayed around here after you got discharged?" Duane asked. "Or, were you from around here before?"

The old man waited a moment before he responded. "I grew up in this little town," the old man said. "Born and raised right here. Couldn't wait to get away. Back then, they let you join at seventeen. I asked my daddy to sign for me, but he wouldn't. So, I said I was eighteen and signed myself in. Thought they might check, but nobody must not have cared. They needed recruits and I looked grown for my age. So, next thing I knew, I was at an army base in Alabama."

"What did your daddy say when he found out?" Duane realized the man still hadn't told him his name. Through the window, he could see the word 'JUNIOR'S' painted backward, in cursive. But, Junior could be anybody. Besides, other than in Arkansas, that wasn't usually a first name.

"My daddy never spoke to me again, even after I was honorably discharged and came back to see him. He had a stroke while I was gone. Nobody told me. He might have been mad about me leaving and told them not to let me know. Or, he may have just decided that he wanted to cut me off. No telling. He was that kind of a man."

"Wow, that's too bad. Well, I bet he was proud of you anyway."

"Umph." He released the pump and lowered the chair to floor level. Swinging Duane around to the mirror, Jim stood to the side as he checked out his cut. Duane nodded affirmatively. The old man took his brush out of his pocket and swept the back of Duane's shirt collar. He separated the Velcro strips, removed the cape, and shook Duane's hair onto the floor. Folding the cape over his arm, he stepped back so that Duane could stand.

"Man, I like this!" Duane continued to turn his head from side to side, admiring his profile in the wall mirror. "I might have to set up a standing appointment with you! What's your name, sir?"

"Glad I could help you. That will be fifteen dollars." The old man looked Duane dead in the eyes. Duane figured he wasn't going to get a name, so he pulled out his wallet and paid him.

"Thank you, sir. I appreciate you fitting me in." Duane looked at himself again in the mirror. "You did a great job! Bye!" The old man nodded. Duane brushed off each shoulder with his hands and then walked out the door. He got into his car and rolled down the windows. It felt like the sun had gotten twenty degrees hotter in that little bit of time.

Starting the car, he looked in his left mirror before putting the car in gear. He saw a person on a bicycle about half a block behind him, so he decided to wait until they passed before pulling out into the street.

Jim was looking out the window. It was past time for his daughter to come so that they could go to their appointment. That's why he had hurried up on that unexpected cut. He seemed like a nice kid, polite. But, Jim didn't trust too many people and was wary of strangers showing up to get their hair cut. You never knew when somebody was going to try to rob you. He felt a cold stab in his chest. What if something had happened to her? Maybe she got hit by a car or something. He began to second-guess his directions to her that morning. "Maybe I should have told her that I would come home and pick her up." Suddenly, that old threat that haunted him for so many years was lurking right there, ready to disrupt his calm once again.

That day was the day that changed his life. She had been late getting home from school. Really late. She liked to walk home with the neighbor kids. He thought maybe she had stopped there to play and lost track of the time. So, he went two doors down to see if she was there. A little boy was in the front yard fixing his bicycle. He said that some guy in a brown station wagon had picked her up as soon as they crossed the street.

Jim panicked. He called the police and had the boy tell them the same thing he told him. He kept trying to call his wife at the public library where she worked, but the phone kept ringing busy. Jim began to imagine all sorts of crazy things. He started to holler at the policeman because he kept asking questions. What did she have on? How tall was she? What color was her hair? Did she have any moles or birthmarks? How could he remember all of that by himself? Why couldn't they just go out and find his precious baby? She had been their late life surprise. He thought the chemicals he was exposed to in Nam had made him sterile. Then, here comes this beautiful little blue-eyed curly-headed baby to crack the shell around his heart and make him feel human again. And, who left the phone off the hook at the library? And why wasn't this cop out there trying to find his baby instead of asking him all these questions that he didn't know the answer to?

As it turned out, Naomi had been trying to call him when he was calling the library nonstop. She wanted him to know that she had her friend, Randy, pick up Candi from school because she had planned to take her to get her hair done for her birthday. The only appointment she could get was for right after school. She wanted to let Jim know so that he wouldn't worry. But, the phone at the house had been busy for a whole hour. Did he accidentally knock the phone off the hook?

Jim was still shaking when the front door opened and Candi stepped into the barbershop. "Hi, Dad!" Candi said, cheerfully. "It's really getting warm out there! Let's hurry up and get to the bank. I think I want to go swimming today!"

"Candi, what took you so long? I was worried about you!" Jim realized that his hands were trembling and his face felt flushed.

"Daddy! Are you okay?" Candi came close to him and touched his forehead, a look of concern on her face. She glanced at the big black clock on the wall. Softly, she said, "It's just 12:10. You told me to be here at noon. I rode my bike around the park a couple of times because it felt so great outside. You know how much I love to feel the wind." Candi patted his cheek and kissed him on the forehead. "I'm sorry I made you worry, Daddy!" She smiled and gave him a light hug. "You know I'm a big girl. Nothing's going to happen to me."

Jim hugged her hard. "I know baby." His voice trembled. "I know. I just worry too much sometimes. But, I'll be okay." Jim grabbed a suit coat that didn't match his baggy casual pants. "Let's get going. We need to be at the bank by 12:30."

Duane had sat in his car watching the girl maneuver her bicycle up over the curb right behind his car. He noticed that she moved like a dancer, very conscious of her form and figure. She looked like she was a model in a commercial for some hair care product where they blow an invisible fan on the girl's hair. Her golden mane was gently lifted by the breeze. "She has to be the most beautiful girl I have ever seen," he thought. As she passed by the passenger window she had glanced at him and then smiled lightly. He felt a rush, like when someone scratches your back in that just right spot. "There it is," he said to himself. When he saw her park her bike on the porch and heard her say, "Hi, Dad!" he put the car into "Drive" and pulled off.

He thought about her all afternoon. Somehow, he knew that she was going to be his wife. He didn't know how he knew, but he knew. And, she was the daughter of the man with no name. Wow, he was going to have to figure out how he could ever see her again, especially since her father wouldn't let him make another appointment.

Duane ran a couple of errands before he realized how hot the day had become. The weatherman had predicted that it would get close to eighty degrees that day, but Duane thought it had to be at least ten degrees more. He didn't go to the beach much on a weekday. Usually, that was a weekend activity and he went with some of the guys from the base. But, the thought hit him that maybe he would go on down to the beach today and cool off in the water. That might take his mind off of this girl he didn't know but had fallen in love with in five minutes, or less.

When he dropped off his purchases at home, he grabbed his trunks and a towel. Passing by the mirror, he caught another glimpse of his haircut. "Not too bad," he thought. "But, when have I ever gone swimming on a day when I got a fresh haircut?" Still, Duane found himself in the car, heading south toward the beach.

Business at the bank took longer that Candi thought it would. Jim was trying to get his finances in order so that Candi could know what was going on. She thought he was overreacting to turning seventy. Even though her parents were at an age that some people might have considered old, Candi was always so impressed with how they seemed to stay current and healthy. Other than being nervous now and then, her dad had no health problems and worked every day. And, her mom was like Pollyanna – nothing ever discouraged her. She was always upbeat, happy, smiling, and positive. Candi was sure they would both live a very long time. That's why she didn't want her dad to think that he needed to include her in his financial business. He wasn't going anywhere any time soon. But, she wished she were.

Maybe it was because they had her in their forties. Maybe it was because of that stupid incident when she was a kid and her dad thought someone had kidnapped her. Whatever it was, her dad's tendency to smother her made her feel panicky herself. She hated to think about it, but she thought she was starting to have anxiety attacks at the prospect that she would have to live with them all of her life. So, her escape was riding her bike as much as she could, and swimming at the beach when she wasn't riding. Anything to get away from that house or the barber shop and feel liberated by the wind, the sun, and the water.

She spent a few minutes sweeping up the shop when she and her dad got back from the bank. She felt guilty about wanting to break away. She knew her dad loved her and meant to provide the best for her. So, she felt like she had to do something to justify her leaving as fast as she could to go swimming.

Kissing her dad goodbye, she walked out of the door and closed it gently behind her. "He'll be busy real soon. The regulars are about to get off of work from the fishery." Candi hopped on her bicycle and headed down Conch Street, straight for the beach. She had packed her gear before she left home. The weatherman had said it was going to be hot today.

Duane stopped in the bathroom and changed his clothes, then went back to the car to drop off his bag. He hid his car keys under the passenger floor mat. Walking toward the beach, the grass felt cool. He decided to jog. The water was calling to him. When he hit the hot sand, he began to run faster. It was coming up between his toes, burning and stinging. He dug in his heels and lifted his toes; but no matter what, the sand was burning his feet badly while bits of black, brown, and off-white shells poked the bottoms. Seagulls sat comfortably on the shore, watching him with bored curiosity. "Why didn't I wear my shoes?" he thought. "What was I thinking about?" "That girl," his thoughts answered. Duane laughed. He was right.

Finally, he hit the water and ran straight in before stretching his body out on the water. The cool, frothy waves carried him back. Duane reached out to the next wave to carry him out further before he began to stroke. He went out about fifty feet. The water felt so good on his back and arms. He turned over and began to backstroke. Looking up at the sky, he thought, "God, You are amazing. This world is beautiful. The people you make are beautiful. Especially that girl." Duane chuckled. "Man, this is not me," he thought. "I got it bad, acting like some lovesick school boy. I'm a man! I gotta get over this. Besides, I have too many things to think about right now."

Duane began to focus on the decisions he was facing. Should he stay in the army? He was thinking about becoming a computer programmer. The college offered a two-year degree, and his GI benefits would pay for everything. The timing would be perfect. But, he didn't know if he wanted to stay down here or go back home. That was going to be a hard choice. The ocean seemed to be on his side. It was giving him a gentle massage, supporting him while he thought without forcing him to think.

The beach looked empty. This was the way Candi liked it. Even though she had no reason to be bashful, she preferred to swim in solitary settings. Just her and nature. Sometimes, when the beach was really crowded, she would go ahead and swim because the drive to get in the water was one that was difficult for her to suppress. But, she didn't like the way the guys would google her, and she also didn't like the way the women would roll their eyes at her. "This is perfect," she said to herself. Slipping her swim shoes on, she sat down at the shore and let the water draw her out. That was her favorite way to start her swim. It felt like she was asking the ocean for its permission to welcome her, and it was responding by opening its door and letting her in. It was not in her nature to be intrusive. That was another reason why she liked to swim in private.

As Duane allowed the waves to carry him back, he thought about what life might be like for him if he stayed in this community. It was pretty nice, all things considered. He knew he could get a good job at the fishery, but would prefer something in an office working with computers. Still, he could be content to wait his time. But, things would be easier if he had at least one good reason to really want stay here.

Out of the corner of his eye, he saw something swimming toward him under the water. It looked like a large fish. "Shark!" he thought, then brushed that fear away. No one had ever spotted a shark in these waters! He began to swim toward shore. Whatever it was, it was approaching him. Suddenly, a head emerged from the water. Long, wet gold hair was plastered to the side of her face. It shimmered in the sunlight. She turned her head to the right as she took a breast stroke. As she opened her eyes, she spotted him. She looked startled. Her lips formed, "Oh!"

Duane swam swiftly toward the shore. "I think that's her!" He wasn't sure what he should do, but he knew she was as surprised as he was to see someone swimming out there. Suddenly, she flipped around under water and began to also swim to shore.

"Here we are," Duane said. "This is the address of the parsonage. Are you ready?" He turned to Candi and looked deeply into her eyes. She smiled.

"Mr. Murray, I love you with my whole being. I am honored to become your wife. I have saved myself just for you. I am ready to love you for the rest of our lives. It's so easy to say yes. Yes."

Stepped in the Water; Water Was Cold

"For the lips of a strange woman drop as an honeycomb, and her mouth is smoother than oil; but her end is bitter as wormwood, sharp as a two-edged sword." Proverbs 5:3,4

*

When they were children, Victor and Angela were neighbors. Victor's father, Victor Sr., was a very successful attorney. When graduated from law school, he was invited to join a local firm: Chronister, Halyard, and Chronister. The Honorable Judge Willis P. Chronister's father had started the firm in the 1920's. It was now the eighties. Affirmative action was an issue. Judge Chronister had been very impressed with Victor Sr.'s work ethic, sharp wit, and evident potential. As a law student, Victor, Sr. had done quite a bit of research for him and had served as his clerk for two years. Plus, the Judge thought it was time to add a little color to the firm.

Victor, Sr. entered the firm as a junior partner. Within a few years, he attracted a number of wealthy clients and was raised to full partner. With that raise came an elevated status within the community, plus a three-figure income. Victor, Sr. had married his high school sweetheart, Loretta. From the day they got back from their dream honeymoon, they had been living in a modest downtown apartment. With the new position and the healthy raise, they were now in a position to have their home built in a brand new subdivision. Loretta's father was a smart real estate investor and had amassed quite a fortune over the decades. Since she was their only child, they put everything they had into her wedding and then gave the newlyweds a honeymoon in Hawaii on top of it all. Loretta loved Hawaii so much that she insisted down through the years that they revisit their honeymoon hotel every anniversary. They had missed a few, but not many. One year, it was because Victor, Jr. was timed to enter the world during their anniversary week.

He wasn't born on their anniversary. He came two days later. The delivery was difficult for Loretta. She was a fairly small woman, and Victor, Jr. had been a very large baby. Nine pounds, three ounces. But, he was the palest baby she had ever seen. Blue-gray eyes. Transparent skin. "Did they switch my baby with some white lady's baby?" she thought when she first laid eyes on him. But, the tiny wrist band around his plump left wrist had her last name on it with the word, "Boy". "Our boy!" Loretta thought.

"Thank you, Lord!"

It actually wasn't that hard to believe that she and Victor would have a baby that looked white. Both she and he were very light-skinned. She often thought that was why Judge Chronister had been so quick to hire him. Business leaders in the town were getting pressured by race-based organizations to make sure there were black people in professional positions so that the community would not be viewed as racist. What surprised her about her son was <u>how</u> white he looked. <u>Porcelain</u> white. Her mama told her to keep checking his fingertips and the tops of his ears for some kind of color. But, it didn't matter. Victor Jr.'s eyes were the most beautiful combination of blue and green with tiny golden brown specks. She had never seen had eyes like that in her lifetime.

When Victor Jr. was six, they moved into their brand new home in the "white" neighborhood. She had been just a little apprehensive about how they might be received, but Victor, Sr. was confident that they would fit because of the color that really mattered – not black or white, but green! Victor, Sr. always said that money was the great equalizer. It bought you friends and influence; and if you had the resources they had, it didn't matter what color you are.

Victor Jr. was comfortable in the neighborhood from day one. While the movers were carrying in their new furniture, he was going door to door throughout the neighborhood, like a Bible salesman. He went to every home on both sides of the street, methodically knocking on the door, saying hello to whoever opened the door, and then asking if they had any kids. As an only child, he longed for playmates all the time. But, Loretta marveled at how balanced he was as a person. He got along with everyone. He would play alone, play chess with his father, play card games like Go Fish with her, and just make the best of things, however they were. What was more amazing was that everyone loved him.

He didn't know it at the time, but his move-in day introduction to the neighbors was something they never forgot. Years later, when his name would come up in a social or professional setting, someone would generally remark that he was the young man who had met all of his neighbors in one hour by going door-to-door. The most important neighbor he met that day was little Miss Angela.

For years, they were playmates. They went to the same school and usually participated in the same activities. Swimming, plays, and summer camps often found them walking and working together. When they got to junior high, people just expected to see one when they saw the other. They were best friends and were inseparable. There was no evident romantic connection; otherwise, Loretta would have nipped things in the bud. Angela's parents would likely have done the same thing. Victor, Sr., though, secretly hoped that his son would marry this white girl. Why? Her dad owned half of the town. But, Victor, Sr. almost owned the other half. His father had left him a number of valuable holdings, and he had bought up quite a bit of property himself during the recession. Many of his friends chose to do private transactions to keep "For Sale" signs out of their yards or business windows. What was devastating for them was a blessing for him. His family would be well-set for generations. Add to that the common property his son could share with Angela, and the name of "Whitman" would become historical in this town. "What a dynasty that would create!" he often thought.

Different thoughts ran through Dr. Carson's mind. He had been intrigued by the inquisitive little boy standing in his doorway that morning, asking if he had any children. He was drawn to his large, blue eyes with the green and brown shadings. The boy looked white, but he had pronounced black features. However, the boy's confidence was what impressed him the most. "What did you say, son?" he had responded to the boy's question.

"I said, 'do you have any children', sir. My name is Victor Whitman, Jr. and we just moved here. That's our new house over there." He pointed across the street. "I just wanted to know if you had any children I could play with every day."

Before Dr. Carson could respond, a small girl peeked behind his pant leg. Immediately, Victor, Jr. saw her and smiled with excitement. He extended his right hand, right past Dr. Carson. "Hi! My name is Victor, Jr.!" He looked up into Dr. Carson's puzzled eyes. "Can she come outside and play with me?"

"Wait, I'll go get my jump ropes!" Angela dashed toward the back of the house. Dr. Carson turned to watch her run, his mouth fixed to say something but nothing coming out.

"Thanks for letting your little girl play!" Victor, Jr. turned and ran down the large steps and into the expansive yard, where he stopped to wait for Angela to come out. The rest of the morning was spent hopping up and down the sidewalk, each child following the other in turn as they swung their respective jump ropes under their feet and into the air in a rhythmic dance, over and over until they were called into their individual homes for lunch.

By the time she was in twelfth grade, Angela had heard her father tell her more than one hundred times that he did not like her dating that black boy. It didn't matter that he looked white. It didn't look right. Even if his father was probably one of the three most wealthy and influential men in town, even if he was her best friend, he would never – could never – be her husband. And, if she defied him and tried to marry him anyway, he would disown her forever.

Angela would passively nod and affirm to her father that Victor was just her best friend. They had been best friends forever. They just chose each other over anyone else they could call themselves dating, and they preferred each other's company to anything else they might want to do any given day. But, more than anything, they were friends. "Daddy, don't worry about anything."

Angela's mother loved Victor. She wished they would marry. She was more concerned about what might happen if Angela lost Victor's friendship and emotional support. From the day he had knocked on the door as a small child and brought her precious little angel out of a state of uncommon bashfulness and withdrawal into a world full of sunshine and laughter and playfulness, she wanted to make sure that nothing ever disrupted this perfect existence for her. So what if he was what her husband called black. He was a good and caring man. He loved her daughter in a way that did not focus on physicality and possession, but was a gentle presence that affirmed her humanity every day. "What is wrong with our world that would keep my daughter from being happy and protected for the rest of her life, just because that love was coming from someone of a different race? And, what is wrong with my husband? Doesn't he know true love when he sees it? He can diagnose a deadly disease in everyone except himself. Hatred kills everything it touches. He can't let it kill his own daughter!"

They would often debate about who had to go to college with whom. They hated the idea of being separated. That had not happened in the past twelve years of their lives. But, Victor, Jr. knew he wanted to be a teacher, and his parents expected him to go to the historically Black college where they had received their degrees. Dr. Carson had donated and maintained a large endowment to his alma mater throughout the years, so Angela had her place at the state university where she would matriculate as her parents, grandparents, and great-grandparents had done. She was unsure of her proposed major, but her father had told her a number of times that he expected her to also become a physician and take over his practice after she joined him following her graduation. So, with both of their lives already planned out for them, they had to plan how they would function without each other for the next eight to ten years while they went to university.

The day that Angela told her parents that she had applied and been accepted to a historically black college, she thought her father's stiffening was signaling a stroke. She ran to him when she noticed him begin to turn gray-green and sweat profusely. She had been trained in CPR and thought that she was going to have to administer it immediately. She looked at her mother, who had a slight smile on her face, and said, "Do you think we need to call an ambulance?" Her mother took a deep breath, "No, I think he will be fine." Angela's father sat down quickly in the chair that Angela had led him to and gripped the curved wooden arms. He opened his mouth as if he wanted to speak, but nothing came out except a low moan.

Angela had expected a shocked response, but she hadn't thought her declaration was going to disable her father.

Kneeling beside the chair at his shoulder, she spoke gently. "Daddy, I am a woman. I have to make decisions that are best for me. I have thought about this day and night, because I don't want to disrespect or harm you or Mom. But, if I am to be successful in school, in life, I know what I have to do. I need Victor. He is like a part of me. Don't worry; we don't have a physically intimate relationship. But, we do have an emotionally intimate relationship. I love him like I don't love anyone else. I can't explain it. It is like I am a parasite and he is my host. If I am forced to disengage from him, I will die! So, I am choosing to live. I am going to the university with him. I will complete my degree there."

"Don't expect a penny from me!" Dr. Carson's shaking, raspy voice sounded like a curse. "You will never get a dime of my money!"

"Tomorrow, I will deposit a check in your bank account to cover six years of tuition, housing, and living expenses." Mrs. Carson spoke calmly and decisively. "We'll also purchase a brand new car for you tomorrow. Then, we will go visit the campus this weekend and find a nice condo we can buy so that you will have permanent housing during the breaks and over the summers. Does that sound like a plan?" Angela's mother looked at her with a confident smile. Then, she opened her arms wide to welcome her daughter to the comfort of her embrace. Dr. Carson slumped over into his own open hands and began to sob.

Their freshman year was exciting. Victor, Jr. stayed in a campus dorm. Angela would arrive on campus early, meet Victor in the cafeteria for breakfast, go to her classes, and then meet him after her last class to go to the library to study and then back to the cafeteria for dinner. They would joke about who was approaching them on the sidewalk and what their major might be, because they always saw shocked faces when people would get nearer to them. They looked like a white couple from a distance. Most people might have wondered why a white couple was on a small historically black college campus. Then, when people would realize that Victor was really not white, or didn't look all the way white, their expression would change and they would look confused, or look back and forth at him and Angela. She really looked white. That's when they would smile big smiles and say, "Hi!" After the person was past them, they would laugh over a joke only the two of them understood.

That only worked for a short time. Once the students, professors, and campus staff got to know each of them, it was not uncommon for people to wave and holler greetings to them long before they met up with them on the sidewalk or in the cafeteria. They would usually all have a few minutes of conversation before moving along to their destinations. Once again, whenever someone saw one, they expected to see the other. Angela had started to think about what to declare as a major. She knew that she had overcome quite a few emotional hurdles throughout her life, and she knew that she could not have done that without Victor. She thought that she might be able to help others as he had helped her. She thought she might want to become a social worker. She also wanted to find out more about herself, because she knew she had a long way to go, still.

Angela wrote her mother every week. She sincerely appreciated how her mother had stood up for her when she needed it most. She also worried about her mother, but nothing ever signaled that anything was wrong from her mother's letters. It sounded like everything was perfect at home. Angela's father never sent a word of greeting in her mom's letters. And, her mom never said anything about her father. Until her junior year.

The counselor had emailed the professor of her 11:00 class to ask him to tell her to stop by the Counseling Center after class. Angela thought it might be about the appointment she had requested to visit about her internship at the Boys and Girls Club in town. It wasn't. Her mother had called that morning. Her father died last night in his sleep. He was going to be cremated, but there would be a memorial service for the community on Saturday.

Victor slept on the couch at her apartment that night. She was devastated. He saw a side of her that had only been a shadow now and then in the past. She cursed, she cried. She threw things and acted as if she were about to cut herself with a paring knife. She tore up her checkbook. She ripped to shreds an old Billy Bob's Crab House shirt that she said her father had bought when the family went there for dinner. He was afraid to leave her. It was as if some ancient demon had possessed his beautiful friend and turned her into a monster that was bent on destroying everything in its path. She finally cried herself to sleep, but he was afraid to leave her.

Angela packed up enough clothes for a week the next morning, dropped him off at the dorm, and headed home. She found her mother in worse shape than she was herself. That week turned into three months. By then, the semester was close to ending. Her counselor suggested that she just wait and return the following fall. She had petitioned Angela's situation to the dean, and he agreed to drop her grades so that it wouldn't affect her transcript and grade point average. Angela was very appreciative of the counselor's support and promised to contact her in July.

She didn't. Her mother needed her attention around the clock. She hadn't known that her mother had been medication-dependent since long before Angela was born. Dr. Carson's most needy patient was his own wife. She had struggled with having dependants – her husband and her daughter. She lacked the capacity to give more than a surface level of attention and care. That had impacted Angela greatly as an infant and young child, but everything changed the morning that Victor showed up at her front door. Now that her supplier was gone, Mrs. Carson needed another caregiver. Angela had to fill the role, even though she needed great care herself. And, he was nowhere near to provide what she needed more than anything – a source for her own survival.

For the first two weeks of Angela's absence, Victor kept himself busy between school and her apartment. He had promised her that he would check on it every day. He cleaned things up and then found himself looking for reasons to spend less and less time there. Soon, his "checks" consisted of unlocking the door, looking inside, and then quickly closing and locking it back. He would call her each evening at six o'clock. Her mother would be asleep and they could talk. Angela sounded desperate for him the first six weeks or so. But, there was no way he could get home. They already had spring break. Dead week was coming up, but he was committed to a department project that would only leave him a few hours to himself that week, not enough time to drive down and then get back.

Soon, her voice sounded more and more detached. She would ask routine questions, but with little interest in his responses. She had originally asked about all of their friends and told him to let them know she missed them and would be back soon. Later, she would have to be reminded who someone was when he would pass on their greetings to her. The past few weeks, she hadn't answered when he called at six, but would call him back around nine, saying that she had fallen asleep and was sorry she missed his call.

One day, she called him. It was about five o'clock, and he thought that she sounded unusually cheerful. He felt good, hearing her voice and thinking how much she sounded like she used to, maybe even better. "Victor, can I ask a big favor of you," she said, midway into the conversation.

"Of course! You know I will do anything you want me to do!" he responded eagerly.

"I think I need to stay down here and take care of my mom. I'm not sure that I can leave her right now. Would you be able to find some time to go to my apartment and pack up my clothes and other personal things and then send them to me? I'll send you some money for the shipping. I know you're really busy right now, but I can't figure out how to get this done any other way."

"You know I will, Angela! I wish I had time to bring them down myself. I really miss you! I never imagined I could be so lonesome. It's as if I lost my arm or my leg. I can't wait to see you again. I really wish your mom was okay so that you could come back here to me. I didn't realize how much I need you." The line was quiet. He waited for what seemed like eternity for Angela to say something. He believed she was still on the line, because he thought he could barely hear her breathing. But, she didn't say anything. "Angela? Angela? Are you there? Angela?"

"Oh, yes. Victor? I'm sorry. Were you saying something?"

Victor felt a piercing pain in his ribs. Her voice sounded unnatural. He felt like something just popped and came alive in his brain; but they say when someone is born someone else dies. What he couldn't decide at the moment was who had done what. "Oh no, I didn't say anything."

"Okay," she said with a clear voice. "So, do you think you could be a darling and do that for me? I'm so sorry. I wouldn't bother you, but I don't have anyone else." She paused, then added, "And I hoped I could count on you."

"Of course you can. I'll get your things to you by the weekend."

"Thanks! Check's in the mail. Talk to you later!" The line went dead quickly.

Dr. Victor L. Whitman, Jr. was one of the most popular professors on the campus of the university. But right now, relationships outside of his immediate family meant very little to him. He had waited four years for Angela to call him. She never did. Not even to thank him for sending her things. He didn't think much about that at first, because he was her best friend. He didn't expect thanks for doing what friends do. But, after a while, he began to wonder what he ever meant to her. Wonder turned to worry, but his mother would see her now and then around town so he knew she was still alive. Worry turned to anger, because he knew he had done nothing to deserve being ignored. It felt like he had ceased to exist in her mind. That is when he vowed to never call her. If she wanted to talk or resume their friendship or account for the emotional trip that took her to this place, that was up to her. He wasn't going to demand it.

Victor went home to visit his parents at least twice a year for Christmas and summer breaks. There was no need to try to get back for his birthday, because they were usually on their annual vacation to Hawaii. But, he started off wanting an excuse to come home, just to catch a glimpse of her. As time went on, the unresolved anger became the dominant emotion when he thought of Angela. And, he wasn't sure what he would do if he should ever see her. So, he decided to do his best to not see her.

Dating other women was not a priority. He was absorbed in his research and his teaching, and the students seemed to love him. Most of them raved about him on their end-of-course evaluations. These affirmations were enough for him to feel fulfilled in himself and his work. There was no need for any additional emotional connections. Besides, having been in a strong relationship with a female since he was a small child, he had not ever had any other opportunities to explore his life as an individual who had the potential to connect with a woman on equal ground with both covering their own space in such a healthy way that they could welcome another stable adult into it without either becoming a victim of the other's deficiencies.

Angela and her mother had moved to a secluded beachfront cottage. The big house in the now middle-class neighborhood felt cloistered. Plus, every time she walked out onto the porch, she could see in her mind's eye two little mismatched children skipping down the sidewalk with their jump ropes. "Who are they?" she wondered each time. Then, she would go back into the house, sit in her father's large armchair, and cry. So, she knew they had to move.

The cottage was colorful and airy. She wasn't sure who had painted it and the first thing on her list of "to-do's" was to paint every room a neutral color. But, after a week or two, she got quite used to the colorful interior. Her mother seemed to brighten up a little, too. They would go out on the small but wide porch and sit. Mostly, they sat in silence. But, every now and then, they would have a lucid conversation. A couple of times, they shared a laugh about some happy recollection.

Her mom took long naps every day. Some were brought on by the prescription she took when she needed it. Others were probably initiated by the cool sea air and the daily lull that came in with the tide around three o'clock each day. While Mrs. Carson napped, Angela would often think. Sometimes, she would write. She began to try to remember why she was so unnaturally angry. Was it her mother, or her father? Was it actually her? Some expectation of entitlement? Loneliness? Boredom? Defiance? If the problem was something inside her, shouldn't she have the power to expose it so that she could fix it? Sometimes, she felt she did; but, most of the time, she knew she didn't.

One morning, Angela woke up fighting her way out of a realistic dream. She had seen a boat far in the distance. It looked like a luxury liner, but when it got closer she realized it was just a small motor boat. There was a man standing at the helm holding the steering wheel. He was tall and had on a pointed hat, not a captain's hat as would be expected. He was waving and his mouth was moving, but she couldn't hear anything he was saying. The hat had a small propeller on top, and as he pulled up toward the shore the boat turned into a small red sports car. It was a convertible and he was now standing up in the back seat with an open Bible in his hand. It was like he was preaching to her from the back of the car on the seashore. His mouth was still moving and his right index finger was pointing at her, up and down, but she couldn't hear a word of it, though it seemed like he had something important to say. She was getting frustrated. A large alligator came out of the brush and tried to eat the car. The man acted like he didn't see it. He just kept on pointing and preaching silently. The alligator bit the tire and it started to go flat. She screamed at the man in the dream, "It's going to eat you! Stop talking and look! It's going to eat you!" She decided to attack the alligator since the man wasn't listening.

She felt like she was running fast but she wasn't reaching the alligator no matter how hard she tried. Suddenly, she found herself standing outside the car. The man, who had her father's face, reached out his right hand to her and said, "Jump in the car." Right then, the alligator turned toward her and began to move quickly in her direction. She grabbed her father's hand and tried to jump up into the car; and as she looked back, the alligator had its mouth open, ready to snap down on her foot. That's when she woke up.

That afternoon, the waves carried a gift out on the peace of the sea. The gift was from Angela. It was her father. She had said a small prayer: "God, help me to forgive my father, my mother, and myself. None of us are perfect. But, all of us deserved a chance to be happy. They say, 'if you love someone, you will let them go.' I choose to let Victor go. I choose to let myself go. I choose to let my father go."

The ashes of a stubborn, loving man's days gone by drifted out to sea on the afternoon tide. A dream of the hope of the peace which could come drifted over Angela's spirit. Hope. Did she dare?

It Chilled My Body, But Not My Soul

"Go to the ant, thou sluggard; consider her ways, and be wise."
Proverbs 6:6

✢

Philip Chatworth was a big man, not only in his physical frame but also in his own eyes. He knew how hard he had worked to get to where he was in his profession, even though some people didn't recognize him as respectable professional. Still, he provided the resource many people needed. It wasn't his fault that they paid him more than they should have for his product: money. Philip was a pawn shop owner and sometimes a small loan arranger. A couple of times, he had been accused of being a loan shark. He really didn't mind what anybody called him. He was making a pretty good living doing what he did best.

From the time he was a young child, Philip had been taught to think "big". That meant to look beyond where he was right then – barefoot, living in a ramshackle house with dirt floors, eating sugared and buttered cocobread sandwiches for breakfast, lunch and dinner – toward a place in his future where he was a successful businessman with everything which accompanied that lifestyle.

Philip's parents were humble but hard-working. They had come to America from Panama in the '70's, determined to make a good living for themselves and their four children, two girls and two boys. Philip was the baby of the family. With his pretty brown mahogany skin and his "old man" eyes, he could charm a rattlesnake out of his rattles. And, coincidentally, that was the type of person Philip felt most comfortable hanging around – the snakes of the world.

His parents were both employed by a local hotel resort. His mother cleaned rooms and his father oversaw the kitchen. Within a few years, they had each worked their way up to management status in both areas. Patricia supervised the housekeeping staff and trained all new inductees in the best practices for making the guests look forward to returning the following season. Abram was a seasoned cook and knew how to put his professional touch on everything from seafood to barbecue. His fruit drinks were so much in demand that local townspeople would often come to the hotel just to get an evening fix of one of Abram's mixes. Philip watched their work ethic and learned.

The children were never left alone. Patricia got up early to report to work by 4:00 a.m. She would make sure the children's school clothes were ironed and ready for them to put on. She would lay out the breakfast food for the day so that Abram could cook it quickly. She would kiss each child goodbye as she passed their pallets in the kitchen. Some mornings, Philip would wake up just so he could smell his mother's sweet milky vanilla scent before she left for the morning. That slight smell would stay with him the entire day.

Abram's shift started at 2:00 in the afternoon, right before the children were released to come home from school and thirty minutes after Patricia's day ended. He would get to work about an hour early so that he could follow Patricia around while she did her duties and spend just a little time talking, teasing, and laughing with her. They had been in love since they were twelve, and married since the age of fifteen. Their oldest child, Preston, was born the next year. The twin girls, Violeta and Christiana, followed. When Preston was ten, Philip arrived as a welcome surprise.

Patricia still couldn't figure out how she could have carried a baby full term and not known she was pregnant. Of course, it could have been because she was a fairly large-framed woman. Also, she was always busy working and caring for her husband, home, and children; so discomfort in the evenings was just a way of life for her. But, the night that Philip was born was unusual.

The family had gone to her auntie's birthday celebration that day. It had been an all-day affair, starting at sunrise and going until well-past midnight. There was lots of eating, cooking, dancing, and singing. Abram and the men of the family had roasted three large pigs in a pit covered with gigantic palm fronds. The smell floated across the entire cay. All kinds of fresh fruit were piled on clapboard tables – pineapples, bananas, mangoes, papayas, coconuts, on and on. Sweet rolls, rice, fish, chowders, conch, pulled meats, food everywhere. The music was hypnotizing – steel drums, guitars, hands clapping, dancing singles and couples, this was what she loved about the island life. So, she had herself a time! She ate until she couldn't eat any more. She danced until she fell out on the ground. The babies were passed from relative to relative. Preston ran around with the other children, playing hide and seek, dancing to the music, running from the tottering old uncles, and laughing until they rolled on the ground and finally fell asleep. Abram was in his element, cooking, singing, dancing, and socializing. Things couldn't be any better.

When they got home early that next morning, she collapsed into her pallet, exhausted. Her stomach was queasy and uncomfortable, but she thought it was probably because she had eaten and drank so much. She tried hard to go to sleep, but couldn't. Finally, she got up in the middle of the night to go to the bathroom. She had awakened from a cloudy sleep and wished she could just suppress that urge until morning when the path to the outhouse would be better lit. But, she realized she couldn't wait. Thinking it was something she had eaten, she rolled off of her pallet to her feet, lightly kicking Abram as she stood up. He grunted just a little, lifted one tired eyelid, and then rolled over.

Walking down the dimly moonlit path, she realized that there was a pull in her thigh each time she lifted her right leg. Things didn't feel quite right. She was having a hard time catching her breath. She began to stumble; and before she knew it, she had slipped to her knees on the ground. A tight band grew from her back all the way around her stomach. She gripped the patch of grass that was beneath her fingers. As she arched to raise herself back up to her feet, she felt warm water flow from her vaginal area. "Oh my, I'se peed myself!" she exclaimed through clenched teeth. "Oh, oh!" she cried suddenly. She found herself straining as if she were having a difficult bowel movement. Strong pains as rhythmic as the steel drums she had danced to a few hours ago began to pound inside her body, dancing and stomping to a beat all of their own. Her strong hands groped at her upper thighs in an attempt to either stop whatever was coming out or to pull the piercing cramps from her crotch and end the waves of pain that were raging in her gut. Before she could even begin to process what was happening to her body, a wet and cheesy dark brown baby slid out into her claw-like hands.

"Abe! Abe, come help! I'se had a chile, boy! Come quick!" She groaned as she collapsed to her knees on the warm, sandy ground.

Abram was suspended in deep sleep. Patricia's piercing call roused him sharply. He jumped to his feet and looked around, frenzied. "MaMa! MaMa, where is you, me love?"

"Abe, come quick! I out in de yard!"

"In de yard?" he questioned as he rushed out of the door of the small raised-frame house. He stood briefly on the stoop to acclimate his eyes to the morning mists, and could see nothing standing except the palm trees. "Where you?" he called. Suddenly, he heard a mewling sound and a slow, soft moan. "MaMa? MaMa? Where is you?" He began to run down the path to the outhouse.

"Right ova heah," she replied softly. Abram stopped suddenly and looked down in the grass. There lay his beloved Patricia, cradling something squirming and wet. At first, he thought it was a baby goat. Then, he heard the mewling sound once again. "That sound like a little baby chile!" he said to himself. He knelt beside her quickly and began to cradle her in his arms. "What is dis, MaMa? It look like a baby! Whose baby is dis, MaMa?"

"It be ours! It come so quickly! I thought I has to go pee, and this come out right heah on dis here path. I don't know why. I didn't know I was with no chile!" She gripped Abram in desperation as he was lifting the baby from her cupped hands, umbilical cord still attached. "Abe, dis heah a real little baby?"

"It be a real baby, MaMa. Wait here. You be fine. I go get a knife to cut dis heah cord. He be fine." Abram lay the infant on her stomach. It wasn't moving much. Abram knew he had to cut the cord quickly. Rushing to the house to grab his knife, he felt like he was still in the dream. A baby? How could that be? He knew her body like the back of his own hand. There was no way she could have been expecting a baby and he not know it. But, she had gained a little more weight recently and had seemed to act a little more tired than usual. "Get yo self together, black boy! Hurry and take care of yo woman and yo baby!"

Rushing back to Patricia, he thought about how he must quickly cut the cord, wrap the baby, and help his wife pass the afterbirth. He had seen the process many times. His own mother had fourteen children. He had seen his first three children born. He knew what he must do. He tore off his nightshirt on his way back down the path. Cutting off the tail, he split it into two strips and knelt beside his wife. Tying both strips about five inches apart, he deftly sliced the cord between the ties, and then tightened them as much as he could, stopping the quick flow of blood. Patricia began to moan in discomfort as the afterbirth began to pass. He quickly wrapped his newborn son in his nightshirt, bundling him tightly, and laid him facedown on Patricia's stomach. He needed to massage her abdomen as he cleaned the baby's mouth between applying pressure to her uterus. Patricia began to squirm, so he placed more pressure to the top of her abdomen. Soon, she pushed as if delivering another baby and the placenta rushed out in a flood of blood.

Philip's birth scenario was a foreshadowing of his character. He was a slickster, a charmer, and a surpriser. He was often a cheater, too. If someone wanted to pawn something of great value for a small amount and it was something he really wanted for himself, he would "lose" the item and keep it. Then, he would act very apologetic, offer a pacifying explanation, and then pay them far above their pawn refund but far below the value of the item. He was smart enough to not do that too many times. He didn't want people to get suspicious and not trust him. He also wanted to maintain his good business name. But, when he saw something he wanted more than anything, he had to have it, no matter what the risk.

As a child, Philip was the brightest star in his class. He was always the teacher's pet and never got blamed for any of the mischievous acts for which the other children got whippings. He always had an alibi. He had been picking a bouquet of flowers for the teacher, or washing the chalk dust from the blackboards, or watching out for the little dog that always showed up at the school during lunch time. He was never in the vicinity of the shed where the window was broken, or on the field when a little boy's eye was blackened. He was always performing a kind act for a teacher or an animal. Or, so he said. His classmates knew better. They knew how he tortured the poor little dog until it yelped so loud that the teacher woke from her nap to come running, only to see Philip petting it and soothing its leg while scolding the other children for throwing rocks at it. No matter how much the children denied that they had done anything and outlined in detail Philip's beastly actions, the teachers always believed Philip and punished the other children. Even when his brother or one of his twin sisters received the punishment, they never implicated Philip. Never. Not even to their parents. He seemed larger than life. Hadn't he just appeared one morning without any notice, like some created being? Hadn't their parents always treated him like a gift from God that no one expected but everyone appreciated with awe? So, all of his life, Philip had the privilege of living with no consequences; for if one could do no wrong, why would one suffer consequences?

Philip's mesmerizing personality transformed his humble existence. He would never be stuck without options. He would always be able to create the door he was destined to walk through. His confidence in that assurance always made a way for him out of no way. When he graduated at the top of his high school senior class, lack of income did not stand in the way of college entrance. Even though he had known nothing about scholarships and how to apply for them, he selected the nearby university as the place he wanted to continue his education. He had saved up close to one hundred dollars by betting on trivial things, such as how many people would pass by the window where he and his best friend, Brian, were sitting while they sipped their ten-cent sodas. Brian could not imagine how Philip would know the answer to such things and figured the odds were in his own favor, so he would bet up to fifty cents against Philip. However, Philip would hit the number right on the head and Brian would have to pay up! "How could he know such things?" Brian would often wonder. "That's impossible!" But, what he didn't know was that Philip was a student of patterns. He knew who was coming from where at that time of day. He had watched for months the habitual behaviors of downtown workers, trash haulers, policemen, Wednesday shoppers, and could estimate within two or three who would be moving down that sidewalk at that time, as they did every day. And, he was accurate ninety percent of the time. So, when he set his bets with Brian, and other unassuming victims, he wasn't just guessing. These were definitely calculated bets. Because of that, he won ninety percent of the time.

One Monday morning, he took that one hundred dollars and purchased a twelve-dollar bus ticket to the city so that he could visit the university he planned to attend. He knew no one, but figured there should be someone there who ran the school, and he planned to find that person and talk with him. Four hours later, he found himself in the office of the president. He had arrived on campus two hours before, figuring out his route by striking up casual conversations with people he met along the way. Each person gave him another tidbit of information, stringing together a trail which led to the welcoming receptionist in the alumni hall. When she blushed at his extended hand, he knew that he had hit the gold mine. She herself had escorted him to the president's secretary. Not having an appointment was just a consequential roadblock. She understood his mission. So did the president. By the time he left campus and was headed back to the bus stop in a cab, he had secured a full scholarship which would later be extended for the next four years and allow him to earn a master's degree in business along with a weekly chair at the president's Sunday dinner table.

Once again, Philip had graduated at the top of his class and had struck off on the road toward great success. Nothing could stand in his way – except his own pride and self-consumption. He had an unseen enemy, and it created his demise. His first professional position was with an investment firm, Continental Stocks, Inc. He had charmed the senior partners in his interview. They were highly confident that he would perform well and increase the trading value of the company's stock in no time. He did not disappoint them. In fact, he garnered such a large percentage of stock within five years that he began to think of starting his own firm, taking only a couple of his most dependant clients with him. He left with the blessing of the senior partners, for they felt a strong allegiance with him and responsible for mentoring such a successful young man. A young intern who had just graduated from university asked Philip if he could start at ground level in Philip's new venture. Philip welcomed him, confident that he could mentor him as his former employers had done for him.

Things started off well for Philip and his new aide, Tucker. Philip's reputation had preceded him, and he soon had a stable of steady clients. He made wise investments for them and brought high-yield short-term returns, so this greatly increased his clientele. Within a year, he had a new building for his business and seven additional advisors on staff, four of them interns. This kept his payroll low and his income high, but it also gave him the ability to hone their sharp skills as he taught them almost everything he knew. He and Tucker, as primary principals, became very wealthy men in no time at all.

But, all good things must come to an end. Philip had maintained many of his Panamanian connections throughout his life. The family would venture back to the islands every five years or so as he was growing up. Somehow, he would always meet someone who thought himself as wise as Philip, manipulating money in many of the same ways, and figuring out how to use it to make more. One such friend was Halstead. He knew how to pick up a dollar with his right hand, rub it between his palms, and turn it into a ten-dollar bill in ten seconds flat. What the man or woman watching that feat of legerdemain did not realize was that the ten-dollar bill had come out of his or her own pocket! Needless to say, Halstead became one of his best island-home friends.

Philip had included Halstead in some of his professional ventures when he began his own securities firm. Halstead proved his faithfulness by returning to Philip and his clients extremely large returns on their investments. He would put their money into international ventures such as war goods, drugs, and secluded island properties purchased by European businessmen who raided third world countries' natural resources and needed a place to hide their financial assets. Philip was riding high on the current that Halstead created until that fateful day when two men in black suits and black ties knocked on his office door. They were couriers from the securities commission. They were there to let him know that he was being prosecuted for investment fraud. Their professional twins had just delivered the same message to Halstead, all the way in Panama. But, if Philip was willing to tell everything he knew about Halstead's dealings and liquidate all of his personal assets, they would forego the federal prison prosecution and let him go with probation.

True to form, Philip folded. What was Halstead's life in comparison to his? He knew he could start again. But, with his trading license revoked, he didn't know how. He decided to pay a visit to the judge to request that his probation be reassigned to his hometown. After a fifteen-minute conversation, that was a done deal.

That was three years ago. Philip reestablished himself as a reputable businessman once again. A topic of frequent conversation was just what kind of reputation he had, but Philip was not fazed by what others thought of him. If he could get money, he could make money. What better way to make money than to take something that someone valued, give them a small percentage of its value, charge them three times the loan to hold it for them for a few days or weeks, and then return it to them – most of the time – and let them know sincerely how much you appreciated their business.

Tucker had known from the first time he met Philip that he possessed the key to his future. If he could learn the things that Philip knew, if he could practice the business skills that Philip taught him, if he was able to just sit at his feet and soak up his wisdom, he would be just like Philip one day. So, he had gone back home with Philip to support him in whatever new venture he embarked upon. Tucker did learn everything Philip could teach him. Soon, Philip trusted Tucker like he trusted his own right hand. Tucker settled comfortably into the town and began to develop his own social circle. He had acquired expensive tastes over time, and the money he made with Philip allowed him to live out his dreams. New home, new car, fashionable clothes, and attractive women – everything he wanted was at his fingertips. He worked in the pawn shop every day of the week. Philip had started to go to church on Sundays. That was a big surprise. But, he had met the pastor at the barbershop one day and the two of them really hit it off. What a strange relationship! They would go out for coffee and sit, drink, and talk for hours. The townspeople and the church people would observe them walking down the street laughing and hitting each other on the shoulder and wonder what these two polar opposites could have in common.

Over the years, they developed a strong bond; and though it may have hurt the pastor, it only helped Philip. He began to look into himself, rather than just at himself. While Philip was growing into a different type of person from how he had been all of his life, Tucker was growing into Philip's old spot. As Tucker noticed Philip talking and acting more ethically, he began to worry. The money had been very good, and Tucker was afraid the pastor was talking Philip out of being the keen businessman Tucker needed him to continue to be if he was going to accumulate the wealth he wanted for himself. So, Tucker started to make some side deals to cover himself in case things went belly up again.

Tacking two or five percent onto a loan wasn't that big a deal. Plus, Philip never noticed and probably wouldn't have cared if he did. Hadn't he created Tucker to be his clone? After a while, that measly five percent wasn't enough; Tucker had plans. If he was going to become independently wealthy, he needed more. Ten percent on top of Philip's lucrative fee seemed just about right.

One Sunday morning when Tucker drove up to the pawn shop, he saw Philip's long black Lexus parked beside the back door. "What is he doing here today?" thought Tucker. Parking his tiny red Miata beside the Lexus, Tucker unlocked the shop door and walked in, calling Philip's name.

"Good morning, sir," said Philip. "Come on in my office, and have a seat." Philip patted a chair that was beside him at the desk. Tucker noticed that Philip had three accounting books open. A spreadsheet page was open on the screen of his desktop. He took a deep breath.

"How you doing, Phil? I'm surprised to see you in here today. Thought you might want to relax, man! Hit the beach or something, cause you sure are a hardworking dude. Making that money!" Tucker laughed, forcefully and nervously. "What is going on?" he thought.

"I said, 'sit down', man!" Tucker could hear the edge in Philip's voice and he sat down quickly. He looked up at Philip and could see the vein in his left temple throbbing. But, when he looked in Philip's eyes, he looked very calm. "I've been going through my books," Philip continued, "and I'm seeing some things that are making me wonder." He turned to face Tucker. "You know I'm going to wonder. I'm just a wondering kind of guy." He held a strong gaze, eye-to-eye, with Tucker.

Tucker laughed loudly. "Yes, you are Phil! You are a wonderer!" He expected Philip to laugh, and was a little fearful when Philip just responded with a deadpan stare. "What's the matter, Phil? Why you so serious this morning?"

"Ah, I'm always serious when it comes to my money. Don't you know that, man? Don't you know that I keep good track of what I have and know when I've lost a penny?" Philip turned serious suddenly. "Where's my money, Tuck?"

"What you mean?" Tucker stammered. "Your money? Your money is where it always is! Your vault. Your bank. Why you asking me where your money is?"

Philip continued to sit there calmly, but Tucker could see his hand gripping the knob on the arm of his chair. It looked like it was about to form a fist. Tucker needed to be ready to move at a moment's notice. Philip began to talk in a measured clipped tone. "I am asking you where my money is because I know that you know. When you stole my money you put it somewhere, so you have to know where it is. Is it in your car? Maybe in your house? Your bank account? A shoebox under your bed? Your wallet? You've been taking about fifteen percent of my take and putting it away somewhere. I have proof. I have you. What I don't have is my money. What do you think about that?"

Suddenly, Tucker began to cry big tears. He started to sob and shake like a small child who knows he is about to get a sound spanking. He began to try to explain something in the midst of his breakdown, but all Philip could make out was "I" over and over, then "my" repeated between racking sobs, and some other unintelligible gibberish that was beginning to make Philip feel sick to his stomach, even though it was somewhat comical. He thought, "This big old kid made the worst mistake a man can make. To try to use another's power as if it is your own is like putting on a man's clothes and thinking his wife will mistake you for him just because you're wearing his suit. You're setting yourself up for a slap and a kick in the behind."

Right then, he remembered something the pastor had told him last week. They were sitting in the book store, enjoying a cold glass of sweet tea and talking about how the wisest man and the richest man who ever lived had come to the conclusion that wealth and wisdom are nothing but vanity, things that feed the ego but not the soul. Looking at Tucker blubber and slobber, collapsed in a chair on the verge of a nervous breakdown, worried that he was about to be arrested and have to go defend himself from the rogues in the city jail, he realized that he had created the sin he wanted to purge. Tucker had learned his tricks. He had been an outstanding pupil. He had matriculated to a level of excellence in his chosen profession, and all along Philip had been his proud professor. So, what would he do now with his protégé?

As Tucker was about to grasp his ankles and begin washing his shoes with his tears, Philip stood up. "Tucker, Tucker, stop all this, man. Look, get up. Get up. We can talk about this." Tucker looked up at Philip in shock. He had been expecting the worse. "Look, Tucker, I can't be too mad at you anymore. You only did what I had taught you to do. I guess I just wasn't expecting you to do it to me. But, when you learn to cheat, you can't help but do what you've been trained to do. Come on, man, get up." Philip put his right hand under Tucker's elbow and lifted him up. Tucker looked at Philip with combined fear and amazement. He wasn't sure who this Philip was, and he didn't trust him. He knew that he had been cheating him, and he knew how much Philip loved his money. There was no way he was getting out of this! Why hadn't he thought about the consequences before?

"Listen, Tucker. You are a brilliant young man. Anybody who can turn a trick on me has skills I didn't teach them. Yes, I've done all right with this business, but I hadn't really thought about what I'm doing to people. I'm going to have to think some things through, make some changes. But, you don't need to stay caught up in this mess anymore. It's time for you to go your own way and do your own thing. Just do it right. Don't get caught up in graft and start to travel a dead end road. Get yourself on track and make a good life for yourself. How much did you get out of me?"

"Huh?" Tucker left his mouth hanging open.

"How much money did you skim off of my customers? Tell me!"

"About ten thousand," Tucker said softly, moving slowly backward toward the door, anticipating the soon-coming wrath of Philip's rage.

Philip, instead, looked very pensive. "Ten thousand? That should be enough to get you started." Tucker lifted his eyebrow quizzically. Philip continued, "You have made me about a hundred times that much, so I think that is fair. Let me know if you need a letter of reference to a securities firm, and I will be glad to provide one. Even though I had a fall, I do have a lot of former colleagues who appreciate my skills and value my judgment. If I tell them they should hire you, they will." Philip extended his right hand, inviting a handshake. Tucker hesitantly responded. However, when Philip shook his hand firmly, Tucker became more enthusiastic in his own handshake and began to smile. He looked at Philip expectantly. Philip looked at his watch. "Hmmmm, nine-thirty! It looks like you have time to make it to church service today. That's where I'm going. I think God is trying to tell me something. Guess I'll go hear the rest of His message." He cleared his throat and looked Tucker dead in the eye. "Care to join me?" he asked. Tucker knew it wasn't really a question.

"I'll follow you," Tucker replied.

Follow Me Down to the Jordan Stream

"And I beheld among the simple ones, I discerned among the youths, a young man void of understanding." Proverbs 7:7

*

"Patty-cake, catch a snake, let him go before he break." Steve couldn't figure out what made him remember that crazy rhyme his mother used to repeat over and over whenever she had to look for him before she gave him a whipping. He might be hiding under the porch, trying to avoid the inevitable. He would hear her voice, sing-songing that ridiculous rhyme in a mocking tone with a strangely humorous lilt, and it would make him more nervous the closer she circled toward him. He always thought he had the perfect hiding place, but she always found him. Then, she would pull him out by the arm and beat the literal mess out of him with one of those long switches she would braid using three or four thin tree branches.

Historical memories had been nagging him all day while his tired brain replayed that tune like monotonous elevator music. He had spent most of the afternoon trying to recall what current event triggered it. In the process of trying to walk that back through, he also began to try to figure out what it even meant. "Catch a snake? Before he break? Was she trying to say I was a snake?" He chuckled. "Did she stop short of beating me to death so she wouldn't break me? Oh Lord, I am putting too much thought into this stupid rhyme when I really should be trying to solve this issue. I guess I'll just have to call Mom and ask her these things."

Steve pulled in to the parking spot nearest the store door. He often told himself that one day he would take the advice of the talk show doctor and park in the farthest location of the lot to make sure he got his daily exercise. He wasn't too worried about that though – yet. Even though his dad died eight years ago of a heart attack, his mother was still in pretty good health, so he was counting on her strong gene pool to be dominant when it came to his health. So far, he had done fairly well.

After his father died, his mother changed a lot. It was only the three of them, and those two treated him like a little pet for the majority of his life. All he had to do was be there. He didn't make a big impact on their lives or their relationship, he thought. They acted like best friends who were willing to let a third wheel tag along all the time.

His upbringing was old school, but textbook. They would practice the same discipline procedures all the time, faithfully. He was never given any more or any less of a punishment based on the severity of the act. If he disobeyed by not taking out the trash, he would get twelve hits with the switch. If he broke his mother's heirloom bowl after she told him not to touch it, he would get the same twelve hits with the switch. And, if he ran away and hid in order to avoid those twelve hits, she would sing that now-haunting song while she looked for him, every time. He got to the place where he hated the song more than he hated the switching.

"Maybe that is why I'm thinking about this song today. Maybe I need to call Mom, and this is the Lord's way of telling me that." Their weekly conversations had become less frequent after he started dating Beverly. Mom didn't approve of her. Maybe it was because she was more jealous of his time and attention since Dad died, or maybe she didn't like Beverly because she was white.

When he first took Beverly to meet her about a year ago, his mother told him she did not approve of him dating a white girl. She was in the kitchen and talking so loud that Steve was afraid Beverly heard the whole conversation. But, when they came out of the kitchen with some snacks, Beverly was sitting on the couch with her earphones attached to her cell phone, listening to her music and smiling at both of them when they entered the room. So, he hadn't brought it up with Beverly and she hadn't brought it up with him. He hoped that she hadn't heard a word.

Steve wasn't sure what his mother had against white people. He knew she and his father had white friends and that they socialized with white couples in their neighborhood. He had gone to school with white students and many of them were his friends who had frequented his house during their growing-up years. His mother never treated them any differently than they treated him, and he thought she liked all of them because they would stay for dinner and spend the night from time to time. He couldn't imagine any reason why she wouldn't like Beverly. Bev was sweeter than any girl he ever met. She was kind, gentle, easy to talk to, funny, caring, intelligent, and everything a mother-in-law should want in the next woman in line to take care of her son.

He and Beverly met in their college chemistry class. Both were seniors and had put off this course until the last minute. Neither was very confident in their ability to do well at memorizing the table of elements or conducting lab experiments without blowing up the classroom, so they would often joke with one another about what the results of their work might be and how much damage it might do. Eventually, they began to plan study time together in the library.

Steve had a roommate who turned out to be a great tutor for both of them; so many late nights were spent at Steve's apartment, reviewing for the next day's exam. What impressed Steve most about her was how she behaved on those nights. She never lowered her standard of character. So,

Steve made sure that he showed her the respect she earned. And, even after years of dating and ridicule from his friends and roommates, their relationship had maintained a level of complete trust and emotional respect. They were saving themselves for each other in marriage.

After his last conversation with his mother, he had prayed for days about how he should deal with this conflict. He had even shared that they had not engaged in any form of premarital sexual contact, and shouldn't she respect Beverly for being that kind of woman? What did skin color have to do with virtue and self-respect? He had even quoted Dr. Martin Luther King! But, when he finished the phrase about the content of her character being more important than the color of her skin, his mother had slapped him.

"How could you quote Dr. King and praise a white person, especially a white woman, in the same breath? Boy, have you forgotten what your ancestors fought and died for? Do you know what white people have done to your people? How could you even think about praising a white woman in my presence? I used to work for those people! I know how they look down their noses at us! I helped make them rich, selling their overpriced furs to more white people who already had closets full of them and then watching them double the price when one of my people wanted to buy just one on layaway. If you think you're going to bring a white woman into my family and continue my blood line with her tainted, weak-minded blood, you got another think coming! If you do it, it will be over my dead body!"

He couldn't even think of anything to say after that. He wanted to insist to her that she did not even know Beverly, that Beverly was a great person and she would be proud of any grandchildren that he and Beverly had. He wanted to say that if Beverly was black she would be bragging about her to all her friends. He wanted to remind her that this was not what he had been taught in Sunday School when they faithfully took him to church. He wanted to say a few more things, but couldn't say anything. So, he had just walked out of her home and hadn't called or visited since.

But now, it was nagging him. It must have been. Otherwise, he wouldn't have that whipping rhyme circulating in his subconscious today. Or, maybe the Lord had put it in his mind. Either way, he knew he needed to at least call her and try to straighten things out. But, he also knew that no matter what, he loved Beverly and would not give her up for anyone.

As he entered the store, he noticed that the young guy was at the cash register again. Steve liked that guy's attitude. He was funny, but you could also tell that he had a good head on his shoulders. He had done a great job of reorganizing the store and putting things in convenient places. Steve had been coming here for a long time and could remember how frustrated it was to pick up cereal on one aisle and coffee on the other. Weren't they both breakfast foods? Things were so much easier now when the coffee, tea, cereal, and breakfast bars were all on one aisle so he could zip in and zip out. Besides, why would Mr. Bob think that breakfast bars and candy bars would go together? Oh, well, that's how some people's minds worked. As a psychologist, Steve understood this; but sometimes, things people did still didn't make any sense.

"Hey, Steve! Good morning. How are you today? Just coming from the gym?"

Both men laughed. "Hey, Lincoln! You know me, man. I get my early morning workouts the best way I can. Thought I might squeeze something in after I have my coffee and a few clients this morning. Will you be free to join me?" They shared another good laugh on that one.

"I'll see if I can schedule that in for later today," Lincoln responded. "Is this all you have today? Were you able to find everything you needed?"

"Yes, thank you, man. I'm good with a breakfast bar and some juice this morning. I have to compliment you! You're doing a great job with this store. I remember when Mr. Bob had things set up like a crossword puzzle. You didn't know where one theme started and another one ended. You'd find bread in the produce department and he'd say something like, 'Well, you never know when somebody is going to walk in the store thinking about making a peanut butter and banana sandwich. You gotta remember the customer comes first!' If he really believed that, he would have put things where the customer could find them! But, you have done a super job!"

Lincoln smiled and shook Steve's hand warmly. "Thank you, Dr. Steve. It makes me feel good to hear you say that, because this is my dream job. People laugh when I say that. Some of them frown because they think I'm not setting high enough goals. But, what would they do if I wasn't doing what I love to do?"

"They'd be finding the ice cream in the automotive supplies aisle because people like to eat ice cream cones when they take a ride along the beach road!" The men laughed again as Steve picked up his bag. "All right, man. I'll probably see you tomorrow after my workout."

"You do that, Brother! I look forward to seeing you," Lincoln said, then paused. "By the way, do you have any time you could see me on a professional basis? Well, I'm sure you probably do, but should I call your office to see?"

Steve looked at Lincoln for a moment, then replied, "Of course, man, of course! Look," he said, while pulling out his business card portfolio, "here's one of my cards. Call me when you get some time, and I will set up a conversation appointment. First one's on me!" He smiled warmly at Lincoln.

Lincoln took the card and looked at it closely, then put it in his shirt pocket. "Thanks, Dr. Steve. I really mean it. I'll give you a call. Soon."

"Sooner the better," Steve said as he walked out the door. He thought to himself, "I wish I had someone who I could just talk to about this problem with Mom. Who does the 'psychia-trick' for the psychiatrist?" He chuckled. "It would be great if life was just that easy. But apparently, it's not."

Steve's office was just a few blocks from the store in a building which had been renovated and now housed four fairly new businesses. There was an optometrist office on the west side of the building. Steve had the opposite suite on the east side. Upstairs, two family practice physicians occupied the entire second floor. The third floor was a law office. So, if someone saw you enter the building, they assumed you were either crazy, going to have a baby, get some new glasses, or divorce your mate. Typically, none of the above was true.

Beverly was a partner in the law office. They both had completed school in the same year. Even though she had gone into law and him into medicine, they shared many of the same interests and chose to support one another as they finished in tandem. It had just worked out that he was able to secure office space in the same building where her firm had set up its offices as soon as the renovation was completed. "See, that's another confirmation that we are meant to be together. And, we're both grown people who can make our own decisions about our future. We don't have to listen to anybody else!" Yet, he could hear his mother's voice singing, 'Patty-cake, catch a snake, let him go before he break!' "Yes, Mom, please let me go before I break!" he spoke aloud.

Steve walked into his office and noticed how brightly the sunlight was shining through his large front windows and landing on the leaves of the philodendron that sat on the receptionist's desk. He noticed how tall the ficus tree was growing and how the waxy leaves seemed to stand out, one by one, yearning for more sunlight and strength. "Good morning, Tracy!"

"Good morning, Dr. Fannister! Your first appointment should be here in a half-hour. I called to confirm yesterday, and her file is on your desk. Do you need anything? Fresh coffee? Juice? Water?" At each item, Steve shook his head no. Finally, she said, "Ms. Sumner has already given you a call." Tracy smiled and winked. "You might want to call her back right away."

"Thanks, Tracy," Steve headed into his office. Before he sat in his chair, he dialed Beverly's number. "Good morning, Attorney Sumner," he tried to disguise his voice.

"Good morning, Dr. Fannister! Thought you could fool me?" She laughed loudly. "How are you feeling this morning? You seemed like you had a lot on your mind yesterday."

"I did. I do. But, don't you worry about me. How's your day going?"

"It looks like it might be fairly busy, but I sure would love to set a noon appointment with you so that we can go get some lunch and talk about how lonesome I feel when I don't see you for twelve hours."

"That sounds like a real plan, because I would like to present to you, counsel, that I feel the same way, if not worse. And, if I won't be prosecuted for this confession, I may just die if I can't spend at least one hour of quality time with you today."

"I will hold your confession as privileged between an attorney and her client, and I will agree to the plan of reconciliation. Let's stop by the store, pick up some sandwich makings, and have a short picnic on the beach. I think that will do both of us a lot of good. Agreed?"

"Agreed!" Steve replied. "All right, my love. I will meet you in the lobby at 11:55, unless you want me to come upstairs and pick you up."

"See you in the lobby! Love you."

"I love you too, Bev. More than anything. Goodbye." Steve hung up the phone. "Mom, I wish you were a fly on my wall. Beverly is the best thing that has ever happened to me and if she will have me, I will marry her. There are only three people in the world who have ever meant anything to me, and she is one of them. You must accept that."

Suddenly, he knew what he had to do. Today. He immediately pushed the intercom button. "Tracy?"

"Yes, Dr. Fannister."

"Tracy, please hold all of my calls for the next twenty minutes. I need to make an important phone call."

"Yes, sir."

As he hung up the phone, Steve prayed. "God, I know that your Word said I should honor my father and my mother, because that is the only commandment with the promise of a long life. And, I want a long life because I would like to enjoy it with Beverly, our children, and our children's children. I also want my mother to be part of that love and celebration. But, I can't figure out why she won't accept the woman that I love and want to be my wife just because she is white. Even with my schooling and years of professional experience, I can't figure out my mother's psyche and the single issue she has with Beverly. I know this is not of You. I know I need Your wisdom to address it with Mom and keep peace between her, me, and Beverly. So, please go ahead of me and this phone call. Please let Your Holy Spirit speak to her heart and her mind and prepare the way for this conversation. Please support me as I attempt to do this decently and orderly. Please let me have good news for Beverly when we go to lunch today. Please just work all of this out, in my life and in my mind. I can't be what I need to be to help others like Lincoln if I can't help my mother and myself. I have committed my life to You, and I trust You to work this out. You have never let me down. So, thank You, Lord. Amen."

Steve dialed the familiar phone number, the only one he had consistently known all of his life. As the phone rang, many thoughts ran through his head. He could hear his mother repeat in a raspy tone, "Snake, snake, snake, snake." The ringing stopped. She picked up. "Hello?" she said.

"Hi, Mom. It's me, Steve. Sorry I haven't called you in a while."

"Steve? Steve? It's good to hear your voice, son! I was thinking about you this morning when I woke up!" She chuckled. "Actually, I think I dreamed about you."

"Did you, Mom? What did you dream?" The psychiatrist in him kicked into gear. "You know, sometimes our dreams are telling us something about ourselves or an issue we need to figure out." Once Steve said it, he wasn't sure how she might respond. But, she agreed quickly.

"That is so true, son. Well, I have been thinking about this dream all morning. See, I was trying to get to some water. At first, it looked really close. It was clear and looked like it would be warm. There were other people who were wading in it, and it seemed like they were having a good time. I was inside a room looking out through a large window. I wanted to be in the water. So, I went out of a door that at first seemed to lead directly to the water. However, once I passed through the door I saw that there were two paths to the water. The one on the left looked like it was the one that would lead easily to the wading area. The one on the right, which was where I stood, was the one that could get me to the water, but it I would first have to go down a steep cliff. I hadn't seen the cliff when I was inside the room. But, since I was there and the water still looked inviting, I decided to try to get down the cliff.

As I started toward the cliff, I had to pass under some tree branches. Someone was beside me coaching me on. They told me to look up. When I did, I saw a very large red lizard, maybe the size of a crocodile, crawling through the tree branches. It passed over my head and scared me, but the person coaching me said it was okay, it wouldn't harm me. As I moved closer to the water, I noticed that I would have to go down a steep drop to get to the water. It looked like I could do it if I could slide and stop and then maybe jump into the water. But, when I looked to my left, I could see that if I took that path, I could just walk right into the water. As I was trying to decide if I wanted to stay where I was and try to get to the water that way, or go back and take the easier way on the left, I woke up. Son, you're the doctor," she chuckled. "Does it mean anything if you can remember a dream once you are awake?"

"Wow, Mom, there's a whole lot going on here!" Steve laughed. She was quiet on the other end. "Well, Mom, if I can apply a little clinical analysis," he laughed lightly, "I would say that you are struggling with making a change. You want to do it, but it is a challenge. You are willing to do it the hard way if you have to, but you are seeing what might be an easier way to do it. There are risks involved, maybe because of old ideas or emotions that are tempting you to be fearful. But, a guide is directing you forward, letting you know that the things you fear cannot harm you. You have a choice; but either way, you are headed for the water and it represents a pleasant change. You will be warm, you will be comfortable, and you will be with the people you desire to be with in a situation you will enjoy. You just have to take the leap."

The opposite line was silent for some seconds. He heard what he thought might be a slight sniff. He was about to call to her when she said, "Son, you are a very wise man. I wish I could take some credit for that. But, I will say that your words have confirmed my thoughts today, and I would like to apologize to you sincerely for my words and actions from the past. Hopefully, I can share more with you one day about that. But for now, please forgive me and let Beverly know I would love to visit with the two of you any time you can fit me into your schedule. I'm looking forward to getting to know her better. I miss you. I love you." Her voice began to quaver.

"Mom, I love you too, and I will always be your champion. I exist to kill all the red lizards in your life. You have made me the man I am, and you have made my day. Thank you." Steve was praying when Tracy buzzed him to say his appointment had arrived. He was ready for everything that God had in store for his family.

61

There is a River of Life Flowing Out of Me

"Receive my instruction, and not silver; and knowledge rather than choice gold." Proverbs 8:10

*

Sunrise on the coast is something that, once you see it, you never forget it. When Jimmy woke up that morning, he realized that the light haze of pre-dawn was slowly lifting, and if he moved very swiftly, he would beat the sun out to the shore. He turned first to look at his wife of six years, Mary. "Lord, thank You for this woman! She has stuck by my side through thick and thin. Please give me the wisdom and the resources to make her know the sacrifice was worth it. Amen!"

He went to the bathroom and then the closet. He pulled on the shorts he wore yesterday and slipped his feet into his flip-flops. Still wearing the old t-shirt he slept in, he stepped out the door and headed for the seashore. A few gulls were up with him, waiting for the sun to wake up the insects and small sea creatures that would be their breakfast.

Truth be told, this was his favorite part of the day. It exhilarated his spirit to watch the world wake up. The sun coming over the eastern horizon, mirrored on the swift-moving wave caps, made him feel part of a well-orchestrated pattern. God was saying, "Time to wake up, Creation! I'm turning on the light!" He always felt excitement to know he was ready even before the call came.

Jimmy sat on the sand and rubbed his forearms, warming himself before he rose to make one quick lap from his favorite spot to the pier and then back. As he was heading back, he saw the bright rim of orange and yellow begin to expose itself to him. "Hello, sunshine!" he thought. "It's so great to see you!" His heart began to race slightly. He felt anticipation of greatness every time he witnessed this moment. "God, You are truly mighty. To create something so dependable, day in and day out, and never let the mere sight of it become routine is amazing. And, You've been doing it faithfully for eons. This is why I serve You! And, I know that You are in control of all things and can work miracles by Your great grace and power! Thank You for loving me!"

As Jimmy stood and marveled at the works of God, his doubts about how he and Mary would survive this latest attack of the enemy began to diminish in the brilliance of God's love. Something leaped from his spirit into his mind. "God can do it! That's all I needed to realize! It's not up to me or any man. God has already done it!" Praise rose up in his chest and burst from his lips. "Thank You, Lord!" he began to holler at the top of his lungs.

A few gulls flew up from where they posed on the shore, and he started to laugh. Jumping up and down on the sand, he cried louder, "Thank You, Lord! Thank You! What you have accomplished in just a short time in my life is a miracle, so I know that You can work miracles and do what no man ever thought was possible! You will be with us in court on Friday! You will go before us and touch the hearts of the attorneys and the judge. You will work all things out for good! Whew! Thank You, Jesus, in advance for this miracle!" Jimmy stayed out on the beach for a while longer, just keeping his mind focused on the beauty of nature, the power of God, and his gratitude for all God had already done for him.

When he came back into the house, Mary was sitting at the kitchen table, sipping from her cup. The aroma of fresh-brewed coffee drew him to his cup, which she had placed in front of the chair across from her. He kissed her forehead gently. "Good morning, beautiful," he whispered. "Why you up so early?" He ruffled her hair and laughed.

Mary stretched and lifted her right leg to the chair, hugging her knee. She smiled. "I heard you get up, so I thought I'd do that too. Plus, I wanted to make you coffee for a change."

"Aw, girl, you're just too good to me!" He reached across the table and squeezed her hand. She looked deep into his eyes. He could see a flicker of concern on her face. "Look, this isn't the first time we've invited God to create a miracle for us! And guess what? He's never yet refused an invitation! He has shown up every time!" He laughed. Mary joined in, rising from the table.

"Yes, He has. You are sure right about that! So, I'm not worried. I just wanted to make sure you were okay."

"I'm just fine! You know it's hard for me to survive without some exciting trepidation every now and then!" He laughed heartily. "But, no, I'm not afraid. I'm just waiting for God to surprise me!"

"Me, too!" She leaned over and put her arms around his neck. He stood up and kissed her, then snuggled his nose in her neck.

"Baby, I thank God for you! And, I want to thank you for trusting the God in me."

"Of course I do," she said softly. "I, of all people, know God gave you to me to take care of me, and He gave me to you because He knew I needed you. So you see, I have to trust you, because I have to trust God."

"Girl, your brain is working like that this early in the morning? How did you say that, *I have to trust you because I have to trust God*?" Girl, you are deep!" Mary laughed and tried to hit at Jimmy. He danced away playfully. "You are too much, Girl!! You got it going on!!" He ran toward the bathroom as Mary followed, laughing.

Work that day was challenge after challenge. He couldn't find his badge when he got ready to enter the resort complex. That had never happened before. Jimmy was such an organized person and never made errors. That is why the gate supervisor wanted to let him in anyway, but that would have been a policy violation and he didn't know if it might be a quality management set-up, so Jimmy had to go back to the car and search for it. He finally found it under his sun visor. "How could that have happened?" Jimmy was puzzled. "I never even use that thing, and I know I didn't use it yesterday. Plus, I had my badge yesterday. That makes no sense whatsoever!" But, Jimmy was glad that he did find it, so he decided to try to figure that out later.

Jimmy had worked almost every position during the five years of his employment at the resort. Shuttle driver, front desk clerk, hospitality room monitor, pool security guard, and events facilitator. He had been promoted to the position of concierge last year, and that seemed to be the just-right fit for him. He loved to meet people and do all he could to help them have a good time while staying at the resort. He loved to overhear the conversations among successful people as they shared their secrets for gaining and keeping their wealth. He loved to joke around with the little children and the teenagers who ran through the resort and played in the pool. The bottom line was that he just loved his job, and that was it.

Unfortunately, he had not made enough money in those five years to keep up with their expenses. They had shown up in town with little money and no real connections. All they had going for themselves was faith. They both loved the water and warm weather. They both knew they wanted to put down roots in a place where they could raise children and enjoy life, maybe one day living in a beachfront condo. Both believed in following the leading of God, and when their car ran out of gas in this town, they both agreed this was their sign to stay.

Things worked out well. The gas station attendant told them about a house that was for rent under unusual circumstances. The owner's family had lived there for many years. Both of his parents had died many years ago. He and his three siblings had all moved away. He had a successful investment firm and lived in another city. He was willing to "rent" the home to someone who would fix it up and keep it up for as long as they wished to live there. All they had to do was pay for all the improvements, maintain good care of the home, pay the yearly taxes, and allow him to come and check on the condition of the home whenever he was in town. Eventually, he moved back to town, but kept the agreement with them because he was impressed with the great care they had given to the home.

That was a blessing! But, there were other bills which they incurred over the years and had been unable to pay. Mary had three miscarriages in a two-year period. With each, she experienced extreme complications. She lost one ovary due to an ectopic pregnancy. That resulted in a very expensive hospital stay. With the last attempt at pregnancy, scar tissue in the uterus caused her to experience excessive blood loss; so once again, she had a hospital stay of a few days. Jimmy hoped that the hospital would give them more time to make monthly payments on the bills, but he received the notice last month that they were taking them to court this Friday, demanding a total of $360,000. On his meager wages, there was no way – short of a miracle – that he could come up with that kind of money. So, he had watched, waited, and prayed for a miracle.

This was ridiculous! Here he was, five days away from judgment, and he was happy about his circumstances. People might call him crazy, but he called himself maintaining an attitude of faith that God would reward with a blessing. So, when the lady accused him of damaging her luggage, he smiled and said, "Ma'am, I am confident that I didn't damage it, but I will be glad to check the camera to see who did." He noticed her face flush, but went directly into the security office with a smile to check the monitors. What he found was that she had dropped it down the stairwell after she had impatiently decided to take it to the lobby herself.

The camera showed her waiting for the elevator, looking frustrated and tapping her foot. She then grabbed the suitcase and dragged it to the stairs. The next camera picks her up in the stairwell. She bumps it down one flight of stairs, turns on the landing, then begins to head down the next flight. Somehow, the handle on the luggage twists and breaks, so the suitcase spins around on her, hitting her leg. She hops around for a moment, which was a little amusing to Jimmy. She kicks the bag, then tries to pick it up and carry it. She makes it for one flight. The next thing you notice is her leaning over the railing. She begins to walk down the steps and it is obvious that the suitcase is nowhere to be seen. When the camera at the lobby level picks her up, she is pulling the suitcase up to the concierge desk and then ringing the buzzer for Jimmy. He arrives and lifts her suitcase onto the luggage rack. Ten minutes later, his supervisor approaches him to question him about the damage.

His supervisor's conversation with her was a humorous one. She feigned denial until he showed her the video footage. She wasn't very happy with either the supervisor or Jimmy when she left, but Jimmy was glad that at least his reputation remained intact.

His last experience of the day was his most trying. An older gentleman had been staying at the resort for a ten-day vacation. He was probably too old to have been traveling alone and had displayed some erratic behaviors during his stay. He would order multiple meals at one time from room service, then act as if he did not remember the order when it arrived at his door. He would walk into the gift shop about twenty times a day and ask the clerk about the same sun hat each time. How much does it cost? Does it come in any other colors? How does she think it looks on him? She really wanted to just give it to him, but knew it would count against her inventory. So, she just patiently answered those three questions sixty times and kept a smile on her face. He would ride the shuttle into town and back without ever getting off, just smiling and nodding. The gentleman had called the service desk about 7:00 that morning to say he would need a ride to the airport at 10:00. Jimmy had the shuttle driver ready and waiting at 9:45. The gentleman did not show. Jimmy called his room, and he said that he didn't plan to leave that day. So, Jimmy cancelled the service.

At 10:30, the gentleman showed up in the lobby with his luggage. He apologized for being late and said he was ready now to go. Jimmy reminded him that he had told him he was not going to leave that day. The man said he did not recall that conversation, and he needed a ride to the airport right away. So, Jimmy called the driver and told him to come right back to pick the gentleman up. At 10:50, the driver pulled up to the door. By this time, the gentleman had fallen asleep. Jimmy woke him up to tell him that his ride was here to take him to the airport. The man asked why. Jimmy patiently told him that he had requested a ride to the airport, and it was here. The man said he didn't need to go to the airport, as he was staying at the resort.

Jimmy liked the old man, but he was becoming frustrated at the consistent change in plans. He was also worried about the man's safety if he was going to travel alone. He asked the desk clerk if the man had listed any next relative, and she said he had not. He returned to the gentleman, who had fallen asleep once again. Jimmy shook him gently and asked him if he had airline tickets. The man said that he had driven to the resort; however, Jimmy knew he had arrived by airport limousine, so he had flown in.

Right when Jimmy was about to phone the police, a well-dressed young woman walked over to the man. "Grandfather! What are you doing down here? I told you to wait in your room for me to check you out! I've been looking all over for you!" He smiled and reached out to her as a young child would to a parent when he wants to be picked up. "Now, you just sit right here and let me finish taking care of your bill. My goodness, you had a hearty appetite while you were on vacation! This sea air must have stimulated your appetite!"

As she walked back over to the desk, Jimmy stepped up to her. "Excuse me, miss? Is this your grandfather?" She smiled and nodded yes. "Well, I am very glad to know that he has someone to take care of him. I was beginning to get worried that something might happen to him if someone wasn't with him to make sure he got where he needed to go."

"Thank you for even caring about him. He has been independent all of his life. The very thought of supervision makes him even more stubborn. So, we agreed to let him vacation alone, but I have been staying at the resort down the beach so that I can keep an eye on him. I've never been too far away." She smiled with a knowing twinkle in her eyes. "I have to treasure these days and the memories they bring, because I'm not sure how much longer we will have him with us. Still, we never know. He has a way of fooling us from time to time."

"I can believe that," Jimmy chuckled. "Well, I'll go say goodbye to him." Jimmy stepped over to where the gentleman was sitting. His eyes were closed. Jimmy lightly touched his shoulder. "Sir, I think your granddaughter is just about ready for you all to leave. I'm glad you have someone you can depend on to look after you. You're a blessed man!" The old man opened his eyes. He looked at Jimmy with a piercing blue gaze.

"Thank you, son. You are, too. Here." He handed Jimmy a card. Jimmy turned it over. It was a lottery ticket. Jimmy laughed. The man smiled.

"Well, thank you, sir. But, I don't gamble." Jimmy started to hand it back to the old gentleman.

"I don't either, Sonny. This isn't a gamble. This is a know." He pushed the ticket back at Jimmy and tapped his own forehead with his forefinger. He looked up at his granddaughter, who had just approached them. He cleared his throat. "Are you ready, Missy? I am." He looked back at Jimmy. "My work here is done. Good bye, son. Thank you for all you have done for me. Thank you for what you will do for others." With a spryness that Jimmy had never before noticed, the older gentleman took his granddaughter's arm and walked out to the shuttle. Jimmy stood there and watched them get in and drive away. He put the ticket in his pocket with a laugh and then went back to work.

Mary had fixed a great meal of fish stew, fried oysters, a tossed salad made with fresh greens, and cornbread. Jimmy had been ready for dinner and a hot bath after a day like the one he had experienced. Over their meal, they laughed heartily about the story of the woman with the damaged luggage. Mary had him verbally replay the camera footage of her picking up the suitcase and putting it on the luggage rack, looking around, and then going to the desk. With every retelling, it became more and more funny! Mary teared up a little bit when he was talking about the older gentleman. She felt sorry for anyone who didn't have someone to care for them. After Jimmy finished that story, Mary asked, "So, where's the ticket?"

Jimmy hadn't really thought about it since he had placed it in his shirt pocket. "You know what, it's in my pocket."

"Well, go get it!" Mary said.

"Why? We don't gamble! I'm not going to count on something like that to give me money when other people have wasted their money to make a lottery!"

"Didn't the Bible say the wealth of the sinner is laid up for the just? Anyway, I just want to see it. Plus, you spent no money on it. And, what if God planned to use it to bless us? You said the old man said it wasn't a gamble, it was a 'know'. And what does that mean? Was he talking about faith? You know, the substance of things hoped for and the evidence of things not seen? Something you 'know' with no evidence? And, what if he and his granddaughter were angels unaware?"

"Mary, slow your roll!" Jimmy laughed and rubbed her head between his hands. "You're thinking too much! Look, we trust God, not lottery tickets. I had meant to throw it away before I even got home. I don't like even touching those things. I know that God is going to work a miracle, but He doesn't need any help from the lottery." He kissed her on the forehead. "It's been a long and crazy day. I'm going to take a bath and get in the bed. I'm tired, and worried that tomorrow might not be any better."

Jimmy headed into the bathroom. Mary sat at the table for a few minutes, thinking. What if they were angels that were sent to minister to her and Jimmy? She knew that Jimmy had strong faith, but there were times when he missed seeing the spiritual element because he needed to know the black and white of a situation. But, faith isn't always black and white.

Mary stood up and started toward the bedroom, then stopped. "Lord, I know this ticket is technically Jimmy's property. The old man gave it to him. But, I don't want him to throw it away. Wednesday is two days away. What would it hurt to hold on to it until then? That's when they announce the lottery winners. If it's not a winner, nothing is lost. If it is, everything is gained. I'm not going to count You out. Please forgive me if this is stealing, but I don't believe it is because he would be the first to say that what is his is mine. Plus, if it is a winning ticket, he will thank me for the rest of our lives. Especially on Thursday."

Two days later, Mary felt so disappointed, embarrassed, and foolish! To go against what she knew were her husband's wishes, taking something from his pocket and praying that it would be a winning ticket that would save them from financial ruin seemed now the very thing that made God laugh at their circumstance and have her build all of her hopes up for nothing. She looked on herself in disdain as she recalled how she had grabbed the ticket at 10:00 that night, sitting quietly and nervously as she listened to the television announcer read off the numbers. None of them matched. But, she knew there was a Powerball number that could win it all for them. There still was a chance! She had felt a strong confidence all day, as if God was confirming in her spirit that He was going to work it all out! Now, that last number! Lord, please let it match!

It didn't. Nothing at all matched. They were losers. It was almost too much for her to bear. All of her hopes had been resting on those numbers. Now, she felt that she had nothing. She cried and prayed herself to sleep that night, wondering how Jimmy could snore so peacefully with Friday only two days away and no plan for their situation, except to keep trusting God.

Lincoln brought the stack of newspapers into the store and placed them on the end of the counter when he arrived around 6:30 that Thursday morning. He did his usual routine of circulating the store and checking on things, then went to open the front window shades and let the sunlight in. A ray of light shone on the front page of the paper where the lottery numbers were printed. "Oh no!" he said to himself. "I forgot to deliver that envelope to the concierge at The Lobster Bay Resort. Where is that envelope? Let me run it over there right now!"

He remembered the couple who came in on Monday afternoon, the dapper-looking old man with the young beautiful lady. They had come into the store, arm in arm, and purchased some water and breath mints. When they got to the counter, the man asked him how he was doing, and if he knew where The Lobster Bay Resort was, to which Lincoln responded that he was fine and yes, he did know the Lobster Bay. The lady then asked Lincoln for four Powerball tickets and an envelope. She paid for them, placed them in the envelope, sealed it, and wrote, "Concierge, The Lobster Bay Resort" on the front of the envelope. She gave Lincoln five dollars and asked him to please deliver the envelope to The Lobster Bay Inn on Wednesday evening. How could he have forgotten to do that?

Jimmy got up Thursday morning with a song of joy in his heart. He was laughing and singing and dancing around the house so much as he got ready for work that Mary couldn't help but laugh with him. The depression that had tried to attach itself to her last night slid off like a loose scarf. By the time he walked out of the front door, she was singing and smiling. No matter what, they loved each other and God loved them.

As Jimmy was walking up to check in at the back doors, Lincoln had arrived at the front doors. He knew that he only had a few minutes to put the envelope into the hands of the concierge and rush back to the store so that his early morning customers would not be inconvenienced. Lincoln entered the lobby and headed toward the front desk clerk. Jimmy came down the hall and smiled at Lincoln. He had seen him many times at the store, but didn't know his name.

"Good morning! I know you! I've seen you at the store." Jimmy smiled and extended his hand. Lincoln shook it. "What can I do for you this morning?"

"Hi, man! Yes, I do recognize you! Wow, maybe you can help me. I need to drop something off to the concierge and hurry back to the store. Can you tell me where I can find him?"

"You're looking at him!" Jimmy laughed. "I'm Jimmy. I'm the concierge. You have an envelope from me? Who is it from?"

"It's from an older gentleman and a young woman who stopped by the store on Monday afternoon. They bought some lottery tickets and asked me to bring them to you. I was supposed to bring them last night, but time got away from me and frankly, man, I just forgot! Please forgive me!" Lincoln handed Jimmy the envelope. "Here they are!"

Jimmy accepted the envelope. "Thanks, man! I hope this didn't take you out of your way!"

"Aw no, this is no problem! I just wish I would have made an on-time delivery! Anyway," he pulled the newspaper out of his back pocket, "here's the winning numbers right on the front page. Check them! Those two seemed to think this was real important, life or death. I'd like to see if I had any part in making a winner."

Jimmy laughed loudly and slapped Lincoln on the back. "Man, if I won anything it would be a miracle!"

"Let's see!" Lincoln urged. Jimmy paused for a moment, then responded.

"Okay, man! Let's see." He stepped up to the counter of the concierge desk. Lincoln followed. Lincoln opened the paper and put his fingers on the numbers. "All right," Jimmy said. "I'll scratch and you read."

Jimmy took a dime out of his pocket and began to slide it over the silver film that covered the numbers. He read them, one by one, as they were disclosed. "Seven, five, two, two, zero."

"You have three matches on that one, man! What's the Powerball number?"

"Forty-three," Jimmy read.

"Forty-three? Forty-three! That's a winner, man! That's the winning number!" Lincoln jumped up and down. "You hit the Powerball, boy! You're the winner!"

Jimmy looked up in disbelief. "What do you mean? I hit the Powerball?"

Lincoln grabbed Jimmy by both arms and looked him dead in the eye. "You're a millionaire! You have the jackpot number! Wow! I can't believe this! And the tickets were bought in our store! Mr. Bob is going to be rich! Me, too!!" Lincoln lifted his arms high in the air and began to prance around the desk like a boxing champ.

By now, the other employees were gathering around, trying to make sense of Lincoln's excitement. Jimmy was standing there, his mouth and eyes wide open. "God, am I dreaming?" he thought. "Is this my miracle? Yes, it is! You waited until the last minute and came in the back door with a blessing! Thank you, Lord!" Jimmy began to jump up and down and cry out, "Thank You, God! Thank You for this miracle! You made a way out of no way! Thank You, Jesus! Where's the phone? I need to call Mary right away!"

Lincoln walked toward Jimmy, and Jimmy tackled him in a strong embrace. "Thank you so much, man, for bringing this to me this morning! You can't know how much this means to me and my wife today! See, we have to go to court tomorrow. We're being sued for $360,000 which we did not have. But, thank God for this miracle! They will know that we can soon pay it all off. God is so good, and He used you today to deliver a blessing! I appreciate you!"

"Man, I'm just glad I listened to my mind this morning and brought this right over! I'm happy for you. And, don't forget – you've got three more tickets to check! Those might be winners, too!" He patted Jimmy on the back. "Take care, man. I hope I get a chance to know your wife. And, your God! I need these kinds of blessings in my life."

Jimmy grabbed Lincoln's hands and shook them hard, then looked straight into his eyes. "Man, I know God laid this plan out for both of us. There's something He wants to do in your life, too. Bless you, brother! Listen, I'll be coming by the store to see you soon." Jimmy laughed and hugged Lincoln warmly, then wrapped his arm around Lincoln's shoulders as he walked him toward the door. "But first, I've got to call my wife!"

But the Master of the Sea Heard My Despairing Cry

*"Give instruction to a wise man, and he will be yet wiser;
teach a just man, and he will increase in learning."*   Proverbs 9:9

*

For years, Lily had to live with the will to fight temptation and the urge to give in every time – to food. She was a normal, healthy baby and a fairly slim child. But, things changed when she started seventh grade. For some reason, she began to gain weight, at least ten pounds a month. Her pediatrician told her parents that it was probably something hormonal and she would grow out of it. She didn't. It seemed like she craved food and ate even if she wasn't hungry. She would eat a full breakfast and lunch, and then piece together a full meal of leftovers as soon as she got home from school. By the time her mother got home from work and cooked dinner, she was ready again for another full meal. When she started high school, she weighed 400 pounds.

It was a good thing that she was outgoing and friendly, or high school would have been miserable for her. But, Lily was active in almost every organization at school. She had a major part in all of the plays and musicals, she was on the debate team, she attended all of the sport events year round, she was an officer in student government, and she was a teachers' pet. Everyone loved Lily. Teachers were always giving her candy as a reward, or taking her out for a hamburger lunch at the nearby fast food restaurant. They meant no harm. They just wanted to make her as happy as she made them and to motivate her to keep up her great work. But, these kinds of rewards translated to more weight for Lily so that by the time she graduated high school and left home for college, she weighed an extremely unhealthy 452 pounds.

Lily remembered vividly the day she walked into the dorm room she was to share with her roommate from the West Coast. She had been so excited about going away to go to school! She bought new clothes, new room decorations, new bedding, and new shoes. She couldn't wait to meet new people and begin living the college life. The 452 pounds stuck in her mind as she recalled the day she first met Rachel, who was already in the dorm room. She had walked in, lugging all of her belongings, with a big smile and a warm greeting.

"Hi! You must be Rachel! I'm Lily, your new roommate! We are going to have so much fun!" Lily had not anticipated Rachel's response. Rachel rolled over and sat on the bed, staring at Lily with her mouth open wide. Then, she stood.

"What is wrong with you? How much do you weigh?"

Lily immediately became defensive. "Nothing is wrong with me. What's wrong with you? No manners? No home training? And, since you asked, I weigh 452 pounds. What's that to you?"

"Whoa, I'm sorry! But, I didn't expect you to look like this." Rachel waved her arm around the room. "How are we both going to fit in this little space? I'm sorry, but I don't think I can do this!" She sat back down on the bed and looked Lily up and down.

"Well, you don't have to do this!" Lily glared at Rachel. "Look, I'll go see if I can find another room, maybe with someone who isn't so self-centered."

"Good luck!" Rachel started to laugh and then rolled back over onto her stomach, reopened a magazine, and began to leisurely read.

Lily stood in the doorway for a moment and just looked at Rachel, not sure what she should do but confident that if she stood there too long, she might do something that she would regret later. Gathering the belongings that lay around her feet, she turned clumsily and walked away, leaving the door wide open. Tears smarted her eyes as she lumbered down the hallway toward the elevator. How unfair! It wasn't her fault that she was overweight. Or, was it? She thought about the big breakfast she had that morning, so excited about her first day living on a college campus. Wasn't that a reason to celebrate, and hadn't food always been the best way for her to host her own personal parties?

Lily had never felt ashamed of her weight. She had embraced it and even enjoyed it because it was the product of the love of her life, food. It was everything to her, physically and emotionally. It brought her happiness, comfort, and good memories. It was like a faithful companion that had never let her down. Even though it wasn't good for her, it was good to her. And, it had never hurt her the way some people had.

But, she couldn't get Rachel's disgusted expression out of her mind. Lily had gone directly to the resident assistant and reported what had happened with Rachel. After he looked at her for a few seconds, he cleared this throat and told her that he thought there might be one more single room still available and he would see what he could do. Single room? Lily thought that college life was about having a roommate to share your day with, study with, maybe even fight with. Well, she had already done that part, so she was looking forward to exploring the other two areas. But, she didn't say anything, because she thought that if she could just get a room, everything would be okay for now.

Thank God, there was a single room at the end of the hall, so she moved in there. Things worked out pretty well. It had its own bathroom and shower, so she wouldn't have to compete with any of the other girls on that wing of the floor for those two conveniences. Still, it seemed like something set up for handicapped people, and she wasn't really happy about that. There was nothing wrong with her that a good celebration wouldn't fix.

By the end of her first semester, Lily was very popular and involved in campus life. She had many international friends and often dreamed of what life might be like when she was graduated, earning great money, and able to travel around the world. She loved the foods that her new friends would cook and share with her and was excited at the prospect of visiting foreign countries and testing all types of international cuisine. Just the thought of travel and food made her extraordinarily excited, so she would eat something she loved in order to celebrate that goal.

Her brother called her on the morning of her last final to tell her that she would need to go to the airport and pick up her ticket to fly home because her father would not be able to drive up to get her for the Christmas break as he had planned. Lily didn't mind that; she loved the thought of flying. It fit right in with her future goal of world travel. It was the first time in her life that she would be on an airplane. Was she all right with that? Her brother was just a little worried about her. Lily assured him that she would be fine!

She packed up everything before she went to class. She breezed through her final and then hurried back to the dorm to get her bags. Looking around the room, she thought about how much she had matured in the past few months. She was able to live alone without feeling homesick. Many of her classmates had quit school already and gone back home, but she had survived. She had always been a survivor, she thought. No matter what had happened to her, she had pulled herself together and avoided being a bother to anyone. She wished she could convince her brother that he didn't have to worry about her. But, she supposed, that is what big brothers are supposed to do.

"Then, why didn't he do it when it really counted…" There is was again, that quiet little voice that often plagued her thoughts. She fought the urge to answer it this time. It wasn't worth it, and she didn't have time to deal with the things she had worked so hard to box up and pack away years ago. The problem now was that the box kept trying to pop open like a giant Jack-in-the-Box, and she was losing the strength to keep pushing the lid down. Still, she heard the words coming out of her mouth, "He couldn't. He didn't know. And if he would have found out… well, I don't even want to think about that. But, I'm okay. I'll be okay. And I don't want him feeling guilty for something I should have done."

On the cab ride to the airport, Lily began to think about the day the abuse happened. She really didn't want to, but looking out the window, it seemed like the weather was exactly like it had been that day. Just a little cool, with moisture in the air. Skies somewhat cloudy. All the elements of a drowsy day. Nick's friend had come by looking for him. Lily had opened the door when he knocked. It was mid-morning and she had slept a little later than usual on that Saturday. Dad was on a weekend fishing trip with some of his buddies. Mom had gone shopping. Nick was doing some odd jobs for one of the neighbors. Lily had grabbed an old bathrobe when she heard Brian knocking. She had asked who was at the door, and then opened it when he said his name. She didn't know him all that well, but she knew that he and Nick hung out sometimes.

Brian stepped into the house, even though she told him that Nick wasn't home. She had kind of suppressed what happened next, because it was very confusing for a thirteen-year old. He had looked at her for a moment, and then asked her if anybody had ever kissed her. While she was trying to figure out what he was talking about, he grabbed her arms and forced his mouth on hers. What happened next was something she had tried all of her life to forget.

By the time she got to the airport, she was famished. The sky cap helped her check her luggage at the curb, and walked her through the process of picking up her boarding pass. All the while, she felt like she was in a trance. The thought of food was prominent in her mind. She really didn't care whether or not she made it on the plane in time. She just had to have something to eat. Now. The sky cap was very polite and helpful when he realized that this was her first time flying. He walked her into the terminal and helped her check in. He told her where to sit and wait for the announcement that they were ready to board. As he turned to leave her, she called, "Where can I get something to eat?" The way he looked her up and down angered her for a moment, but the urge for food was stronger than his judgment of her. She repeated, "Sir, where can I find something to eat?"

He smiled slightly. "Just go back the way we came, but head to the right toward Terminal A. The food court will be right there. Just don't forget how to get back!" He walked away.

"Thanks," Lily said sarcastically. "What should I do? Drop crumbs like Hansel and Gretel? Eat my way back?" Of course, he didn't hear her, but she heard herself and felt a little frustrated. "Why are my eating habits any of his concern? If I want to eat that's my business." Lily shifted herself back up to her feet. "And, I'm about to take care of business right now!"

Within fifteen minutes, she had found the food court and was headed back to her departure gate. She purchased enough cheeseburgers and fries to tide her over until she got home. She'd heard about the small airline meal portions, so she had to be full to avoid being angry during the flight.

Lily was not familiar with the boarding process, but she began to suspect something might be wrong. Even though she was supposedly seated in the third row, she had to wait until everyone else boarded before the flight attendant escorted her toward the door. "Ma'am," she started, "you appear to be over our weight restrictions, but we are going to see if we can accommodate you on two back seats. Whoever made arrangements for you did not purchase the required extra seat. However," she smiled warmly at Lily, "today is your day! We don't have a full flight, and we're heading your way anyhow, so we will make it work."

Lily smiled back weakly, but she wondered why this was such a big deal. She wasn't that big, that she should need two airplane seats! But, reality set in when she finally sat down. She barely fit into both seats put together. "Is this what 452 pounds looks like?" she wondered. "And, is this why people have been looking at me crazy for the past few months?" Lily felt like she wanted to cry, but she hadn't done that in so long that she almost couldn't remember how it felt.

She had heard that people typically got nervous during the takeoff and the landing, but she felt strangely calm. She watched the stewardess demonstrate what they should do in case of an emergency, but her mind was far away. A sadness was descending on her, and she was having a difficult time shaking it. She thought it might be due to leaving all of her friends for a month, but she really knew what it was all about. She was going to have to deal with the demon called "food addiction" and she wasn't ready. Plus, she felt that if she was, she would feel as if she were being unfaithful to the love of her life. There went that soft voice again, "Love doesn't abuse."

Lily closed her eyes for what felt like a few moments. She was awakened by the sound of wheels moving down the aisle. As she opened her eyes, she saw the stewardess standing in front of her, smiling. "Would you like something to drink with your sandwich?" She handed Lily a tray with a roast beef sandwich, a bag of chips, and two cookies. She waited for Lily to reply.

"Could I have two colas?" Lily asked. The stewardess paused for a moment.

"Two?" Lily continued to look at her with a questioning glance. She gave in. "I guess so, even though we're only supposed to give one per person. But, with a small flight today, I guess that will be okay. Here you go." She handed Lily a cup of ice and two cans of cola. Lily smiled.

"Thank you so much!" Lily said, setting them on the table tray to her right. As she opened the sandwich tray and the first can of soda, she looked out of the window. The clouds were fascinating! They seemed to form white mountains and rivers. They created an alternate universe, one she might not mind living in for a while. It looked pure, untampered, virtuous. Everything she was not.

The bite from her sandwich tasted dry. She felt tears rising. Her throat was closing. She grabbed the can of soda and tried to gulp it down. That made her cough. The coughing made the tears start to flow. "God, what is wrong with me? I mean, really, what is going on? I need You, Lord!" Through the stinging tears, she could see waves of clouds that looked like one gigantic soft, fluffy mattress. She wanted to jump out of the window and just lay on them, comforted by their softness and support. But, she knew they were deceptive. They were nothing but water and air. They couldn't support her. If she landed on them, she would fall straight through to her death.

"Okay, Lord," Lily said. "I trust You to heal me of whatever I'm trying to pacify with food. Help me, please." Lily finished her meal and closed her eyes. Scenes from her past began to flash through her mind like slices of a movie clip. Brian scaring her with that forceful kiss. Brian placing his hands all over the private places of her body. Brian holding her hands down, hurting her shoulder joints when she tried to fight him off. Brian pushing and pushing against her while he smashed her mouth so hard with his left hand that her teeth and jaw hurt. Brian laughing and telling her that he would know if she told anybody about what happened, and then he would kill her brother and act like it was an accident. Brian promising that he had a gun and he and Nick had been out shooting before. Brian walking out of the front door and her sobbing, then running upstairs to take a shower that burnt her skin so bad that she almost told her mother. But, she didn't. In fact, she didn't tell anyone, ever. She loved Nick. She couldn't stand the thought that Brian would hurt him worse than he had hurt her. So, she kept her mouth shut except to eat and satiate her pain with the joy of food.

"It's all right," she heard, over and over, as she opened her eyes. "It's all right. You are strong. You can forgive. You can reclaim your life. You can move forward. It's all right."

"It is all right," Lily said, aloud.

Lily determined that she would try her best to allow this new understanding to open up another chapter in her life. She was going to tell her family tonight what happened with Brian. She was going to begin, even during this holiday season, to change her eating habits. She was going to make an appointment with that psychiatrist that Nick said worked in his building and see if he could help her get started on dealing with this eating disorder. She was going to set some goals for her weight loss. No! She was going to begin losing weight and training so that she would be ready to run in the local marathon next fall. She would do it, with the help of the Lord. And never again would she need two seats on an airplane.

"Lord, please, tell me again that I can do it!" Immediately, the lights in the cabin flashed. The seatbelt indicator came on above her. Lily looked up. For a split second, that icon made her think about security. She laughed while tears began to flow down her cheeks. "Thank you, Lord! I get the message. You have me protected. I don't have to worry. I just have to trust You."

"Ladies and gentlemen, please make sure that your trays are up and secured and that your seatbelts are fastened. We are preparing for landing. Flight attendants, please check the cabin for our descent."

"I am prepared for landing," Lily thought. "Finally, I'm prepared to be grounded in reality. I'm prepared to equip myself to fight the past and become the woman I am created to be. I'm prepared to make change happen. I'm a little scared after being stuck in this place for so long, but I am so ready to be home. I don't know how things will work out, today or tomorrow. I don't even know if I can stick to my plan. But, I'm looking for a way out and this may be the day. It might be a lot harder than I think it will be, but it's worth a try. I hope I can do this. I think I can do it. I'm really nervous, but I'm going to give it a try."

Lily was shaking when she slid from her seats into the aisle. She was the last one to leave the plane. She thought about her plans and the strength she felt deep inside. With a big smile on her face, she thanked the attendants and pilot, and then stepped quickly into this new world where she had landed.

Throw Me Overboard; I've Got a Hiding Place

"The Lord will not suffer the soul of the righteous to famish; but He casteth away the substance of the wicked." Proverbs 10:3

*

"Laurie, would you please put that report on my desk as soon as you are finished with it? The stakeholders' meeting is at nine in the morning, and I'd like to look it over before I have Margaret make the copies." Mr. Turner stepped inside her door, waiting for her response.

"I sure will, Bob. I just needed to finish up a couple of slides for my PowerPoint, and then I'll get right on it." She hated how he always tried to make his stuff seem so much more important than hers. Didn't she know what to do? Hadn't she been doing this job long before he was hired? How come Margaret couldn't have just done the whole report? Why did everybody expect her to do all of her own work plus all of their work and get everything done by the same deadline? She felt herself getting more frustrated, so she just swung her chair around and stared at him. "Did you need anything else?"

Mr. Turner stepped completely into the office. He shut the door behind him. "Laurie, I'm not sure what went on here before I came. But, I do know why the corporate director hired me. This unit was performing poorly. Production was low. Employee morale was low. If data was gathered, it certainly was not reviewed. Our performance rating is improving, and I am going to make sure that continues. If you are willing to be part of the team and help turn things around, that's great. If you don't think you're up to that, I understand. I will write the best referral letter I can to help you move on to a place where you will be more comfortable. But, if you are going to remain with this team, I need to trust that you will follow my lead and do what I need you to do when I need you to do it. Is that understood?"

"Who do you think you are, Bob, to tell me what I need to do in order to keep my job? I was doing this job long before you came, and I will keep doing it the way I know it needs to be done after you are gone. I'm not afraid of you. You can't fire me! And, write this in your quality review: from this moment on, I refuse to do any part of your job. You take care of your business. I'll take care of mine. How's that? Is that understood?" Laurie could hear her own voice escalating, but was struggling with trying to control it. She didn't want everybody in her business, but she could see people gathering in the window outside of the closed door.

"Who do I think I am, Laurie?" asked Mr. Turner in a calm and measured tone. "I am your direct supervisor, the site manager, assigned by the corporation with the responsibility of totally managing this site. I give the assignments to all thirty-six employees who work here. And, any employee who refuses to perform any duty as assigned may be terminated for insubordination. I believe I heard you say that you refuse to do the assignment that I have given you. Is that correct?" He looked directly into Laurie's eyes. She just stared back with her eyebrows raised and a stubborn look on her face.

"That's what I said!" Laurie emphasized that last word with a turn of her chair back to face her desktop. She began to create a new slide in her PowerPoint.

"Then you leave me with no other recourse. Laurie, please shut your computer down. Clear your possessions from your desk and this office. Your services are no longer needed at this firm. I will call security to escort you from the building in ten minutes. I will forward all separation documents to you within twenty-four hours."

Laurie swung back around to face him. She was livid. Her face began to flush as she struggled to her feet, stuttering. "What? What are you talking about? You can't fire me! I will sue you for everything you are worth, which isn't much! What did I do? You can't be serious!" Mr. Turner was already moving toward the office door, his cell phone in his hand.

"Security? Hi, Tom. Would you please report to Ms. Riley's office? She will need an escort from the building. Thank you!" He turned back to Laurie. "Yes, I am serious. Our team is recovering from a very toxic state of disorganization. Right now, you are a virus that is threatening to destroy all the great work we have done. I can't let that happen." Mr. Turner opened the office door wide. "I will prepare a letter tomorrow which will outline your severance package. Good day, Ms. Riley."

Mr. Turner closed the door behind him. Besides everything that was churning in Laurie's brain, she could hear him talking to Tom, the security guard. She and Tom were good friends. How embarrassing! How was she going to walk past all of her coworkers in their offices on her way out? What would she say if anyone asked her a question? How would she say goodbye to all of these people who had been her friends for so long?

Laurie's legs were trembling as she sat back down in her chair. Her shoulders felt weak. She put her head in her hands and began to cry. She couldn't think of a next step. All she could think was, "How could I have let something like this happen?"

Her door opened. She waited for a moment, then lifted her head and wiped her face with her hand. Reaching for a tissue, she saw someone in the corner of her eye.

Tom cleared his throat. "Laurie?" She hid her face in the tissue and nodded her head. "Laurie, this is hard for me, too. Can I help you get your stuff packed?"

"Tom, how can he do this to me? I knew he didn't like me from day one. Didn't I tell you he had it in for me? Oh, Tom, what am I going to do? I don't have a job? I can't come back here anymore? Oh, Lord!" Laurie began to sob uncontrollably.

Tom came over to her desk and sat on one corner, facing her. "Laurie, pull yourself together for a minute. You've got ten minutes to pack up your belongings. I'll help you. I'll walk you out and take you home if you need me to. But, don't waste your time crying. We can talk about this later. You know I've been telling you how you have to take care of yourself and maybe see a doctor. People can't have insomnia for days and still work off of no sleep. It makes you crazy!"

Tom was moving around the room, picking up knicknacks, pictures, personal items, and her business cards. He took a canvas satchel he found hanging on her coat rack and started to load those things into it. Laurie opened a couple of drawers and began to dump them into an empty copy paper box. She continued sobbing as she worked. Tom finished his gathering and stood to the side as Laurie took her diploma off of the wall and set it beside the box. When she went to lift her laptop from her credenza, Tom came to examine it.

"Sorry, Laurie, but you can't take this. It belongs to the firm."

"Tom, are you kidding? This has all of my personal stuff on it! How can I at least not take it and download my own folders so that I can save them? They won't let me do that?" Laurie was crying, begging.

Tom shook his head, sadly. "This can't leave the building." Tom looked at his watch, "And, our ten minutes is up."

Laurie looked at the window beside her office door. Mr. Turner was standing there with his cell phone in hand. Tom glanced up and saw him standing there, too. Tom nodded at him.

"Come on, Laurie. It's time to go. I don't want him calling the police. I'm with you. I'll carry this box. It's going to be okay." Tom opened the door and looked at Laurie, his eyes full of empathy and concern. He said softly, "Let's go."

Tom walked her to the parking garage and then to her car. He loaded the box and bag into her trunk. He helped her into the car, asked her if she was sure she could drive herself home, gave her a hug when she nodded that she could, and told her that he would call and check on her later. When he closed her driver's door, patted it, and walked away, Laurie waited until he got on the elevator before she began to cry.

It wasn't a sobbing, shaking, screaming cry. It was a slow flow from an anguished well deep inside her consciousness. It connected to a lake of desperation which had been growing larger and larger inside of her for decades. The lake would rise and fall on a seasonal schedule. Sometimes, she remembered, she had been so happy – feeling like everything was perfect and could never go wrong again. But then, the dark storms would come. She would become doubtful, paranoid, self-destructive. She would lose friends. She would hurt people. She would hurt herself. And, there was nothing she could do about it.

The sound of a police car siren shook her. Laurie put the key in the ignition and turned on the engine. She fastened her seat belt and engaged the gearshift into "Drive". She backed slowly out of her assigned stall, then began the long descent down each of the eight parking levels in the garage. With each round, she thought about the things that may have led to this place. Mr. Turner was so insensitive! How could he pile so much work on her and not expect her to crack? All these years of valuable service she'd given to the company! How was she going to fight this firing? Her last two evaluations hadn't been that great, but didn't they tell her they would give her a chance to do better? How soon could she get another job if she had to? How soon would her severance pay start? What would happen if she couldn't get another job? How could she pay her bills?

When she turned out onto the street, she saw a team of emergency vehicles blocking the street to the right. Even though that was the way to her apartment, she decided to turn left. She really wasn't in the mood to witness anyone else's misery at the moment, but she breathed a quick prayer that nobody's house had caught on fire and nobody was dead. Those thoughts caused her mind to drift back to that day, way out in the country.

Laurie's grandparents were the loves of her life. Her mom was a high-power attorney who worked very hard to leave the small town where she grew up and garner enough scholarships to attend a prestigious university and eventually earn a law degree. Laurie's father was a professor at the university. He was older, handsome, and persuasive. When Laurie's mother completed her undergraduate work and was accepted for law school, she received another surprise on the day that her acceptance letter arrived. She found out that she was pregnant. Of course, the professor was married and had a family with grown children. There was no way he was going to leave his wife and family for Laurie's mother, but he was willing to provide monthly child support and an annuity that would be cashable when Laurie turned eighteen. It took her through college and only ran out two years ago.

That last summer with her grandparents was miserable for Laurie. It wasn't because she didn't want to spend time with them. That was something she looked forward to every June. It was because she had been arguing with her mother about finally seeing her father. Her mother had shown her a picture of him from one of her old yearbooks one day, only because Laurie had a tantrum and told her that she would hate her forever if she didn't let her see her father. But, Laurie wanted to see him in person for once in her life. Why couldn't her mother make that happen? Why couldn't that short trip be part of their summer vacation on the way to her grandparents' house? What was so difficult about driving to his town, parking in front of his house, walking up to the door, ringing the doorbell, and just looking at him when he opened the door? Her mother kept telling her that it wasn't that easy. Why not?

So, she had slipped into a very deep depression that summer. Her grandmother thought she was going through those hormonal changes that all thirteen-year-old girls experience. Her grandfather couldn't entertain her like he had in the past. He had slipped on a patch of ice that winter and broken his hip. He had healed up fine, the doctors said, but something was still wrong with him. He didn't want to go anywhere or do anything. He sat around the house and slept while the grass grew high and the summer heat burned up the little garden that he used to tend so meticulously. Had it not been for kind neighbors, the yard would have been overgrown and a breeding ground for snakes.

Laurie was terrified of snakes. Even thinking about it now made her shudder. Little garter snakes looked like gigantic pythons to her. She would do anything to avoid even seeing a snake, so she too stayed inside most of the summer. One day, though, the neighbor arrived early in the morning to cut the grass for her grandparents. There had been fifteen straight days of temperatures over one hundred degrees, so he was determined to cut the grass and beat the afternoon heat. Laurie had taken to going outside in the early morning to walk in the grass while it was still wet with dew. She didn't walk far, though, because she was afraid that snakes might be hiding in the areas of the yard where the grass was ankle-high.

The neighbor began to tease her about playing so close to the house. He asked her why and she told him that she was scared of snakes. He laughed heartily, and then asked her did she know how country folk got rid of snakes. She said she didn't. He told her, "We burn 'em out!" Then, he ran toward her, wiggling a small twig as if it was a snake. Laurie was terrified! She began to scream and run around, flailing her arms and shouting for her grandmother, while the neighbor laughed and chased her.

Laurie's grandmother came running out onto the porch, scolding both the neighbor and Laurie. However, Laurie was inconsolable and collapsed in her grandmother's arms, sobbing hysterically. The neighbor tossed the stick into the grass, turned to Laurie and said, "Boo!" and then headed to his tractor to cut the grass.

Grandmother had fussed at her for crying because she was scared.

Grandfather couldn't protect her. He had slept through the whole thing. The neighbor terrified her, and the snakes did, too. Laurie decided she would have to protect herself. She knew that Grandmother had matches. She kept them in an empty aluminum salt shaker beside the stove. After she had calmed down enough for Grandmother to go in to check on Grandfather, Laurie snuck into the kitchen and took three stick matches out of the salt shaker. She put them in her pocket and vowed she would always keep them with her in case she saw a snake in the yard. If nobody would take care of her, she would take care of herself.

The last thing Laurie remembered was going outside early that evening, looking down, and seeing a snake. Her grandmother later told her it was the stick that the neighbor had thrown into the grass. By the time her mother arrived the next morning, the house was burnt to the ground. Thank goodness, her grandparents were able to get out safely, but the extreme heat had caused the dry grass to ignite quickly and spread to the house. Due to its age and wood frame exterior, it went down in flames within minutes.

Before she realized it, Laurie was pulling into her garage. As she sat there, she thought about how much trouble she had caused everyone she had known and cared about in her lifetime. Her father didn't know or want her. Her mother had been so angry with her after that incident that she had emotionally shut her out. She was kind, but detached. She had never had a real boyfriend. Men had always come up with excuses for not dating her more than once. Tom was the only male who had maintained a friendship with her in her whole life, but she sometimes felt his commitment was grounded in pity. Her co-workers seemed to like her, but none of them had ever invited her to their social events.

Laurie began to wonder about the purpose of her life. She hadn't done anything good for anyone, not even herself. Both of her grandparents had been dead for a few years now. Her mother had taken a job in Vermont. They exchanged cards on holidays and birthdays, but never spoke on the phone. She felt like a castaway on an island. No one knew who or where she was, and she didn't see any reason to keep fighting and living. No matter what, she would never get off of the island.

She remembered hearing that if you leave your car running in the garage once the door has closed, you will fall asleep and die in your sleep. After so many nights of insomnia, a good sleep was just what she needed. That would eliminate all of the problems in her life. Her mother didn't care whether she was dead or alive. There was no job to go to where people would wonder where she was if she didn't show up. She could trust Tom. He would come to check on her. When he found her dead, he would see to it that she was cremated or something and he would be sure that her belongings were donated to some charity. When, or if, her mother found out she was dead, she would be fine with Tom's arrangements.

It all was beginning to make a lot of sense to her. Maybe this is how her life was supposed to go. A fitting end to a frazzled existence.

Laurie lowered the garage door and revved the engine. She took off her seatbelt and leaned the car seat back. She rested her head on the back of the seat, closed her eyes, and took a deep breath. She felt her body begin to relax. A couple of tears had crept into the corners of her eyes, but she didn't feel like crying. She felt like sleeping. Behind her eyes, lines and arcs in black and green and orange danced in patterns that looked like a kaleidoscope. She saw her mother's face fleet through her mind. There was her grandfather, sitting on the porch of the country house in a rocking chair. Grandmother was standing in the doorway with a gingham apron tied around her waist, drying her hands with a red and white tea towel. She was smiling. Laurie thought she could smell sugar cookies baking. She drifted to sleep.

Her neighbor had seen exhaust smoke coming from under Laurie's garage door. He hadn't thought much about the fact that the door was open a few inches, even though that was unusual. He actually assumed something inside the garage was on fire. So, he called 911 right away and waited for the fire truck to arrive. It wasn't until they manually lifted the automatic garage door that he saw the long tree branch attached to her left rear fender. It was stuck in the aluminum rim of the door frame. There had been a storm the night before. Tree branches had fallen into people's yards, on sidewalks, and in the streets. One must have been overlooked in the morning cleanup. Laurie probably drove over it, catching it up high in her fender. That incident of negligence saved her life. Miraculously, the branch had kept the garage door from fully closing. A fireman spotted Laurie in the car, turned off the ignition, and pulled her outside, applying resuscitation while his partners got the oxygen started.

The first sight Laurie saw when she woke up was Tom's concerned face. As soon as she opened her eyes, he jumped up. "Nurse! Nurse! She's awake!" he hollered out into the hallway. The nurse hurried into the room and checked Laurie's IV bag. Coming around to the side of the bed, she pulled a small flashlight out of her pocket and shined it into Laurie's open eyes. Laurie blinked quickly.

"Hi, Laurie," the nurse said. "Do you know where you are?" Laurie moaned softly and turned her head to the side. Tom leaned forward and looked at her closely.

"Laurie, it's Tom! How are you doing?" Concern chiseled deeply in his face, he gripped the side of her bed with both hands.

Laurie moaned again, then said, "I think I'm gonna throw up!" The nurse moved quickly to get a pan. Laurie began to wretch.

Holding the pan under Laurie's mouth and patting her back softly, the nurse said gently, "Go ahead, this is common. You might have a bad headache, too. Thank God you're alive." Laurie continued to vomit. Tom grabbed a face towel and took it to the sink to wet it with warm water. He came back and wiped her mouth and face. Laurie looked at him with grateful eyes, then closed them and moaned again.

"She'll be okay," the nurse said to Tom. "She will just need some time to get over the effects of the carbon monoxide." Tom smiled at her, weakly. "Can I count on you to keep an eye on her?" The nurse gave Tom a wide smile.

"Oh yes!" Tom said. "I'm not going anywhere."

"Great!" said the nurse. "I'll be right out here at the station if she needs anything else." She looked at her wristwatch. "We will bring her something clear to eat and drink in about an hour if she doesn't have any more vomiting spells. Just let me know."

"Will do!" said Tom. The nurse checked the digital readout screen above the bed, entered some data into the computer, checked the IV bag again, and then patted Laurie's feet as she left the room.

Laurie stirred, turned over in the bed, and looked at Tom solemnly. Tears began to flow down her cheeks. Tom pulled a chair close to the bed, sat down, and leaned over to look at her closely. She made him feel like crying.

"I feel so ashamed, Tom! I had hoped to end everybody's problems today, and here I am making more problems. I'm so sorry!" She began to sob softly.

"Laurie, it's fine! You don't have to apologize. I'm here for you. You don't know how I felt when the police answered your cell phone. I had called to check on you, and so when I didn't hear your voice on the other end of the phone, I freaked out!" Tom began smoothing her hair back, his hand shaking. "I drove to the hospital in a panic, thinking about how I couldn't bear the thought of something happening to you that I couldn't prevent! I hated to let you drive home by yourself today. But, I couldn't leave the job. You stayed on my mind all the rest of the day. I prayed that you would be all right!" Tom broke down and began to sob. Laurie lifted her right hand, full of intravenous ports, and laid it on Tom's head.

"Tom, I've hardly ever prayed before in my life! How do you do it so you know it works? It's a miracle I'm not dead, and now I'm wondering if God did me a favor today, or if He just didn't want me yet!" She laughed a little through her tears.

Tom lifted his head and reaching across her stomach, he gripped both her hands. "God loves you, and He does want you; but yes, maybe not today. He may have wanted to wait until you wanted Him as much as He wants you. And yes, He did give you a miracle! Do you even know what happened?" Laurie shook her head no. Tom continued, "Somehow, the garage didn't close all the way! There was a stick stuck in the frame of the garage door. It was attached to your fender. You must have picked it up as you were driving home and it kept the door from closing all the way! A stick saved your life!"

"That is a miracle," Laurie murmured. "A stick changed my life when I was around thirteen. It made me burn up my grandparents' house. I was thinking about that today. That memory was one reason why I just wanted to end it all. I haven't done much good in my life, starting with that incident." She lifted her head to look Tom straight in the eyes. "Tom, do you think that God was telling me that if He can use a stick to set me on a path to my purpose, then He can use me, so I can't die yet?"

Tom smiled as he drew Laurie into a gentle embrace. "Yes, I can believe that, and I can believe that He has placed us in each others' lives for a reason. Maybe if we start figuring all of this out through prayer, then everything will work out well for us and the people we may be able to help in the future. What do you think?"

Laurie gazed in his eyes for a long time. It seemed the events of the day were passing like a parade in front of her, reflected in the twin pools of his gentle brown eyes. What did she think? Could any good come out of her? Maybe, with the help of Tom. And the Lord. Maybe it was time to find out the answers to all of the mysteries that existed in her life. Maybe it was time to start living.

"I think that I can trust you. I think that is a good idea." Laurie grabbed Tom's hands. "I think that I'm ready to learn how to pray," she said softly, closing her eyes.

Peace, Be Still

"When pride cometh, then cometh shame: but with the lowly is wisdom."   Proverbs 11:2

*

"When I see the love lights in your eyes, shining bright, showing me the way to your heart, to your heart; I know that everything will be all right, that it's all been good, so good, right from the start, from the start. This love is so good." Willie smiled and nodded his head. "Hey, I like that! Let me write it down."

He reached for his tablet and began to swiftly record his thoughts. Willie loved his music. It was really his life. He hadn't done much more than write songs and sing for as long as he could remember. When he was a little boy, his mother and father noticed that he had a fixation on the radio. As a toddler, he would pat the top of the radio, his signal for someone to turn it on. They would have to rotate the tuning dial until it landed on something that made him want to dance! He would stand in the same spot, bouncing up and down, his fat little knees bending out and in to the rhythm of the music.

Willie's school teachers were very impressed with his musicianship. He had learned to play the piano when he was six years old. A neighbor was a retired music teacher. Even though she was close to seventy, she still loved teaching, and she really loved working with Willie, or "William" as she, exclusively, called him. She had future visions of him playing an elegant black grand piano on an expansive stage at Carnegie Hall, wearing a black tuxedo with tails, his stiff white shirt fronted with a perky collar and a shiny black bow tie. The name "Willie" didn't quite fit this picture, so she decided to call him by his formal, given name.

Willie not only loved the lessons, he also loved his afternoons with Mrs. Bridges. She always smelled like roses. Her breath was sweet, as if she had just sipped some lemony iced tea. She would give him two cookies and a small glass of milk if he could show he had practiced every day by playing his lessons without any mistakes. That was his motivation to learn to play the piano well – those cookies! They were delicious and always warm. They had little sprinkles of sugar on top of them. He would savor each bite, letting it melt in his mouth until the sugar and butter swirled into a taste ball that slowly dissolved until nothing was left but a few crystals of sugar on the tip of his tongue. While he took his time enjoying his cookies after each lesson, she would tell him about what her life was like when she was a little girl.

She told him that she was light-skinned, which made some people treat her special when she was a child. But, she said, it also made some people not like her. "Those little girls I went to elementary school with told me I thought I was 'gooder' than them. I would just look at them while they would stick their tongues out at me. I would think to myself, 'I guess I <u>am</u> gooder than you, because I know to say 'better' instead of 'gooder'. But, I wouldn't say it to them. I wanted them to be my friends." She would always laugh at this part. Then, she would continue. "Later on, in high school, some of them were my friends. Especially Martha. She and I went to the university together. She was a good friend!"

Willie couldn't figure out why she would always tell this same story, every week. She would repeat it, word for word, and narrate it as if it were a part in a play. But, he really didn't mind listening to her voice, and he enjoyed eating her cookies, so he didn't want to make her mad by interrupting her to tell her that he had heard that story before – many times.

Willie really loved something else more than the cookies – he loved listening to himself create the sounds that she had shown him how to make. Each note represented a symbol and a color in his brain. He would sometimes go to sleep by arranging the symbols within blocks of the colors to frame out a line of a song, or even an entire song. When he would sit down each day at five o'clock to practice, he would save some practice time at the end to pull up his colors and symbols behind his closed eyes and try to replicate them using the piano keys.

One day, he felt his mother standing behind him. He stopped playing and turned around. She put her hands on his shoulders. Her hands were warm and damp. She had been washing dishes. "What was that song you were just playing, Willie? It's not in your practice book. I liked that song. It was really pretty!"

"Oh, Mama, it was just a song I had been thinking about, so I decided I would learn to play what I saw in my mind. You like it?"

His mother's voice sounded like she was about to cry. "Yes, son, I really do. It is beautiful. Play it again."

Willie felt like he had made his mother sad, but she had said that she liked the song. "You sure, Mama? Did the song make you feel sad?"

"No, son! I'm not sad at all. It made me feel good, and happy. It made me feel proud of you."

Willie smiled. "Okay Mama. I'll try to play it again." He concentrated until he could see the symbols in the color bars again. He placed his hands on the keyboard and began to play. He could hear his mother breathing behind him, then heard her take a few steps. The springs in the armchair creaked. He continued to play the notes he was seeing and hearing in his mind. Finally, he stopped. He felt like he had run a long, long way.

Mama came and hugged him around his shoulders. "Thank you for playing that song for me," she said. "I love you, son."

"You're welcome, Mama! I love you, too!"

All through elementary school, his teachers would ask him to play for his classmates when it was time for music instruction. Willlie didn't mind at all. In fact, he felt privileged to be asked to perform, so he always played his best. Sometime, he would also slip in one of the songs he had composed. Everyone always enjoyed them, too.

In time, Willie had a featured spot in every holiday program at school. Even community members who had no school age children would show up for the school's music program to hear Willie's performance. Mrs. Bridges' dreams had come true – minus the baby grand piano and the tux with tails.

When it was time to go to junior high school, Willie's parents made a decision that would change his life forever. They decided to send him to the state school for the blind. They were concerned that his educational needs would not be met in the local school because they didn't have personnel trained to help him learn advanced coursework in Braille, and it would be difficult to get appropriate resources for all of his subject areas at that level. They spent quite a lot of time talking with social workers and school staff, and made several visits to the school for the blind before making up their minds. Willie didn't care much either way. In fact, he was pretty excited at the thought of finally being able to play sports like football and baseball. But, along with missing his parents terribly, he was going to miss piano lessons with Mrs. Bridges.

There was a great surprise, however, awaiting Willie. The high school students at the school for the blind had formed a band the previous year. They were badly in need of a piano player. When Willie was heard tickling the keys one day after music class was over, he was seen as a gift from above. From then on, Willie and the band spent all of their free time rehearsing. Other students and even faculty members would often sit in on their rehearsals, enjoying themselves as if they were at a concert. Soon, they were featured throughout the community and would perform on call whenever visitors and benefactors came to the school.

One spring afternoon in his senior year, Willie was called from his trigonometry class to come to the headmaster's office. Grabbing his cane, he made his way quickly. He knew he couldn't be in trouble for anything, but this was the first time in his six years at the school that he had been summoned to the office during the school day. He wondered what might be the trouble.

"Come on in, William," Dr. Stevens said as his secretary escorted Willie into the office. "Have a seat, please." He placed his hand on Willie's left arm and directed him toward a chair. Willie sat down and rested his cane against his right knee. He knew that there were at least two other people in the office along with him and Dr. Stevens. He waited for Dr. Stevens to continue to talk.

"William, we have some visitors with us today. In fact, they have heard a lot about you and your great music skills. So, they came here today to meet you. William, please meet Dr. James Starks and his daughter, Melinda."

Willie stood up tall and extended his hand. Dr. Starks, a short, pudgy man with fat little hands grabbed Willie's hand. Willie smiled and shook his hand warmly. "I'm glad to meet you, Dr. Starks," Willie said.

"William, this is my daughter," replied Dr. Starks. Melinda Starks stepped up to her father's side. Willie turned slightly to his left and extended his hand again.

"I'm glad to meet you, Melinda," said Willie. He could tell she was a small girl. Her hand was little and very slender. It trembled just a little, but she returned Willie's firm handshake.

"Thank you. I'm very glad to meet you, too. I've heard a lot about you." Melinda's voice was soft and quiet, but also very warm.

"Uh, oh!" Willie exclaimed. "I hope it was all good!" He laughed and she joined in.

"Oh yes, all good!" said Dr. Starks with a hearty laugh. "That is just why we are here."

"Please everyone, sit down," said Dr. Stevens. "William, Dr. Starks has something he would like to share with you." Willie turned toward the direction where he knew Dr. Starks and Melinda were seated.

"William, I would like to offer you a scholarship. I have been reviewing your transcript and I see that you are an outstanding student. I believe that you are a worthwhile investment!" He chuckled and continued, "I would like to place my money on your future. I would like to offer you a full scholarship to state college with a hope that you will major in music and make my daughter's dreams come true!"

"Sir?" Willie was not sure what Dr. Starks was talking about. Why would it matter to him what Willie's major was? Why would he need for it to be music? And, what would Melinda have to do with any of that? He just met her!

Dr. Starks laughed again and then said, "I know, I know! That is just my way of saying that Melinda plans to major in vocal music and her dream has always been to be part of a band. She heard your band play last month at the state music competition, and she has been talking about it ever since. Well, the truth is that she has been talking about you ever since. So, if I can make her dream come true while I'm paying for your college education, I'm all for it! How about you, son? What do you think?"

Whenever Willie thought about that day, the day he met his true love, he always repeated a phrase Mrs. Bridges used to say to him: "The Lord works in mysterious ways, His wonders to perform!" She had told him that on the day he left to go to the school for blind students, consoling him as he sobbed and clung to her, knowing he would miss her while he was gone away. She told him that on the day that he called to tell her that he and his band were going to be playing on television! They had been invited to provide the entertainment for the governor's inaugural ball. She was so excited and said she was very proud of him! She later told him that she had watched the news and seen him on the piano. She said it wasn't Carnegie Hall, but it was close enough! Finally, she reminded him of that when he shared that his college education was scholarshipped by a generous benefactor named Dr. James Starks.

She hadn't lived to see him graduate from college. She died at age ninety-six in November of his senior year. He had come home for the funeral, which was right before the Thanksgiving break, and he had played the piano for her memorial service. He felt like she was there, smiling at him with pride and her approval. Music was leaping through his mind like rainbows and bright lights. He could almost see her dancing!

But, his last memory of her alive was the day he took Melinda to her house on one of his visits home. He and Melinda had gone on to state university together. As he anticipated, he met up with some serious young musicians and they all formed a band that soon gained notoriety and a wide following. Melinda didn't land the spot as the lead vocalist, but she was one of four girls who sang back-up. Still, she was happy to just be near Willie. She wanted to take care of him because she had fallen in love. He had, too.

The band was playing for the local high school's prom. It was the school that Willie would have attended had he not gone to the school for the blind. He still had lots of friends in the town and everybody knew him, so he had received a warm welcome back. When they arrived in town that morning, Willie told his members that he was going to see his parents while they got things set up for the evening's gig. Melinda drove him to the house.

As she pulled up in front of the home where Willie had grown up, she admired the order of his early life. The white picket fence looked like Mr. Davis had painted it yesterday. The yellow clapboard house with fresh white shutters and colorful flower beds on every side looked like it had been staged for the cover of a home and garden magazine. She and Willie made their way up the steps to be greeted with hugs and kisses by Mrs. Davis. Melinda could see why Willie was so loving. He couldn't help but be if he grew up around this much love.

She had a lot of love, too, but it was love that she could manipulate. She always meant well, but she knew that if she cried just a little, she could have whatever she wanted. Her parents were married for fifteen years before she was born. They saw her as a miracle, a gift. They had given up on ever having any children. So, when she finally came, they smothered her with gifts and indulgences from day one. "Well, one real positive came from it. I got Willie!" He was the truly bright spot in her life, even though he was jet black. She loved the contrast in their skin tones, though. Here she was, lily white. Sometimes she got strange looks when the two were out and about, but she loved it. People had to admire them. She was beautiful, and he was too. In fact, Willie was gorgeous. His skin was so smooth that it looked like it had been buffed to become a smooth black tone, like dark burled wood. You just wanted to touch him, roll your hands across his face and arms. Polish them just a little more. He was tall and well-framed. Nice head, strong square shoulders. Being blind was just another aspect of his engaging personality. And, it didn't matter at all to her or to him. She felt like he loved and respected her as much as she did him.

When she first talked with her father about her idea of him arranging for the two of them to go to university together, he knew that Willie was a musician, but not much more. The first time that her father realized that Willie was black was the moment that Willie walked into Dr. Stevens' office. However, he had already agreed to offer him a scholarship, so he couldn't go back on his word to his precious Melinda. She was counting on that!

Dr. Starks had not said much as he and she walked to where their slate-gray Lincoln Town Car was parked in the lot on the south side of the administration office. They had gotten into the car and turned on the air conditioning to cool them down after their short walk in the spring heat before he said anything. "Baby, I think you left out one critical detail." Dr. Starks laughed just a little.

"What, Daddy?" Melinda replied coyly. "That he's blind? I thought that you knew this was a school for sight-impaired students." She smiled.

"Melinda, you know exactly what I am talking about." He put the gear shift into "Reverse", turned to look her dead in the eye before he shifted his head to glance out of the rear window. "You didn't tell me he was a Negro."

"Was? Daddy, he will always be a Negro. What difference would that make? You taught me to love everyone. You said that there is no difference in men based on their skin color. You have always shown me that you treat everyone fairly. If there is a reason to avoid someone, it is because they have a character flaw, not because of what they look like on the outside. Blind? Black-skinned? What's the difference? If he is good enough to give your money to, why can't he be good enough to give your daughter to?"

"Now wait, Melinda!" Dr. Starks began to stutter. "What do you mean? This arrangement was about you having the opportunity to access your musical goals. We weren't husband shopping today!"

"We weren't?" Melinda spoke the words firmly while she looked at her father with a serious expression on her face. He began to turn red and sweat, even with the air conditioning streaming forcefully through the vents. Melinda started to laugh and jiggled her father's upper right arm. "Daddy, don't be so serious! I am just teasing you! Relax, Daddy! Oh, I'm so glad everything worked out! I can't wait to be the lead singer in a band! Daddy, you have made me so happy today! You are the best Daddy in the world. I love you so much! Thank you, Daddy!"

Melinda knew the first time she touched Willie's hand that her assignment in life was going to be to take care of him, to look out for him, to help make his life meaningful and purposeful. She didn't know why she felt that way, and she had no idea whether or not he would ever agree with her, but deep in her heart she felt that becoming a life partner to this man was her destiny.

Just a few weeks into the fall semester of their freshman year, it was evident that Willie did agree. Soon, Willie's focus became school, music, and Melinda. She didn't mind that she was last on his list of priorities. She was happy to just have a place on the list. Melinda's parents grew to love Willie and his parents loved Melinda, too.

After a quick breakfast the morning of the band's performance at the high school prom, Willie turned to Melinda and said, "You know what? You have never met my first music teacher, Mrs. Bridges! Mom, is Mrs. Bridges still living in her home?"

"Yes, she is! I have tried time and again to talk her into moving into that nice retirement complex south of town, but she said that she plans on living in her house until she dies!" Mrs. Davis chuckled. Willie laughed.

"I believe that! She's too spunky to stand living in a rest home! Come on, Melinda, let's go over there. I want her to meet you!" As they walked the half-block to her home, holding hands, Melinda wondered what Mrs. Bridges was like. Willie had described her cookies many times, but that didn't help her know how she looked. She also wondered if Mrs. Bridges would like her.

A small, white-looking woman opened the door when Willie knocked. She peered first at Willie and then at Melinda, then looked right back at Willie. "William!" she exclaimed in a sharp, high bird-like voice. "William, I'm so glad to see you! Come on in, son!" She grabbed him by the hand and pulled him inside the door. Then, she reached up high to give him a big hug. "I'm so proud of you, William! You are in college now? My, my! Time has gone by so quickly!" She stepped to the side and looked at Melinda. "William, please introduce me to your guest?"

"Oh, yes, Mrs. Bridges! I'm sorry. This is my girlfriend, Melinda

Starks. Melinda, this is Mrs. Bridges, my favorite girlfriend!" Willie began to laugh and squeeze Mrs. Bridges tightly.

"Now, now, William!" Mrs. Bridges acted as if she was struggling away. She pushed him gently to the side and faced Melinda. "Ms. Melinda? How do you do?" She looked her straight in the eyes. "You are dating my William? Well, all I have to say is that you better come correctly! Humph!"

Willie threw back his head and laughed loudly. Melinda had been a little scared by Mrs. Bridges' comment, but when Willie laughed, she managed a weak but nervous smile as she looked at Mrs. Bridges' stern face. But within a split second, Mrs. Bridges was laughing, too. Melinda knew then that everything was all right; so she joined in, relieved to see Willie so happy in the presence of his two "girlfriends".

Melinda had not come to Mrs. Bridges' memorial service with Willie. She wanted to come, but she was completing an internship at a company that managed musicians. She had chosen to major in the business side when she realized that her career goals to become a recording star were not as realistic as she had hoped when she was a teenager. But, she knew the great potential that Willie had. Not only could he sing and play instruments, but he could compose the most beautiful music anyone ever heard. She didn't want him to ever be taken advantage of or misused by some unethical manager, so she was going to take care of him herself.

The two of them made a fantastic duo. He trusted her, and she truly did have his best interests at heart. After all, her future was intertwined with his. If he was successful, she would be, too. Still, it didn't matter to her if they lived in a box in some alley; if she was with him, that was all that mattered.

When Willie came back from the service, he seemed to be even more inspired to write music. He began writing a song a week, it seemed. Melinda was very busy with her own school work and her internship, but she still managed to get his songs copyrighted as soon as he would complete one. Here they both were, just a few weeks away from graduation, working hard and supporting one another. Willie just wanted to make music and play what he created. If he could do what he loved, she was willing to support him by doing what she did for the one she loved.

One night, Willie asked her a question she had never considered. They had just gotten finished with a band gig. She was dropping him off at home when he turned to her. "Linnie?"

"Yes, Willie?"

"Define a slave for me."

"A slave?"

"Yes. What does 'slave' mean to you?"

"Willie, what kind of question is that?"

"Linnie, don't make this hard. Please, just satisfy my curiosity.

What does the word mean to you?"

"Well, I guess it means someone who is forced to work for someone without being paid, against their will. Does that make sense? Why are you asking this question?" Race had never been a topic of conversation between them, not their race or anyone else's. "What does it mean to you?"

Willie paused for a minute before answering. Melinda was beginning to feel apprehensive. She wondered if he was feeling smothered by her, maybe manipulated? Was he looking for a reason to break up? She didn't know what she would do if he told her he didn't want to be with her anymore! She felt her anxiety rise, and her heart began to beat rapidly.

"I guess I was thinking about how you might feel being tied down to a blind man for the rest of your life. I hadn't been looking at things through your eyes," he laughed a little, then added, "pardon the pun." Melinda grabbed his hand. "I guess what I'm saying is, I don't want you to ever feel sorry for me. This me is the only me I have ever known. But, I can feel your beauty. I know that you are a woman any man would want to marry. You are the woman I want to marry. I've been wanting to ask you for such a long time!" He lifted her hand to his lips and kissed it tenderly. "But, I don't want to make you feel that you have to take care of me, like a slave. Against your will." He paused. "I want you to know that if you don't want to hook up with me forever, we will still be friends, forever! And, no hard feelings!" Willie dropped his forehead on her shoulder.

Melinda kissed him softly on the forehead and exclaimed, "Willie, I love you so much I could burst! I have been waiting so long for you to ask me to marry you! I have prayed for this moment! Yes, I will be your slave, just like we are slaves to Christ! I will be joined to you exclusively because I love you more than anyone on this earth! You are the man that God created for me, and I am the woman He created for you. Hey, we're the modern-day Adam and Eve!" She began to laugh and cry at the same time. Willie wiped her face with his thumbs and then cupped her chin in his hands. She placed her palms on his cheeks and felt his warm tears in her hands.

"Miss Melinda Lynn Sparks, will you be my wife, to have and to hold forever? Will you love me and stand with me as we walk through whatever God has planned for our lives? Will you be willing to change your name to Mrs. Melinda Lynn Davis?" Willie began to laugh, and Melinda joined in.

"Yes, yes, yes!" She laughed through her tears. "Oh, yes, Mr. Willie Davis. You will never ever get rid of me. No Emancipation Proclamation in the world will ever convince me to leave you. I am your best girlfriend forever."

Willie woke up the morning that he had waited for so long with a brand new song for his soon-to-be brand new bride. It had come to him in his dreams, full of rainbows and sparkles and explosive arcs that looked like the Fourth of July all night long! It celebrated the love that only those whose focus is on the truth of love can experience, a love that only God can give and sustain. A love that is not bound to external features, or financial resources, or physical attractions, but a love that is the essence of the plan and the power of God.

Willie began to sing, *"When I see the love lights in your eyes, shining bright, showing me the way to your heart, to your heart; I know that everything will be all right, that it's all been good, so good, right from the start, from the start. This love is so good."* Ah, yes! She *had* opened up his eyes wide to see the only thing he ever desired to see, even though he had never seen anything before. He saw her love in all its splendid lights and prismatic colors — shining vividly, glowing brightly. That sight was the only one he ever wanted to see, and it was good! *So* good!

Wade in the Water

"A virtuous woman is a crown to her husband, but she that maketh ashamed is as rottenness in his bones." Proverbs 12:4

✳

Rosemary had told Brady that she would just be gone for a couple of weeks. She was the only one that Florence had been asking for during the month that she had been in the hospital. At first, Rosemary was just being polite when James would call her every evening to give her an update on Florence's condition. After all, she was her sister. But, after about two weeks, she began to get irritated. Why was she coming back into her life with all of this mess?

It had been years since she had seen Florence, let alone even thought about her. She had hoped that Florence felt so guilty for what she had done to her by seducing Brady that she would leave them alone from here on. But then she went and lost her mind, so they put her in the mental hospital. And now, at least according to James, she had been crying all day every day for weeks, begging them to bring her Rosemary to her. *Her* Rosemary? When had she ever been *her* Rosemary? Hadn't she been Grandma's favorite? Didn't Daddy always act like he loved her best? Stop! She had worked hard to get past all of this emotional baggage, pushing it down into the deep recesses of her psyche so that she wouldn't ever have to deal with those nagging doubts again. And now, here comes Florence, back from the dead!

Brady bought her a round-trip ticket when he looked at her face after the last phone call from James. He could tell that she was in a state of indecision.

"Look," he said, "if anybody should be mad at your sister, I should. She set me up like a bowling pin, with her crazy self. But, I can't stand to see you so miserable. Go check on her. See if you can help her. God knows, He's the only one who can. But, it may do her, and you, some good."

Rosemary realized that he was right, and she appreciated that he cared enough to help her make up her mind. But, the damage that Florence had caused to their relationship had affected her and Brady more than he would ever know.

Rosemary was a wounded woman. She had dealt since childhood with abandonment issues. She knew her father didn't believe she was his child, but what hurt more was how her mother treated her. She acted like

Rosemary was a nuisance. She made it very clear to her that she did not like her at all. In fact, Rosemary could recall times when her mother would say, "Child, you have worked my last nerve! Get out of my face! I don't like you anyway!" Then, she would push Rosemary into her room and slam the door. It would be dark before Rosemary would venture out of the room, just to find her mother passed out on the couch, drunk and snoring loudly.

So, when Florence "seduced" Brady and Rosemary had a hard time believing that he was so drunk that he didn't know what was going on, that broke her completely. Her own sister, the one who had survived their parents' dysfunctions to make it to adulthood, the one who had stood with her at her rush wedding, the one who had kept her morale high while Brady was away at war, was the same one who took both of her legs out from under her when she violated her marriage. To this day, Rosemary also saw Brady equally at fault. She had told him that a couple of times when they argued about it while the incident was fresh. But, he was so repentant and so apologetic for getting drunk and making himself susceptible, that she let it go when he seemed on the verge of a nervous breakdown. But, what about her? Hadn't she been on the verge for her whole life?

When Rosemary began to convince herself that there was no one she could trust or completely love with full abandon, she began to allow herself to enter into relationships outside of her marriage. Typically, it was nothing more than going out to lunch with guys at work. It didn't matter if they were married or single. She just enjoyed socializing and forgetting for a while that she had past issues that kept her from nurturing the same warm interchanges with her own husband. She convinced herself early on that these meetings were harmless. They weren't doing anything but laughing, talking, flirting, and eating. What she wasn't allowing herself to realize was that she was constructing her initial contacts with the men she was interested in by devising plans that would allow her to have that first interaction.

She would notice an attractive man. For a few days, she would plan how she would arrange to meet him. She would mentally rehearse the conversations they would have at dinner. Her real pleasure was seeing everything come together like clockwork, exactly the way she had envisioned it. She often thought, "Wow! The human mind is a phenomenal thing. I guess that scripture Pastor used to quote is right. 'As a man, or woman, thinketh in his or her heart, so is he or she'. Umph! I really think that is supposed to be interpreted and applied from a positive aspect, but it must work either way! At least, it's working for me!"

Since she met Easter, though, things had started to loop out of control. That was another reason she was glad to be leaving for a few weeks. Lately, she remembered a saying her Grandma used to repeat when it seemed like somebody was backsliding. She'd say, "Don't let the devil ride, or he will want to drive!" Ah, that devil named Easter Long was trying his best to work his way over to the driver's seat. At times, she felt like she was the victim of a carjacking.

He was a fascinating Black man! Intellectual, smooth, a gorgeous smile, smelling good all the time, well-read, a lover of jazz who knew what to say and how to say it. He was a regional manager newly assigned to her district. The first thing she wanted to know was who named him Easter.

"My mama!" He exclaimed with a laugh. "I was born bright and early on Easter Sunday morning! I was her only baby and she was my number one girl! Wasn't no daddy to argue with her, so Easter I became and Easter I am today. Easter Sunday Long!"

"Wow! What a name! What a story!" Rosemary laughed with evident excitement while she shook his hand and looked into his dreamy brown eyes with the long thick black lashes. "Boy, you are fine!" she thought. His lips were thinly sculpted and he had a small dimple in his chin. All of his muscles bulged in just the right places. When he moved closer to her, she felt her knees get weak, and leaned into him slightly.

"Uh oh! All right?" Easter put his arm around her waist and lifted her up slightly, laughing.

"Oh, yes! Sorry! I think my heel turned a little." Rosemary began to feel flushed. She wasn't ready yet to ask him her next question, 'Could we go out for lunch?' She didn't think her knees would stand it. She decided to wait until later.

'Later' came the next morning. True to her plan, he told her yes. That was the beginning of three months that took her beyond her own limits, into a relationship that was exciting and terrifying at the same time. Easter had no boundaries. Rosemary was finding him difficult to control, but still couldn't imagine how she could end this relationship. Worse, it seemed like Brady didn't notice anything amiss. One night, she was out with Easter until three in the morning. She knew that she would be in big trouble. But, when she snuck in the back door with her shoes off, she found a note on the counter from Brady. Opening it apprehensively, she breathed a deep sigh of relief when she read his message that her dinner was in the microwave. He knew she would not feel like cooking when she came in from working late. He loved her. He was tired and going on to bed. She dumped the meal in a plastic bag and then dropped it into the trashcan, walked on into the bedroom, and found him lying in bed, snoring.

Rosemary undressed, feeling nauseous. She took a long hot shower, scrubbing herself hard for about fifteen minutes. She put on her gown and climbed into bed, wanting to cry herself to sleep, but no tears came. She was ashamed, but she was angry. Why couldn't Brady have been awake, waiting at the back door, acting like a mad man, asking her where she had been until three o'clock in the morning? Why couldn't he have cared?

Rosemary woke up in the middle of the night, fighting her way out of her sleep, feeling like someone or something was smothering her. She looked over at Brady, still snoring. As she closed her eyes again, she could hear her Grandma saying, "Don't let the devil ride. He'll want to drive."

As soon as Rosemary boarded her flight, her head began to pound. At first, she thought it might be cabin pressure because the two infants on board were screaming as the plane increased its altitude. When she closed her eyes, she began to see her sister's face. It looked swollen and bruised. Her eyes had dark circles under them. Her gums were toothless and she was mouthing, "Help!" in slow motion, like a giant fish sucking in oxygen. Rosemary opened her eyes quickly and looked around to see if anyone was watching her. She was shaking and a few tears had squeezed their way out of the corners of her eyes. "Get yourself together, girl!" she said to herself. "You're supposed to be going to help her. You're the one who needs some help!" That thought made the tears come faster. She put her sunglasses back on, even though the window shade beside her seat was down. She wanted to cry hard, but the gentle release of teardrops down the sides of her cheeks was also helping to relieve some of the pressure of the headache. "I guess this will have to do for now," she said to herself.

Rosemary began to think about her conversation with Easter yesterday. He had known that she was going out of town to check on her sister, but he didn't find out until yesterday how long she planned to be gone. He was furious! You would think he would want to support her in this very difficult task. Instead, he began to accuse her of trying to see someone else, to sneak away to hook up with an old boyfriend. He threatened to tell Brady about them so that he would know what kind of woman she was. She tried to laugh it off, to reposition herself into the place of control she had enjoyed in her previous relationships, to assure him that there was no old boyfriend, that Brady had been her only relationship before she married him. It was like talking to a steel door. He was not budging.

Rosemary halfway expected to see him in the airport lobby this morning when Brady was waiting for her to check in. Easter had threatened to do a lot of things, and she knew he was crazy enough to attempt to follow through. He knew she was leaving from the airport, but he did not know when or by which airline. Still, he was highly resourceful and could find out what he needed to know if he wanted. Thank God, he was nowhere to be seen. Thank God. Rosemary wondered if it really was divine intervention, and then checked that thought. Why would God be interested or willing to help her in this adulterous situation? Didn't the Bible say that He would judge whoremongers and adulterers? She sure remembered that verse! It was drummed into them in Purity Class down through the years. Keep your panties up and your skirt down. Keep your knees crossed whenever you are near a boy. Say no to the devil. Save yourself for marriage. If you fornicate or commit adultery, God will judge you. Well, she had saved herself for marriage, and look what that got her. A man who played on her with her own sister, the one who she was going to save now; now when she was totally at the opposite end of the spectrum, committing adultery and fornication in ways that would make God blush when He ran her evil deeds before her own eyes on Judgment Day! "Lord, help me!" she breathed, and then fell dead asleep.

A mid-morning fog had arrived to welcome Rosemary home. She rented a car at the airport. With Brady's military veterans' discount and the insurance company discount combined, weekly rates on the compact car were next to nothing. Plus, she didn't want to be dependent on James to get her around while she was in town. Rosemary watched the highway closely. Some of the road she remembered; but with the growth of the town they had been doing a lot of construction. She didn't want to miss her turns.

She decided to go to the beach road first. Even with the fog, she wanted to just be back on her ocean. She recalled how much walking in the sand, feeding the sea gulls, wading in the waves, and smelling the salty air had refreshed her many times in her growing-up years. She remembered the picnic lunches that Grandma used to pack for her and Florence. When they were really little, she would take them to the beach herself every Friday when they got home from school. They would swim until they couldn't stand up. Then, she would rub the sand off of their legs, put a towel on the back seat of her long split-pea green "Deuce and a Quarter", and take them to get an ice cream cone on the way home. When they got to be in their teens, she would pack a lunch for them any day they had finished their work and wanted to go for a swim. They would walk to the beach with their brown paper bags, swinging the bags happily between them, and reminding each other of her instructions to only swim near the lifeguard.

Rosemary thought that those were some of the best days of their lives, long before Florence started having those migraines and nightmares and begged to sleep with her every night. What was she going to do? Protect her from something imaginary? Something in her dreams that no one could see? Rosemary pushed those thoughts away. "I just want some time to clear my head out on the beach!" she thought. "That's all! Then, there will be plenty of time to worry about Florence and her crazy self!"

She managed to find the old turn off to the beach road in spite of all the road construction. She found a spot where she could just sit in the car and look toward the water. The fog was still very thick, and she wondered if she had missed hearing about a change in the weather. It looked like some kind of storm could be brewing. But, just sitting near the water began to bring back those old feelings of comfort and peace. "I wish Grandma was still here. I just need to talk to somebody. Not that she would understand the mess I'm in, though." She laughed to herself. "Not that anybody could," she thought.

Rosemary had planned to stay with her brother-in-law, but now she was thinking twice about that. Not that she didn't like him. He was a very nice man, a pastor. He had just the right mannerisms for a pastor, too. He was gentle and kind, always glad to listen, and always ready to pray. If he wasn't such a close relative, she may have considered talking to him. She wondered what he would say if she began to confess her faults to him, like Catholics do to their priests. "What a mess that would be!" she chuckled to herself.

She remembered that there was a nice resort right on the ocean. A young man and his wife had bought it and fixed it up last year. A friend had stayed there when she had come back to town to visit her mother, and she told Rosemary about how comfortable everything was there. The sun was beginning to clear the fog to the point where Rosemary could distinguish the white caps rushing the shore every few seconds. She quelled the urge to get out of the car and make a dead run toward the sea, yearning for the waves to scrub her and rinse her and make her feel clean and new and young again.

She opened the car door. A few walkers passed her and made their way to the sandy shore. Her eyes followed them on their route down the shore line. The further away they walked, the smaller they became. The fog was lifting back toward the sky. In her peripheral vision, something loomed large. Turning, she noticed a hotel about eight stories high. "I wonder if that is the one that Lisa was talking about?" she thought. She could see that there was a direct, fenced-in walkway that led from the rear of the hotel down to the beach. It looked inviting. Small patios surrounded the fencing on both sides. "Maybe this is a message. A sign. 'I'm clearing the fog, Rosemary, so that you can see your way.'" Rosemary laughed at herself suddenly becoming God-conscious. But, that did help her make up her mind. "Okay, God," she said aloud, "I'm going to take You up on that. I'll check into this hotel and see what comes next."

She was greeted in the front drive by a nice-looking young black man. He could have been bi-racial. His hair was slightly straight and he had the most beautiful gray-green eyes. "Good afternoon, ma'am! Welcome to Princeton Acres Resort! May I get your bags for you?" Instantly, Rosemary felt like a tourist, a visitor, in town for a vacation. She smiled broadly.

"Thank you! I don't have a reservation, though."

"No, problem, ma'am! I will take you right in to the front desk and we will get you all set up with a comfortable room. Did you have a good trip here? Will you be staying long? And, if you give me your keys, I will be glad to park your car for you and then bring the keys to the desk to you."

"My goodness, you are very helpful!" He smiled and Rosemary laughed. "Thank you! Yes, I have had a good trip so far. I'm not sure how long I will be staying, but for at least a couple of weeks, I think. Thank you for offering to park my car."

By this time, he had taken her to the desk and introduced her to the clerk, Regina. Within a few minutes, he was back from parking the car and helped her into the elevator that would take her to her room. He told her about all of the hotel amenities and showed her the features of the room. He invited her to the manager's reception every evening from 6:30 to 8:00 and urged her to call the desk any time if there was anything that she needed. She felt pampered already. That had been a great idea to stay at the hotel!

After refreshing herself a little, she called Brady to let him know she had arrived and would be staying at a hotel and not with James. He sounded a little concerned about her staying by herself, but seemed relieved after she told him that she was right on the beach and she felt like that in itself would do her a lot of good. She asked him how his day had gone and he didn't say much, but told her that he missed her before he hung up.

Next, she called James so that he would not be looking for her. She wasn't sure how he would take her staying at a hotel and not at his house. She didn't want his feelings to be hurt, perhaps thinking that she was refusing his hospitality. His phone rang and rang without him picking up, so she left a short message for him and asked that he call her back when he got a chance. Most likely, he was at the hospital with Florence. He'd probably call when he got home.

Florence. Guilt began to nag Rosemary. She probably should go see her now. That is why she came back home, wasn't it? This wasn't a vacation; it was a mission trip. She shouldn't be selfish. She sat down on the side of the bed to try to either talk herself into heading back out and going to the hospital, or to lie down for a few minutes to rest after her flight. Guilt won. She might as well go to the hospital now. She could stop and get a sandwich on her way. There was no telling how long she would end up being there, because there was no telling what she would find when she got there. So, she would get something to eat and then check on Florence. Taking a deep breath, Rosemary slid her tired feet back into her shoes, picked up her purse, and headed out of the door.

In the lobby, she saw a tall young white man. She could tell he was the manager or something. "Oh, I bet he is the new owner," she thought. "Seems like a nice guy!" He smiled as she came closer to him.

"Hello, how are you?" he asked.

"Hello. I'm doing well, thank you," Rosemary replied.

"Great!" he said. "Have you found everything you need?" He

stepped toward her and extended his hand. His concern seemed genuine and sincere.

She shook his hand. "Yes, I have," she replied softly. "This is a beautiful hotel, and my room is very comfortable. I can't wait to get on the beach and enjoy the water. This place brings back a lot of memories for me!"

"Are you from around here and visiting the past again?" he chuckled warmly, looking deeply into Rosemary's eyes.

"As a matter of fact, I am! I have just come back to see my sister. She's in the hospital. I'm on my way there now."

"Oh, I'm sorry to hear your sister is ill. Well, I hope that you find everything well when you get there. Can we help in any way?" Again, he seemed to really care about her.

"Thank you," Rosemary replied. For some reason, she felt like she needed to cry. "I should be back soon. Goodbye." As she stepped through the front doors and into the bright sunlight, she realized how much she had missed Tisdale Beach. The fresh, salty smell of the sea air seemed to open up her head. She felt alert. Soft stirrings from days long gone by made her arms tingle. Somehow, she felt more alive than ever before. "Maybe I'm just hungry," she said to herself, drifting back into the cloud of negativity that always hovered right behind her. "I'll stop and get a sandwich before I head to the hospital."

Once she got back on familiar ground, she realized how little the town had changed. In spite of all the road improvements, new houses, and small strip malls, she recognized many familiar landmarks. The library. The elementary school. The Methodist church. All of these held familiar memories and brought warmth and comfort to her spirit. She stopped the rental car in front of Mr. Bobby's store. She hoped she could still remember the odd places where he put things like bread and meat. "Maybe they have a deli these days with pre-made sandwiches," she thought as she stepped out of the driver's side door into the quiet street.

The first thing she noticed when she walked into the store was how bright and organized it looked. It smelled clean, and there was a large selection of fresh fruit on display right inside the door. The aroma of apples, oranges, cherries, peaches, plums, and pineapples made her mouth water. She made a mental note to plan to stop back by tomorrow and pick up things that she could put in the small refrigerator in her room. A handsome young man approached her with a box of snack crackers in his hand. He set it on the counter and then greeted her with a big smile. So warm, so comforting. She felt like he was embracing her with his hauntingly-beautiful eyes. He didn't even know her! But, he acted as if he did. Why was everybody being so nice?

"Good afternoon! Can I help you find something?"

Rosemary smiled. "Good afternoon. I was wondering if you have any deli sandwiches and maybe some bottled juice?"

"Yes ma'am!" He said with authority, and then turned to lead her to the deli fridge. She saw quite a few selections. She picked out a chicken salad inside a whole wheat croissant.

"This looks good! Thank you." She followed him to the cold drink cooler. That chilled grape juice was calling her name! "Wow, this was painless!" She laughed, "I can remember the days of fumbling through this store, going up and down the aisles, looking for things that were in one place last week and could be any place this week! Mr. Bobby sure didn't know how to organize a store!"

The young man turned to look her in the eye, flashing that big smile again. He had the cutest dimples! "You know Mr. Bobby? Mr. Bobby is a cool dude!" He slipped into a deep, rolling laugh. "Mr. Bobby let me go ahead and make this a customer-friendly store, and I love him for it." He continued to chuckle. "The patrons do, too! So, I haven't seen you around here before," he said as he led her to the checkout counter. "Are you back visiting?"

"Something like that," Rosemary replied. She took her wallet out of her purse and waited for him to ring everything up. "Actually, my sister and her husband still live here. Both she and I grew up here, living with our grandmother. I found out that my sister is sick, so I came back to check on her. I just got here today." Rosemary became self-conscious, feeling like she was talking too much. He probably didn't want to know her life story. He was just making small talk until he got her money. But, he responded immediately.

"Oh no, I'm sorry to hear that! I hope she gets better soon. It can take a lot out of you when your family member is sick. I know how it is. My grandma died a few months ago. My grandpa is still working hard to deal with that. But, life goes on. Well," he said as he bagged her items, "at least she is still alive. And, as my pastor says, 'where there is life, there is always hope!'"

Rosemary nodded, feeling oddly optimistic. "It sounds like your pastor is a wise man."

"He is, probably one of the wisest men I know. His wife is sick, too, and I know that weighs really heavy on him. He has been taking care of her for a lot of years, and he's been through a lot. But you would never know it, because he is always trying to help somebody else. He never complains. He shows his wife so much love that all the ladies in church get jealous." He laughed again. Rosemary smiled and nodded. "He is one of those people that act like you expect Christians to act." He stopped and looked at Rosemary. "Hey, if you're going to be here on Sunday, you should come to my church and hear him preach. It'll make you feel better!" He laughed.

"That's our church motto, even though it's corny. 'Come to Metropolitan, it'll make you feel better!" He laughed again as he looked closely at Rosemary.

"I just might do that," she said, as she accepted her change and picked up her bag. "Thank you!" She turned to walk to the door, then looked back toward the young man. "What is your name?"

"I'm sorry! I'm Lincoln, and welcome back to town."

"Thank you, Lincoln!" Rosemary said. She walked out the door. An older woman holding the hand of a small child walked past her to the door, smiling warmly at Rosemary. Rosemary smiled back as she held the door open for them. The small child looked up at her and smiled, too. Then, he wrapped both of his little arms around Rosemary's legs and hugged her tightly. Rosemary wobbled for a moment. Her heart leaped into her throat. She was visibly shaken by this open show of affection from a child who didn't even know her.

Sensing her discomfort, the older woman began to scold the child, pulling him closer to her. He looked puzzled, then looked back at Rosemary, his eyes beginning to fill with tears. Rosemary put her bag on the steps, stooped down, and gave the little boy a big hug. "Thank you," she whispered. When she stood, she looked at the older woman and smiled a weak smile. She shook her head up and down. The woman smiled, touched Rosemary's hand, and then stepped into the door.

Rosemary sat in the car a few moments before she engaged the engine. What a weird exchange. Why would a child who didn't know her hug her out of the blue? Even worse, why would she hug him back? She wasn't the hugging type. What was happening in her life today? Things seemed more out of control here than they were when she was with Easter. And, she hadn't meant to even think about him.

Fifteen minutes later, she pulled into the parking lot at the hospital. She intended to eat her sandwich in the car, but somehow lost her appetite after thinking about Easter. She decided to take it inside with her. Heading up to the large automatic doors, she made up her mind to do her best to be positive and supportive toward James. As Lincoln talked about his pastor, she knew he had been talking about James. Her pastor, James' uncle, was the same. "It must be a family trait, or maybe a Godly man trait!" she thought. "Maybe I do need to go to church on Sunday. I've have enough of these other kind of men."

The elderly volunteer at the information desk gave her the room number and directions to the elevator. As she made her way toward her sister, she wondered what she would find when she got to the room. Would James be there? Would Florence look like she had in her dream on the plane? Would she be out of her mind? Would she even know that Rosemary was there?

The hallway smelled of antiseptic and wintergreen alcohol. There it was. Room 422. The door was slightly ajar, but Rosemary still knocked. She heard a man's voice say, "Come in." Rosemary felt dread and hesitation, but she pushed the door forward. As she stepped into the dim room, she could make out a brown couch and two orange armchairs. There was James, sitting in a rocking chair next to the bed.

"James!" she exclaimed, walking toward him. He opened his arms and she embraced him warmly. "How good to see you!"

"Sis! I'm so glad you're here!" He buried his head in her shoulders. For a moment, she thought he was going to cry. He stepped back to turn her toward the bed. "Look who's here, Flo! It's your big sister! Rosemary's come to check on you!"

Rosemary turned her glance slowly toward the head of the bed, fearful of what she might see. Her life had shifted to slow motion with this scene like a frame in a slow-moving picture show. Her eyes focused sharply on the face resting against fluffy white pillows. "Florence," she breathed, moving closer to the bed. She touched her sister's beautiful face, running her hand from the forehead to the chin. "Florence, I'm here." She cupped her right hand around Florence's head. Florence's eyes opened wide. Rosemary could see tears forming in the corners. Like she had in the dream, Florence was mouthing Rosemary's name. "That's all right, baby. Don't worry. I'm here now." She kissed her gently on the forehead. "I'm here."

Rosemary turned to James, wanting to ask so many questions but yet knowing that no answers were necessary right now. He had his head bowed in his hands, his shoulders slumped. He was obviously crying. "God, what is it that you have for me to do?" Rosemary felt like she was at a fork in the road. She could take a path that would lead her away from her past and put her in a position to help those who needed her right now. Or, she could continue traveling the way she had been and do her duty, just to eventually return to the mess she left behind.

"Lead me in a plain path, O Lord…" Those words came to her mind. She couldn't remember the rest of the verse, but maybe she didn't need that part yet. Maybe she just needed to get on the plain path right now. Then, wherever else she needed to go next, the Lord would lead her. That type of divine control might be what she needed right now. As if in an answer to her dilemma, she heard Florence speak. "Rosemary!"

When Sorrows Like Sea Billows Roll

"Hope deferred maketh the heart sick, but when the desire cometh, it is a tree of life." Proverbs 13:12

*

Stretching herself out full in her bed, she took a long yawn before swinging her right foot over and on to the cold wood floor. She shuddered for a moment and then drew herself to her feet and headed for the bathroom. "Just another day," she thought. The closet floor, which was carpeted, felt great. It welcomed her every morning at five o'clock. It was comforting, embracing, and it warmed her spirit. That is why, no matter how tired she was, there was a strong energy awaiting her every morning in her "prayer closet", and she lived for it.

This morning, she first meditated on the verse she read last before going to sleep the night before. It had stayed with her throughout the night, as if it was making sure she understood the message it was bringing. She has been reading in Matthew 16 and gotten to the verse where Jesus told His disciples that he would give them the keys of the kingdom of Heaven. That is where her brain put up the stop sign. She couldn't think about anything else, even though she did finish reading the chapter. She and the girls had been going through a rough season. She had faith to know that everything was going to work out all right; but at the present time, it looked pretty bad. The engine in her car had blown up last week, which should not have been a surprise since it had 245,000-plus miles on it. Still, she had been hoping that it would keep on rolling until she could afford to buy something else.

Yesterday, she received a notice that her check was going to be garnished for a credit card bill that her ex-husband ran up after they separated but before they divorced. Even though she knew he had done it just to spite her, she had prayed her way through the bitterness and anger that tried their best to take root in her spirit. She was past being embarrassed. So much had happened in the last eighteen months that nothing surprised her anymore. Still, she wasn't sure how much more she could take. That was why she was so committed to her five a.m. prayer hour. No matter what happened the day before, she found that she could face her present day with peace if she started it with prayer.

As she laid out flat on her face, her nose resting on her crossed arms, she began to thank God for all of the blessings He had given her and the girls. The apartment they were living in was a miracle. She had been so afraid that they would see her credit report and refuse to approve her application. But, the manager ended up saying that he would be glad to work with her and she had paid her rent on time every month, so she felt like that would help her rebuild her credit. Even though the car broke down, the bus stop was at the end of their sidewalk, so both she and the girls felt alright about riding the bus to work and school.

Her ex-husband had begun to call the girls again. They hadn't heard from him for about four months and were worried if he was okay, or if he was mad at them, or if he had forgotten about them. But, after the phone call two weeks ago, he had been calling them on a regular basis, every two days at the same time of day. They began to watch for his calls and he hadn't disappointed them yet. Even though he and she had issues, she was determined to not let that affect his relationship with his daughters. So, she was thanking God for helping him to be a good dad, now.

In spite of her optimism, she was still worried about how she was going to handle her bills with this upcoming garnishment. "That is going to take a miracle! I know they don't change those things once they start. I just can't see how our budget will survive if they take half of my check to pay for his credit card bill!" She began to feel sick to her stomach but tried to suppress it because she knew that would be like doubting God. "Please, Lord, help me! Please fix this situation!"

"Why are you worrying?" She heard a soft inner voice say. "Don't you think I can fix this, too?"

Cheryl began to cry, but also to praise through her tears. "Yes, Lord, I know You can do anything! I know that You have power over every situation that I could ever encounter. Please increase my faith, and help me to believe! You have already given me authority over every situation that the enemy can create to distract me. You have given me the keys of the kingdom. I have access to Your resources! Faith is the power that will open the door. Yes! I am coming out of this with victory and a testimony! Thank you, Lord! I know I can walk this through because You are walking with me! You are carrying me. I survive because of Your power. Everything will be all right. Thank you, Lord! Amen!"

Cheryl rolled over on her back and drew her knees up to her chin. "I'm not going over into a fetal position anymore! I'm looking up!" She opened her eyes wide and kicked her legs straight out, then sat up. "Yes, Lord, I am going forward in Your strength today!" Rising to her feet, she raised her hands and jumped up and down a couple of times, laughed at herself, then headed to the bathtub to start her water.

"Girls, it's time to get up!" she called. Stephanie was fourteen, a freshman in high school. She had a sharp mind and loved school. She was also very fashion conscious, so she was usually the first to get to their bathroom. She wanted plenty of time to get ready so that she would look her best when she walked out of the door. Celeste, at eight, wasn't quite so worried about what anyone thought of her wardrobe. Cheryl often had to send her back to her room a few times each morning to pick out a pair of clean shorts or the t-shirt without the holes, or to make sure she had on matching tennis shoes. All in all, though, she was blessed to have two very sweet and resilient daughters who loved both her and their dad equally. She saw so many positive attributes in their character that she was excited about the young women they would become in the future.

She herself was very blessed to get a job at the hospital so quickly after they had come to town. The reason they settled here was not because of family ties or knowledge of the community. This was where the car had started to overheat on their way to her grandmother's home two states away. She really didn't want to sink all of her money into fixing the car again, so she decided to spend the night at a resort hotel on the beach and take the afternoon checking out the job market.

Once she and the girls settled into their room, they walked down to the beach. It was fun walking up and down the seashore, picking up all sizes, types, and colors of shells. They then had a tasty lunch in the hotel restaurant. After lunch, she told the girls that she was going to go out for a couple of hours, so they should stay in the room and either watch television or take a nap. They were a little tired, and with their bellies full, they gave her no argument.

Pulling up to the front doors of the hospital, she had prayed a quick prayer. "Lord, if it is Your will for us to settle here for a while, please give me a strong sign. I don't want to be out of Your will, but I also want to be wise and use the resources You have given me to get to my next stop in life. Thank You." She parked her car in an open space. She noticed that it seemed like a busy hospital, but the parking lot wasn't overcrowded. She wasn't sure if that was a good sign or not. If it was overcrowded, that would mean that they likely needed more help. She decided to just go inside and see what would happen.

"Good afternoon!" she said to the young receptionist seated at the information desk. The young lady smiled. "I was wondering if you could direct me to the personnel office?"

"Yes, Ma'am! It is just to your left, right beside the elevators." Cheryl followed her directions to the job that secured her family with a nice apartment the very next day and some cheap car repairs done quickly by the receptionist's father. Cheryl knew that God had been on her side in these transactions. It just happened that a registered nurse had resigned the day before because her husband had just gotten a great job in another city. Cheryl was hired on the spot. The resort manager owned an apartment complex, too, so he was willing to let her rent a three-bedroom, two-bathroom apartment once he met her and the girls. It seemed that God had put his stamp of approval on her settling here for now, and she was relieved to be supported by such good people.

So now, even with the threat of garnishment, Cheryl had a hard time allowing herself to become depressed. She had seen what God could do and she believed that He would not disappoint her now. She and the girls headed to the bus stop. They were busy talking about news that their father had shared with them when he called last night. He was planning to get married! The woman he was dating had two small boys. The girls were excited about having brothers, finally. Cheryl was a little puzzled at their reaction. She thought they would be jealous of a new woman and new children in his life, especially since he wasn't around spending time with them. Then, she checked her attitude. "Isn't it good that they aren't reacting emotionally to his news?" she thought. "I could have some whiny, petulant adolescents on my hands, needing me to validate their worth to their father and me. Instead, I have some mature young women who only want their father to be happy and who have enough love to welcome a woman and children that their father has chosen to love into their own circle of love. That's amazing! I guess I just need to count my blessings!"

The bus pulled up within seconds. They all boarded quickly and paid their fares. The two girls made their way midway down the aisle and sat together, and Cheryl sat down beside an older man a few rows closer to the driver. He smiled a wide grin, showing off the spaces where he had lost a few teeth. She smiled back and then turned to check on the girls. They were chattering happily. Cheryl sat back.

The schools were adjoined on the same campus. Celeste was in the fourth grade. The elementary school was the largest of the three schools. Between the elementary school and the high school was the middle school. It separated the two girls from each other during the school day. Stephanie attended the high school. When the girls got off of the bus, she walked Celeste to the front door of the elementary school and then travelled the equivalent of a half-block to the high school. Sometimes, the girls would see each other coming and going to lunch, as all three facilities shared the same lunch room. After school, they would meet up again to take the bus home.

Once the girls got off of the bus, Cheryl would begin to pray for the patients she knew she would care for that day, and even for some who had been released. She felt like that prayer helped her to be prepared for their needs each day. Today, Mrs. Patterson was weighing heavily on her mind. She had begun to do better since her sister had come to visit her last week. It seemed like her mind was clearing up and she was speaking better, but she was crying a lot. The doctor had changed her medication, so Cheryl thought that may have affected her hormonally. However, when her sister and her husband were not there and Cheryl would come into the room,

Mrs. Patterson would want to talk to her about her parents. At first, Cheryl had listened politely, but then she began to notice some patterns in Mrs. Patterson's questions. "Did your father ever tell you he loved you and you were his little girlfriend? Did your mother ever get drunk and say crazy things to your father about you? Did you ever dream that you were kissing a man who looked like your father? Did your father ever sleep at your feet to protect you from monsters, though you would still wake up fighting off the monsters?" The questions, interspersed with crying spells, went on and on, and Cheryl never tried to answer any of them. She just listened.

"Lord, please help Mrs. Patterson find the answers she needs so that she can be healed of the hurts of her past. She needs to be whole. Her husband needs for her to be all right." The bus pulled right up to the front doors of the hospital. Cheryl rose from her seat, smiled at the old man, then thanked the driver as she stepped off of the bus.

She checked her mailbox after she clocked in for the morning. There was a small pink message slip with a name and a number on it. "Coker Law Office, 337-555-5935. Call asap."

"Oh, Lord, what can this be now? As if I haven't got enough to deal with! Is this more of Brian's bills? I know I've made arrangements for all of mine." She was beginning to feel a little vexed, wondering when she would ever be able to break free from these issues. "Help me, Lord! I don't want to make this a bad day for myself by worrying. Let me go find someone to cheer up!" She picked up her charts and stepped into the hall.

"Good morning, Mr. Lewis! How are you doing?" She smiled cheerily as she moved toward his chair. She checked his vitals and gave him his medications. She saw six more patients before she came to Mrs. Patterson's room. There was a soft conversation going on as she quietly stepped into the room. Rev. Patterson was sitting in a chair close to the right side of the bed. Mrs. Patterson was sitting up tall against her pillows. She looked up and smiled at Cheryl as she walked into the door. Her eyes looked very clear. Cheryl noticed a peaceful expression on her face. She had never seen her like that before.

"Good morning, Cheryl." Florence opened her arms as if she wanted a hug. Cheryl walked to the side of the bed, facing Pastor Patterson who was seated on the other side of Florence's lap. He was smiling, but he had tears in his eyes. Cheryl laid her stethoscope and blood pressure cuff on Florence's knees. She reached over and gave Florence a warm hug.

"How are you feeling this morning, Mrs. Patterson?" Cheryl looked at her and then at Pastor Patterson, who was gazing at his wife in amazement.

"This morning?" Florence responded in a clear voice. "This morning feels like the first morning of my life. I feel as if I have emerged from a dark fog. I feel like my mind is clear for once in a long time. I feel like a new person."

"Wow, and you haven't even had your medications yet!" said Cheryl, chuckling a little.

"Yes, I have, Cheryl. I've had something that doesn't come in a bottle, though. Do you have a few minutes?"

"Of course," Cheryl said, moving closer to the head of the bed. "What happened?"

Florence reached over and grabbed her husband's hand. He smiled at her, and a tear escaped the corner of his eye. "It's all right, baby. This is your testimony, and we know that God works miracles. You see, Ms. Cheryl, God delivered my wife last night of demons that have tormented her since she was a little child. All it took was exposing the enemy, forgiving those who hurt her, and praying for her sister. Through that, she got her own freedom. You see, it wasn't that she was crazy. She was heart-sick." He looked at her and smiled, squeezing her hand tightly. "But, she's all right now."

"My sister came to visit me yesterday," Florence continued. "I had just awakened from another nightmare when she came in the door. The dream had been so vivid. I could see faces of real people, people that I knew. I saw my father, standing over me, drunk. He was crying and apologizing for mistreating me. It was like I was watching a movie. He began to shrink until he looked like he was five inches high. He was crying so hard that he began to melt, so I picked him up and put him in my pocket." Florence's long, slender fingers demonstrated in sign language-like gestures the events of her dream, acting like she was placing the man deep into a pocket. She continued talking, "Then, my mother appeared from somewhere and began to laugh at him and tease him. She kept calling him 'little man'. All of a sudden, my sister walked up. She was a giant. She picked up my mother and shook her, then she picked me up and cradled me like a baby." Here, her well-manicured fingers once again dramatized the shaking and the cradling. "She had my mother in her left hand, shaking her like a rag doll, and me in her right hand, holding me like a baby doll. My father was still in my pocket crying. There was so much noise and confusion that I started screaming, 'Stop! Stop!'". Florence's hands moved swiftly to the sides of her head. She looked like she was on the verge of hysteria. Cheryl extended her palms to Florence, and Florence grasped them tightly. After a moment, she continued her narrative.

"All of a sudden, a strong wind started to blow. When I looked into the wind, I saw my husband's face and his lips rounded, blowing forcefully. He blew my mother out of my sister's hand. He blew my father out of my pocket. I could see them disappearing, carried off with each gust of wind that he blew. My sister and I embraced each other tightly so that we wouldn't blow away, but instead of moving us, the wind was removing things from us. Our clothes became ragged and blew off of our backs, but new clothing appeared in their place. Our hair blew out straight. We began to laugh and jump up and down. The wind felt warm and refreshing. At that point, I woke up. And, my sister was walking in the door. When I saw her, I just wanted to hug her, tell her I loved her, and apologize for all of the hurts I had caused her to feel. She cried and told me she loved me, too. She apologized to me, also. I felt so clean and new. I know that God used my husband to pray for me when I couldn't pray for myself." She nodded at Pastor Patterson, and he began to speak.

"You see, Ms. Cheryl, while my wife was sleeping, I was praying. Yesterday morning, I felt such a burden for my wife that I had stopped on my way to the hospital, parked my car, and prayed until I felt drained. I knew that something had to change in her life. The devil had to let her go! When I got here, she was asleep, but I continued to pray over her while she slept. I believe I was ministering to her in her dream! That wind she felt was the power of the Holy Ghost, setting her free from the bondage of her past. And, not only did God deliver her, but He delivered her sister, too!"

"Praise God!" Cheryl exclaimed! "Do you know that I have also been praying for you, Mrs. Patterson? In fact, I was just praying this morning that God would help you be well so that you will be able to help your husband in his ministry! Wow! I truly know now that God will answer prayers, and He can work miracles!" She hugged Florence and then came around the bed to hug Pastor Patterson.

"Thank you!" he said. "I don't know what the doctor will say, but I am believing that I can take my wife home today!"

"He's scheduled to be by on his rounds in a few minutes," Cheryl said, "but I know that when God starts a work, He finishes it!"

"Amen!" said Florence, softly. "Cheryl, I want to tell you about my sister Rosemary, too. She won't be back to share her own testimony. She has gone home this morning to reunite with her husband and to get some situations straightened out in her own life. But, she left in a different way than how she came. She had backslidden. She had built up anger and resentment toward me because of things I had done to hurt her. But, when we were able to forgive one another and pray for one another, God restored her and changed her life, too. She called her husband from the room to let him know how the enemy had deceived her, and he forgave her. He said he knew all the time, but his love for her had kept him from hurting her. That is real love, isn't it?" Florence looked at Pastor Patterson with respect and warmth in her eyes. "I guess I have a lot to learn, huh?"

"But, I'm here to learn with you," said Pastor Patterson. "We will make it together."

Cheryl began to cry. "I came in today, hoping to bring a blessing to you. But, you both have blessed and encouraged me. I'm dealing with some issues in my life, too, but I am praising and trusting God to work it all out. I know if He can do it for you, He can do it for me and my girls." As they held hands, Pastor Patterson began to pray for Cheryl.

"Father, in the name of your precious son, Jesus, we first want to thank You for Your miracle-working power! You have shown us what You can do when we trust You! Now, I raise up before You the needs of Your faithful servant, Sister Cheryl. I ask that You meet those needs in a great way. Show her Your power this day! Work it out, and make it another miracle in her life. Amen!" All three wept and praised God. There was a soft knock on the door. Cheryl stepped away to open it. Her supervisor was standing in the doorway, a concerned look on her face.

"Cheryl, you have an important phone call at the nurses' station. You need to come and take it now." She turned quickly and walked away.

Cheryl stepped into the bathroom to wipe her face and blow her nose first, and then she asked the Patterson's to excuse her. She followed her supervisor to the desk phone. "An important phone call?" she wondered. "What can it be now?"

"Hello? Yes, this is Cheryl Bass." There was a male voice on the other end of the line. He identified himself as Attorney Arthur Coker. She remembered that was the name of the law firm she was supposed to have called this morning. "Oh, yes, I did get the message to call you, but I hadn't had a chance yet," she explained, fear beginning to build up in her gut. "Yes, I did get the notice of garnishment. Did you realize that debt belonged to my ex-husband and he incurred it long after we separated?" Cheryl was praying while she talked, praying that he would understand and have some mercy on her, praying that he would please show her favor! "Oh, you did find that out? He told you? He's going to settle it? The garnishment has been lifted? Excuse me, please!" Cheryl put the phone down on the desk. She almost couldn't believe what she had just heard! "Thank You, God! Thank You for this miracle!" she said in her spirit, eyes closed and fists clenched passionately! She picked the phone back up. "Thank you so much, sir!"

Mr. Coker concluded the conversation with his congratulations and the assurance that he would not just mail the confirming paperwork to the hospital human resources office but would fax it immediately if she would provide him with the fax number. He chuckled and thanked Cheryl as she thanked him and blessed him over and over before they each hung up.

Cheryl had other patients to see, but she could not resume her rounds before she hurried back in to tell the Pattersons about how God had answered their prayers so quickly! She was confident that Florence would be released shortly, and she wanted to be sure she knew where their church was located so that she could visit them often and put down her roots where the waters were troubled.

God's Gonna Trouble the Water

"Every wise woman buildeth her house; but the foolish plucketh it down with her hands." Proverbs 14:1

*

"Mommy, please tell Celeste to hurry up! I have to be at choir practice on time! Miss Loretta said that she will help me with my solo, and we're supposed to be singing that song tomorrow. I can't be late!"

"All right! Celeste, get your other shoe and come on!" Cheryl lifted her car keys off of the hook beside the back door of the kitchen. She knew that Stephanie was getting frustrated, but she also knew that Celeste hadn't been feeling well that morning. Still, she was glad that both girls enjoyed singing in the choir at Metropolitan. They had been welcomed into the church family from the first Sunday they visited and she had been blessed herself by being under Pastor Patterson's leadership.

Stephanie had already gone out of the back door and was standing beside the passenger's side front door waiting for her mother and her sister. She was such a beautiful young lady. Tall, stately, built like an athlete. Her skin was coffee-colored and smooth. Her face was flawless. She had never had a single pimple, and many girls her age envied her for that. She had natural self-assurance that allowed her to always appear composed but never seem aloof. Her hair was jet black and long. Often, it looked like a wig due to its thickness and straightness. Cheryl had never put any chemicals on either of the girls' hair; she did not need to, because of the strong Native American genetic traits that both she and their father carried.

Stephanie's focus on fashion made her always look like a model, set to parade down the walkway. Today, she had on a short brown plaid skirt, a collared pink shirt with a gold, knitted scarf wrapped around her neck. Knee-high socks and brown and white saddle shoes completed the outfit. Her nails were done in a deep, bright pink and she had yellow and pink hair clips holding up her hair on the left and right temples. She had put on her tortoise-shell-rimmed sunglasses while she stood impatiently beside the car, waiting for her mother and sister.

She didn't mean to be mean to either of them, or to make them think they were inconveniencing her in any way. But for her, singing was a very serious matter. In fact, it was what she hoped would be her vocation one day soon. She knew she could sing well. She just wanted to learn how to do it better. Ms. Loretta had been in town visiting her parents when she decided to come to the church and sit in on the youth choir rehearsal while her sister played the organ for the choir. That was last Saturday, when they had introduced the song that Stephanie was selected to lead.

From the moment Stephanie opened her mouth to echo the lines as the choir director demonstrated the lead, Loretta knew that this young lady had a special gift, an anointing to sing gospel music. The tremor, the smoothness, the range, and the soul in her voice rang true in Loretta's spirit, for she of all people knew what it took to communicate commitment to your faith through your natural praise instrument, your voice. So, when the rehearsal was over, Loretta went to the young lady and introduced herself. She told her that she used to sing in this same choir, but had left many years ago to pursue a career in show business. She had come back to visit her family for a couple of weeks, but would come to practice next Saturday if Stephanie would want her help on the lead. Stephanie was so excited that she reminded Loretta of the young groupies who used to throng her every time she left a performance during her prime.

For the first time since the incident occurred, Loretta felt like she had a purpose. Once again, she could mentor someone younger to grow and do many of the things she herself had learned as a successful musician, yet without making the mistakes she had made; mistakes which left her where she was today. So, all week, she rehearsed with her sister some of the rifts that she was going to teach Stephanie on Saturday. There was something supremely therapeutic about learning music so that she could teach music, and she woke up Saturday morning excited about the venture ahead.

On the way to the church, Cheryl made a mental list of the errands she could complete while the girls were at rehearsal. Sister Patterson had called her last night to see if she would stop by sometime on Saturday. There was something she wanted her to look at before Sunday. She also wanted to go by and check on Brother Reynolds and make sure that he had some fresh milk so that he would continue to take his medication with something on his stomach. She decided that she would just stop by the store and pick up some milk on her way to his house. It didn't hurt him to have a little extra on hand. Plus, she always liked seeing Lincoln and hearing one of his corny jokes. He always asked about the girls, which she thought was very kind of him. She felt like he was a good old friend that played the important role in her life of making her laugh, which she really needed to do on a regular basis. So, she decided that would be her first stop after dropping the girls off at church.

At some point, she was going to have to wash the car. It had rained on and off all week, and now the exterior of her "new" car was all dusty. She didn't know if this was a job she wanted to do by herself or if she wanted the girls to help, so she wasn't sure when she would do it. But, she needed to do it. This car represented yet another miracle performed by a merciful God! She still wasn't quite sure how things had worked together on this one.

A little over six months ago, she had gone to the hotel on the first day of the month to see her landlord, Jimmy, and pay the rent on their apartment. When she arrived, she saw his wife Mary first. They had been so kind to her and the girls this past year. She and Mary embraced, and then Mary whispered to her, "Guess what, Cheryl? We're going to have a baby!"

Cheryl hugged her hard, congratulating her on this good news. Mary asked her to quiet down. "I've just come from the doctor, so Jimmy doesn't know yet! Please don't say anything! I came straight over here to tell him."

Mary sat back down in the chair on the opposite side of Jimmy's desk. She patted the chair beside her, signaling Cheryl to take that seat. Mary grabbed Cheryl's hand. "See, we have been trying so hard for years to have a baby. We gave up about five years ago, just left it in the Lord's hands. So, I thought I had the flu last week because I couldn't keep anything down all day long. I got pretty weak a couple of days ago, so I called my doctor and he got me right in. Jimmy's been so worried about me, but he had a meeting today so I told him not to worry, I would drive myself. Girl, you can't imagine how shocked I was when the nurse told me I'm pregnant! I'm five months along! The doctor assured me that I'm past the stage of miscarriage, and everything looks great! I'm almost afraid to get too excited, but I believe God is going to bless me to carry this baby full term. I just have to have that kind of faith! It's been a few hours, but I'm still in a state of shock. Look at me, rambling on and on, making no sense!" Mary began to laugh, and then hugged Cheryl.

"Look, I know everything is going to be all right! Jimmy is going to be so excited! I'll leave and come back later. I was going to drop off my rent check, but I guess I could just put it in an envelope and leave it here on his desk. When he comes in, I know you two will want to be alone." Cheryl stood up and moved toward the door.

"Hello, ladies! My, my, what have I done to deserve this view? Two of the most beautiful women in the whole wide world, gracing my humble office! What's the occasion?" Jimmy came in the door, almost bigger than life. He hugged Cheryl and then embraced Mary, kissing her on the cheek. "How you doing, Girl?" he murmured softly. "You look better. Are you feeling all right? Did they give you some medicine?" Jimmy sat on his desk, facing Mary. She sat back down into the chair.

"Uh, well, I'll be leaving," said Cheryl. "I just came by to pay my rent." She handed Jimmy the check.

He took it with a nod, then motioned for her to sit back down. "Thanks, but don't go anywhere. I might want to take both of you to lunch. Besides, Mary has been sick for a couple of days. We think she had the flu. You might need to keep an eye on her, make sure she is out of the woods. I don't know what I would do if anything happened to her." He smiled and pinched Mary's cheek. "You do look much better!" he exclaimed. "What did they give you?"

"Some good news! We're going to have a baby!"

When Jimmy recovered from his shock, he was ready to change the world. After listing all of the things he was going to do and buy for the new baby, he declared that Mary's two-year old car wouldn't do anymore. Their baby needed a lot of room. They were going to buy a utility vehicle, today! He turned to Cheryl, who had been observing Jimmy's processing with great amusement.

"Cheryl, can you and the girls use a new car?" he asked. When she answered that they could use a car, period, he took Mary's keys from her purse and placed them in Cheryl's hand. "Here you go! God bless you! Just clean it out and put Mary's things in a box. Drop them by the house later. I'll have the registration and title all ready for you then." He turned to Mary and gently lifted her from her chair to her feet. "Come on, Girl! Let's go car shopping!"

That was a day Cheryl would never forget. She saw, once again, the grace of God at work in her life. She hadn't begged for a working vehicle, but God knew her situation. Not only did He bless her with another car, but He gave her the car, free! And, He allowed her to witness the blessing of a child to two of the most deserving people she knew. Now, they were all enjoying their blessings! Baby Joy Marie was a newborn beauty, and Jimmy and Mary were so happy.

All of their rushing paid off for Stephanie. When Cheryl and the girls pulled up in front of the church, Loretta and Maxine, her sister, were parking in the lot. Cheryl recognized Loretta from television and media shots. She decided to park the car and go meet her. Plus, she wanted to thank her for taking time to work with Stephanie. As soon as Cheryl turned off the engine, Stephanie was out of the car and running toward Loretta. She gave her a big hug and told her that she had been practicing all week! She was ready to work! Cheryl could see Loretta laughing and teasing with Stephanie. She looked so happy! They both did. Celeste was talking to Sister Maxine. Cheryl recalled that Celeste told her last week that she wanted to take piano lessons. Cheryl said a quick prayer of thanks, that God had given each of them a place in this church family.

Loretta was so relieved inside to have received such a greeting from Stephanie. Ever since she woke up that morning, she had been so afraid that she was extending herself more than would be welcome. She had gotten herself out there before. She didn't want to be more excited for Stephanie that she was for herself. She didn't want to become bossy and manipulative and then drive her pupil away. She had to be careful about that. But, to see Stephanie's excitement now and to hear her say that she had been working on this project all week on her own made Loretta feel needed. That was something she had not felt in a long time.

She sat toward the back of the church during the beginning of the youth choir rehearsal. She just wanted to allow herself to feel the moment, become immersed again in the aura of the environment. This church had always been a comforting place. She didn't realize how much she had missed it until she came back. There was something about just being in the sanctuary which made her understand why it was called a "sanctuary", a place of safety and rest. This was the most relaxed she had felt in years. In fact, this was the most "Loretta" she had felt in years.

"Why did I ever leave the church to sing?" she thought. Looking at the young teenagers in the choir stand, she could almost see her own face in the crowd. One of many who emerged as one of the chosen few, those who had a special gift to sing and were chosen to represent the group as a soloist. Her gift had not gone unnoticed. When she was sixteen, she competed in a local talent show and won the grand prize. One thousand dollars and a free recording. Most winners became one-time wonders. Not Loretta. She became an overnight success. She recorded a song that she and Maxine had written for the event. It was a hit! She was invited to perform on "Soul Showcase", a nationally-syndicated show that featured prominent Black music artists every week. After that appearance, her career took off. Recording offers came in from everywhere. She began to open for many of the major artists of her time. She was invited to tour the performance circuit as a featured soloist. But, these roads took her far from her gospel roots, not to mention far from the Biblical teachings which had guided her early life. Still, no matter where she was on a Sunday, she had maintained her commitment to visit a local church or at least watch a church service on television. But, that wasn't enough to keep her strong, and she eventually gave in to the strong temptations that lurked continually around the circles in which she travelled.

Loretta met Don in one of those circles. It was a small one, made up of drug addicts and their best friends – drug suppliers. She had always been a person who felt she could take on projects, take something a little rough around the edges and make it better. Most people did that with real estate. Loretta tried to do it with people. Tried, because it never worked. Not once. Years ago, she had an epiphany that had changed her practice. She realized that she was trying to play God in others' lives. She was attempting to be the rescuer, the life changer, the savior. God told her clearly that she was doing a poor job of being Him, and he sent that message through Don.

He had a sad life story. Neglected and abused as a small child, he had been passed from foster home to foster home. His last parents had been naturalists who lived in a remote compound. He was home-schooled through high school and only escaped when he left at seventeen to go to college. Even though they had one more year of support checks coming for him, he never contacted them again. He didn't care about the money. He was free. Plus, he had learned a new way to support himself. Pharmaceutical sales.

Due to the early trauma he experienced, medications were mailed monthly to the home, a requirement for his foster care by the state. However, his foster parents did not believe in anything but holistic care, so they hid his medication and treated him with natural herbs. Whenever the case worker visited, Don was instructed to tell them that he was taking his "medicine" and feeling well. Actually, he was feeling good and had very few psychotic episodes. But, he knew where his foster father was stashing the pills that he was supposed to be taking, so when he left for school he took a suitcase full of many years' worth of pills with him. He was nervous about being on his own and taking care of himself. Plus, he was not sure how things would be if he felt an episode coming on and could not find the herbal remedies his foster parents had provided to him, even though his prescriptions followed him to college so that he was able to refill them each month, as well.

When his roommate found out that Don had a large supply of medications that other students would search for on the streets, he turned Don on to an easy way to support himself in luxury during his college years. Of course, he would have to cut the roommate a share for providing him with customers. But, Don was a smart young man and figured that was a small price to pay for what he would be making.

He soon had a stable base of customers and worked hard to become a personable provider, eager to meet their needs in a professional way. Loretta's friends liked doing business with Don. That is how she met him.

He was always amazed that she could be a social observer, yet never take part in any of the addictive activities in which her friends indulged. She was the designated driver, the sober supervisor, the level head at all times in any situation. Don admired her stability, along with her sense of humor. So, when he would show up with the party favors, he would spend his time with her after setting up the table. He grew to enjoy her conversation, and she seemed to like being around him, too. Even though he was nervous, he asked her out on a date. She accepted his invitation. After that, they became a couple and enjoyed many happy times together.

The relationship deteriorated when she started to pressure him to drop the drug business and use his exceptional skills in a legitimate career. He wasn't ready, or willing, to lose his lucrative profits. He had personal goals that had not yet been realized – the dream home, the dream car, the dream lifestyle. He wanted her to share in this world with him; in fact, he was doing it for her now. Her desire to control and change him angered him.

He had never had a real mother, and he really wasn't looking for one now. He wanted a woman who respected him and allowed him to give her all the things that he believed would make her happy. Why wouldn't she just let him be himself? What was wrong with him that needed to be changed?

Loretta recalled that this was the point when his personality also began to deteriorate. He swore up and down that he never used any drugs, he just supplied them to others. He said he was like the Jewish grocer who would not touch a slice of ham, but would sell pork all day to anyone who wanted it. So, when he began to demonstrate paranoid behaviors, or to flip from caring confidence to extreme destructive anger within a matter of minutes, Loretta questioned whether or not he was using drugs. She would give him her speeches about how he needed to change, to leave this business and these friends, to move away and get a new start, to do something with his life, and talk to him until he would blow up and say something hurtful to her.

The last time that happened, she told Don that their relationship was over and she was leaving town. He would never see her again. She had not anticipated his response. He first exploded in a round of fury, throwing things and cursing loudly. He stopped just short of threatening her, but she could tell that he was extremely angry. She did not want to show any fear, but she was worried about what might happen next.

Instead of escalating, he sank down on his knees and began to cry. He grabbed her legs and held on to her, as if to prevent her from walking away, crying like a baby. His nose was running, he was shaking like a dope fiend in detox, holding on to her for dear life, all the while begging her to not leave him. Loretta had never seen this side of Don's personality and she was very afraid. She cared about him, but she didn't trust his mood swings. So, she had forcefully and heartlessly broken his grip on her legs and run away from him as fast as she could, never looking back. She could hear his voice calling her name in between sobs, but he did not pursue her. She imagined him still kneeling on his living room carpet, a crumpled heap, crying and calling her name.

She stopped the social aspects of her career immediately, so she rarely saw anyone who would have known about her relationship with Don. One day, though, she ran into an old friend in the mall. During their greetings, Don's name came up. Loretta just listened politely with a pasted-on smile. As it turned out, Don had seemed to disappear. No one had seen him in a couple of months. Had she? Loretta nodded no, and then waited to see what else might be said. Even though she didn't want to see him, she still cared about him. "Somebody said he's crazy now!" was the last comment that the old friend made. They parted, each telling the other how good it was to see them again.

For a while after that news, Loretta worried a little about Don. What if he had experienced an episode that had damaged his mental health? Why hadn't he listened to her? They could have still been together, and she could have been there to take care of him. But, maybe she wasn't capable of providing the level of care that he really needed. Anyway, God knew best, so she wasn't going to open herself up to more issues. She would leave things as they were.

Loretta hadn't thought much about him for a long time, but he would pop up every now and then. Literally, it seemed at times. She might be driving down the street and glance over at the driver next to her. For a moment, he would look like Don staring back at her with those strange, piercing blue-green eyes that had so strongly attracted her in the beginning. They would startle her to the point that she would look away quickly; but if she snuck a second glance, no one would be there. Maxine had even told her that she had gotten some strange phone calls about six months ago on the house phone. Some man would call and ask for Loretta, then hang up quickly when Maxine would question him. A couple of times, she thought he had called and just breathed in the phone while she said, "Hello? Hello?" a few times, waiting for the connection to clear. One time when he called to ask for Loretta, she told him that Loretta would be there in about an hour. In fact, they would be at a restaurant three blocks from the church and he could come join them there if he wanted to see her. She was making that up to maybe get a glimpse of him herself so that she could tell Loretta who was looking for her.

Maxine had gone there and waited in the parking lot to see if she saw anyone who looked suspicious. She waited as long as she could. There was a meeting that afternoon at the church for the women, so she didn't want to be too late for that. But, if some strange man was stalking her sister, she sure wanted to know what he looked like so that she could warn her sister to be on the lookout for a man fitting that description. However, no one even drove into the parking lot to walk toward the restaurant during the half-hour that she sat there, fifteen minutes on either side of the time that she told him they would be arriving at the restaurant. So, she assumed that it was a prank caller who had no intent of following through on his commitment.

She started her engine and headed toward the exit. Entering the street, she noticed a crazy driver zigzagging through traffic in the opposite lane. She figured it was a teenager trying to show off. But, as the car swung into the turn lane, she could see an older man with glasses on behind the wheel. He looked deranged. For a moment, she wondered if he could have been the caller. She tried to remember as much about him as she could and wrote it down as soon as she got to the church. Funny thing was, Sister Patterson had described some crazy man who had followed her to the church parking lot and threatened her that same day. Maxine had often wondered if he and Don were one and the same. When she shared those few details with Loretta later on, Loretta couldn't confirm that it could have been Don, but she still wasn't sure that it was not Don.

Sitting here in church today, hearing her sister make that organ "sing", and watching the young people praise God in their own way made her yearn once again for the old days before her life got off track, before the drama with Don, before she had to clear away trash in order to enjoy the peace of a good church experience. "It's not too late to come home," Pastor used to say at the altar call when they were children. Oh, how she wished that was so for her. Career-wise, relocating back home would mean instant professional suicide. All of her connections were on the coast. She'd never be able to secure the gigs she presently had if she moved home. But, was home a location as much as it was a state of mind? Was the call to come home moreso a call to come back to the spiritual place that put her in right standing with God?

Her sister began to play a song from their youth choir days, and she and the choir director joined in two-part harmony. Loretta felt an undeniable urge to take her part and sing. Before she knew it, she had left her seat at the back of the church and was walking forward toward the organ, adding her rich alto to the choir director's soprano and her sister's tenor. Some of the children had stood up to listen, but Loretta was oblivious to anything except the words of the song. *"He's calling you, come home. The door is open. The light is on. Oh, wandering child, don't rest alone. Just come on home. Just come on home."*

Instead of heading to the organ, Loretta's feet took her to the altar, where she collapsed. All of the burdens of her past seemed to weigh her down there. She couldn't move; yet, she didn't want to move. She wanted to stay there until something in her heart changed. She wanted the mist that circulated in her brain to clear. She wanted to sing and feel an anointing again. She wanted to surrender her will to God and stop trying to do His job from now on, for the rest of her life. She wanted to be His child again, and never have to plan or worry or fear anything. She was ready to return to her roots, ready to relax, ready to be free. "Yes, Lord. I am finally ready to come home!" She stretched out on the altar. She was home.

The Winds and the Waves Shall Obey Thy Will

"Better is a little with the fear of the Lord than great treasure and trouble therewith." Proverbs 15:16

*

Pulling her pink turtleneck sweater over her head a little guiltily, Emily could hear the haunting voice of her daughter, Angela, saying, "Put on your sweater before you go out into the cold evening air, Mom. You don't want rheumatism setting in tonight." Same dry words every evening. Emily chuckled just a little as she thought, "Now, who is the mother and who is the child?" Still, she was glad that Angela had stayed with her all of these years, taking care of her when she could have ventured back out into the world and resumed her old life. Emily sincerely appreciated her daughter's sacrifice.

Evenings on the beach were a daily treat for her. Even though it was almost summer, there was still a cool crispness in the air. The waves licked the shore, trying to pick up the last few pieces of sand and shell before going to bed for the night. The sea gulls were after their last meal, too, pecking at tiny sea creatures and picnic leftovers before they finally called it a day. That is why Emily chose this time for her walk. She felt needed, especially by one favorite sea gull. He would come to the porch to greet her each morning as she sat at the small café table and enjoyed her warm cup of dark brown coffee. He would politely accept any crumbs of toast or bagel that she set on the porch rail. She would then bring him the days' end crumbs in the evening so that he could sleep well with a full stomach. This had been her daily ritual since the first week they moved out there. Angela didn't really understand it; but then, Angela didn't always understand her. Sometimes, Emily thought that Angela felt she was crazy. Maybe she was. Things had changed a lot since her husband died. But, she didn't feel crazy. She just felt empty, with no purpose. So, feeding the sea gull brought a daily responsibility to her life.

Sad to say, she looked forward to seeing the gull each day as if it were her best friend, a buddy she could talk and laugh with, share her secrets with. Not that she had any secrets. Nothing much was happening in her life, or Angela's either. Angela seemed happy enough. Just boring. Unfortunately, she had not yet returned to the university to complete her final year of college. Her father had wanted her to become a doctor like him. She had talked for a while of becoming a social worker and helping

126

troubled children find their way to happiness. Emily often thought how ironic that career choice would be for Angela, a troubled child who never seemed to display much happiness. She was nicer than she used to be, Emily thought, but still very pensive now and then. After asking a few times about what might be on her mind and getting no verbal response, Emily had stopped asking. In fact, it seemed that Angela was happiest when she was writing while Emily napped, or pretended to nap. Some days, she would recline on the porch with her eyes mostly closed and she would watch Angela's mouth move while she wrote, often smiling or even laughing, totally engaged into whatever she was creating. That was when she would come back to life, and Emily's soul would rest easy when she could see that Angela from time to time.

Lately, she had seen that side of Angela more than she had ever seen it since her husband died and Angela had returned from school to take care of her. Angela had just gotten a job working with young women who were being acclimated into the social culture of the town in preparation for going on to the university. They were from a small island right off the coast, one that remained secluded in many respects. The language and customs of the island were highly peculiar. The citizens spoke a hybrid form of French, African dialect, English, and Native American called "geechee". While it was a viable form of communication among the people on the island, it was difficult to comprehend in the college setting.

The young women lived in a local apartment complex, residing four to a room. There were twelve girls that she was training right now. She was excited each morning to go and work with them, like a Pygmalion project. She would come home and talk about the transformations she had witnessed each day, and Emily could visualize each girl and her individual personality. Mostly, she was glad to see Angela emerging from the depression that had bound her for the past few years.

These were the things that she would share with her sea gull whenever they would meet. His name was Roland, though she sometimes affectionately called him "Roly-Poly". She often wondered how she could tell him from any of the other of hundreds of gulls she saw each day. There was a bond that had been formed by relationship. Of course, she recognized his distinct marking – the little patch of black right beside his tail which looked like a black diamond on a playing card. But, he was more than just a sea gull to her. He was a faithful friend, and somehow she knew that she was the same to him.

Tonight, as she walked down the shore, she spotted him at his usual perch. He fluttered his wings just a little to signal to her, and she walked over to him with her small bag of fresh bread crumbs. She sat down on the branch of driftwood that she usually occupied next to him. She laid the crumbs out in a line as always, then talked to him as he ate them, one at a time. She felt comfortable with him in a way that she had never felt with her husband, Dr. Carson. He had always been so controlling, so bossy. She assumed that was his way of taking care of her. But, he had kept her from feeling life, and alive, for so many years.

As a young bride, she had been extremely fearful on her wedding night, nearly to the point of panic. She had not known what to expect. Her mother had talked about marital procedures as something mysterious and scary. She had talked of blood and pain, of men turning into monsters for an hour before they regained their senses, like a Dr. Jekyll and Mr. Hyde. She enjoyed the thought of being the wife of a physician and she knew how important that status was socially. But, she was terrified of what her mother had described as her potential first sexual experience.

Being a physician, he had sensed her nervousness and brought sedatives on the honeymoon to administer in case they were needed. They were, in fact, needed that night and nearly every night since. Emily had grown accustomed to the calm they brought and became addicted within about three months. It wasn't until her husband died that she was aware of all she had missed for twenty-five years.

These were the things that she shared with Roland. Her sadness at not being there for her daughter during her growing-up years was what plagued her the most. She was just beginning to cultivate a friendship with Angela. They had laughed and shared more in the past few months as Angela had been working with her island girls than they ever had. In fact, she looked forward to her daily conversations with her daughter and hoped that she could meet the girls one day soon before they went off to the university.

Roland seemed to understand everything she was telling him. He would nod at the appropriate times, and his head would bounce up and down rapidly when she would laugh. At first, she thought it was her imagination! But, it happened all of the time. It was as if he was human and could understand well, even though he could not talk. She could feel his sincere concern for her and his enjoyment of the time they spent together. Even if she was wrong, she thought, she was glad that at least she could feel for the first time in a long time.

That night, as she made her way back to their cottage, she wondered if Angela had anyone she was close to the way Emily was close to Roland. Who did Angela share her secrets and dreams with? Years ago, she knew that Angela had followed Victor off to the college for young Black students, and she knew that Angela had dreams of marrying Victor back then, even though her husband had promised that would only happen over his dead body. He was almost prophetic. He died; but so did Angela and Victor's relationship, apparently. She noticed that every now and then Angela would reread one of Victor's early cards, one that he had mailed to the old family home. For years, though, she knew that Angela had no new communications from Victor, and Emily imagined that such a handsome young man was now married with a family of his own. Poor Angela. She had lost so much to care for her mother. "What could I do to repay her?" Emily thought.

That thought plagued her throughout the night, but she awoke the next morning with a plan. As she shared her coffee moment with Roland the next morning, she talked with him about what she planned to do. He nodded in enthusiastic approval as he picked up each of the crumbs she had lined out for him. "Yes, then! I will do it! I'm so glad you agree, my Roly-Poly! Do you really think it will work? You do? I do, too! All right, and I will let you know tonight how this first step works. If things go right today, I will have some exciting news for you tonight!"

Angela stepped out the back door. She had heard her mother's voice and thought some visitors had walked up through the gate, coming from the beach. There was no one there. Just her mom sitting at the table and a sea gull perched on the rail. "Mom, are you talking to that gull again? I swear, you need to get out into the real world! Meet some people. Go places and do some things." Angela had said that many times before and expected her words to once again fall on deaf ears.

"Angela, you are right! I think I will get dressed and go into town with you this morning. Would you drop me off at the library while you go to work with your girls? I could stay there for a couple of hours, browsing the shelves and maybe doing a little reading before you're ready to take a break. Then, you could bring me back home, or we could have some lunch downtown. Maybe I could meet the girls you are working with?"

Angela walked over to her mother and looked deep into her eyes, her brow wrinkled into a gigantic question mark. She touched Emily's forehead. "Mom, do you feel all right?" Emily nodded, optimistically, an odd smile on her face. "Did I hear you say that you want to go to town? Mom, you haven't been away from this house since I don't know when!"

Emily got up from her chair and moved purposely toward the door. Roland flew up and perched on the stair rail. "You are so right! That's why it's time for me to get busy and do something I haven't done in a long time. The weather is beautiful!" Emily looked out toward the ocean and took a deep breath. The sky was clear and blue, the waves were frosted white, and life was teeming all around her. "It's time I started living again, enjoying this world God has blessed me to wake up each morning and see. So, I want to go to the library. Will you take me?" Emily smiled and kissed her daughter on the cheek, then breezed past her into the kitchen and headed toward her bedroom."

"Sure…" Angela said as she tried to figure out what was going on with her mother this morning. "I wonder if she's gotten her meds mixed up," she thought; then, she corrected herself, "I wonder if she has even taken her meds this morning!" Oh well, it couldn't hurt her to get out and about for a couple of hours. Not much had changed downtown in the last few years, so she was sure no harm could come to her mother at the library. Angela decided to get dressed, too, and see what would happen with this day.

Emily seemed very bright and alert on the drive into town. They passed many golf courses that used to be farming areas a few years ago, and Emily commented on the changes. She saw a snow cone shed with a colorful tiki roof on the side of the road. "Angela, do you know how long it's been since I've had a snow cone? I think it was probably back when I was a child! Oh, do you think we can stop by there this afternoon on our way home?" Angela was warmed by her mother's animated conversation. This was a side of her personality that Angela had rarely seen and she was enjoying this glimpse of what appeared to be a spirit rising like a phoenix from the ashes of a detached life.

"Sure we can, Mom. I heard it's supposed to be warm today, finally. This might be a nice afternoon for a snow cone. But first, let's plan how we will do this business this morning. I'm going to drop you off at the library." Emily nodded. Angela continued, "You will stay there until I return in two hours, come inside, and pick you up. You will not go out of the library and walk around town by yourself. You will wait for me to personally come and pick you up from the library. Is that correct?" Emily nodded again, an excited smile on her face. This disturbed Angela slightly. "Mom, what in the world are you up to? Something about this sounds fishy to me! I hope you are not planning to do anything crazy!" Angela's voice broke just a little. She was unsure of her mother's motives, and she couldn't figure out why she didn't trust them. But, she could not imagine her mother doing anything risky on purpose.

Sensing her discomfort, Emily reassured her quickly. "Angela, don't worry!" She placed her hand on her daughter's right arm. "I know I seem crazy most of the time, but today I can swear that I am in my right mind!" Emily laughed and Angela joined in, reluctantly. "I am still a young woman, relatively speaking. I have energy and a good strong mind now. The sea air has done me well. Coming off of years of medication has done me well. Spending time with a doting daughter has done me well. I woke up this morning knowing that it is now time for me to take part in creating an environment that will do me well. That road starts at the public library, exposing myself to books and resources that will enrich my life and challenge my mind. I can meet new people and reconnect with old friends. I can talk to someone other than you and a sea gull." She stopped to smile and wink at her daughter. She thought she spotted a tear in Angela's right eye. "I'll be all right," she reassured Angela. "Trust me. Please."

Angela took a deep breath and thanked God for this change in her mother. She had really been worried about her mother's mental state and didn't want to think she might have to consider closer supervision for her. Her mother looked so much healthier physically, and she was relieved to hear how lucid her thoughts were now.

They pulled up to the front doors of the library. Already, school age children were streaming in, some alone and some with their parents. She could see Emily smiling as she looked at them. "All right, Mom! I trust you. I'll be back in two hours. Maybe we can have lunch with the girls today. I'll see what their plans are, and maybe you will have a surprise when I get back." She leaned over to kiss her mother's left cheek. "I love you."

Emily turned to her and smiled as she patted her daughter's face. "I love you too, Precious. See you in two hours."

As soon as she entered the library, she headed straight for the check-out desk. She saw a high school-age girl standing at the counter. Emily smiled as she approached her, and the girl responded with a wide smile. Emily asked her if she knew of anyone who could help her locate someone using the computer.

Victor happened to be in his office when the phone rang. He was scheduled to sit in for another professor who taught a summer course, but his friend's plans had changed at the last minute, so he called to let him know he was off the hook for that assignment. When Victor heard the phone, he wondered if his friend had changed his mind again and now needed his help.

He was shocked to hear a shaky voice on the other end, a woman identifying herself as Emily Carson. He knew it couldn't be a prank, because there would not be a reason for anyone to use her to prank him. But, he noticed his heart beat faster as she was talking to him, explaining what had happened in her life and Angela's over the past few years. He sat at his desk as she talked, feeling as if he had slipped into some alternate universe and was watching his life move slowly before his eyes as she shared her medical issues and the sacrifices her daughter had chosen to make in order to care for her. He fought emotions of rejection as she talked about Angela's current difficulty in moving on with her life. He had the same problems. Who had called Angela to advocate for him? Plus, how could he forgive her for cutting him off as if he were a stranger, someone who meant nothing to her? Why had she coerced her mother into trying to manipulate his emotions once again?

"I was talking to my friend Roland about this last night. Don't laugh," Emily paused and Victor did not respond, "but Roland is a sea gull! He visits me twice a day and we have some very stimulating conversations. Anyway, I realized how much Angela gave up of her own life to take care of me after her father died. I asked Roland how I could repay her, and he affirmed that I should at least try to reach you, try to give her one more chance at a happy life. I'm ready to become independent now. I can let her go. I just wanted to let you know that." Emily's long monologue ended there. Victor felt like he should say something, but could not think of a response.

He cleared his throat. He tried to think of what would be appropriate to say, but everything that was buzzing through his mind sounded like commercial clichés. Something rose up through his gut and met a single word that was standing out in his mind in capital letters: FORGIVENESS!

"Mrs. Carson, I first have to confess that I am totally floored, hearing from you today. I had put Angela out of my mind for so many years due to the way we separated. I felt that she had rejected me for some reason, and that thought has tormented me for a long time. I still don't know the answer to that question, and I guess Angela is the only one who does, unless she shared it with you. I know things changed for your family when your husband died, and I was very sorry to hear about his death, even though I knew he didn't like me and didn't want me and Angela to be together. I have worked very hard to forget these things and now I am having to face reopening this wound to my spirit. I am not sure what you want me to do for or with Angela. I am not even sure of what I want to do." Victor paused at this point, and thought he could hear raspy breathing on the other end of the line.

Emily began to speak, her voice quavering. "I'm sorry, Victor!" He could hear the strong emotion in her words, and imagined that she was crying.

Suddenly, Victor let down his defenses, on the verge of crying himself. "No, Mrs. Carson, I am the one who is sorry. I should have pursued Angela more aggressively. I should not have let her shut me out. I knew where you all lived. I could have shown up and demanded that she be true to the love that we shared with one another for so long. I should have pressed past all of her self-protective barriers and convinced her that we could conquer anything in life together, that we could have both taken care of you, that we could have built a life based on courage and faith. As her man, her protector, her covering, I should have done that; but I didn't. I got my feelings hurt and hid like a wounded dog under the porch, licking my wounds. Well, I am so glad you called today." Victor wiped the tears from his eyes with his fist and picked up a pen. He opened his note pad and prepared to write. "Where do you and Angela live? Give me your address, and I will be there this evening! Don't tell her that I am coming. I want to speak for myself tonight. I want to apologize to her for not being the man she needed me to be."

Sitting in the lobby, waiting for Angela to come back and pick her up, Emily could hardly contain her excitement. She was hoping that Angela had convinced the girls to join them for lunch. She needed some distraction to keep her from letting the cat out of the bag and even making Angela suspect that she was hiding something from her. But, Emily really couldn't wait to get home and have a conversation with Roland tonight after Victor had made it to their cottage and he and Angela were reunited. Emily had no doubt that was exactly what would happen! The chance that she could have located Victor so easily would have been a slim one. In fact, the way things worked out was one of the greatest miracles she had ever experienced! The young lady at the check-out desk was a student at the university, home for the summer. She had just completed a course taught by Dr. Victor Whitman. He was, in fact, her favorite professor! Of course she knew how to reach him! She quickly found the department's phone number by pulling up the university website on the Internet, then dialed the number and asked the secretary to ring the professor's office. And now, the rest was history!

Emily amused herself thinking about the kind of exciting life she could lead as a detective story writer like that lady on the television show named Angela, the same name as her own daughter! What stories she could share with Roland each day! Maybe he could be her sidekick and help her solve the mysteries, like Lassie used to do with Timmy! In fact, that relationship proved that humans and animals could share a special bond that allowed them to communicate in a genuine way. Supportive care, reciprocal communication, problem-solving, all things were possible when you had good friends!

Angela walked into the lobby, shifting her out of her pleasant reverie. Emily stood and walked over to greet her daughter with a big hug. "Love," she thought, "is a wonderful thing!"

When Peace Like a River Attendeth My Way

"Pleasant words are as an honeycomb, sweet to the soul and health to the bones." Proverbs 16:24

*

"Sundown", a word that held special significance for Robert and Rita. These were the sundown years of their lives. They knew that after sixty years of marriage, the road ahead of them was shorter than the one behind. Plus, they had enjoyed their evening walks on the beach for many years. They would wait until about fifteen minutes before sunset and then set off down the beachfront, heading west. As they walked, the sun seemed to be walking with them. They would review the events of the day and plan out their tomorrows. They were still hoping for a number of tomorrows to share many more sunsets.

Both had been blessed with good health and youthfulness, in spite of their advanced years. They had successfully raised three children, two sons and one daughter. By now, they had a number of grandchildren and a few great-grandchildren. Family reunions were a joy. They had many opportunities to share their life experiences with those who were coming along behind them. Rita was still the favorite cook at these gatherings and she was praised for the dishes only she could make – the chowders, the hot rolls, the pound cakes and cobblers! She welcomed anyone who wanted to learn her secrets into the kitchen, but hers was a pampered crew! They assumed she would always be around to cook and bake. She hoped they were right.

Robert was highly respected in the church where they were married and had raised their children. As the head deacon, he had been appointed to that honorable position in his early thirties. That was a little more than fifty years ago. He was still very active in the business of the church and had not missed a Sunday service in more than forty years. Vacations were few and far between. Why go anywhere when you already lived right on a beach? He hardly missed a mid-week service in that same period of time, too.

But, the real passion in his life was his precious rose, his Miss Rita. They met when her parents moved to town after her father had been released from his two-year military stint. She was just three years old, but that didn't keep the two of them from clicking immediately. Her parents had been visiting the few "colored" churches in town. One particular

Sunday, they selected Metropolitan. As soon as they entered the door of the old sanctuary, Robert's mother rushed over to greet the new mother and her child who appeared to be the age of her small son, Robert. These two women became instant friends. The same could not be said for the toddlers. Rita had spotted the stuffed brown sock monkey with bright red lips that Robert was clutching in his left hand. His right thumb was stuck dead in the middle of his mouth. Rita walked right up to him, pulled his thumb out of his mouth with her left hand, and snatched the toy out of his hand with her right. Robert began to wail and sat down at his mother's feet with a temperamental thud! Rita sat down beside him and hugged him, but kept a firm grip on the monkey. Later, when they talked about this incident that their mothers resurrected almost every time the families got together down through the years, they continued to wonder how the monkey ended up in Rita's belongings when they got married and then moved into their first small apartment with them. Did she ever give it back? Neither could recall that she had.

They were the counselors to every young couple in the church and had been as long as they could remember. Their marriage was the model. Their love and respect toward each other was evident. Their parenting practices had stood the test of time. All three of their children had done very well, and each came back to town on a regular basis to check on their parents. Any reason was a good one for a family gathering. The church family valued their wise advice; and if either of them made a suggestion, it was a done deal.

It had been obvious a few times that they had disagreed on a matter. However, their "arguments" were more like comedy routines. There was so much love and laughter interspersed within their debate that onlookers would often wonder if this interchange was staged in order to entertain the viewer and demonstrate how a couple could disagree without fighting. What a great lesson for many young couples to learn! Then, they would always kiss each other at the end of the discussion, healing and loving as they moved forward to the next conversation.

It shouldn't have been so easy to look like teenage lovers at eighty-plus years of age. The latest fashions looked appropriate on both of them. They seemed to have expanded with the times and remained contemporary in spite of their advanced ages. They even had a little sports car that Robert purchased brand new off of the showroom floor five years ago. They could be seen cruising down the main strip on summer evenings, drop-top down, waving to their many friends and neighbors. But somehow, they managed to make it home before sundown so that they could still take their customary stroll down the beach, saying goodbye to another day.

Their children had been working on a plan for three years and had enlisted almost the entire town to help carry it out. They wanted to celebrate their parents' sixtieth anniversary in a big way. There had been a recommitment to their vows on their silver anniversary. You would have thought that a royal couple was getting married with all of the fanfare that accompanied that event. Tickets were given for a grand cruise throughout the Caribbean, but those tickets were still in Robert's safe. He couldn't figure out how to fit a fourteen-day cruise into six days so that he wouldn't have to miss a Sunday morning at Metropolitan.

This kind of old-school commitment was exactly what endeared the entire community to Robert and Rita. That is why anyone who was asked to do anything for them was ready and willing to give their all. But, keeping it a surprise was going to be the hard part.

Their daughter, Delores, was a highly-respected event planner in Los Angeles. She was the preferred choice of many well-known performers and artists. She had gone to college with the intention of owning her own business, so she earned her masters in business administration. However, she could not decide just what type of business to own. She knew that many great cooks had come from her family, so opening a restaurant would be a breeze. Still, there was more that she wanted to include in her venture. So, she decided to network with businesses that provided the wide array of services that individuals would need if they had to plan a banquet, a wedding, a reception, a concert, an open house, or any type of event anyone could imagine. If they could communicate their need, she would find the means to meet it.

She had built her business reputation on her ability to follow through with exceptional quality, finesse, and timeliness. People don't care what you say you can do if you don't do it to the best of your ability. That was a lesson her parents not only taught her, but more importantly showed her all throughout her life. So, as soon as her name and reputation hit the streets of L.A., she was in! And, her business holdings and reputation had increased exponentially down through the decades. When you contracted with "Dee-Light-Full Dee", you knew your event would be a featured occasion in the media and tabloids the following morning.

Dee had been coming to town more often than ever before to solidify the arrangements for her parents' special day. All they knew was that the children and their multiple levels of grandchildren would be in town to attend Metropolitan with their parents on their anniversary weekend. There would be a great family reunion at the dock house on the oceanfront. The meal would be catered so no one could request their favorites from Rita. Every weekend that Dee flew in, Robert and Rita assumed she was coming to firm up those arrangements in person.

However, she had other plans. The Sunday service and family celebration were just the tip of the iceberg. She had requested that the mayor and city council rename a city street for her father, and they had agreed. The governor was going to be in town to be the grand marshal at the parade that would take place in their honor on the Saturday preceding the Sunday service. A former local band was going to reunite for the gigantic block party that was staged for Saturday night, taking over the entire downtown. They would be the opening act for a major blow-out band that owed her a favor. She was confident that people from all over the state would be there, and those who couldn't come would wish they would have been there.

Her brothers, one a very successful doctor in Atlanta and the other a well-known corporate attorney in Boston, had also been doing their part for this memorable anniversary to celebrate two of the greatest people anyone in this part of the world had ever known. They knew how much their parents valued education: their own, that of their children and grandchildren, as well as for all of the children in the community, especially those in the church. For years, their mother had been volunteering at local nursery school programs, reading to the young preschoolers. She was a firm believer in reading to a child every day. She knew that she had done this with her children, and each of them had been an early reader. These pre-school skills had helped them to advance quickly once they entered public school.

So, her sons were contacting all of their wealthy and influential friends, asking each to make a sizeable donation to the Rita Fay Walker Early Education Experience. They knew it would take at least three million dollars to build a facility that would meet all of the needs of all of the preschool children in the community, so they asked each of their friends to ask five of their friends for a donation, as well. Already, they had pledges for two-thirds of the money needed to build and equip the school, and they were confident that the rest would come through within a couple of months. If not, the balance would come out of their own pockets. This was the least they could do for this woman who had made them the men they had become.

While their Dee was working in the forefront, and sons Rob and Nick were doing their part in the background, Robert and Rita were trying their best to act like they had no idea what was going on. After Dee's second turnaround trip to town, her parents began to suspect that the kids were planning some grand surprise for their anniversary. Pretty soon, all of the phone calls and swiftly-aborted conversations clued them in to something in the works. Many evenings as they walked down the seashore, they would laugh aloud at their children, wondering how witless they assumed their parents could be! Robert and Rita didn't know all of the details, but they did know that Friday, Saturday, and Sunday were going to be full of dignitaries and celebrities.

Thank goodness they did have some inkling. Their children would have given them heart attacks with this level of surprises! Their evening walks were punctuated with lots of laughter over how they would have to be resuscitated in the town square when the fireworks went off simultaneously and lit up the sky like a forest fire, or at the church when some famous televangelist showed up to preach the morning message. What would Pastor do when Rita keeled over? How would the fire chief respond when Robert collapsed, grabbing his chest, as the mayor dropped from the sky in an air balloon? Would he remember his CPR training? Many a good, belly-shaking laugh shared between the two of them led up to their sixtieth anniversary memorable celebration.

Early in their marriage, in fact not long after Rob, Jr. had been born, they had made a promise to one another. Robert had a job that demanded great focus and a lot of responsibility at the local airplane assembly plant. Back in those days, Black men were not selected for this level of job, both because of the pay and the responsibility. However, from the day he was hired, Robert stood out from his contemporaries, and not because he was trying to show off. That was just one of the basic traits of his character. He would be outstanding, no matter what the setting. At this same time, as a new mother, Rita put her everything into the care and nurturing of their newborn son. So, they decided that they would give all of their energy and attention to their daytime duties during the day, and then dedicate all of their energy and attention to each other by the time the sun went down. It hadn't worked every day, but maintaining that focus had helped them to do that almost every day. In their sundown years, they had added in the concept of including that daily evening walk into their commitment to their respect of the day and each other. Watchfulness to daylight transitions and faithful commitment to romantic traditions made each day special and kept their relationship sacred in each other's eyes.

When Rita came home from a day of volunteering at the YWCA day care and seemed just a bit distracted, Robert sensed that she was carrying a burden that had nothing to do with the two of them. He fixed her a tall glass of iced tea and sliced a fresh lemon, placing a couple of wedges in her glass. He carried it into the bedroom where she was sitting on the bed, her hand holding the heel of her right shoe. She looked up and smiled. "Hi, Sir!" She greeted him with a smile.

"Miss Rita, what is on your pretty little mind?" Robert asked, smiling back. She just looked for a moment out of the window, studying the sky as if searching it for an answer.

Robert waited, glass in hand, until she dropped the shoe and sat back, resting her shoulders on the headboard. She then accepted the glass and placed it on the nightstand. "Honey, I met a little child today who just stole my heart! He is the cutest little person in the world! His smile melted me." She turned to her husband; he could see the agony in her eyes. "He's a little foster child. No parents. His mama gave him up. Left him in a trash can in a bathroom three years ago. I couldn't believe it when I heard that story." Robert could see tears forming in her eyes. He knew how much she loved children. However, with so many grandchildren and great-grandchildren, he wasn't sure why one new little child would affect her so deeply. She continued, "It's not like he is so different from any other child," as if she was reading his mind, "but he came to me today and climbed up into my lap with a book. He has these big brown eyes that have that old person 'knowing' look to them! He just looked at me, he didn't say anything, just looked. Robert, he just looked at me like he was saying, 'Help!'"

Rita started to cry. Robert sat beside her and hugged her close. "It's all right, Miss Rita! You'll go back and read to him again. Why, you could do it tomorrow if you wanted to. What's the matter?"

"I'm just wondering if I'm going to have time to do everything I know I need to do for every child who needs it! Robert, I am eighty-three years old! Who knows when I'll have to stop due to health reasons or taking care of you or something else beyond my control! Him and the other babies like him are going to need me for at least another three years!" She sat up straight and grabbed her husband's arms. "I need to know that I'll be there for him. I won't abandon him like his mama did. I will be there to read to him every day until he learns how to read. I just need to know that is how it will be, Robert! I'm scared, Honey! I'm so scared that my sun will go down before my work is done!"

"Miss Rita, we have shared a wonderful life together. We have raised a beautiful family and enjoyed a peaceful walk along the sea of life. We may have stumbled over a few shells along our way. Hot sand may have burned our feet many a day. But, we've kept on walking. And from what I hear tell, a whole lot of people have been following in our footsteps in that sand. Our children, our church family, people in this town, they are all marking our steps. Don't you know that somebody is watching what you have been doing for years, going to these places and reading to the babies?" Rita nodded, listening intently. "Then, you have to know that somebody is following in your footsteps. This won't end when the Lord takes you up and your footsteps end. Girl, when the footsteps are gone, the footprints will still be there. That baby will have you to read to him as long as you are here to carry out that duty. When you are gone, there will be somebody else in place to read to him and every other baby and it will go on and on."

Rita realized that she had been modeling this very plan all of her adult life. Robert had just given words to what her spirit already knew. God had allowed her to watch her own mother and grandmother do what she learned to do. She had walked it out so that her children and their children would see how to give your all to the world that God placed you in.

Whatever your hands found to do, you were to do it with your whole heart and all of your might! That is what Rita and Robert had seen their parents do, and that is what their children had seen them do. The responsibility of walking out a life of giving and caring was what they modeled every day. Looking back, Rita could see so many following her, walking in her steps, doing what she had taught them to do.

"You are so right, Robert. One monkey doesn't stop the show. Just like that little monkey I took from you eighty years ago." They both started to laugh. "See, I saw you looking like a little baby when I walked into that church. I knew you weren't going to survive if I left you standing there, sucking your thumb and playing with toys. So, I took both of them away from you, according to your mama and my mama. But, I gave myself to you. That one monkey I took was replaced by me." She and Robert finished their hearty laugh. "But," she continued, pointing to herself, "this monkey will be snatched away one day. And when she is, the show will still go on."

Robert grew very serious for a moment, then grabbed her hand and pulled her to her feet. "Put your shoes back on, Miss Rita. It's time to go for our walk. And my prayer is," he said as they headed for the back door, "that when that day comes, we will both walk hand in hand toward our sunset and let the Father take us away and set us up on a high place where we can just sit back and watch that show." He smiled at her, giving her a big hug and kiss as they turned to walk with the setting sun. "Oh, yes!" he said, swinging her hand like a teenager, "that sure ought to be a great show!"

Laughing with every step, they blended completely into their sunset.

Billows May Roll, Breakers May Dash

"A foolish son is a grief to his father, and bitterness to her that bare him." Proverbs 17:25

*

Swoosh…hummm….swoosh….hummm…swoosh…

Fred's internal motor was engaged in automatic, his mind locked in some grainy area fixtured between his feelings and his imagination. He counted to one thousand, then turned. By the time he reached one thousand again, his body relaxed for the smooth ride back to shore. He had been doing this training routine for so long that it was just a standard part of his daily schedule. Wake up. Empty his bladder. Put on his trunks, shirt, and shoes. Get into his Jeep. Drive to the boat dock. Put his shoes and shirt in the driver's seat. Walk to the shore and plunge into the first whitehead that crests to greet him. Swim out one thousand strokes, swim back one thousand strokes. Seven days a week for twelve years. He had never missed a day.

Fred was proud of his persistence and strength. Often on the drive home he would recall the day when the entire town had been evacuated due to a hurricane warning. He had stayed behind. He had swam that morning in hurricane waters. It was a battle of will, him against nature. He won, but he paid a high price. Weeks of tortuous nightmares almost made him regret entering the water that morning. If he could imagine the worst part of hell, that would seem like a summer vacation in comparison to what he experienced. Somehow, he had locked his brain into its automatic, conditioned state and pushed his mind and his muscles past hundred-pound waves to complete his regimen. The experience was one that he had not talked about since, but he had thought about it a lot. Almost daily.

Fred was confident that he would do the same thing again if faced with the decision. Nothing in life would beat him. He would dig deep within himself to find the stamina he needed to defeat any enemy, human or natural. Never again would he be called "weak". He was a different person today than the boy he had been at sixteen. He had a strong mind, but his body had not always stood in balance to his brain. In fact, during junior high school, he was a poster boy for the caricature of the ninety-pound weakling. Still, he loved school because he excelled in the academic aspects. Always at the top of his class, athletes would befriend him because he was a great "study buddy". In exchange for their fraternity, he would show them how to get the answers and then share his answer while they nodded and gave a knowing, "Aw yeah, I understand!" Soon, he knew they really didn't; they just wanted to be able to copy his answer.

The truth came out when he could not avoid physical education any more. It was in high school, the second semester of his junior year. He had to take the class in order to graduate. With his wide friend base, he felt safe now from the teasings that had humiliated him in junior high school. Those terrible words that drove him to want to kill made him fearful even today of ever thinking about a relationship or marriage. Yet, they also drove him to create a new exterior that would likely intimidate anyone who would even think about taunting him.

Back then, though, his physique was deformed; and that was pointed out to him again on the first day of class, as soon as he had taken off his shirt to change into his exercise uniform. It was almost as if the boys had staged it. There were at least fifteen of them who formed a semi-circle that appeared in front of his eyes as his shirt was being raised like a curtain to reveal the scene on the stage. Pointing, hooting, laughing, rolling on the concrete floor, hand-slapping, teasing words, cruel words, the barrage of attack was intensive, almost as bad as the waves that tormented his muscles during the hurricane swim. He thought he was about to lose his mind. There were times when, looking back on that day, he believed he really had lost his mind.

That night, he had to make a decision. He could stay home the next day and cry some more into his pillow, beating it with his fists and pleading with God to let him wake up in a different body tomorrow. Or, he could do something about it. He had tried to explain it to his parents, why he didn't want to go to that school any more. They were so busy with their small motel that all they could do was hum and nod, acting as if they were listening when he knew all the time that they were just passively responding because their minds were on other things that would keep a roof over their heads, food on the table, and the motel from going belly-up.

His dad was the owner, manager, grounds man, handyman, and concierge. Mom was the desk clerk, room maid, cook, and launderer. He was expected to go to school, come home and do his homework, wash the dishes, and take out the trash at the end of each day. That way, there were no additional employees to hire who would cut into the profits that the family so direly needed in order to keep the old motel going. It was a preferred spot for a number of seasonal patrons who had been visiting them for years, so they were able to survive financially as a family. But, it took everyone pitching in and doing their part.

At sunrise the next morning, Fred got up and headed straight for the lawnmower shed. He found a couple of mower rims that weighed about fifteen pounds each. His dad had a couple of metal rods that fit fairly well into the holes in the middle of them. With some slight rigging, he constructed a set of barbells within about an hour. He lifted for about three minutes before he had to put them down. But he was proud of himself. He had resolved his problem on his own and had a plan to continue to lift until he saw some results. He felt like this might be God's way of answering his prayer. He would have a different body as of today, even if his external physical characteristics did not yet match how he saw himself in his mind.

Faithful to his routine, he began to see some results within a couple of months. He had continued to go to the locker room to change for class. He wasn't going to let them think they had beaten him. Their teasing waned after about a week. In late spring, though, he noticed some of the guys staring at him again. "Oh no," he thought, "here we go again!" This time, though, something was different. Some looked surprised and some looked angry. Fred couldn't figure out what was going on.

"Hey, Fred, what'd you do? Buy yourself some muscles?" Terry, the class clown, came up to him and grabbed his biceps, pressing down hard. "Wow, man, that's a brick! You been in the gym?" Fred thought he could detect a faint level of sincere admiration in Terry's voice. Fred was surprised, but he was also proud that his hard work was noticeable.

That scene ended all incidents of teasing. From then on, the guys were trying to compete with him, trying to show off their biceps and abs. That motivated Fred to work out harder, evening and morning, to stay a step ahead of his new competition. It paid off in great dividends for him. Girls began to notice him, smile at him, pass him notes. A few even asked him out. But, inside he still felt like that ninety-pound weakling who knew that ridicule by a girl would be the kryptonite that would destroy him completely. So, he was polite and extremely personable, but he always ended up saying, "No." His fallback excuse was that he had to work at the motel. That was true, but not every night. After a while, they just stopped approaching him, realizing that he had other priorities and the dates they hoped for would never happen.

His motivation now was not to impress anyone, male or female. He wanted to keep the vow he made to himself long ago and hold himself to the high physical standard that he had set on the morning that changed his life. He would never again be called, or seen as, *weak*.

Fred parked his Jeep in front of the small motel room that had become his apartment. He was glad that his parents understood his need for privacy. After all, he was almost thirty years old. He was also glad that they just let him live rent-free on the family property. Most parents would want their grown son to be out of the house and working on building a career for which they had gone to college. But, in spite of his high intelligence and ability to perform well in school, Fred was so consumed with his daily routine that he opted to just stay and work odd jobs at the motel and live with his parents. He did work as a lifeguard during the swimming season, and his stunning body kept his end of the beach busy. He had ended up making a record number of rescues so far in the years he had worked as a lifeguard, and he was not sure how many were feigned and how many were real emergencies.

After taking his shower and dressing for the day, Fred went to the motel lobby to check on his mother. She hadn't been feeling well since mid-winter. A bad bout of influenza had kept her down for about two weeks. The doctor had told her that she was fine at her last checkup, but she still seemed to lack much of her usual energy. "Hey, Mom! How are you feeling this morning?" She walked over to Fred and kissed him on the cheek. That surprised him just a little.

"Good morning, Freddy. I think I'm feeling a little better today." She laughed a little at the puzzled look on his face, then stepped back. "What? The kiss? Son, these last few weeks, I have been thinking more and more about how little I showed you how much I love you during your growing up years." She sat down in the high chair behind the desk. Fred leaned on the counter. She continued, "Me and your dad were working so hard when you were little, trying to take this gift of an opportunity and turn it into a goldmine! We dreamed of saving our money, tearing this down," she said, waving her hand around the room, "and building a beautiful resort that would soon attract the rich and famous!" She laughed loudly.

"Well, Mom, you never know. That could still happen!" Fred smiled at her, optimistically. She patted him on the hand.

"Son, both you and I know that your dad and I will likely spell out our golden years right here, doing the same things that we have done since you were a little baby. And if we do, that's okay. But, I want more for you."

Fred squirmed just a bit. He didn't want to think about doing anything more than what he was able to emotionally manage right now. He didn't want to have to begin defending himself to his mother. He wasn't yet strong enough for that conversation.

"Anyway," she continued, "I've been thinking about how much attention and love I owe you. You have been so good about checking on me and taking care of me this winter!" She looked deep into his beautiful blue eyes. "Will you let me start catching up on my payments now, Son?"

Fred leaned over and kissed her in the middle of her forehead. He felt a gush of relief. "Mom, you don't owe me anything, but I'll take a kiss on credit any time! Now," he continued, standing up straight, "what's for breakfast?"

He wasn't scheduled to lifeguard today, but he still wanted to get back to the beach. The feeling of panic he had experienced when he thought his mother was about to push him to do something he didn't feel able to do had left him with a nervous energy he hadn't felt in a long time. He was usually the one who was prepared for whatever came from any direction. He had never anticipated a charge from his mother, though his father had broached the topic now and then when he turned twenty-one. Fred looked back on his conversational evasions with pride. It felt like he was sparring with his dad using his verbal reasoning, and he was so believable that his father had conceded to Fred's spoken plans like a bull when he is deflected by the red cape, not knowing that the toreador's sword may not be far behind.

He first thought he might just walk back to the beach so that he could expend some of that nervous energy, but at the last minute he decided to drive. Jumping back into the Jeep and entering the sunshine the shade had masked, he was glad he had not chosen to make that trek by foot. He would have been sweltering by the time he reached the shore.

He parked in a shady spot and stepped out onto the warm sand. He had not planned to swim, just to walk, so he headed toward the east. Most of his time was spent in his favorite swimming spot unless he was on guard duty. It was refreshing to see some new scenery. His eyes looked as far down the beach as he could. Very few sunbathers or swimmers were out on this end today. He relished the sound of the waves crashing on the shore, their foamy gray crests high and looking like fingers grasping for a hold on the air and then on the wet sand. Losing their grip, they slid back out in the ocean to regroup themselves for another try. Over and over this bid for gain played out. "Keep on trying," he spoke to them as he passed, "and one day you will succeed!"

He paused to quiz himself, "What are you talking about? Why would watery fingers need to be successful at pulling something out to sea?" He thought that might depend on what they were reaching for, whether or not it was to destroy that thing or to take away from it something it didn't need to hold on to anymore. He thought about why he had endured his tormented swims until they became therapeutic. What had the water been carrying him out to? What had it been taking away from him that he didn't need to hold on to? Just as he thought he was about to get the clarity of his experiences in the water, he spotted something that appeared to be out of the usual.

His practiced skills as a life guard automatically clicked into play. He scanned the shore to see if anything appeared awry. His pace quickened, and then he began to run. There was a dark pile up on the shore, toward the grass. It looked like clothing or maybe a blanket. It formed a small hump. He shifted his head directly to the right and spotted something floating on the water. It could have been debris, but really didn't look quite right. Immediately, he ran up the shore toward the water and dove right in.

Dragging the body from the water, he noticed that she was slightly warm, but still clammy. He laid her on the sand and immediately began to press hard on her abdomen. Sea water and mucous began to trickle out of the side of her mouth. He kept pressing, pausing after three strong pushes, over and over until, like a geyser, a flood of sea water gushed straight up from her open mouth. She began to cough spasmodically, and he turned her quickly to her left side. Water continued to spew out with each cough. He knelt beside her and watched her closely, talking to her and telling her that she needed to get it out and everything was going to be all right.

When it appeared that she was breathing regularly in between the periodic shakes and spasms, he ran up to the shore and picked up the army blanket that was laid on top of some other items – a book, a metal cup, and a comb. He ran back down the beach and wrapped her up quickly, then picked her up and carried her to the Jeep. She was still coughing and sputtering, at times gagging and choking on her spit. As he drove, he kept talking to her, telling her to hang in, they were on their way to the hospital, she was going to be all right.

He made it to the hospital in record time. He had hoped the police would try to stop him so that he could ask them to radio an ambulance to meet them. He was afraid she had swallowed too much water and would die. But, with no additional aid, he got her into the emergency room and stepped to the side, believing that he had reached her in time and she really was going to be all right.

The policeman at the hospital took down Fred's account of what happened. Fred didn't know her and he wasn't sure if he had ever seen her before on the beach. In fact, she looked like many of the young ladies who often paraded past his watch station; blonde, blue-eyed, slender. But, she was one whose call to him was authentic. She was a true emergency. Had he not showed up when he did, she would have been dead, carried out to sea by those grasping fingers that were either taking her away because she needed to go, or trying to cleanse something that needed to live.

Fred stayed in the waiting room until the nurse came out to let him know that they had stabilized her and she would likely be all right. It might be touch and go for another few hours, but they would monitor her vital signs and keep a good eye on her. Fred thanked her for the update and left. Sitting in the Jeep, he decided that he would go home and get cleaned up and then come back and check on her later.

Fred continued to check on her, morning, noon, and evening for the next two days. She seemed to still be in a daze the first morning. He introduced himself and told her that he was the one who pulled her from the water. She had looked at him with a detached gaze and then closed her eyes. He told her that he knew she needed her rest, so he would come back later. She didn't respond. The same was true when he came a couple of hours later and then in the evening. It was as if she knew someone was in the room with her but did not have the will to acknowledge their presence. That second day was identical to the first. When Fred drove home on the evening of the second day, he told himself that he would not return to the hospital. She was getting her color back and he was confident that she would survive. There was no need to keep trying to talk to a girl who obviously wanted to be left alone.

It was almost eleven o'clock. Fred had just drifted to sleep when the phone in his room rang. His mother was on the other end. "Freddy, the hospital is on the line. They need to speak to you right away."

"Oh no," he thought as his mom connected the call. "Maybe she took a turn for the worse!" He was beginning to feel panicky. "Hello?"

"Hi, this is Robin, station nurse at Memorial Hospital. Is this Mr. Fred Clark?"

"Yes, it is. Is everything all right with the patient I brought in two days ago?"

"That is why I am calling, Mr. Clark. I have someone here who would like to speak with you. Please hold on for a moment."

Fred could feel his palms become extremely sweaty as he waited for the voice of a doctor on the other end of the phone. He sat down in the desk chair, anticipating what he knew would be bad news.

"Hello?" The weak, soft, feminine voice disarmed him. "Hello? Is this a Mr. Clark?"

"Yes, it is," he replied. "This is Fred. Fred Clark."

"Mr. Clark? My name is Lindsay. I'm the girl you saved two days ago. I'm sorry to call you so late." There was a soft sob.

"That's no problem! I'm just glad to hear your voice and glad to know that you're okay!"

"Thank you, Mr. Clark. I wouldn't be if it wasn't for you." Lindsay began to cry, and Fred could hear her trying to catch her breath between sobs.

"Hey, it's going to be all right! I'm just glad I was there to be able to see you and get you out of the water in time. Everything happens for a reason. I know that. Look, why don't you get a good night's sleep and I'll come have breakfast with you in the morning. How does that sound?" He paused, hoping he hadn't said too much or gone too far.

Things were quiet on her end for a few seconds, then he heard a very soft, "Okay. I'll see you tomorrow." He heard the click of the phone. Fred held his phone to his ear for a few seconds longer, still trying to process what just occurred. He heard another click. "Mom," he thought, "listening on the motel main line! Oh well," he finished, "she might as well know the whole story. That will save me having to explain my plan tomorrow."

Poached eggs and dry toast never tasted so good. That was all the doctor was giving Lindsay until her digestive system settled back to normal, and Fred didn't want to eat his usual protein-hearty breakfast in front of her. So, he drank weak tea along with her and enjoyed seeing this frail young woman begin to take on some life. She shared that she had been living in town for a while with some friends but had no real relatives around this area. She had run into some problems and decided to go for a swim to clear her mind. She got to the part about her journal, then looked around in panic.

"Did you happen to bring any things with you, things that were on the beach?" She looked frantically around the room, as if she had just remembered that detail.

"What kinds of things?" Fred questioned. All he could remember was grabbing a blanket that he saw lying on the shore.

Lindsay sat straight up in the bed and spoke quickly, "I had my diary. It's a journal that looks like it could be a book! I had a cup and my comb. Oh no!" she exclaimed, "Please don't tell me that they are still out there!" Suddenly, she slumped back into the bed. She began to tear up. "Oh well, I guess if I would have drowned, someone else would have found them anyway. Too bad."

"Lindsay," Fred said, standing up, "I do remember seeing those things under the blanket on the shore, up by the grass line. Look," he said, walking toward the door, "I'll go out there right now and see if they are still there. I'll bet they are. That's a pretty quiet stretch of beach. Most likely, nobody's been down there since we were there. I'll be right back with the goods!" He smiled and waved, looking at her sad face trying to muster up a weak smile in response. "I will be right back. I promise." Then, he whispered, "See if you can wrangle a hamburger out of them for me for lunch!" He winked at her and she smiled and winked back. "Yes!" he thought, and headed for the Jeep.

He didn't get his hamburger for lunch, but the vegetable broth was tasty enough. She had been so happy to see him walk back in with her things! Her face lit up and her cheeks flushed. Finally, a little color to her face! He could tell how beautiful she was, but she had seen a lot of neglect. Her hair was dry and uneven, full of split ends. That told him a lot about her diet. Her skin was sallow with a pale yellow tint. He could tell that she had not taken very good care of herself for a long time. Was it because she didn't want to, or because she couldn't? He didn't know yet, and he didn't want to ask too many questions. But, he had a plan.

Over lunch, she shared that she was a writer and had come out to the coast a couple of years ago to get the inspiration she felt she needed to start a novel that had been a seed in her imagination for many years. She had made a few friends. A couple of them were pretty nice, but one tried to use her to negotiate some shady business. She had gotten in deeper than she felt comfortable and had been looking for a way out, but didn't have much money and really didn't have any family to go back to. So, she had just been trying to make it as best she could.

She loved to walk on the beach, sleep on the beach, and write on the beach. She had been out there for a few weeks, sleeping on the blanket and working on her novel. She would catch fresh seafood in a little net and cook it on the beach. She didn't need a lot of food to survive. She would get fresh water in her cup and kept a comb on hand to make sure she didn't scare any little kids that might wander down her way. But, she hadn't seen anyone in weeks, and that had done her good.

On the morning she nearly drowned, she had finished a major section of her book, which left her feeling exhilarated and happier than she had been in a long time. She felt like she needed a long, relaxing swim to close out this chapter in her life and get her mind cleared to start the next segment of her writing. She had just walked straight out into the water, clothes on, for a baptism of sorts representing the close of the old and the promise of the new. The water was so warm and welcoming, deceptively gentle, and before she knew it, she had been drawn out into waters so deep and choppy that she could not make her way back.

She had swam with all her strength to get back to shore, but she was small and weak and couldn't fight the strong fingers that seemed to be pulling her farther and farther out. Panic set in and soon she was fighting a losing battle. She lost consciousness and didn't wake up until she was in the hospital. She vaguely remembered someone carrying her out of the water. In her delusion, she told Fred, she thought it was Jesus. She could hardly see Him, but she felt Him. He was warm, strong, speaking to her firmly. He cradled her and she felt safe. She said she remembered thinking, "If this is what death is like, I can't imagine why I was fighting it. This is so peaceful!"

The hospital social worker had spoken with her on the evening of her second day. She had told her about the young man who had been coming every day to check on her. Lindsay wasn't sure about much that happened after she went into the water. She felt like an amnesiac. That is why she didn't recognize him and wasn't willing to say too much to him. She had been trying to avoid her friend, Byron, and his friends for about two months. She looked Fred dead in the eye. "Drying out," she said. She continued to say that she thought he might be one of that crowd who she just didn't recognize yet.

It wasn't until the nurse told her that Fred was one of the lifeguards that she knew she had to call and thank him for saving her life. "I don't want you to think I'm one who adheres to Asian customs. Just because you risked your life to save mine, you are not to feel responsible for me for the rest of my life." Lindsay laughed. "I kept hearing your voice saying I would be all right. And now, I believe that. I'm going to find a place to park myself so that I can get healthy, finish my book, and prepare for this new phase of my life."

Lindsay didn't know it, but Fred was thanking God deep inside. Purpose was a powerful driving force in this natural world. Had he not followed God's leading to go back to the beach, he would not be sitting here today with Lindsay. She would have been in the coroner's office, likely an unclaimed corpse. And, he would have been a breathing version of the same in his apartment at the motel. God is good.

"Lindsay, I can't do much more for you right now than be a friend," he said as he placed his empty soup container on her tray table, "but please let me be that. My parents own a motel on the beach. We're never full. There is a nice room on the southwest end. It's a kitchenette. It would also be a great place to write a book. There's a little wooded area right beside it, great for picnics and naps. When you get released from the hospital, why don't you plan to park your blanket, cup, and comb there and finish your book? No strings attached. Plus, I know it would do my mother a lot of good to have someone to take care of again. She's a great lady who would really enjoy your company. What do you say?"

Sweaty palms turned to shallow breathing. "Please, Lord, no rejection!" Fred began to feel slight panic again. He prepared himself for the worst. But, what he wasn't prepared for was the flood of tears that came from Lindsay's eyes, preceding her tight grip on his shoulders as she hugged him in desperation.

"Are you really Jesus? You have to be Jesus! You have saved me again, and I am so grateful!"

Master, the Tempest is Raging!

"The name of the Lord is a strong tower: the righteous run into it, and is safe." Proverbs 18:10

*

Artrella was the last of Mama Gee's relatives to yet live in the low country. She still had not heard the story that made a definitive connection between this hundred-year-young woman and her own family blood line, but it did not matter. Artrella loved Mama Gee as if she had been her own birth mother, and no genetic definitions would change that. Everybody on the island called her "Mama Gee", but Artrella had the distinct privilege of being her sole caregiver. Mama Gee had lived with Artrella's mother and also her grandmother before they each died, and for decades she had been in the center of all of the family doings. As long as Artrella could remember, Mama Gee had been. To have inherited this position of honor on the island, that of providing shelter for the stately matriarch whose life experiences had spanned a century, was a great responsibility that carried with it much community respect. It was like having the Ark of the Covenant residing under your roof. Blessings came in abundance, favor was overflowing, and Mama Gee's wisdom was unparalled.

Jet black skin as smooth as a cocoa bean, Mama Gee still had a sharp twinkle in her eye and a tight jaw line that belied her ancient state. Her arm muscles were still taut, likely due to exceptional conditioning during her many decades of hard work. Her yet-thick tufts of stark white hair were usually tied up in kaleidoscope-colored bandanas, somehow always matching her fashionable red, green, yellow, blue, orange-splashed, indigo-dyed Gullah dresses. Her square white teeth were still strong, and she was only missing a few of her original set. She looked like a classic mahogany carving when she sat in her rocking chair, resting for a moment before she stirred up some new action that would keep her entertained for at least a few hours.

There was a round patch of smooth, brown dirt set in the middle of a grassy knoll in the front yard of the family home. This was where Mama Gee loved to perch in her antique rocking chair and hold court every evening around six o'clock. She wasn't bossy, but she was certainly authoritative. Anyone on the island who had an issue to be settled knew when and where to meet with her. There may be an audience, but Mama Gee knew how to deal with you and your problem without embarrassing you, and how to teach a lesson to the entire community in the process. Sometimes, her court would consist of a history lesson, generational stories preserved from time immemorial. She may talk about their homeland on that dark continent of Africa. She might call the roll of the ancient ancestors whose names and acts of valor had gone down in the annals of time.

The island was settled by Africans who had been transported to America to serve as slaves. Mama Gee's parents had been among that group, one of the last to arrive before the institution of slavery was abolished. She was born on the sundown side of legalized slavery. Two years after she entered this world, the Emancipation Proclamation was signed. Her parents had met on the island. Her father already had a family that he had been abducted from on the Ivory Coast. Her mother had been brought over as a teenage girl and sold on the auction block in Savannah, Georgia to the family of a congressman who represented that state. Her plight was not that bad in the congressman's home, according to what she told their only daughter, Georgia; but when two male slaves killed each other in a knife fight over her, she was ferried down the ocean to the island to await her next sale. In those days, the island was a holding place for slaves; sometimes, it was also a hiding place.

Mama Gee loved to say her pappy was a runaway. She could still see his wide, dark black face with the flat nose and large, flat lips. When he smiled, ivory teeth looked like straight white blocks hanging from fleshy pink gums. When she was a child, she would do whatever it took to make her pappy smile. She was happy when he was happy. He hated the white people. He remembered the wife and babies he had left behind. He loved them and would bring them into their island family in his conversations, his celebrations, and his prayers. Four little stick dolls, one big and three small, were kept in a pouch made out of a goat's stomach. That pouch was kept in a small clay pot with a lid. Her pappy hid it in a hole he dug in their main living space. Sometimes, he would hold it and cry. When he died, Mama Gee put it with her things. She still had it.

Her mammy met him by chance. He had run away from the last white man who bought him but never got him to the farm. He had choked the white man to unconsciousness on the ride back in the wagon; snuck up behind him and put his shackles around his neck, pulling harder and harder until he fainted. Before he jumped off of the wagon and ran, he made sure the man wasn't dead. Later, Sami told Jennie, Gee's mother, that he wasn't sure why he checked on him. He just remembered thinking that hating doesn't always have to mean killing, too.

Sami had run until his legs gave out. He was afraid to swim with the irons on his wrists. He found a raggedy fishing raft in some bushes. He pushed it out with the tide and said a prayer. An east wind came up and began to blow hard. He lay down and fell asleep, content to accept whatever happened. When he awoke, he found that he had grounded in a cove. He got off of the raft and pushed it up the shore to some bushes. Looking around, he saw a mountain with some small caves in the walls. In no time, he had settled himself in one of the caves, built a fire, blocked the mouth of the cave with the remnants of the raft, and killed and eaten a couple of snakes.

Jennie had seen him float in. She didn't want to react too soon, because she needed to find out some things first. Patrollers were always sneaking out to the island, trying to steal slaves to sell illegally. She didn't know if he was there to do good or to do bad. Day after day, she kept an eye on him. She knew where he was living and hunting. She could tell his footsteps were heavy, based on the prints he left in the sand. She could see that banana trees and coconut trees had deep marks on them at points where a person would be reaching to pull down the fruit or hit it with a stick. He looked like a man who needed some help.

She showed up on the shore early one morning. Just as the sun was coming up, she could see his shadow moving down the path on the mountain trail. She didn't want to hide and surprise him. She wasn't sure what he might do. So, she stood dead center in the path to the ocean. She wanted him to see her long before he reached her. That would let her know whether he wanted her help or not, and would further identify for her whether or not he was worthy of her help.

Getting the shackles off was the easy part. Getting him to trust her was extremely difficult. He couldn't speak the language well, and she didn't do much better. However, her time in the congressman's house had been a great start to her formal education. She was very bright, a quick learner. The congressman's eight-year-old daughter fancied herself a teacher. So, when the tutor would finish her lessons in reading and writing, she would hurry to practice her new learning with Jennie, teaching her everything she had learned while Jennie baked her biscuits and cookies and fruit tarts.

Jennie could tell that Sami was a loner, but he needed a few good meals and a little medical attention. So, as she led him by hand back to her palm frond-covered shack, she also collected some leaves and bark that she knew would make a healing poultice to put on his wrists, along with treating the boils she noticed on his feet and legs. Either he trusted her completely, or he figured he had nothing to lose.

The Civil War broke out, leaving the island inhabitants forgotten. No one ever came looking for Sami. Jennie's old master never sent anyone to fetch her and bring her back to the auction block. So, they and all of the other citizens developed their own society on the island, and life was great. Jennie seemed to be the appointed mayoress of the community. She had knowledge. She could read and write. But, she also still had close memory of her time in the homeland and could still speak in her tribal tongue. She was a bridge between the old and the new, the native land and this strange new homeland. Jennie didn't mind. She was a born leader and a strong black woman.

Jennie was the storyteller and historian of her day. Many of the stories she would share with the islanders at their evening meetings were the same stories that Mama Gee shared with those who gathered to listen as she sat in her rocking chair and dispensed her wisdom and tales. The children's favorite was the story of Cracklin' Joe, the one who would come in the night and eat the toes of the little ones who did not obey their mammys and their pappys. "He sneak in de kicchen way an he be cryin to we, 'where dem bad little ones wat don' want dey toes tomorrah?' Lemme snatch dem out de window an' fly they ovah to de' big wide Mammy dat live in de underneath of de big blue an' drop all o' dey down deep in de big wide arms of her! Oh, but her teach dem bad 'ems!"

Here, the children would holler, as if on cue, "No, no! We no wanna go be dropped in da big blue!", meaning the ocean.

Mama Gee would continue. "If dem not wanna be dropped in da big blue, den I take one toe!" Here, she would lean forward in her rocking chair, spreading her arms wide over the children. All of the children would jump up and begin to run around in circles. Those who had heard the story before were pretending to be terrified, but laughing wildly as they ran. Those who hadn't heard it, or sincerely believed that Cracklin' Joe was going to pay them a visit tonight, were running around looking fearful. Some of the little ones were just running and crying because others were. Parents were happy, because they knew they would all have obedient children for at least one day.

This was one reason why Mama Gee was so vital to the island and the main reason why Artrella was so fearful to share her dilemma with Mama Gee. All her life, Artrella had wanted to be a nurse. She had learned a lot about natural, island remedies from her mother, grandmother, and Mama Gee. Much of the island herbology provided precedent for traditional prescriptive medicine. Remedies that town folk purchased from a pharmacist had natural versions all over the island. Leaves, roots, herbs, barks, flowers, grasses, and numerous other floras had proven to be effective healing agents for centuries.

But, times were changing. Many young island residents had left their roots to go to the large cities so that they could go to school and get jobs that would provide good support for their families. Quite a few had come back to share their stories of success, and Artrella was anxious to take advantage of a great opportunity that had come her way.

A doctor in town had stopped her one day when she had taken the ferry in to sell some of her herbs. He had been a customer for about six months, needing an herbal base for a patient who insisted on a holistic prescription. He praised the quality of her herbs and the excellence with which she blended her bases, as well as the professionalism she showed in packaging them. He had asked her where she learned her skills. She told him about her mother, her grandmother, and Mama Gee. He was impressed. After that first conversation, he reserved time for a visit with her each time she made her delivery.

Dr. Stephen Hall saw a great deal of potential in Artrella. She was intelligent, knowledgeable, personable, and caring. She would make a great nurse. For him. What if he scholarshipped her education? She would bring a whole new element to his practice. Traditional and holistic medical care. That would appeal to clients across the entire area. Plus, it was a service that was not available anywhere, so there was a void in the market that the two of them could fill.

When he made the offer to Artrella, she thought she was dreaming. She would love to be a registered nurse and work one-on-one with a doctor as a practitioner in his office. And, to be able to practice herbal medicine in a traditional office would be a dream come true! But, what about Mama Gee? There was no way she could leave her, and there was no way Mama Gee would leave the island.

Tonight, as they gathered at the circle, these thoughts weighed heavily on Artrella's mind. Dr. Hall had brought it up again today when she went to town. All the way back, on the ferry, she thought about his parting words. "You will have to make up your mind soon, Artrella. The registration for the new semester begins in two weeks." Two weeks. Such a short amount of time. But, she knew some things couldn't be rushed. She was still young and had a lot of time to work on her goals. Mama Gee was one hundred years old, and who knew how much time she had left to enjoy life?

Before anyone could ask a question that would initiate Mama Gee's instruction, she began to talk. She talked about her father and her mother, about Cap'n Jack who was the white slave with one leg, about Aintie Pinkie who had twenty-eight children. She retold the story of Pidgin, the giant who was tall enough to pluck the coconuts off of the top of the tree. The children loved to hear about him and how he used to shake the island when he snored.

Then, Mama Gee began to talk about change. She talked about how she and her mammy and her pappy lived in a little shack. Then, they moved to a clapboard house set up on cinder blocks. She lived there until she got married and moved with her husband, King David, to their own little tarpaper shack. They lived there for many years and raised their six children, five of whom died before they reached the age of five. The last one was a victim of smallpox when he turned seven. She came home from the field one day to see her little house consumed in a blazing fire. Her husband was sitting in the yard, crying. He had a vision in the heat of the day. He had to come home and purge the house of the evil spirits that killed his babies. The next day, he walked straight out into the ocean and never came back.

That was when Mama Gee began staying with Artrella's grandmother and grandfather. When they died, she moved in with Artrella's parents. When Artrella's parents eventually died, Mama Gee moved in with Artrella.

"It's time for a change, peoples! We Gullah got to be people of the island and people of the mainland. We caint be left behind no more. The babies must all know how to make good money and build up our lives. I'm ready for change." The gathering got quiet. "Artrella, I want to finish out my days in the town. And, don't you argue with me! I know what I sees. I may be a hundred, but I think there's a few more good years in me!" She clicked her teeth. "See, they's still ready to do some more eatin'!" Everyone joined her in a laugh.

"As long as the ferry rolls, I'll have me a ride back. But, I feel ready for a change. I'm ready to go." She leaned back in her rocker and closed her eyes. The islanders knew they were being dismissed. As they drifted away, Mama Gee fell asleep, dreaming of Pidgin; and soon, she too was snoring.

It's Gonna Rain, It's Gonna Rain!

"He that hath pity upon the poor lendeth unto the lord; and that which he hath given will He pay him again."   Proverbs 19:17

*

Hall Plantation was a popular tourist site. In the eighties, it was registered as a national historic site. Great effort had gone into restoring it to its antebellum state. The multi-columned veranda was an elegant place to host weddings and receptions. The expansive yard was often filled with dining tables draped in white linen and decorated with fresh, colorful bouquets for spring and summer events.

If one chose to pay the exorbitant fee and rent the home itself, they would have a fifty-foot ballroom, a large industrial kitchen, and five side rooms which could easily hold three hundred people each. Glassy marbled floors, artistically-muraled walls, colorful stained glass windows, and original, richly polished hardwood trim made this an elegant setting and one of the few structures of its authentic quality left in the town.

The sole descendent of this affluent family had left it all behind a long time ago. He had grown up in the sixties and was tempted to become a hippie, but knew he'd better wait until his daddy died. You see, his father had been a close confidante to the grand wizard of the Klan, and he had been expected to follow in his footsteps as the only son. His mother had chosen to closet herself in a perpetually medicated state, and took frequent cruises to a variety of ports in order to enjoy her medicine with others of like mind, painting and writing poetry under the supervision and care of personal physicians. Stephen became a loner early in life. He didn't like his mother's friends, though he loved her; and he didn't like his father or his father's friends.

Stephen's best friend was the family cook, Mabel. His second best friend was Daisy, her daughter. Close to the same age, they surprisingly shared the same interests. Many a summer day was spent tramping through the woods on the plantation grounds, catching a variety of butterflies and picking native wildflowers to bring back to the house and mount with stick pins. Once dried out, the kids would carefully place them in cellophane envelopes and label them with white sticky adhesive tape.

Even though Stephen did not like his father, he loved his father's office. That is, until the day he and Daisy were working hard to set the last two butterflies into the album that would show off their collection. She was perched on her knees in the leather chair that was always next to his father's desk. Stephen was sitting across from her in his father's desk chair, looking like a miniature version of Captain Hall. This is the scene his father witnessed when he walked in to pick up an envelope. Captain Hall stuttered and shuddered at the sight of the two children working together. He was all right with them playing every day while Mabel watched and fed them both, but that little pickaninny would never step foot in his office ever again. When he snatched her by the arm, dragged her to the kitchen, and threw her hard at her mother's feet, Daisy had lost all desire to ever step foot again into the house, let alone into the office. That day, Mabel quit her job as their cook. Stephen's heart was broken double.

It was years before Stephen forgave his father for this act of racial barbarism. After his father died, Stephen hoped Mabel would forgive them, too. He delivered to her an envelope with his father's name in the return address corner. It contained three thousand dollars in cash. The note he enclosed was signed, "Debt paid in full for services rendered to an ungrateful idiot, Captain Samuel Hall." It never came back, so Stephen assumed she accepted the gift in the spirit with which it was given.

He never found out what became of Daisy. He hoped that somehow she had been able to attend medical school, like him. He hoped that he would run into her one day at some medical convention so that they could go back and pick up where they left off. Stephen was in love with her, really was in love with her – as only an adolescent boy can be in love. When he began college, he prayed that he would run into her on campus. He didn't. But, there were many other beautiful brown girls who caught his eye. Being in the South, he didn't want to make them uncomfortable by approaching them in a romantic way. But, he was able to generate many good friendships with black guys and girls alike. He felt most comfortable with them, possibly because that was the social base to which he became accustomed during his impressionable years.

After his mother died, he figured he should at least date eligible girls in case one might be suited to be his wife. He was alone in the world now and companionship was important to him. The problem was, though, that he was not attracted in the least to white women. They were intelligent, charming, beautiful, resourceful, cultured, and well-connected socially, but none did anything to make his toes curl or his blood flow faster. He knew a few that he could settle down with if he just had to, but life would be boring and that would be unfair to them.

Stephen would often laugh at himself. He wondered if he had developed this preference just to irk his father, even in his grave. Sometimes when he would see an attractive black woman and imagine her as his wife, he would immediately break into laughter thinking about his father rolling around in his casket, over and over like a hamster on a wheel. If she would smile back, he would be laughing so hard that he looked to her as if he were daft, so she would roll her eyes, swing her head, and walk away. "She must not be the one," he would say to himself, laughing again at his own ridiculous wit, "so slow your roll, Captain!"

He wasn't in a rush to get married, but he was strongly motivated to secure his medical practice. He used part of his inheritance to purchase a small building downtown. He remodeled it and rented out sections to other up-and-coming professionals who were servicing the town. There was a bank, an optometrist's office, a psychiatrist's office, a law office, and his suite that he shared with one other physician. They were doing great business, and he had been approached last week by a barista who wanted to open a little coffee shop in a corner office on the first floor. He was feeling an excitement and exhilaration about his life that he had not felt in a long time. It wasn't about making money. He had enough of that to last a lifetime, and then some. What was stimulating to him was an opportunity to help a young black woman who wanted to become a registered nurse go to the university and finally realize her dream.

Something about her was intriguing and familiar. It seemed that he had known her before, but there was no way he could have. He was strongly attracted to her, though she looked nothing like Daisy. In fact, she looked the opposite. Daisy had light brown skin with a few tiny freckles dusted across her nose, deep green eyes, and blonde highlights in her chestnut hair. Artrella was the color of coffee with thick cream, that rich caramel color that made her chocolate brown eyes stand out strongly from her face. Her nose was tiny and thinly-sculpted. Her hair was straight and deep brown, long and heavy with gentle waves at the temples. He had caught himself daydreaming about her twice last week, and after that had purposely gone to sleep at night repeating her name over and over in order to call her back into a new dream.

He realized it was not Daisy's exterior that he was yearning for, but something that he connected with in someone entirely different in age and looks from Daisy. It was the character, the persona, the inner qualities that Artrella displayed which reminded him of Daisy. Her strength, her commitment to caring for those who were sick and needy, her willingness to experiment to find the best cures and then to package them with care and precision, those were the qualities that he had known in Daisy even at a young age, and those were the qualities that he now admired in Artrella. These qualities had been strongly evident in every woman that he fell in love with, except his mother.

His mother's funeral was a hoax. He couldn't remember what he had done to anger her doctor so, but he did remember the scene he caused when they refused to open the casket after they supposedly claimed her body from the cruise ship. Where was the body? The doctor reported that she had slipped on the deck and tumbled into the ocean. When pressed for more details, he disclosed that she appeared to be under the influence of something earlier that evening and may have fallen over the side rail due to her instability. The death certificate, signed by both the ship's doctor and captain, stated that the cause of death was "accidental, likely due to an unattended fall over the side of the ship." Unattended. As long as he had known his mother, she had been attending to her own demise.

When the entire town showed up at the plantation to pay their last respects to the wife of Captain Samuel Hall, Stephen suspected they were coming to see a woman who had been a phantom to most of them all of her years in town and also to feast on the funeral dinner that was sure to follow. So, Stephen had gone all out to plan an occasion that would never be forgotten. The rector of the Presbyterian Church was set to share a few words of condolence in the great cotillion hall. The doctor who had accompanied her for years on the numerous cruises she had taken was slated to give the eulogy. Mother's casket was to be displayed on the veranda for the town to review as they passed out of the house and into the yard for the funeral dinner prepared by the best caterer of Southern coastal cuisine in the county.

The rector's words were inspiring and comforting. Many tissues dabbed many a tear. Many matronly well-wishers made eye contact with Stephen, silently expressing their pity and concern as the rector spoke of God's presence and comfort to those who find themselves forsaken by mother and father.

After that, everything went downhill. When the doctor began to talk about what a loving and caring woman Mrs. Hall had been, Stephen began a coughing spell that he could not control. The more the doctor talked, the louder Stephen's coughing became. Sweating and blushing deeply, the doctor had to sit down since Stephen made his words intelligible. Miraculously, the coughing stopped as soon as the doctor took his seat.

At the end of the service, the rector asked that the congregants remain seated as the casket was wheeled to the veranda. Then, they would all be able to pass and leave their respects as they moved to the beautifully-set tables on the lawn for lunch. The organ music began, and Stephen stepped behind the mortician as he and the pall bearers rolled the casket to the veranda. When the casket was situated, Stephen asked the mortician to open it. The mortician looked extremely flustered. He told Stephen that he had received instructions to keep the casket closed.

"By whom? I am the next of kin. I secured your services. You receive your instructions from me. Open the casket!"

"Dr. White said the casket was to remain closed!" The mortician looked around nervously. "Dr. White, Dr. White!" He spotted the doctor walking toward the front door. "Dr. White, Dr. Hall is asking that we open the casket." He paused, hoping that Dr. White would step into the conversation.

"Dr. White, please explain why my wishes are not being followed in this matter," said Stephen.

Dr. White cleared his throat. Beads of sweat gathered above his upper lip, betraying his commanding tone. "Son, I have decided that the casket will remain closed. Your mother is not in a proper condition for viewing."

"Sir, I have determined that no matter what my mother's state, the casket will be opened and this community will see the woman who they always knew about but never knew. As her son, I shared the same fate." He turned to the mortician. "Sir, open the casket. Now!"

What happened next was one for the historical records. Mrs. Hall had been retrieved from the ocean after a two-day recovery effort. Sharks and other sea creatures had consumed a good part of her body. In fact, not much at all was left. The mortician had been instructed to just place the pieces inside the casket, seal it, and deliver it to the home for the funeral. No embalmment had taken place. No order was made in arranging the leftover body parts. No clothing draped the remains except a sheer shroud that had been soaked in formaldehyde to control the order of decay during the services.

Stephen waited until he saw the lid of the coffin lift and the mortician step to the side. Then, he went back inside to shake the hands of consoling well-wishers as they passed out the door to view the body and then go to enjoy the lunch. When the last of the attendees had shaken Stephen's hand, he moved toward the front door. Looking out onto the lawn, he noticed that very few people were seated at the lawn tables. He wondered if the cooks and servers had changed the arrangements at the last minute. "Why isn't anyone listening to me today, of all days?"

He moved toward the casket to take his last glance at the woman he had never known well, the woman who had given him life and now reclined in death. He stepped in front of the casket and looked down. What greeted his sight looked neither human nor animal. It looked like someone had taken the head of an octopus, the body of a squid, and a variety of offal from other large sea creatures, wrapped them in a sheer tablecloth, and placed them in a casket. Stephen was horrified! He looked at the mortician, who was raising his shaking hands as if to say, "You told me to do this!"

Stephen viewed the lawn. All of the cars that had been parked on the grounds were gone. Servers were posted at their stations with no one to serve. The sight of his mother's remains had caused all four hundred people to lose their appetites and go home to gossip about what the other eleven hundred who had known his father and mother had missed.

Stephen turned back toward the mortician and nodded his head in resignation. As he passed the now-closed casket, he whispered, "Rest in peace, Mother. And, I pray that my soul may do the same."

He could not explain to himself why this event had interrupted his thoughts of how he was going to help Artrella achieve her personal and professional goals. Were they actually his personal and professional goals? Did the two align? Was he trying to force her into a situation where he could become her Svengali and control her life for his own purposes? Perhaps that is why he had thought of his mother. Maybe he was following the same pattern of manipulating others in order to satisfy his own needs and wants. He did have her genes. Some personal tendencies and character traits could be the same.

Who was he to think that a bright and beautiful girl would need him in order to be successful? Was it that he actually needed her to finally feel that he had accomplished what he was destined to do? All of his growing-up years had been spent swimming upstream, enduring humiliation, and living down his father's racist reputation. What was he still running from? What was he running to? Why was he continuously running?

When Stephen opened his office door, he could hear his phone ringing. It was early morning, not yet office hours, and he had a service to handle his emergencies so he decided to let it ring. Something nagged him, though, telling him to pick it up.

"Hello? Dr. Hall's office."

"Stephen, it's Artrella. I'm planning to come into town today. I'd like to visit with you. Would you have any time for me?"

"Time?" He paused, then said, "Artrella, please come. And yes, I have all the time in the world." Hanging up the phone, he finished, "In fact, I have a lifetime."

The Billows are Tossing High!

"Wine is a mocker, strong drink is raging; and whosoever is deceived thereby is not wise." Proverbs 20:1

*

Sherry adjusted her glasses before checking the map again. She should know how to find this building, as many times as she had been in this area. The pickup was scheduled for 2:30, and it was 2:26. She had never before been late picking up a client.

"Come on, now, girl. Look around. You have to be missing something." Glancing through the driver's side window, she suddenly spotted the address, three numbers positioned high above the awning. "There it is!"

Sherry swung the minivan around in the middle of the street and pulled into the access drive just as the young man was walking through the automatic glass doors. She parked the van and exited her door, crossing around the back of the van to greet him.

"Good afternoon, sir, and welcome to our humble town!" she said with a laugh, extending her right hand. He was quite tall and had an air of authority about him. His close hair cut made it difficult to determine his age. But, his body was well-sculpted and he looked to be in good physical condition. She wondered why he was in town, why he wanted a tour, and how long he was planning to visit. There would be plenty of time to find out!

As she pulled back into traffic, she made small talk. "What a pleasant day to see all of the sights! We'll try to get in as much as you like today. Do you plan to be here long?"

"Not long," he replied, with a smile. "In fact, I'm just here for a couple of days. But, I have heard so much about your fine town and the beautiful beach, that I wanted to see as much of it as I can while I'm here."

"Business or pleasure?" She was hoping he would say business. That would mean he wasn't coming to meet up with some woman he had been talking with online.

"My business is my pleasure!" he replied with a hearty laugh. "I am an evangelist. I've been invited to preach at Metropolitan Community Church this weekend. There is a Saturday evening rally planned and then a Sunday morning service. Perhaps you've heard about it?" He leaned forward from the back seat over the console between Sherry and the front passenger seat,

163

his long arms draped across both front seats.

"No..., I can't say that I have." Sherry cleared her throat. "Dang!" she thought. "I never imagined he was a preacher. He probably has a fat little wife and ten kids running around a parsonage somewhere. "My work as a tour guide keeps me pretty busy," she continued, "working seven days a week!" She added that last part almost guiltily.

"Well, I want to be the first to invite you to the services!" he exclaimed, sitting back. He patted his knees as he stretched out his long legs. "I'm sure you know where to find the church! But, I don't, so can we drive past it at some point while I'm taking my tour?"

"Sure!" Sherry responded, scratching her brain to recall where she had seen that large billboard sign advertising Metropolitan Community Church, 'It'll Make You Feel Better!', but she figured after driving around a while, it would come back to her.

They worked their way through downtown as she pointed out many of the historic buildings in town square. She showed him where a Civil War battle had been fought, with the Union Army emerging as the winner. He asked her to stop so that he could take a picture of that site. She took him to the library and narrated the story of how it had been burned down and then rebuilt after the first black child had been given a library card. After cruising slowly past a few more buildings, Sherry made her way to the highway.

"Can we roll these windows down? I'd love to get a whiff of some good old sea air!" Her passenger was already pushing the automatic button on the left door.

Sherry quickly switched off the air conditioning. "He really doesn't know what he's asking for!" she thought. "Sure we can," she answered him, "but this time of the afternoon is pretty hot in these parts! I tell you what," she said, formulating a quick compromise, "let's just drive down on the beach for a while. It's about ten degrees cooler there than it is here, so you'll get the best of all worlds."

"That sounds good to me!" he exclaimed, rolling his window back up.

"Thank goodness!" she thought, as she switched the air back on. "I know the customer is always right, but I may have had to argue with him a little on this one had he insisted!"

Sherry parked her van at a little motel so that they could walk down the beach front. She knew it would be safe there. Plus, the elderly owners were good friends of hers. For as long as she could remember, her family had taken two weeks of vacation at their motel every summer. She and her siblings played and swam with their son, Fred. Her mother and Mrs. Clark became great friends, corresponding with each other throughout the year. They all looked forward to the visits, and by the time she was a teenager it seemed that they were attending a family reunion each year.

Fred Clark was the same age as her two younger brothers, so she hadn't known him very well until she became an adult. Now, he was like a little brother, though he wasn't little at all. She admired how he had built himself up to be so buff, like a body builder. He didn't participate in any contests; but if he had, he would have won hands down. He looked just that good.

As soon as they stepped on the beach, Sherry began to share the history of the area. She had memorized dozens of stories about this place that she had adopted as a second home. Halfway through her second story, she paused. She realized that no formal introductions had occurred, and she felt like that formality should be corrected at this point. They were having fun, laughing and talking, exchanging bits of trivia. Shouldn't they know each others' names?

"Pausing for a commercial break!" Sherry said, raising her hand with a laugh. "I just realized that we don't even know each other's names!"

"Well, I was wondering when you were going to ask me to share that bit of information!" He laughed, too. "I'm a well-bred East Coaster whose mother would cringe if she thought I was going around introducing myself to strange women without their invitation. So, rather than have that happen, I was willing to patiently wait for a formal introduction."

"We sure wouldn't want to have your mother cringing," Sherry replied, "let alone your wife!" She extended her hand. "I'm Sherry Hughes."

He shook her hand warmly. "I'm Theodore, aka Teddy, Washington." He bowed slightly. "Glad to meet you, Sherry Hughes!"

"And, I'm glad to meet you," Sherry curtsied, "Theodore Washington!" She laughed.

"Please call me 'Teddy'," he rejoined. "And, no wife."

"All right! Well, now that we have the formalities covered, let's resume our tour guide narrative!" They both laughed and continued down the beach. Teddy had a lot of questions and Sherry was glad to be able to answer them all. She could tell that he had done his research about the area, so she asked him about his interest in this place.

He explained that his great-uncle had started the church that his mother's cousin now pastored. He had heard many stories during his growing-up years of the generations of preachers in his family. One of the greatest was the founding pastor of Metropolitan. His preaching style was strong and convicting. He loved and cared for the people in his congregation as if they were his own children. He would come back home once a year and run a revival and the entire town would turn out to hear him preach. In return, one of his relatives would come to Metropolitan once a year to run a revival. This was Teddy's first invitation. He knew that the congregation was very familiar with his family, and he had done his homework so that he could be familiar with theirs.

Walking up and down the beach on that warm afternoon left both of them a little thirsty. Before their next stop, Teddy suggested that they stop and get something cold to drink. For any other client, she would likely have suggested the upscale cocktail bar that she frequented almost every evening; but since he was a minister, Sherry immediately headed for a nearby café.

When they pulled up to the café, Teddy asked if they had time to go inside and be served there rather than sit in the parking lot and wait for a carhop to come and serve them. Sherry agreed. Passing through the front doors, Teddy picked up one of the colorful sightseeing brochures in the stand next to the newspaper racks. He took it to the table with them as they were seated by the waitress.

"Would you like tea, lemonade, or co'cola?" the waitress asked as she waited to write down their order. Teddy looked quizzically at Sherry, and she mouthed 'lemonade'.

"Two lemonades, please," Teddy told the waitress, smiling warmly.

"Lemonade it is, then! Anything else?" Sherry shook her head 'no'.

"No, thank you," answered Teddy. "That will do it!" For the next twenty minutes, they sipped their lemonades and talked about what led them into their individual professions.

Sherry's story held no great mysteries. She had fallen in love with the town during her family's summer visits. She loved everything about it – the history, the community spirit, the food, the beach, the landscape, and the fact that she considered this place more of a home than the place where she was born. When she graduated from high school, she chose to attend a college close by so that she could come to the town whenever she had time. On one of her many visits, she had applied for a summer job at the library. One day, a docent asked if she would be willing to provide a tour of the town to a group of her friends who were visiting. They had been attending a conference nearby, come down to visit her, and wanted to see the historical highlights that were around town. Sherry, with her bubbling personality and wit, along with her expansive knowledge of the local history, jumped heartily at the chance to do something she was sure she would love.

She was a big hit with the group. That gig led to many more. Soon, her weekends were full of tours. She made enough to register her business, get a license, purchase a minivan, and support herself well by working seven days a week. She was well-respected in the town and promoted many of the businesses that advertised her services. She had been doing this steadily for the past three years, and had lately been thinking of purchasing another vehicle and hiring an employee so that she could take a break now and then.

As Teddy was watching her talk, he noticed how excited and

animated she was. She certainly did not look as if she was overworked or frustrated with her busy lifestyle. She smiled a lot. She spoke with confidence and optimism when she talked about her plans for her business. "She must really love what she does, just like I do!" he thought.

Sherry paused and looked at her watch. "Oh my! Have I been talking about myself for that long?" She drained the last bit of lemonade through the ice at the bottom of her glass. The slurping sound made her chuckle to herself. Lifting her eyebrow, she looked at Teddy with a smile, just a little embarrassed. He smiled back.

"No problem! I can tell you about my path to greatness while we're riding out to Hall Plantation." He tapped the brochure on the table between them. "This may be the last local highlight we'll get in today." As they stood, Teddy pulled a couple of dollars out of his pocket and laid them beside his glass on the table. The waitress was hovering nearby.

"Thank you!" she exclaimed, as she moved to lift the glasses, napkins, and tip off of the table.

"You're welcome!" Teddy said. After stopping at the cash register to pay their small bill, they moved toward the door. Teddy opened it for Sherry to exit first, and then followed. As they approached the car, he said, "Do you mind if I sit in the front? It's a little hard for me to hear you all the time if I'm in the back seat. That is, unless it's against company policy." He opened the driver's door for Sherry after she automatically unlocked it.

Stepping up into the seat, she said, "Well, I'm the company so I make the policy. Of course it's fine. I want to be able to hear your story clearly, too. I'm always fascinated to hear why people choose a sacrificial lifestyle."

"Well, fasten your seatbelt!" Teddy exclaimed, as he shut her door firmly. Coming around to the passenger side, he opened the door and continued, "I'm always glad to tell people why they should choose a sacrificial lifestyle!"

Sherry turned the van onto the main road that would take them to Hall Plantation. She estimated it would take them about a half hour to get there with traffic as it was this time of day. She settled back to hear what Teddy was going to share.

His childhood was typical. Two parents. God-fearing home. Three sisters and two brothers. He was the youngest child. Both of his brothers were pastors, but he had not chosen to settle down with one church. He preferred to evangelize, like three of his uncles. He had never been married, but he had been engaged once. She made it clear before the wedding that she needed stability. The life of an evangelist was too financially unpredictable. He agreed, accepted her ring back, and let her go. They were still friends, even though she eventually married and had two children.

He had been a star basketball player throughout high school and college. That had paid for his education. He had majored in drama with a minor in English literature. He was an avid reader and enjoyed writing as a hobby. He had performed in a few gospel plays and had even auditioned for some off-Broadway parts one summer. But, there were too many things congruent with that lifestyle that conflicted with his Christian principles. So, he decided to let God direct his life.

Sherry cringed just a bit when he mentioned God. She hoped he didn't notice, but he did. "What's the matter, Sherry? Don't you believe in God?" he asked.

She recovered from her engagement in his story. "What kind of question is that?" she thought. With a quick smile, she answered, "Of course I believe in God! Who doesn't? People who say they don't believe in God are lying, because how would they know that there was a God to not believe in if they didn't know about God from the Book that He wrote, the Bible. Of course I do!" She congratulated herself on her quick thinking.

"Ummm, that sure sounds good," complimented Teddy. "But, belief means that your heart and your brain are in sync. You believe because you have stated that you believe in your heart. Have you done that?" He looked at her eyes in the rearview mirror. She turned to him and smiled. Then, she looked at her watch.

"What time did you say revival starts, Rev. Washington?"

Teddy chuckled. "Touché, my dear! All right, back to my story. I realized very quickly that my life's blood was doing the very thing I was just doing with you. I lived to talk of my faith. I loved to share the Word of God with anyone, anywhere. I could be in the mall, on the basketball court in the middle of a pickup game, at a restaurant, it didn't matter. I have never been intimidated by people or places. God made it all. If He gave me an assignment to minister to the president, I would be overjoyed to do it. We all need a Word from the Lord."

Teddy went on to explain how God had directed his life. He led him to commit himself to working with his uncle's ministry as an associate minister. He would go out and run revivals throughout the year, then come home to continue his work with incarcerated young men, the homeless, and his ministry for abused women. He had a staff of about forty church members who kept these three mission ministries going when he was away. So far, many people had shared how their lives had been changed and how they had been saved because Teddy had been willing to allow God to direct his life.

They pulled on to the expansive grounds of Hall Plantation. Beautifully manicured hedges, vibrantly colorful flower beds, and green lawns greeted them. Sherry often wondered at all of the slave labor that had gone into cultivating this greenery, along with building such an extravagant structure. The sowing surely was done in sorrow, but the reaping was beautiful and full of joy.

Today, though, Sherry was jealous. She had felt so confident, so proud of herself and all she had done on her own. She had worked hard and had never asked anyone for anything. Yet, she hadn't really helped anyone except herself. She was planning to hire another employee, but hadn't done it yet. Selfish? No. Self-absorbed? Possibly. Was that so wrong? She heard a small voice say, "Definitely." She turned quickly to look at Teddy as she pulled her van into a parking spot.

"What did you say?" she asked in a challenging tone.

He gave her a puzzled look, and then responded. "I was *going* to say that this is definitely a beautiful place! Look at it! I have never seen anything like this in all my life! But, I have to wonder how many of my ancestors sacrificed their life's blood to create such a wonder. Do you know?"

Sherry was embarrassed that she had allowed emotions from her own thoughts to spill over into her conversation with Teddy. "I'm so sorry!" she said. "I think I was hearing things!" She laughed self-consciously. "Actually, I was just thinking that your question was something I have been wanting to research. I'm sure the answer will reveal that many more than we can imagine were forced to do things they never wanted to do. But, the end result of that ugliness is truly a thing of beauty. Would you like to go look at it?"

Teddy was quiet and pensive. "Actually, Sherry, I think I've seen enough. There is something about this place that is both awe-inspiring and depressing at the same time. I feel like I want to cry, but mixed with those tears of sorrow would be tears of joy. There is a scripture found in the Psalms, the 126th I think, that says those who go forth weeping, carrying their precious seed out to be planted, will surely come back again rejoicing, bringing the sheaves as the reward of their labor with them."

Sherry sat silently for a moment. Her quick wit had given way to deep thought. Finally, she spoke. "I think I know what you mean, Teddy. There are times when I just start to think about these kinds of things and I just want a hard, stiff drink to turn my brain off! I see too many of my loved ones' faces in the people I imagine would have built these fine structures, and planted the crops, and tended the animals, and nursed the little white babies. Maybe that is why I have avoided this level of research. It's not funny. It's not anecdotal. I can't distance myself from it to make it seem like someone else's story. It's my story, and that of people who share my bloodline. So, when I see this place and think about what it took to create it, I want to cry for that precious seed! My great-grand relatives who were stolen, molested, abused, enslaved, they are that precious seed! They planted Hall plantation and all of the beauty that now represents it. But, I hear what you are saying, and I guess I need to look for the beauty is in the sheaves." Her eyes began to fill with tears.

He sat for a moment, his right leg on the step of the van with the door partly open. Then, he nodded. "We've come back again. We are the returnees, observing the reward of their labor. And, we are supposed to experience joy, seeing all of this beauty," he said waving his hand. He turned to look again at Sherry, totally attuned to where he knew she was emotionally. "But, where's the joy, Sherry? Where's the joy?"

"Isn't there a scripture in the Bible for that, Rev. Washington?" Sherry placed her right hand on top of his left hand, which was resting on the console beside her. Her voice was filled with emotion. She was beginning to wish her lemonade had been a hard one.

He turned back to her with a smile.

"You know something, Sister Hughes, I think you are right! And, thank you so much for reminding me! I needed that help right now! Can you say 'Amen'?" Sherry laughed and mouthed an 'Amen!' "I believe that in that same chapter there is a familiar refrain: 'The Lord has done great things for us, and for that reason, we are glad!' You have reminded me that we should not focus on what is wrong with a situation. We must keep our focus on the Lord. There is no wrong in Him. In spite of bad things that happen in our lives, we have to continually keep our eyes on God, Who only does great things! Then we will stay glad! And, that's where the joy always is, Sister Hughes!" Within those last phrases, Teddy had incorporated a traditional syncopated, sing-song delivery common to old-school preachers delivering a call that anticipates a response. Sherry was engaged in spite of herself.

"Amen!" Sherry stated loudly, wiping her eyes, clapping her hands, and shaking her head back and forth like she had seen old church mothers do when she was a child. Both of them began to laugh. "And I know that joy is just what I need." She paused and her voice revealed that she had become thoughtful once again. "I guess I've just had a hard time finding it."

"Maybe it's because of where you have been looking?" Teddy looked at her with a smile and one thin eyebrow raised.

A long time ago, a friend had told her that peace didn't come in a bottle. Right now, she was realizing that joy didn't, either. She felt the need for a restart. This just might be the time.

"You may be right, my friend," Sherry responded. She looked out the window, and then looked at Teddy. Nodding her head up and down, she started the van. Teddy closed his door and fastened his seatbelt. Sherry placed the van into drive and began to reverse their course, heading back toward town. Smiling at Teddy, she said, "I guess you're right. I need to refine my search. So, Reverend, what time did you say the revival starts?"

Down By the Riverside

*"Whoso stoppeth his ears at the cry of the poor, he also shall
cry himself, but shall not be heard." Proverbs 21:13*

*

"Kenneth, it's me, your mother! Please call me back as soon as you
get this message! I've been trying to reach you for three days!" He could
hear the stark frustration in her voice, but he still wasn't ready to talk to her.

Vanessa was a nice girl and she came from a good family. He thought
she and his mother would hit it off right away. They had a lot in common.
Both were business majors in college. Both had strong, magnetic
personalities. In fact, it was seeing many of his mother's positive
characteristics in Vanessa that led him to ask her out on the first date.
Now, the rest was history.

"Yeah, and our relationship could be history, too," Ken thought.
Vanessa had not returned his calls since the fiasco with his mother at
dinner. He couldn't believe how his mother had acted toward Vanessa.
She, an intelligent community leader, was always kind and polite to
everyone. How could he have known that she had another personality
when it came to a woman who could show her some competition for his
affections? But, hadn't she been the one to tell him that it was about time
for him to begin looking for a wife, get his life on track and start making
plans for his future? He was confused, and apparently confusion was an
inherited trait.

Vanessa's father was a prominent attorney. Ken had met him once
and was surprised at how quickly they hit it off. He was a solid man who
inherited his firm from his father. In his early fifties, he was yet vibrant and
youthful. During the whirlwind weekend Ken had spent at Vanessa's
parents' home, they played tennis in the morning, golfed in the afternoon,
played chess in the evening after dinner, went to church on Sunday
morning, and picnicked on the private lake in the afternoon. Ken was
treated like a member of the family, and he had hoped that his mother
would respond to meeting Vanessa in like fashion.

The afternoon luncheon had started off well. Ken made reservations
at the resort restaurant and selected a table that looked out on the ocean.
The afternoon was beautiful, like a page from a vacation magazine.
Vanessa looked gorgeous, her long black hair swept up in a loose chignon
held together by a carved coral comb. She wore a tropical flowered dress,
light and flowing. Ken thought she looked like an angel. "This could be

my wife," he said to himself as she approached the table where he was standing and his mother was sitting.

Introductions also went well. Louise, his mother, was the mayor of their town. She knew everyone, or at least one of their relatives. Very excited to meet Vanessa, she was extremely cordial as she sized up the lovely young lady who could potentially provide her with the yearned-for grandchildren in the future. Her questions were animated and her probing was gentle. Where had Vanessa gone to school? What were her hobbies and interests? Who were her mother's people? It was obvious that Vanessa's family had white ancestry in the bloodline, but it would have been rude for Louise to go there directly. So, she took the scenic route to find out what she needed to know.

As it turned out, Vanessa's mother was related to a black family in town, as Louise suspected when Vanessa shared her mother's maiden name. By that time, they had finished their shrimp salads and were awaiting the entrée. Ken was happy that the two ladies were connecting in conversation. Vanessa complimented Louise on how much the town had grown during her leadership. She could recall a visit when she was a teenager. Old-time country stores comprised the main street, and the town had boasted such a quaint character. Yet, now that the major department store chains were opening up stores downtown, a far more cosmopolitan crowd frequented the city, bringing new life and attracting young people to relocate there. Louise beamed with pride that Vanessa would even connect her to Tisdale Beach's newfound successes.

By the time they were enjoying their dessert of *dolce de leche* cheesecake, the two women were planning a shopping trip for the next day. Ken was ecstatic! When he first met Vanessa, he knew somehow that she was the one. That one was a chance meeting, and almost of a storybook nature. He had walked out of the bank on a windy day. He was carrying two envelopes in his hand. One was to be dropped in the mail and the other was to go into his briefcase. It was a large check that he was going to deliver to a broker for an investment he needed to make. His portfolio was very healthy due to his careful scrutiny of stock values each week. He found that he could earn good returns if he did much of the stock investigation himself. So far, his hard work was paying off. He had gotten a good lead on a pharmaceutical firm and had followed its activity for the past two months. It looked like this was the perfect time to invest his money and see if it would earn what he anticipated it should over the next quarter.

All investments are subject to how the wind blows. That day, the natural wind was blowing strongly. So strongly, in fact, that it blew the envelope with his check in it out of his hand and carried it across the street just as he was depositing the other envelope into the large blue mail box.

Ken dropped his briefcase on the ground in front of the mailbox and took off after the other envelope. Lithe as a ballet dancer, it pirouetted across the grass into a parking lot. A car was turning into an empty space. The envelope seemed to become attracted to its tire. It blew right up against it and stuck. Ken tried to keep his eye on it as he made his way toward the car. He noticed that as the envelope flattened onto the pavement, its corner became stuck right under the left rear tire.

"Great!" he exclaimed as he ran up on the rear of the driver's side just as a female leg extended from the open driver's door.

"What!?" The young woman recoiled in fear, gripping her handbag as he rushed up to the wheel. "Help! Help!" she hollered as he sank down on his knees, pulling at the envelope that was secured beneath the tire.

"What?" Ken responded. "Oh, no, ma'am, I'm not trying to do anything but get this envelope that blew out of my hand!" He motioned to the envelope on the ground. It was not budging. He tried to wiggle it out from underneath the tire, but that wasn't working, either. He looked up at the young lady and she appeared to be fumbling with a container of mace that was attached to her key ring. Ken jumped up.

"Ma'am, please! I'm not trying to harm you! Look!" He pointed to the envelope on the ground. She still didn't seem to believe him, but she did look down. "See? I had this envelope in my hand," he pointed down, panting. "The wind blew it out of my hand and it flew across the street. I was over there mailing another envelope." He pointed toward the mailbox, where his briefcase was still laying on the sidewalk. "Look, there's my briefcase. I dropped it when I had to chase this envelope. It has a check in it that I was going to take to my broker. Oh my," Ken sat down on the pavement. "This is probably too much information for you." He looked up at her, pleading. "Please, I just need to get this from under your tire. I'd pull it harder, but I don't want to tear my check. Would you mind backing your car up just a little bit so that I can pick up my check?" He smiled a sheepish smile.

"I think I've heard everything," she replied in a doubt-laced tone, "but I think I believe you. I'll back the car up a little." She put her keys back into the ignition and turned on the car. Ken held on to the check while she moved the car back a few inches. He didn't want the wind to start its game all over again.

Their conversation continued over coffee. He felt so bad at inconveniencing her that he thought at least he should offer to buy her a cup. Plus, he wanted more time to convince her that he wasn't some weirdo who was about to victimize her by sneaking up on her getting out of her car. Beyond that, she was probably the most beautiful girl he had ever seen, so he didn't want her to get away without him doing his best to get to know her better.

That had been about three months ago, and now he found himself beginning to get serious about her. He thought she might feel the same toward him, too. She had initiated the meeting of the parents by inviting him up to their coastal home three weeks ago. He scheduled a lunch with him, her, and his mother as soon as he got back from the weekend at her parents' home. He wanted everything to be perfect. He was ready to move forward in their relationship and in his life.

It all started when Vanessa mentioned a celebrity she recently met at a charity event promoted by her father's law firm. Louise politely asked about the charity which provided support to single mothers who wanted to go to college. That led to questions about the law firm. When Vanessa mentioned her father's first name, Louise turned into a drone missile. How old was he? Where did he go to school? How long had he been a lawyer? She asked Vanessa everything except for his social security number and his mother's maiden name.

Throughout this interchange, Ken had become more and more distrustful of his mother's motives. Was she just going out of her way to make Vanessa uncomfortable? What had been a cordial, even friendly, conversation had immediately turned into a hostile interrogation. This was a side of his mother that Ken had never seen. He was ashamed that, on the first occasion Vanessa had ever met his mother, she was also a witness to Louise's uncharacteristic behavior.

Vanessa couldn't wait to leave. As soon as Ken paid the bill, she extended her hand to Louise, thanked them both for the lunch, and walked out of the restaurant before Ken could ask his mother to excuse him. She was in her car by the time he sprinted behind her to the parking lot. He had to knock on the window to get her to keep from driving away.

"Vanessa, I am so sorry! I don't know what came over my mother! I had no idea she would act that way!"

"Ken, I think she was sending me a message, loud and clear. I'm not the woman she would have selected for you. I would never come between a man and his mother. Thanks again for lunch," she paused and then weakly smiled. "Take care!"

As Ken stood helplessly beside her door, she rolled up her window, put on her sunglasses, placed the car into gear, and drove away.

He was so angry with Louise that he did not go back into the restaurant. He was afraid of causing a scene that would end up in tomorrow's newspaper. "Mayor and Son Have Major Altercation in Local Restaurant." He could see the headlines. So, he drove home along the beach road to cool off and then went inside to call the two most important women in his life. Neither answered.

Louise was having a panic attack. She had been afraid to follow Ken and Vanessa out of the restaurant, afraid of what she would say or do.

How could either have known? What would happen if her fears were true? How many men in this part of the state could have that same name, or even gone into that same profession?

She stopped in the ladies' room on her way to her car. She wanted to make sure she avoided her son, plus she was not composed enough yet to meet any of her constituents with a smile. She stayed in the stall for a long time, glad no one else entered the bathroom needing to use the space she had claimed until her heart stopped pounding. "What is wrong with me?" she thought. It was as if her past was emerging like a giant monster, and she didn't have the strength to attack it, let alone kill it right now.

Louise felt a migraine coming on. She knew she only had about fifteen minutes to get home before it totally disabled her. She hurried out to her car and got onto the freeway as quickly as possible. As soon as she entered her garage, darkness was descending over her eyes like the garage door lowering. She stumbled into the house, grabbed a bottle of water on her way to the bedroom, took her strongest medications from the cabinet, and guzzled them down before the lights went out.

Hours later she awoke feeling like a sledgehammer had hit her on top of her head. She lay in the bed for a few minutes until the first wave of nausea passed. "Oh God, it's been so long since I've had one of these. I don't know how much more I can take!" Tears began to stream down her face. She knew she should relax, but she really felt like tensing up into a fetal position and moaning herself back to sleep. "This just can't be!"

In spite of every effort to fight the process, her mind went back to that night in college. She was at a fraternity party. She had been campaigning for student government president, and while handing out her flyers run into her direct opposition. Oliver Simons. A tall, handsome black man, suave and silver-tongued, he had been running a campaign based on fluff and empty promises. She, in contrast, was intent on effecting policy that would benefit women and non-traditional students. Early polls showed, though, that he was projected to be the winner by a slight margin. So, she decided to campaign on his territory and hopefully sway some of his voters to select their president for the intelligent reasons. That is why she accepted the invitation of a fraternity brother to attend the party. She would meet people who could be influenced by her intellect. That might be all she needed to win the race.

She wasn't counting on someone spiking her punch as a joke. She didn't realize that she would be the target of a sick prank and end up in a remote room, the victim of a group rape attack. She also wasn't prepared to see a face rise from the darkness each time she relived this experience in a nightmare brought on by a monster headache that occurred first nightly, then every few weeks, and finally when she least expected it over the years. That face, as it turned out, matched that of Oliver Simons. He was at the party. He snickered as she campaigned assertively until the drugs in her drink made her unintelligible. He was there, somewhere, when the attack on her took place.

She had not reported it, ever. She was afraid that people would think she had made her accusation in retribution against Oliver when she lost the campaign. Also, she had run as a young woman of principle, one who was upright and stood in stark difference to her opponent's character. To have it come out that she got drunk and had sex at a frat party would have cost her the support base she had built in her campaigning. So, she bore her shame in silence until she could hide it no more. Five months after the attack, it was obvious that a baby was on the way.

Kenneth knew part of the story. She told him that she had gotten pregnant with him in college but had decided to raise him without his father's support. When he was a small child, he had been very inquisitive about his father. At some point, she must have satisfied him with some vague answer, because he stopped asking and had never asked again.

But now, this issue had reemerged. Looking at Vanessa, she could see Oliver's face again! The same facial structure, hairline, eyes, it was the face from her nightmares. Could her son possibly be in love with his own sister? She had to know; but more importantly, Kenneth had to know.

Louise tried to call him for three days, but he refused to answer. The migraine left her so ill and with such a strong aftershock of a headache that she had been afraid to drive, so she stayed in all weekend. But, she knew she needed to talk to Kenneth to explain things, because he had never before seen her behave the way she had at their lunch. So, Louise decided that she would drive to his office early Monday morning and sit down with him to explain what happened, if he would be willing to hear her out.

As soon as Vanessa left the restaurant, she had driven straight home. Her parents had been asking her to come up to the house and spend a few days. She thought that now might be a good time to get away. She had been swept up into Ken and their developing relationship. She felt that she had possibly lost some objectivity about her own life. It might do her good to get out on the beach and breathe some salty air to get her head back on straight. She stopped home and picked up some clothes and toiletries, then headed to her parents' home.

They were surprised to see her, but glad that she had come to spend time with them. She unpacked, then grabbed a book and a blanket and headed for the beach. She stayed out there until sundown, reading as long as she had light. By the time she made her way back to the house, her parents had already eaten dinner and were sitting beside the pool enjoying each other's company.

"I wish I was a teenager again, living here with you guys!" Vanessa smiled and sighed deeply as she snuggled her way between the two of them on the edge of the pool.

"I don't think so!" Oliver exclaimed, hugging his daughter. "We have prepared you well for the real world, and you're doing a great job on your own. Still, you know you will always be our baby girl, and you can always come home when you need to!"

"I know, Dad," Vanessa said. "But, thanks for reminding me!"

"I was hoping we would be planning a wedding for next summer, getting you hooked up to someone else who could cater to your every whim!" Oliver laughed, looking at Vanessa with a sly tease.

A tear began to roll down her face. It was soon followed by a deluge. Vanessa began to relate to them the event of the day, revealing finally that Louise had been extremely rude to her and had gone out of her way to show her son that she was totally displeased with his choice of a girlfriend. The problem was that Vanessa was clueless as to why!

When Vanessa mentioned Louise's name, Oliver became extremely thoughtful. Could it be the same Louise Campbell he had known in his college days? Was the world really that small? He thought about how she would not have known him well enough to take anything out on his daughter. Yes, he had won the election for student body president, but that was decades ago and no reason to hate Vanessa now. She seemed like a very intelligent young woman back then. He couldn't imagine that she would hold a grudge for that long just over an election. He might need to schedule a meeting with her himself to see what was really going on.

Early that next Monday morning, he asked his administrative assistant to call Louise's office and set up an appointment for him as soon as possible. His firm was a silent contributor to an organization for which she served on the board of trustees, so he told his assistant to reference that organization if she were asked about the nature of the appointment. As it turned out, Louise would be available at one o'clock that same afternoon.

When Ken reported to his office on Monday morning, Louise was sitting in the reception area. His receptionist had gotten her a cup of coffee and she smiled at him as he walked in the door. His first impulse was to turn around and walk back out, but he didn't want to cause a scene. "Good morning, Mother," he said tersely.

"Good morning, Kenneth. Do you have a few minutes to spare for your mother?" Louise had painted a politician's smile on her face, and stood to follow him as he headed for his office door.

"Of course! Alicia, please hold all of my calls. Thank you." Ken stepped over the threshold and held the door for his mother to follow. As soon as he closed the door behind her, Louise collapsed into the plush red leather chair in front of his desk, holding her head in her hands as she began to cry.

"Oh Kenny, I am so sorry! I wish I could explain to you everything that is going on with me right now! This is terrible, and I never imagined it would happen! I don't know what I'm going to do!" Louise sobbed uncontrollably.

Ken ran around the desk to embrace her. "Mom, Mom, calm down! What's going on? Do you need to see a doctor? I've never seen you like this before. Please! Tell me, what is going on?"

Louise composed herself and then began to explain to him the dreadful happenings on that college campus years ago. He held her while she relived the rape incident, and cried with her when she related how she had suffered migraine attacks for years because she had not been able to share with anyone what happened.

"Do you remember how you used to ask me who your father was, Kenny? Do you? Well, so much of that incident had been pushed deep into my subconscious because it was too horrible to relive! But, do you know whose face has continued to rise to my consciousness, time and time again? Do you? It was Oliver Simons, Kenny! Oliver Simons, Vanessa's father!"

Louise spit those last two words out like they were a bitter pill. Ken was in a daze. He could not believe what he had just heard. Vanessa's father had raped her mother? Vanessa's father was his own father? He and Vanessa were brother and sister? This was too much to process.

"Mother," he began, incredulously, "what proof do you have of all of this? Was he charged? How could he have gotten a license to practice law if he had a major felony? Why wasn't he in prison or something? This makes no sense!" Ken moved toward the phone. "I have to call Vanessa and get his number. This can't be swept under the rug! If he did this to you, to us, he has to pay!"

"Kenny, no! Please, let's leave this just where it's been buried up until now. I can't handle walking through all of this mess again! But, I don't want to damage anyone else, either. Let Vanessa be. You just have to understand that you and she can't date any longer. You can't have anything else to do with her. It just wouldn't be right, Son! It just wouldn't be right!"

Ken held his mother while she exhausted her tears, feeling her pain and becoming acquainted to the new pain and anger that had just introduced itself to him. He was also beginning to feel angry toward Vanessa. How could she come into his life, bringing all of this confusion? Why did it have to be her car that stopped on his envelope that morning? Why did he have to have fallen in love with his own sister? Whose idea of a cruel joke was this?

Deep inside him was a nagging feeling. Something didn't feel right about this. There had to be more to the story. He would find out. He would go to Vanessa's parents' house and have a visit with her father today.

Driving down to town, Oliver tried his best to recall everything he could about that night thirty-five years ago. He remembered the skinny little girl with the long frizzy hair who dressed funny and was always talking loudly. She had rallied a pretty good campaign against him that year when they both ran for student body president. She amused him. She was a campy kid, one who didn't mind doing the grassroots work to build her voting base from the ground up. He admired that about her. But, he had also known from the beginning that he was a shoe-in, and had run his campaign in that way. All he had to do was show up, and he immediately attracted everyone's attention. That is why he had attended the fraternity party that night. He didn't know that she would be there, too.

Things had gotten a little wild that night, he recalled. Someone had sneaked in some liquor and spiked the punch. The partiers were enjoying themselves immensely. He didn't drink. He never had, so he had been about to leave when he saw one of the guys who had a bad reputation for being one to get girls drunk, take advantage of them, and then broadcast his conquests later on leading Louise down the hall. Oliver remembered being surprised, because he didn't think Louise was one of those kinds of girls. "Oh well," he thought, "you never know." He was about to leave the party himself when he saw five other boys follow that joker and began to suspect that something crazy was about to happen. After greeting a few more people and shaking some hands, he made his way down the corridor where they headed about ten minutes earlier.

Three or four guys passed him in the hallway. He came to a slightly open door and saw Louise lying on a jumbled bedspread. She was crying and waving her arms in the air. He walked over to her and could see that she was drunk, but hurt. She opened her eyes and saw him and then began to sob, "Help! Help me!" He picked her up, helped her straighten her clothes, and then took her out of the house with him. He saw blood on the back of her skirt when he laid her in the back seat of his car. He took her to the hospital and sat her on the bench in front of the emergency room door. He then drove away, hoping that someone would take care of her.

He had thought about the incident a few times within the months following. He had asked himself over and over why he hadn't told someone, or even followed up with her. He ended up winning the election and assumed maybe he was afraid that someone would think he was trying to take her out of the running by doing something that would stain her reputation. He wasn't sure if that was the reason or not, but he comforted himself with the thought that at least he had taken her to the hospital.

Today was the first time he had thought about her, or the incident, in more than thirty years. Who could have known that their children would meet and become friends? This was unbelievable, but it was fixable. Louise just needed to know the truth.

He had grayed some over the past few decades and had also picked up a few pounds. The hair that wasn't gray had long since taken flight in his brush on its way to his trash can, so the likelihood of Louise even recognizing him was slim. Her secretary was very cordial and offered him some bottled water before she led him into the mayor's office.

Louise was seated behind a long oak desk, covered with a spotless glass top. She rose to meet him and shake his hand. Her reflection in the glass showed a strong chin and a confident smile. She registered no recognition, so he knew that he had to be extremely creative in leading her into the conversation that he knew was inevitable if Vanessa and Ken were to have any chance at happiness.

"Ms. Mayor, I would like to thank you for taking these few minutes to visit with me about the matter that we have in common today. I apologize that I did not give your secretary my name when I made this appointment. Had I done that," Oliver added, looking her dead in her eyes, "I doubt if you would have agreed to this meeting."

"Is that right?" Louise responded, eyeing him warily. He wondered if she was about to buzz for security, so he hurried to his conclusion. "My name is Oliver Simons. My daughter is Vanessa Simons. She and your son are friends. I understand that there are some issues that presently need clarification in relation to the two of them."

Louise felt as if she were going to faint. The blood rushed to her head so quickly that her cheeks flushed. This didn't even look like the Oliver Simons she remembered. He had been tall and handsome. This man looked shorter, plump, and almost bald. Could this be a joke? Was she dreaming or still experiencing a migraine-induced nightmare? She stumbled backward toward her desk chair, holding on to the desktop for balance. She nervously looked down at the handprints she was leaving in her backward trek toward security, feeling as if she were about to be victimized again and not quite sure as to how she should protect herself. Fleetingly, she thought that at least this time there would be fingerprints at the crime scene. Looking down at the glass before she sat down, she realized foolishly that the incriminating prints would be her own.

Seeing Louise in a state of disorientation, Oliver began to talk quickly, first standing and then sitting when he saw that she was listening intently, though weakly. He told her about what he had recalled on the way down to her office. It played like a movie in his mind and he narrated what he saw. Now and then, Louise would nod. When he got to the point where he walked into the room and saw her on the bed, how she reached up to him and asked him to help her, how he helped her straighten her clothes and get out of the room and then out of the house, she began to cry.

"You are the one who rescued me!" She breathed hard. "That explains why I kept seeing your face. You saved me! You took me to the hospital! And all these years," she continued as she tried hard to compose herself, "I thought your face was the face of my attacker! I'm so sorry!" Louise buried her face in her hands and laid her head on her desk. Tears flowed between her fingers and ran onto the desk top, spreading out quickly like molten glass.

Oliver stood and placed both hands on the desk in front of her, leaning in toward her crumpled figure. "Louise," he said, clearing a throat full of emotion, "I don't know what to say or what I can do. I can try my best to recall the names of the guys I saw walking to and then from the room. I'm a lawyer. I don't do criminal law, but I have many friends who do practice it. We can try to prosecute, if you want. Make it right. I should have followed through back then, turned them in or something. But, I didn't want you to think that I was trying to besmirch your character as some cruel campaign tactic. Or, at least that's what I told myself. But, it's not too late. I should have taken care of this then; I should have taken care of you." He shook his head and sat back down.

"Oh, Oliver! I'm the one who should have taken care of myself!" Louise sat up, grabbed some tissue, and heaved herself deep into her chair as she began to wipe her tears and blow her nose. She waved her arm around her. "I take care of a whole city! I go after those who harm our citizens. I fight for policies that will make this a safe and supportive place for people to live! Why didn't I do that in the beginning for myself and my son? And, why did I react so horribly toward Vanessa when she has nothing to do with any of this?" Louise began to cry again. Oliver walked around the desk and stood beside her.

"Ms. Mayor, may I please have your attention for a moment?" He smiled with tears in his eyes. Louise turned to look at him and could see the compassion that she recalled was also in that face so many years ago. He continued. "You are one of the strongest women I have ever met in my life. I recall that about you when we were fighting for the same position. You are a fighter. You are a survivor. You weren't elected student body president, but you were elected mayor! You didn't let one loss stop you, and look where you are today." He paused, smiled and nodded at her, and then continued. "I believe that all is fair in love and war. You and I have already fought the war, and it is apparent that you are the winner! All that our children want is a fair chance at the love part. Are you willing to give that to them?"

"Willing, and ready," Louise replied as she reached out for Oliver's hand. She stood to hug him when he offered his own arms as a lifeline once again. "My mistakes in life have been many. I should have done a number of things differently, but it's not too late to change what I can. Thank you, Oliver, for overriding my ignorance and coming here today to help me overcome my past. This is a deliverance that has been a long time coming. I love my Kenny more than anything in this world, and would have fought an army to spare him from hurt and harm. As it turns out," she said with a tearful smile, "I was almost the atomic bomb that took him out."

"I can compliment you on the fine young man you have raised," Oliver responded, "and I concur that you most certainly pack a strong protective punch, according to Vanessa! But, I also can understand why, and I know that she will, too."

"Thank you, Oliver, for your understanding! Who would have thought that you would have the distinct privilege of rescuing me twice in my life; once from those attackers, and once from myself!" Louise sobbed again, and then breathed deeply as she opened her arms to Oliver, inviting him into her grateful embrace. "Thank you! Thank you!" she murmured, over and over.

"I believe that a Power greater than any of us has ordained the connection of these two families," Oliver said, gently patting Louise on the back, "and I can't wait for us all to share dinner at our home this evening while we all sort this out together. There may be many mysteries in our lives that will never be resolved, but this is one that will hopefully have a happy ending!"

"And, I believe it is within my power as both mother and mayor to decree it is so!" Louise gathered herself with great resolve. She collected her thoughts and her things as she moved past Oliver toward her office door. Opening it wide, she smiled back toward Oliver. "Let's go, Oliver. We have a lot of work ahead of us!" He nodded, and followed with a smile.

I Looked Over Jordan, and What Did I See?

"A good name is rather to be chosen than great riches, and loving favor rather than silver and gold." Proverbs 22:1

*

Joaquin was no stranger to hard work. As the oldest of six children whose parents were migrant laborers, he had pitched in to do his part since he was old enough to drag a burlap sack. His parents were Puerto Rican and had come to America in the early eighties to seek a better life for their family. They began in Florida working in the citrus groves. They migrated on down toward the Carolinas to work the peach fields. Eventually, they settled where they could work farms growing tobacco, cotton, soybeans, wheat, tomatoes, and corn almost year round.

Before he was old enough to work in the fields, he worked at supervising his siblings while his parents labored. The children were almost two years apart in age, so by the time he could go out to help earn income for the family, his brother just younger than him was ready to step into his place. Joaquin was a quick learner and was soon working almost as quickly as any teenage boy when he was still a very young adolescent. He took a lot of pride in his ability to work hard, even though he would go home each day extremely sore with bruises and scratches from head to toe.

His father had an uncommon nickname that he assigned to Joaquin while he was yet a young child. He called him, *Senor.* It was meant as a name denoting great respect, but people who didn't know assumed that his father was saying that Joaquin acted like an old man. He did. He seemed to feel safe himself when providing care and safety for others. His own father recognized and respected this trait. Plus, his work equaled each of his parents' in bringing income to their home.

In addition to the field work he did during the day, he would look for any opportunity to do odd jobs for individuals in the community. Cutting grass, trimming hedges, pulling weeds, burning trash, cleaning fishing nets, scraping boat bottoms, anything was a job that Joaquin would accept with sincere gratitude. More money meant a pair of shoes that would fit his brother, more milk for the two youngest children, or a candy treat for all of his siblings. Sometimes, he would buy some weekday meat for the family. Always, he would give the majority of the money he earned to his father.

In no time, Joaquin had built a regular customer base. He would rotate days and visit each customer to provide a routine service, establishing predictable income for the family. He always made sure to save at least twenty percent of his earnings for the things he might want to do in the near future. Seldom did his plans include personal purchases, but he was always looking for ways to make his parents' lives easier and make them happy with individual acts of thoughtfulness. Now and then, though, he would see something he really wanted and relish the process of saving up for it and then going to make the purchase as if negotiating a long-anticipated reward. It might be something as simple as a yo-yo or something as indulgent as a new pair of long pants for himself. He recognized the need for money and the importance of earning it honestly to build a good life. Joaquin was learning early what it would take for him to realize the American Dream, loving every minute of it!

By the time he was in his mid-teens, he was respected as an independent businessman in his small community of farm laborers. Older workers admired his ability to maintain his own side endeavors while still keeping up with them in the fields. They had high expectations for him. He needed to go to college, create better ways for others to do what they were doing. He would have to make a lot of money to afford to continue his education. Why didn't he get a town job? He could make five times the money he was making in the fields, along with doing his odd jobs.

There was a big bulletin board in the grocery store where the townspeople would post announcements of local events, items for sale, and jobs. Joaquin had gone into the store one day to get some groceries for his mother and sweet treats for his siblings. He glanced at a large poster hanging on the board. "Lifeguards Needed. $50 a Week. Apply at the Boathouse on the Beach."

Fifty dollars! That was more than he could make in two months of odd jobs! Joaquin was a natural swimmer. He had supervised his brothers and sisters at the beach for as long as he could remember. He swam fast and was strong! He knew that was a job he could do well. Plus, just think how quickly he could save enough money to go to college if he could make fifty dollars each week.

All the way home, Joaquin formulated a plan. He would drop off the groceries and take a quick sink bath. He would comb his hair down, scrub his nails good, and put on a clean shirt and his new pants. He would put on the dock shoes that Mr. Crump had said he could have when he was getting ready to burn his trash. They had fit him perfectly and looked great once he cleaned them up. He would not wait until tomorrow to go and apply for the job. He wasn't sure how long the sign had been up, so he didn't have a moment to spare.

The lifeguard lounging in the office looked Joaquin up and down before he got up from the chair and went to grab an application. "Sit down here. Fill that out." He tossed the application at Joaquin, then sat back down and opened up a magazine.

Joaquin was about to ask the kid for a pen, then decided to look around and see if there were any that happened to be lying around. He spotted one on the window sill. Walking over to pick it up, he wondered if this guy was the one who would interview and hire him. "I hope not," he thought. "If he is, I'm in trouble!"

Joaquin completed the application and checked it front and back twice before getting up to hand it to the young man. He cleared his throat. " I'm finished with my application. What would you like for me to do now?"

The guy looked at him as if he wanted to say something smart, but he didn't. As if right on cue, a tall woman walked into the office. She had on a red plaid camp shirt and a pair of khaki shorts. She looked very serious. "Jack, why are you still in here? Your break should have ended fifteen minutes ago. Who is covering your station right now?" She glared at him, placing her hands on her hips.

"What'd you want me to do?" Jack hitched his thumb toward Joaquin. "This kid came asking about a job. I wasn't gonna leave him in here by himself. No telling what he would have done!" Again, he looked Joaquin up and down as if he was a criminal.

The lady also looked at Joaquin and then at his application. "Are you Joaquin?" she asked him.

"Yes, ma'am! I saw an ad for a lifeguard in the store today, so I came straight down to apply." He smiled hopefully.

"Are you the one who has been cutting my aunt's grass for the past couple of years? She is Mrs. Garner who lives on Paradise Place."

"Mrs. G is your aunt? Why yes, I know her!" Joaquin laughed. "She makes the best chocolate chip cookies in the world!"

"I love them, too!" She laughed, and then looked at Jack. "Do you know what, Jack? You could learn something from this 'kid' right here about hard work!" She pointed emphatically at Joaquin. "He manicures my aunt's lawn, in her words, every week and does a better job than many grown men!" She turned to Joaquin. "Is Aunt Sally going to be mad at me for hiring you from under her?"

"Oh no, ma'am!" Joaquin responded quickly, becoming very serious. "I will keep my regulars. I'm just looking for a job that will help me earn money for college. I think I could afford to go to school if I can earn fifty dollars a week!"

"Then the job is yours, Joaquin! When can you start?"

Joaquin congratulated himself as he danced all the way home. His parents were so happy that he was going to be able to make so much money and maybe be able to go to college! They didn't really know what that type of possibility would mean for their family, but they were ecstatic because Joaquin was ecstatic!

Working at the beach every day became a great blessing for Joaquin and his family. His younger siblings were able to swim all day if they wanted because he was there to supervise them. He became a leader among the summer workers. He was a good organizer and a strong team player. He was willing to work extra hours whenever he was needed. He was very patient with the young children and very respectful toward the teens and the adults. Even Jack had come to him to apologize when he realized what a jerk he had been the first day they met. Of course, Joaquin had no hard feelings. He was on his way toward achieving his goals.

At the end of that summer, Joaquin walked onto the campus of the state university and paid his first semester's tuition, housing, and fees with money he had earned and saved. He was not the smartest student in his group, but he had the greatest work ethic. His reputation for doing quality work-study assignments brought him more opportunities and some scholarship monies. By the time he was a junior, he was seeing a light at the end of the tunnel, as well as helping his younger brother follow in his footsteps.

He entered college determined to major in agricultural studies and business. He became interested in law after taking a business law class, and then switched over to social work after he completed a sociology research project on the malaria epidemic that killed rice field workers in that region a long time ago. He wanted to make sure nothing like that ever affected his family or his friends. Then, he thought that he should probably switch to medicine in order to create cures for things that could harm people. His advisor told him that was what college was all about, weighing all of your interests and opportunities equally. Still, he knew that he had to focus on what would not only help him to be successful but help his family, too.

So, he decided that he should begin where he started. He declared himself a business major. That helped him narrow his course selections and soon he saw how appropriately that major fit his interests. He had been extremely creative in garnering odd jobs to build his own business to service the needs of his community when he was a child. He was interested in improving the business of negotiating fair labor practices for migrant workers, which had piqued his interest in the law. However, the common denominator among all of his interests seemed to be business, so that is where he settled his interests.

Joaquin graduated from the university within the four years he had projected and was left with the question that many parents ask their dependants on graduation day, "Now what?" Joaquin wasn't sure, but he was confident that he would discover that answer soon. His little sister had just completed her freshman year and his brother would be a junior in the fall. Joaquin had already saved their tuitions for the upcoming year. He was almost driven to make sure that the money would be in place for them when they needed it. He decided he would serve as a life guard for one last summer and then begin the search for his life career.

It was the Fourth of July and the beach was packed! Eighty-five degrees outside, hundreds of families were out and about with their picnic baskets and firecrackers. Toddlers, teens, their parents, middle-aged sunbathers and youthful seniors could be seen all over the place, enjoying one another and themselves. The beach was teeming with activity, and all guards were on duty. All needed to be alert.

Jack and Joaquin had the middle stations that day. That was where most of the action seemed to be. Joaquin's mouth was sore by noon, he had been whistling so much at the rowdy little boys who kept dunking girls or knocking down the older swimmers on their way into or out of the water. There were two of them that kept most of Joaquin's attention, a little red-headed kid with freckles and a chunky little boy with a short buzz cut and clowns on his swim trunks. He had made them sit out for fifteen minutes twice. He didn't see parents anywhere. "Maybe they don't want to claim them," he thought.

He checked in with Jack and told him that he was going to take a quick break. He had been in the chair for about four hours straight and hadn't taken a bathroom break yet. He decided it was time to go. Jack looked like he had partied late last night. He had not done much since high school but lifeguard in the summer and work at a bowling alley in the winter. Joaquin had talked with him a few years ago about why he should enroll in college, since that would make a huge difference in his earning power. Jack had just nodded and said he would think about it, but he had made no moves to get started in school. He was turning into a beach bum, Joaquin thought. He was too smart to settle for that, though. Joaquin decided on his way to the bathroom that he would bring it back up with Jack later.

Jack pulled his sunglasses back down and settled into his chair once Joaquin walked away. He was counting the hours until his shift ended. He had been out with some old school buddies last night. They were back in town for the holidays. A couple had moved out of state to go to college, so he hadn't seen them in a long time. Even though he knew he was on duty at ten in the morning, he had partied until almost 2:00 a.m. The warm sun was starting to make him drowsy. He sipped some of his water and decided to close his eyes for a few seconds. They were all planning to get together tonight to celebrate the Fourth with some girls they met last night. One was a really pretty redhead who had acted interested in him. He couldn't remember her name, but he did remember the good night kiss she had given him as they left the bar. He also remembered what she whispered in his ear before she kissed him. Oh yes, it was going to be a good night!

He looked down and saw a little red-haired boy running in circles around the lifeguard stand. The kid was chasing his friend and then kicking sand at a little girl, probably his sister. She was crying and trying to run away from him, but then he started chasing her. Jack looked to the left and saw a red-headed lady walking his way. He figured she was the bad kid's mom, coming to get him. "What's up with the red hair thing today?" he thought. "I wonder if the kid is my girl's brother, and if that ugly lady is her mom?" He started to laugh out loud, and then felt himself drifting, thinking about red hair floating on the ocean and the lady looking like a big yellow shark with big yellow shark teeth. The shark was heading toward the red hair with its mouth open when Jack heard a scream. At first he thought it was the shark, and then he realized he was asleep and someone was really screaming.

Opening his eyes, he saw that the little girl who had been chased by the red-headed boy had run out into the ocean and was bobbing up and down. People along the shore were screaming for him to save her. He jumped off of the stand and swam quickly out into the water. He could see her and then she would disappear. Adrenaline kicked in and he immediately felt her in his arms, but she wasn't moving. People were lined along the water's edge as he walked up on shore, carrying her in his arms. He immediately started resuscitation. He could hear sirens coming closer.

Joaquin was just leaving the bathroom when he saw a large crowd rush past him and head toward the shore. "What is going on?" he thought, moving quickly to maneuver himself around them. As he got closer, he could hear sirens blaring. "Oh no," he thought, running faster, "someone has drowned!"

The officer questioned Jack again about the allegations that he had been asleep on the stand when the little girl drowned. He insisted that he didn't see her through his sunglasses, that he had seen the kids playing around the stand and had seen their mom come to get them. He hadn't gone to sleep. He hadn't seen any little girl run into the water. He hadn't seen any boys chasing her. He wasn't asleep. He was awake and watching. Where were her parents, anyway? Why was he the one being charged with negligence? He was doing his job.

Joaquin could not sleep that night. Regrets plagued him. What if he hadn't gone to the bathroom? True enough, Jack was lazy, but Joaquin knew that. He shouldn't have left Jack to watch those bad kids when he knew he had already sat them out twice. He should have put them out before he went to the bathroom. That poor little girl. Her poor parents! He couldn't imagine how his parents would feel if his baby sister drowned because some lazy lifeguard wasn't doing his job. Joaquin would never let that happen on his watch. But, he wasn't watching this time, and now an innocent life was lost.

Joaquin attended the little girl's funeral, even though he didn't know her. Drownings rarely occurred at this beach. Chris told him over and over that this was not his fault; he wasn't even the lifeguard supervisor on duty that day. She was. She assured him that there was no way he or anyone else could have ever predicted this tragedy. She confirmed to him that he would never have let this happen had he been there. But, he had not been there and it had happened. Therefore, Joaquin had to accept that this was part of God's plan and He would somehow work it out for the good. Joaquin honestly couldn't even imagine how that was possible.

These thoughts ran through Joaquin's mind as he sat through the service. He kept staring at her parents, wishing that this was all a dream for them and things could rewind speedily like a video when you hit the reverse button. Then, he could hold his bladder and tell Jack to go on home and get some rest. He would cover Jack's station until Chris could come and relieve him. He would make those two little boys go home, too. He would make everything okay.

After the pastor talked about the little girl and said some comforting words to her family, the girl's mother asked to say a few words. When she stood and turned to the congregation to speak, her husband stood with her. He had on sunglasses and continued to dab the corners of his eyes from time to time.

"I want to thank everyone who has shown us any kindness and support during this very difficult time. I have to tell you all, I have done a lot of soul searching these past few days. At first, I wanted to blame everyone but myself. I blamed the kids who were chasing her. I blamed the lifeguard who should have been watching her. I blamed the water, I blamed her twin sister who should have been right beside her, I blamed her. I blamed God. I should have blamed myself. I should have kept an eye on her. But, I was too busy being consumed with my own agenda and my own vanity. Trying to get a good, deep tan." She paused and shook her head violently, then continued, "And now, my baby is gone! My baby is gone!" Collapsing in her husband's trembling arms, she began to wail uncontrollably.

As her husband gently sat her back down, the pastor stepped back up to the podium. He said, "Truly, this is a loss that will always be difficult to understand. Why would God allow a small, innocent child die in such a tragic way? Why would He not alert someone, anyone, to see her drifting out toward the deep water and rescue her before she drowned? Why does He allow these events to occur in the first place? Doesn't He love us? Doesn't He care? Doesn't He know what is going to happen so that He can warn us to keep the bad from happening? I didn't plan to share another eulogy today, but I see a healing has to occur.

Yes, God does see and He does know. His ways and thoughts are so far above ours that it is sometimes difficult for us to understand why He does what He does. But, faith in His perfect will helps us be content with

His plan, however He chooses to execute it. So, when we ask the question, 'If God was truly all powerful and all loving and all caring, why would He allow bad things to happen?' Here is the answer that always comes back to us. God's grace is sufficient. God's grace covers every circumstance. God covers us with love when we are angry at Him. God covers us with peace when we want to blame ourselves and others for what He has allowed. God covers us with joy when depression wants to drown us in a pool of self-pity. God covers us with grace to bow to His will and thank Him for the faith to trust Him when we have failed others. God's grace is sufficient."

Joaquin thought on those four words as he drove home. "God's grace is sufficient." The pastor's impromptu eulogy had taught him what grace meant. He needed faith to trust God because he had failed others. But, he also needed faith to trust God to place him where he needed to be so that he could help others best. That was his life calling. He had to care and protect. He had to be there for the people who trusted him and needed him. He had to be accountable for their safety. If they trusted him to be there, he had to be there, just like God was there for him and them. He needed to be like God. But first, he needed God.

Joaquin decided that he would come back to that church again. He wanted to check on the family from time to time. He wanted to be there for the little girl's mother and father. He liked the way the pastor had shared something that Joaquin really needed to hear. This was a friendly place. He thought his parents and siblings might enjoy meeting these people, too. Isn't that what Chris was talking about, that these kinds of events had a way of working out for good, especially when you knew you hadn't done anything to create the tragedy? Could it be that God was using this horrible incident to help Joaquin learn what he needed to do in order to help the people he knew he was destined to help?

Pulling up in front of his parents' house, Joaquin sat in the car for a few minutes. His short life flashed before his eyes. He saw himself as a small child dragging a gunny sack of lemons down a row between the trees in the field. He saw himself trudging through neighborhoods in too-big shoes, stopping at each door, asking if there was anything the homeowner needed done that he could do. He saw himself venturing into the college admissions office with a cashier's check in hand, ready to pay his tuition and start his college career. He saw himself sitting high in a lifeguard's chair, watching a little girl drown.

Joaquin's head dropped to the steering wheel, and he cried until he couldn't breathe. He cried until he felt like a baby, blubbering and begging for help. "Please forgive me, God! I'm so sorry I didn't stop that little girl from drowning. But, if you give me another chance, I will never let that happen again! I will take care of every person you assign to me to watch over. I will make sure all of my brothers and sisters go to college. I will look out for all of the little kids I see anywhere doing anything – swimming, walking to school, crossing the street, anything! Please, give me another chance! Please!"

Suddenly, Joaquin felt a wave of gentle quietness sweep over him. It was as if someone had laid a warm blanket over a shivering infant. Immediately, he was calm and comforted. "Is this what grace feels like?" he wondered. It seemed like he could hear something saying, "You don't have to do anything but trust Me. I'll take care of everything and everyone. That's My job."

That reality hit Joaquin like a revelation! He had spent his whole life taking care of others. His father and mother, his brothers and sisters, his college classmates, his coworkers, his neighbors. That had been his job for so long. Now, it seemed that God was telling him that he didn't have to do that job. It was God's job. All he had to do was be available to do what God needed him to do for others. No wonder he had a hard time deciding on a major in college. He was trying to do it all.

Joaquin felt relief, as if a great weight had been lifted from his shoulders. It had. Finally, Someone was willing to take care of him. Not that he was going to be lazy, though! He loved being a hard, committed worker. It just seemed that now there was a purpose to his assignments. He got out of the car, feeling strongly confident of his next steps. This was greater than the American Dream. This was faith, trust, grace, peace, and joy all mixed together. This was hope for a productive future and an invitation to explore life in a new way.

Joaquin couldn't wait for Sunday. In fact, for him it couldn't come soon enough!

No More Water, But Fire Next Time!

"Labor not to be rich: cease from thine own wisdom." Proverbs 23:4

*

"INTERRUPTING THE PATTERN: EXAMINING THE IMPACT OF WHITE SOCIAL EFFICACY ON BROWN AND BLACK PEOPLES IN THE SETTLEMENT OF AMERICA" *BYZANTINE PAVILION B, 3:30-5:00 PM.*

Dr. Ruth Richards looked at her watch. It was 3:42 p.m., exactly. She was furious. There were only three people in her session, and she had refused to begin until at least seven others showed up. Considering all of the money she had spent in travel costs, hotel fees, and conference registration – even though she was only charged the presenter rate – the small attendance made her very angry. She had long suspected some type of subterfuge related to her work. She often imagined that the F.B.I. had tapped her phone when she started researching what had now become the passion of her lifetime. The facts she had prepared to share were important and critical to the survival of people of color. Two old white ladies and a twenty-something kid with dreadlocks who was fascinated with his cell phone were not her ideal audience.

The young man with the dreadlocks and phone passed her as she stood in the hallway. "Are you leaving already?" Ruth asked.

"Yeah, I don't think the presenter is going to show. I'm gone!" His head remained down as he walked away, apparently texting a message. He didn't even realize that she was the presenter.

"Go, then!" she spoke to herself as she headed back inside the meeting room. "You wouldn't understand any of this anyway!" Stepping up to the front of the room, she picked the microphone up off of the lectern, cleared her throat, and looked at the two old ladies who were still patiently awaiting her presentation. One looked as if she were half asleep already. Wondering if there was any point in continuing, Ruth realized that she should at least say something.

"Good afternoon, ladies. Welcome to the presentation." Ruth cued her PowerPoint slides to begin, handed each of the ladies a packet which accompanied the slides, and stepped back to the lectern. "Today I will share with you my collection from two decades of research based on my dissertation for my Ph.D. in sociology. We will examine how the first whites to land on America's shores began a systematic plan to destroy people of color, both indigenous and ones that the whites themselves transported to these shores from foreign lands to become slaves. It is my position that this plan continues to thrive today through means devised by white men who operate within a supremist mentality. We will examine how jobs, financial status, availability of illegal drugs, de-masculization of men of color, favoristic manipulation of women of color, and the mis-education of children of color are all designed to publicize to society that brown and black peoples in America are to be marginalized in order for the plan of the white American to fully control all of America to be successful."

Ruth had turned the jets on full blast! She hoped to offend the two white women so much within those first few minutes that they too would get up and leave. However, the one who was sleepy continued to nod in and out of consciousness and the other appeared to be listening in rapt interest. So much for her disengagement plan! Ruth continued to share her research with her lone interested party.

As she worked her way through the slide presentation, she noticed that her interested friend was taking copious notes, especially from the slides that showed her data supporting the research. Ruth paused while the slide of the third-grade reading scores correlating with the prison construction projections glared at them on the screen. She wanted this woman to see the ugly side of her white ancestors, see how the game they began in the 17th century was still being played out today. She wanted the woman to ask her questions, to repent, to cry, to beg to support her work as a financial benefactor! She wanted anything except what she was getting – unfeigned interest!

The rhythmic twitch in her right eyelid should have been the clue to Ruth to move on through her slides and end her presentation, but she chose to ignore it. Typically, it was the bellwether that indicated something was about to go seriously awry. In the past, when she overrode it, bad things happened for her. She might curse someone out. She might go off on a rant and find herself facing someone's shocked expression when she finally came back to herself. It was as if her eye was bionic and saw something coming that she couldn't see yet. It would try to signal her of trouble so that she could avoid it. Ruth opened her mouth as her eyelid began to spasm out of control.

"May I ask why you are so interested in my data? I mean, I know that you came to the session for a reason, but what is it about all of this," Ruth motioned to the screen, "that you feel a driving need to remember?" She stepped back, trying to regroup herself before it was too late. She noticed that the nodder had become wide awake and was staring at Ruth with large, round eyes.

"Why, Dr. Richards," the lady drawled in a thick Southern accent, "I have long been pursuing this same line of study in my own work! I was enthused to learn that you were presenting on this topic during the conference! Lawd knows, the world needs to hear this!" The woman paused and looked around. Her table mate was staring at her with an open mouth. The speaker turned back to Ruth and whispered, "It's a conspiracy, I tell you! I'm so glad that you have chosen to disrobe it!"

Ruth considered continuing the conversation, but decided that perhaps she had run into a level of craziness that superseded her own, so she returned to the slide show and resolutely completed her presentation. When it was over, she didn't say anything else to her attendees. The lady who had slept through most of the presentation asked Ruth to autograph her handout as she was leaving. Ruth scribbled something that looked like a childish drawing of a snake and then smiled at her, showing a toothy grimace. The lady smiled back happily and went out the door.

The other lady handed Ruth the stack of handouts that were still on the table. Ruth placed them back into her briefcase. She was starting to get a headache and really did not want to engage in any small talk. Yet, she thought she owed the lady something since she had shown interest in Ruth's work. "Yes?" she asked the lady, turning slightly to make eye contact before she turned her laptop off and began to pack it and the cords away.

"May I ask you a question, Dr. Richards?" The drawl was somewhat annoying to Ruth. It sounded too thick, too fake. Yet, Ruth tried to hide her distaste for the woman's accent in order to finish out these last few minutes of professional obligation.

"Yes, go ahead." Ruth was putting the last of her things into her briefcase and powering off the projection screen.

"Do you recall a Dr. Alfred Campbell at the state university? He taught sociology in the early nineties. He had done a lot of research on inter-racial relationships in America. Much of it had gone missing when he disappeared mysteriously and was later found dead in a cabin on Lake Wishakashee. He had been working very closely with a graduate assistant." The woman looked at Ruth's stunned face as she continued. "If I'm not mistaken," she drawled lazily, "her name was Ruth. Ruth Champion. Know her?"

Ruth had been the first of her family to attend a university. Her older brother had gone to a trade school and become an electrician. He had a license to do what her father and grandfather had done for years and taught him how to do. Everyone was so proud of him, and his accomplishments gave Ruth a lot of hope for her future.

Both of them were good students. When Ruth graduated from high school, she had earned straight A's all throughout her academic career, from elementary school through the twelfth grade. In her senior year of high school, the state had notified the university that they had to offer scholarships to students of color if they wanted to continue to receive the same level of state aid. Ruth's application and transcript arrived on the registrar's desk at just the right time! The registrar rushed it to the admissions advisor, who made copies and forwarded them to the scholarship advisor. Before Ruth knew it, or knew how, she had been invited to be a fully-scholarshipped student at state university in the fall.

She made the most of this gift of an opportunity. She excelled in her studies and was a model student for all of her professors. Dr. Campbell took a special liking to her. She was an excellent writer and her scholarship was impeccable. She enjoyed research and could be a hound when it came down to gathering data. Long hours in the university library were a picnic to Ruth.

Even though he was at least thirty years her senior, Ruth was enamored with Dr. Campbell! He reminded her of her father and her grandfather all rolled into one. He was brilliant, and his mind was what attracted her the most. She felt like she could sit at his feet and listen to him talk for days. Of course, he had no idea that she was infatuated with him. He believed that she was willing to sacrifice her social life to learn everything he could teach her. He began to welcome her into some of his projects, even some that were still just glimmering thoughts in his brilliant brain. One such glimmer was the topic that she had chosen to complete in her dissertation. When she had expressed her interest in helping with his research in the area of the theory of inherently racist practices to control the races in America, he handed her an old tattered satchel. In it was a collection of his notes spanning decades of reading, thinking, and writing.

The last time she saw him, he told her that he was going to go out of the country to do some research for a while. He had been doing work for the government in relation to the examination of a phenomenon which seemed to exist among the original people of America, the Native Americans, and the various initial treatises which the government had created to access lands on the eastern coast of the United States. Certain stipulations and clauses existed word for word in each of the fifteen original contracts, and it appeared that some were created at the same time and written by the same hand, prior to any recorded negotiations with tribal leaders and governmental officials. This had led to his work in uncovering what appeared to be conspiracies to cheat the Native American tribes out of their land from the very beginning. As word of his early work eked out, he received visits from current tribal leaders. Not long after, the trip out of the country was arranged by American government officials. Before he could leave the country, he was found dead in the cabin.

Ruth had been one of the first of his acquaintances to show up at his office once the local news station announced his apparent murder. She ended up being questioned many times by policemen, sheriff's officers, state attorneys, F.B.I. investigators, and a woman who identified herself as a C.I.A. agent. Ruth couldn't say why, but she never disclosed to any of them that Dr. Campbell had given her a satchel. She had thought nothing about it until the C.I.A. agent asked her a few times if she had ever received a packet from Dr. Campbell. Ruth didn't think anything about the notes in the satchel until a few days after that interview. She had gone back through the notes to see if anything in there looked suspicious or had any relevance to Native American contracts, but it was just full of notes about the work she later published as a dissertation to fulfill the requirements for her doctorate in philosophy.

It had been decades since anyone had even mentioned his name to her! She squinted at the woman, trying to see if she could recognize anything familiar about her. Had she been a research assistant, too? Why would she be asking now about Dr. Campbell? Had she resurrected his cold case murder and did she suspect that Ruth might be the killer? Ruth had never been fearful of anyone or anything. She decided to take the woman's challenge.

"I am Ruth Champion, or was. My last name is Richards, now. I'm a widow. Who are you?"

"Do you mean you don't remember me, Ruth? I'm Loralene, Dr. Campbell's secretary. We spent many a day in his dusty book room, poring through volume after volume, looking for research to support his whimsical fancies. I'm surprised you didn't recognize me."

"That's it!" Ruth thought. "I knew something about her looked familiar! But, that voice!" Ruth turned to Loralene and spoke defiantly. "It's been twenty years! And, if I recall correctly, you weren't from the Deep South back then, Miss Scarlett!" Ruth mocked Loralene's fake accent.

"So true!" Loralene exclaimed in her natural voice. "But, I couldn't take a chance on you recognizing me before I could make sure that it was you. I have spent years looking for you! Do you have a few minutes to talk?"

"Not really!" Ruth was angered that Loralene had tricked her in this way. Plus, what questions could Loralene ask that Ruth had not already answered? She was ready to go to her room, take an aspirin and a nap, and forget this day had ever happened. But, as she was turning she caught a glimpse of Loralene's disappointed expression. What would it hurt to give her a few minutes? Ruth changed her mind and sat down at the table. "Okay, Loralene. Five minutes, and then I'm gone. I don't recall us being that close as friends. The only thing we had in common was Dr. Campbell. He's dead now, and I'm supposing that they haven't found his killer, so you think it's me. You have come here with a microphone hidden in your lapel, you will coerce me into a confession, and then will have solved the crime of the century." Ruth began to clap slowly, ending her diatribe in a dramatic fashion.

"Yes, and no," Loralene responded, apparently unimpressed with Ruth's wit. "Yes, we had Dr. Campbell in common. No, they have not yet found his killer. I think I know who it is, though. That's why I needed your help. You were the only one, other than me, to talk with that person. I needed for you to recall, to the best of your ability, the exact phrasing of the question she asked you years ago."

Ruth was intrigued now. Who would have interviewed her who could also be Dr. Campbell's killer?

Loralene looked at Ruth and knew she had her hooked. She decided to continue. "The lady from the C.I.A. was actually a former colleague of Dr. Campbell's. They had done some summer research and had made a verbal agreement to collaborate on a book. Dr. Campbell had me do a lot of research for their project, so I had some slight knowledge of it. The lady was not always professional. Dr. Campbell told me later about some strange things she would say to him, and let me listen in on one phone call in which she thought he was someone else. She kept calling him 'Stanley' and alluding to something they had experienced together the night before. I knew where Dr. Campbell was that night before. We both had been working together late in his office. After that, I told him to end the agreement with her, pull his own work out, give her the manuscripts that related to her research, and call it all quits. He was somewhat amused by her unpredictability, though, so he chose to keep things going. He showed me a few letters she had written to 'Stanley' in which she declared her love for him and talked about their future together. Even in the letters, she would remind him of places they had gone and things that they had done, all events that could not have happened because Dr. Campbell would have calendar entries and meal receipts showing that he could not have been where she said they were.

Eventually, he became fearful of her instability and made a clean break from her. Now and then I would teasingly call him,'Stanley', but stopped when I saw how much it startled him one evening. I think he may have heard from her that day. Anyhow, he asked me to never do it again, and I didn't." She stopped and shuddered. "A few days later, he was found murdered. I think she did it. I think she called him to ask him to bring her something, even though I know he had returned all of her research. I'll bet he went to meet her at the cabin and she killed him, then tried to put it on the government or some European spies, or you." She turned to look at Ruth, "So, what did she ask you?"

"Ask me? I can't remember right now. I would have to think about that. I haven't thought about any of this for so long that I can't even remember what she looked like. Why, she could have been you, for all I know!" Ruth's frustration was beginning to grow. Something about all of this was very unsettling, and Ruth really was beginning to feel weary from the events of this afternoon. Loralene could see that she was slipping away.

"So," Loralene continued, "I took a chance on you being the same Ruth who used to work in our office. I decided to see if you would be willing to help me solve this mystery so that our dear doctor can finally rest in peace. There were no clues left at the crime scene. No fingerprints, no murder weapon. No motive. No suspect. Just a skull that had been bashed in with a heavy object. Poor Dr. Campbell!"

"Loralene," Ruth questioned, "why would that woman bash in his head over a few papers? History has supported what the two of them found. Native Americans have been suing the government for breach of contract for centuries. Have they gotten any wealthier for all of their efforts? The crime doesn't fit the punishment, in my opinion. In fact, I often wondered if maybe Dr. Campbell had a girlfriend, or was dating a married woman. He could be very engaging and his attention may have been construed as flirting by a jealous husband or a jealous girlfriend. But papers? I don't know." Ruth shook her head. "However, I must say that he introduced me to the paranoia of conspiracy theories. I do know that his work was socially challenging and probably did anger many people if they knew what he was researching. Still, I don't know why that would give anyone a reason to kill such a nice man."

Not only did Loralene's voice change as she turned to respond to Ruth. Her entire persona shifted to that of a small child. "You are so right, Miss Ruth, so right!" she exclaimed in a baby girl voice. "Oooh, he was a flirt! He played with my emotions time and time again! I asked him to stop, but he only laughed. He was soooo cruel! He made me sad. He hurt my feelings!" Loralene began to cry softly.

"What in the world?" thought Ruth, as she looked at Loralene. "This woman is nuts!" She almost reached over to pat Loralene on the head, and then thought about how only the two of them were left in the room. Possibly, they were the only two left in the conference area. Glancing at her watch, she realized that it was nearly an hour after the session had been scheduled to end. If she needed help, where would she go? As she was beginning to stand up, Loralene – or whoever she was – reached out and grasped her wrist, covering her watch. Her grip was tight, deadly. Her head was still down and she still appeared to be crying.

"Don't go," she snarled. "Don't leave me yet. He tried to leave me! All these years, I've been looking for you to tell you what kind of man he was. He would have hurt you. He would have used you like he used me. I couldn't let that happen." Loralene lifted her head. Her face looked dark, twisted into a grimace. She reached up and gripped Ruth's other wrist with her free hand, wrestling her down to the table. "You laughed with him at my letters, didn't you? I remember Stanley telling me about you. He said you were smart, smarter than I would ever be. He said the two of you laughed at me!"

As Loralene stood, pressing Ruth down on the table, she began to panic. She wanted to scream, but her own fists were pressing down on her throat. Loralene appeared to be out of her mind. She climbed on the table and straddled Ruth's upper stomach, cutting off her breath. Ruth began to pray, "Please God, please send somebody by to help me right now!" Loralene continued talking.

"He brought a bag of trash, newspapers and old food wrappers. He brought a bottle of wine. He said these were the rest of my papers. We would drink to the end of our partnership and never see each other again. Part as friends, he claimed. How could we be friends?" she raged, turning red and sweating. Sweat drops and spittle were falling from her face and mouth and dropping into Ruth's eyes and face. Her eyes began to burn and Ruth began to cry silently. "So, I broke the wine bottle over his head. It knocked him out, but I knew he would wake up. I took a log from the woodpile and bashed his head in! I was a good researcher, and a good cleaner of facts. I cleaned everything up. The police never found anything. But, I thought he had given you something. I know you knew it was me who killed him. Why didn't you tell anyone? Were you going to wait and blackmail me to pay you to cover up my crime? Were you? I'll just kill you now!"

Loralene pressed so hard on Ruth's throat that Ruth could not move or breathe anymore. She felt her headache slowly drifting away. She felt ropes dropping on her face, then someone beating on her chest. She was drowning now, and a deep fog settled over her like a thick down blanket. Finally, peace.

Ruth woke up. She looked around. Everything seemed blue and hazy. Her head was throbbing, but her thoughts were a blur. Was this Heaven? She could only hope so. She heard voices, someone saying, "Here she is!" She thought maybe it was the angels announcing her entrance into the pearly gates. She began to smile, and then fell asleep again. Seconds later, she started to rouse again. New voices, lots of jabbering. "Heaven must be a busy place," she thought. "Lots of different languages, different tongues. Or, maybe this is how they talk here. They used to say we would see Peter and Paul walking down the golden street in Heaven! Why can't I see anybody?" Again, she drifted back to sleep.

Ruth felt someone patting her hand, and then patting her cheek. The headache was gone. She felt some scratchiness in her throat and tried to swallow. It hurt a lot. Her eyelids felt very heavy and her chest was hurting. This didn't feel like Heaven anymore. Her face felt hot and her eyes were burning. She tried to pry them open, but they did not want to cooperate. She could hear a lot of noises like buzzing and bells ringing. She wanted to wake up badly. She stirred herself, tried to shake herself, but her body felt stiff and a little sore. "Open your eyes," she could hear someone say, or maybe she was saying it to herself. "Open your eyes. Open your eyes!" Ruth's eyes labored to open in slow motion. She looked around her. She didn't recognize anything, and none of it looked like pearly gates or streets of gold. When her eyes rolled to the left, she saw the boy with the dreadlocks and the cell phone. "Oh no," she thought, "here we go again!" Ruth closed her eyes tight.

The following morning, she had a long conversation with the young man. He was a federal detective. He had been tracing Dr. Jocelyn Cameron, aka Loralene, for the three years that he had been assigned to the case of Dr. Campbell's murder. There were some details he could not disclose, he told Ruth, but he had tracked her to the conference, knowing her intent to harm Ruth. The government had many leads and suspicions that Jocelyn Cameron had killed Dr. Campbell, but they had no hard evidence and certainly no confession. She had done an exceptional job of cleaning up the crime scene. But, her mental instability had disclosed a chink in her story, so they had picked that thread and followed it to Ruth's session. He had left when he was sure that at least one of the women in attendance was Jocelyn. He was never far away while Jocelyn was struggling with Ruth, but he couldn't rescue her until he had recorded Jocelyn's confession. He had stepped in right on time to handcuff Jocelyn, resuscitate Ruth, call for backup and for emergency assistance, and get Ruth to the hospital. Lack of oxygen to her brain had kept her in a coma for a day, but the hospital staff said she would be fine. Was there anything else he could do for her?

Ruth's head was spinning. What in the world had happened in the last forty-eight hours? It was going to take her a while to sift through this. But, at least she was alive to start the process toward sorting out her life.

"What's your name, young man? I really do owe you my gratitude. You saved my life!" Ruth's throat was still hurting, she began coughing.

"Don't worry about thanking me, Dr. Richards. Thank Jocelyn. She helped in her own capture!" He laughed. "But, I'm Cliff." He winked. "At least today I am. In my job, I could be Tom, Dick, or Harry any day of the week!" He laughed.

Ruth tried to sit herself up in the bed as she weakly joined in his laughter. "Well, I don't care who you are! You could be Bob Marley for all it's worth! You were right on time to keep her from taking me out of here." She looked at him seriously. "Thank you so much, son. I didn't think much of you when I first saw you in the session and then in the hallway. You were all into that cell phone! I was genuinely offended." Ruth rolled her eyes at him, and gave a sideways smile.

Jeff laughed loudly. "Well, Dr. Richards, you should thank the Good Lord today for this cell phone. It is actually a microphone, a tracking device, and a surveillance camera system. I could monitor Jocelyn's every movement while I was out of the room. That is how I was alerted to come down when she climbed on top of you and started choking you. She might have looked like an old woman, but she is really not that much older than you."

"No wonder she was so spry!" Ruth exclaimed. "I kept thinking that it made no sense that a lady that old could hold me down so hard. I couldn't move! I couldn't even scream for help! She must have known some kind of Asian war moves that immobilized me. I never would imagine that having someone grip my wrists would disable me in such an impactful way! But, it did!"

"Trust me," Jeff assured her, "I have been following this woman for years! She has some slick tricks! But, her show ends when the judge's gavel lands. I'll stay in touch with you to let you know how we will escort you to court for your testimony. Even though I have the recording," he waved his cell phone at her, "your personal witness will seal the deal."

"I am so glad to do whatever I can to help put her behind bars for a long time. I feel sorry for her, though. She needs some help." Jeff nodded in agreement. Ruth continued, "Jeff, please tell me something. I remember some ropes on my face. Was she trying to tie me up, too?"

"Ropes?" Jeff looked a little puzzled. He ran his fingers through his dreadlocks. He had a thought. "Did they feel like this?" He moved closer and lifted her hand to his hair.

Ruth rubbed it on her face. "Yes! I think they did!"

"Ah!" Jeff said, as he lifted his head and smiled. "That was me giving you mouth to mouth resuscitation!"

Ruth looked relieved and then smiled. "Mystery solved!" she exclaimed, then turned her face up toward Jeff, looking a little mischievous. "Well, one good thing came out of all of this! I got kissed by an angel with dreadlocks!"

Take Me To The Water To Be Baptized

"If thou faint in the day of adversity, thy strength is small."
Proverbs 24:10

*

Phyllis could not remember when she began collecting giraffes. She must have been a small child, maybe around nine or ten. The oldest giraffe in her collection was a tiny glass model that was amber and still had an iridescent glaze that looked like a shimmering rainbow when the sun shone on it from the right angle. She kept it in a cherry wood and glass showcase that she had picked up at a garage sale when she was in her twenties. From that first purchase, though, had grown a large collection. At last count, she had more than two hundred giraffes. Some were on her walls, others on tables, mantelpieces, and counters. In fact, there was not a single place in her home where a giraffe was not situated.

Phyllis had not yet figured out why she had such an extreme fascination with these long-necked animals. She knew that she could spend hours on end at the zoo, standing patiently in front of the giraffe habitat, watching them eat and socialize. They were calm and regal. They could use what they had, those long necks, to get whatever they needed. They were uniform in color. All of them got along. They never fought. They didn't have tantrums. They represented great beauty and composure. They were everything she wished she could be.

Since she couldn't do anything else as a child, she decided to surround herself with these positive role models. Even at an early age, she knew that her situation was not healthy and if something within her did not change, she would not end up well. So, giraffes became not only her constant companions, but also her consistent inspiration.

Some of her friends were concerned about what they described as her hoarder tendencies. She didn't see it that way. The giraffes were well organized. Smaller ones were in the bathrooms and all over the kitchen counters. Most of those were seven inches tall or shorter. Those between seven inches and a foot in height were in the guest bedroom. The rest were equally distributed throughout the living room and the dining room, her master bedroom, and the hallways. She had four giraffes that were each eight feet high! She had purchased one from a street vendor one day when she was out and about. It was leather and had cost her close to $300. She had bargained him down from $500, though, so she had felt very excited about that purchase. Another of the tall ones she found at a thrift store. It was iron and sculpted from overlaid rectangular metal strips. She loved to rub its neck. It felt scratchy and smooth at the same time. The final pair of eight-footers was a matching bronze set and a gift from a former gentleman friend.

People never asked her what she wanted for her birthday – they already knew. Her response since she was a child was always, "A giraffe!" Around town, she was known as a shrewd realtor, a savvy business negotiator who could get you what you wanted, where you wanted it, at the best price. But, local merchants also knew her as "the giraffe lady". So be it. Phyllis didn't mind. In fact, it was a compliment. To be associated with such elegant animals was to place her in cherished company.

"Phyllis, Mr. Bolden called again. He is really anxious to meet you at that property today. Are you sure you can't make it?" Her secretary, Kim, had called and left another message. Phyllis knew why she was calling. It was bad business practice to avoid a customer, but she didn't feel comfortable meeting this gentleman alone. He had been very aggressive about setting up a visit to a remote property that she had just picked up. She couldn't quite put her finger on it, but something had not seemed right about his tactics.

The lister had signed his contract with her to handle the property on a Wednesday morning. Before she could even advertise the site under her name, Mr. Will Bolden had called her on her cell phone to inquire about a viewing. He had quick responses to her questions. He knew the lister. He had called him to get her number. He was extremely interested in the property. He wanted to meet her at the site that evening. She had told him that she was already obligated until far into the night, but she would call him on Thursday morning to set something up.

After she hung up the phone, her mind began racing. If he knew the lister, why hadn't he seen the property before it was listed since he was so anxious to view it? Didn't the lister know that he was to allow her to handle the clients who wanted to see the property? Why would he just give out her cell number? And, if Mr. Bolden was his friend, why didn't he tell Phyllis that he had an interested buyer when they began their contract? Too many details related to Mr. Bolden unnerved her, and she wasn't about to recklessly run out to meet with him without having some of her questions answered.

For years, Phyllis had maintained a ritual of reading a chapter in her Bible before she went to sleep every night. There were many times when she would read something that would relate to an issue that was facing her. After Kim's call, maintaining professionalism and serving her client versus giving in to fear and avoiding Mr. Bolden had continued to plague her throughout the day. She couldn't continue to avoid a potential sale. She would have to figure out what she would say when she called Mr. Bolden back tomorrow. She was reading from the second book of the Kings currently. The chapter she read, the nineteenth chapter, was about a time when Israel was threatened with war. God reminded them that He was with them to help them overcome the enemy. She fell asleep with that thought prominent in her mind.

Gary had acquired the property from a friend who needed some quick money. He had given Gary the deed in exchange for ten thousand dollars cash. Gary was glad to make that deal, since he knew he would make twenty times that much by selling it. There was a nice house on the property that was worth at least eighty thousand. The land itself was prime construction property and would sell for at least one hundred thousand without a structure on it. There was a barn and a storage shed, which only added to the value. Gary would earn a lucrative return on his modest investment, and Phyllis would also earn a healthy fee for her services.

So, why was she tripping? She woke up with a headache. Still, she knew she had a professional obligation to fulfill, so she called Mr. Bolden at nine o'clock on the dot.

"Good morning, Mr. Bolden! This is Phyllis Ingram, returning your call. I understand that you are interested in visiting the property on East Orange Road?" She paused, noticing that her voice sounded too bright, too enthusiastic. She sounded fake. Did he notice her nervousness?

If he did, his response did not register it. In fact, he sounded very reassuring and comforting; almost therapeutic.

"Ms. Ingram? Thank you so much for calling me back. I was worried that I would not have an opportunity to visit with you before I left town! My flight is scheduled for five o'clock this evening. I was afraid that I would have to take a chance that the property would still be available when I come back to town next month. But, my experience told me that was a long shot! So, I'm glad that you were able to call."

"I'm so sorry that I couldn't meet with you yesterday, but I can arrange to be out there as soon as it is convenient for you!" Phyllis was mentally berating herself for being fearful and nearly missing a seemingly sure sale. He sounded as if he had already made up his mind to purchase the property. She wondered if he was a developer. If so, price may not be an object and her client would be able to negotiate a good return on his investment. Mr. Bolden's words interrupted her thoughts.

"I could leave now and head that way," he said. "Would that work for you? Would you also be able to bring some paperwork so that we can work up some numbers and save me a little time?"

"Of course!" Phyllis exclaimed. "I will plan to see you at 9:45, and I will bring a contract with me."

"Great," said Mr. Bolden, "and I'll have two cups of coffee with me. Sugar or cream?"

Phyllis laughed. "How about a little of both?"

"Got it!" he said.

Phyllis thought that she should have asked him to bring three cups of coffee, as she had been toying with the idea of inviting Kim to ride along with her. But, she figured that he was a business man, so there should not be anything for her to be fearful about. Plus, she read that scripture last night that said God told the children of Israel that He would take care of their enemies, so they had nothing to fear. "But, they did have enemies," she thought, "and there was about to be a fight."

Phyllis decided to call Kim and let her know where she was going. Feeling a little stupid, she joked anyway, "If I'm not at the office by eleven o'clock, send the sheriff out to check on me!" Kim had asked her if everything was okay, and Phyllis had responded that she was just excited about making some money so that she could buy some more giraffes. Kim told her to be careful and not spend her money before she earned it. They both laughed and Phyllis hung up, then started toward the highway.

The morning was bright and warm. The sun was shining hard on Phyllis' arm. Glancing down on the brown skin with blonde hairs standing up straight at attention to the commanding sunshine, Phyllis thought of how her own coloring reminded her of giraffes. In fact, she realized that her great-grandfather had looked a lot like a giraffe. He was the color of sand with butterscotch freckles. His hair was ruddy and patchy, like a giraffe's mane. He was tall and lanky, with long swinging arms. His hands were large and smooth. They were dotted with something her mother called "liver spots", but they looked like polka-dot skin decorations to her as a small child. She loved to hold his hand and rub his "spots" when he was resting. He had a big, false-toothy smile and often looked as if he were happy but didn't know why.

In Phyllis' early years, he would be prominent in the house, sitting on the porch, walking up and down the street, relaxing in the kitchen, but never saying much. As she got older, he disappeared from the main part of the home. He stayed in an upstairs bedroom most of the time. Now and then, her mother would have Phyllis come up to help her with some task related to his care. That is when she would see him sitting tall in his bed, a white sheet draped across his lap, long arms dangling off the sides of the bed, smiling at her.

One day when Phyllis came home from school, she noticed that the house was very quiet and her mother was sitting in the kitchen with some papers on the table, her hands folded as if she were praying. The telephone was beside her. Phyllis knew right away that something had happened. Her mother turned to greet her, gave her a hug, and said that great-grandpa was dead.

What Phyllis did not know was that she and her parents were dependent on the care her mother gave to her great-grandfather to provide for their existence. The house they lived in was his. The money that provided for their food, utilities, and maintenance was his. Without him to care for, they would have no place to live and would have to manage off of her father's meager earnings. Her parents would need to figure out what they would do now in order to survive.

The plan that her parents devised led to changes that affected Phyllis' life to that day. She thought about the day when she was ten and had to go live with her mother's friend, a lady she called Aunt Nettie. Great-grandfather's assets had allegedly been misappropriated. His estranged son had filed charges against her parents. They were convicted and sent to prison. She was basically now an orphan.

Driving down the county road, Phyllis thought about the day that Aunt Nettie sat with her in court as her mother was escorted out of the courtroom to prison. Phyllis cried, but she was not hysterical. She was confused. How could so much disruption happen in such a short period of time? Her young mind could not process it all, but she knew that things would never again be the same, even after her mother was released in ten years for good behavior. By then, the damage had been done and the past could not be changed. But, on that day, Aunt Nettie had felt so sorry for her that she had given her ten dollars, which was a lot of money back then.

They were in an antique mall. Aunt Nettie was an avid thrift store shopper, and often used that for therapy when she needed to cheer herself up. As she resolutely followed Aunt Nettie up and down the aisles from tiny booth to tiny booth, something caught her eye. It was the way the light shined on an object made of amber glass. Looking at her arm again, she realized that it was the same color as her arm with the same blonde highlights. The little giraffe had captured her attention and implanted itself in her spirit. She had to have it! Aunt Nettie told her she could spend her ten dollars any way she wanted, so she bought her first giraffe. It was so special and made her feel so good on the worst day of her life that whenever she needed a pick-me-up in the future, she would either buy a giraffe or visit the zoo and see one or more.

Considering her large collection, she mused, "I must have needed a lot of pick-me-ups in my lifetime!" Phyllis chuckled. "Oh well, they are beautiful and have so much character. If that is what depression brings me, I welcome it!" Back to reality, Phyllis realized that she was about two miles from the property. She did a mental check on everything she would need to seal this deal today. "I think I've got it!" she reassured herself.

About a mile from the site, Phyllis noticed something she hadn't seen before. Typically, the gray-green foaming ocean on the north side of the road captured her attention. The rocks standing tall in the dashing waves, solid and strong, reminded her of her great-grandfather. But today, there on the south side of the road, she noticed an old barn with what looked like a lot of junk on the outside. At second glance, though, she saw some items that were leftovers from a garage sale. There was a big sign out front, "Big Sale Today!" She made a mental note to stop by on her way back to town. Some of the stuff looked antique and very interesting. Suddenly, something caught her eye. A large, wrought iron giraffe was standing in the yard. It had to be ten feet tall. She just knew it would look heavenly in her garden, right next to her favorite chaise and perfect beside her flower bed. What a surprise it would be to anyone who was in her garden! What a great look it would provide from her back porch, so cozy and adding so much to the setting! It even looked like her! She could imagine herself getting lost in the atmosphere it would help to create so she could enjoy life even more.

Phyllis glanced at her watch. She knew she was less than five minutes away from the site. She had told him that she would meet him at 9:45. It was 9:27. If she hurried, she could at least look at it and then have them hold it for her to purchase on her way back to town. She had to have it!

Fifteen minutes later, she was flying down the road. She had a reputation for being on time, if not early, for every appointment. She regretted leaving herself so little time to get to the property, but she was so glad she had stopped. Not only were they willing to deliver her new giraffe that afternoon, but she was shown two small solid brass giraffes that she had purchased on the spot. She thought she might have some similar to them, but these looked very unique to her. She patted them inside her purse on the seat beside her as she turned up the long drive and approached the house that sat in the middle of the property.

Will did his best to hide his frustration. He had things to do, a flight to catch. She wasn't supposed to be late. He was not prepared to have to wait for her. Where was she? Just as he was beginning to feel real nervousness, he saw dust on the road. He looked at his watch. It was 9:45. He figured he could count that as on time. But, it was too close for comfort. As she parked her car and walked toward his, he reviewed his plan. He could see her as she approached him in his rearview mirror. She was very tall, much taller than he expected. She walked with confidence. She looked like she was very strong. He wondered if she worked out on a regular basis. She carried a purse over one shoulder and had her portfolio in the other hand. She looked like she was ready to take care of business. So was he.

Will stepped out of his car and turned to greet her, extending his hand and introducing himself. "Good morning, Ms. Ingram! I see you are right on time! Your coffee is nice and hot, even though it's pretty hot out here this morning to be drinking coffee!" Will waved his arm in an arc, and smiled at Phyllis as he did so. She noticed his pretty white teeth that almost looked fake. That made her think again of her great-grandfather.

She shook her head and laughed. "Well, let's go inside and see if it's cooler in there!" She went ahead of Will to open the doors while he ducked back into his car to get both cups of coffee. Following her inside the house, which was nice and cool, he sat down across from her at the large oak table in the kitchen. They sipped their coffee as they reviewed the property specifications. Phyllis noticed that his hands were extremely neat and manicured. They looked like advertisement models. She was not used to seeing such flawless hands on a man, not that she was that used to being impressed by any features on any man. He seemed nice, but very business-focused. He wasn't as much interested in the house and other property structures as he was the land value. She wondered if he knew something about the land that she did not. She provided him with the disclosures and sat back to see what he would say.

"As I mentioned to you this morning, I have a flight to catch tonight. I don't like to rush when it comes to spending my money, but I do have to take care of some other business tomorrow so I wanted to wrap this up as much as possible today." Will looked at her with a skeptical eye. "I hope that you are able to take care of things on this end for me."

"My credentials are excellent, Mr. Bolden. If you decide that you want this property, I will do everything necessary to wrap up the deal for you quickly. Do you have an offer that I can take back to my client today?" Phyllis was more than a little irritated that he seemed to question her professionalism. No wonder the thought of working with him had made her uncomfortable yesterday. She must have had a feeling about his attitude. Still, she knew she had to close this deal.

"Yes, I have an offer, but it's not for your client. It's for you." Mr. Bolden moved toward her with his hand in his pocket. Phyllis was feeling confused and somewhat fearful.

"What are you talking about, Mr. Bolden? I'm not selling this property, but I am representing the seller. If there is something about this transaction that will become unethical, I must excuse myself at this point." Phyllis walked toward the door and opened it wide. She stepped outside and waited for Mr. Bolden to follow. He remained in the kitchen.

Phyllis began to regret that she had not brought Kim with her. Mr. Bolden did not look like a serial killer, but then most of them didn't look harmful. She began to imagine herself chopped up and left in the kitchen sink. The sheriff would find her when he arrived around noon after getting a call from Kim. Phyllis thought that she should probably just leave him in the house, head straight for her car, and get out of there as soon as possible. Suddenly, Mr. Bolden spoke.

"Cousin Phyllis, you don't know me, but I remember you. I remember the day you left the courtroom with Aunt Nettie."

Phyllis turned around to look at Mr. Bolden. She didn't recognize him in any way. But, how could he have known about Aunt Nettie? She hadn't told anyone in this town about her, and Aunt Nettie had been dead long before she had relocated. Puzzled, but curious, she asked, "Who are you? How do you know Aunt Nettie? How is it that we are related?"

"I know there are so many questions that I am going to have to answer, Cousin Phyllis. It's been a long time, and I am trying to clean up a large mess that my father created. But, I was determined to do my best to make things right, and you are close to the end of my list of tasks."

"I'm a task?" Phyllis laughed. "I've been called a mess, a puzzle, a bore – but never a task! I don't know you and I don't recall ever seeing you in my life! I don't trust you. Something about you and this meeting had me very nervous. You could be some kind of serial killer, I don't know. But, I tell you what. I'll hear you out, but I'm going to stand out here and you will stand in there and explain to me how you know Aunt Nettie." Phyllis stood in the doorway with her hand on her hip. Her elbow bumped the heavy giraffes in her purse and she nodded. She knew she had at least two weapons if she needed them. She could swing her purse around and hit him in the head if he approached her aggressively. Then, she could run to her car and drive to the barn where they were having the sale. They could call the sheriff for her and he would find himself waking up in jail before he knew it. Knowing that she had an advantage that he was not aware of made her willing to stay and hear him out, if he really had something of substance to tell her.

"Thank you for that, Phyllis. I don't think you will regret it. You see, my father is John Lawson. He was the sole heir to the estate that your great-grandfather, Arthur Lawson, Sr. left. When Arthur died, both of my father's parents were dead. My father had lived in a number of places for many years. He liked to travel and spend his grandfather's and parents' money. His parents had died in a plane accident when he was a teenager. He had stayed with Aunt Nettie that summer and had not been on the plane when it went down as his father was piloting it. He was so angry with himself for not being there with them that he spent most of his life taking his anger out on others. My mother. Me. Aunt Nettie. He blamed us all for something God had chosen to do. He had stopped speaking to Aunt Nettie after his parents' funeral and had left to live on his own at the age of seventeen. He had the money and the social connections, so he made it work. This hurt Aunt Nettie immensely. She forgave him, but told me later that she could hardly bear to speak his name, it still hurt her so much. If she never told you about him, that was probably why.

My mother was a good friend to your mother when they were

teenagers. She knew that my father had set up her and your father to take care of his grandfather, but then had accused them of mismanaging his funds and stealing from him. My father knew that none of those allegations were true. Yet, he ruined three lives with his lies. That was intolerable. My mother and I had come to court to support your mother and even to take you to live with us if need be. But, my father had paid his attorneys to make sure the case was air tight, and Aunt Nettie had already decided that she would soften your loss by making sure you had her love."

Phyllis felt her knees getting weak as Will was talking. How could this have happened? Why didn't she know already? Was she still dreaming? She walked toward the house to lean on the door jamb. The heat was getting to her and she felt nauseous. She needed some cool air, but she still didn't totally trust Will. Why hadn't he just called to tell her this? Why bring her out to some remote property to fill in the blanks in her life story? "If this is true, why go through all of this drama to tell me this?"

Will reached out his hand to her. She did not take it. He dropped it to his side, sat down in the chair, and continued. "I had to see you personally to know that it was you before I could share the essence of my visit. I knew that I would recognize you, your freckles, your height, your coloring. Do you wonder why I am the only known heir to Arthur's estate? Why your mother and father could not claim benefits? He was your great-grandfather. That means that one of your parents should have been his grandchild. But, they weren't. Do you know why, Phyllis?"

Phyllis realized at that point that this issue was something she had thought about a little when she was younger. Was Arthur really her great-grandfather? Had they just had her call him that out of respect because they lived in his home, even though he was no real relation? But, how could they explain how she could share so many of his physical features if they weren't related?

It was as if Will was reading her thoughts. "Phyllis, we're not really cousins. You are my younger sister."

Phyllis felt herself collapse in the doorway. What was happening to her? Her life was dissolving before her eyes. Everything that she knew or thought she knew about herself and her family suddenly seemed like a dead log floating down a stream, passing by and not worth recovering. "What are you talking about, Mr. Bolden? Please stop! This is a cruel joke, and I don't feel very accommodating right now!"

Will got up from his chair and walked over to her. He took her by the arm, lifted her to her feet, and walked her over to the table. She sat down and laid her purse heavily at her feet. Now, she knew why she didn't trust him. He had not been honest. He had not had the courtesy to warn her that he was on a mission to disrupt her life at 9:45 in the morning. That was not fair of him, she thought.

"I'm sorry, Phyllis," he said, sitting down across from her. "I'm sorry about how this has played out, but it is very important that I tell you what I came here to share. My name is William, but my last name is not Bolden. It is Lawson. I was afraid you might recognize it as Arthur's last name. I need to let you know that my father was not a very ethical man. He had hired your mother to care for his grandfather before you were born. It was a beneficial situation for your father, as well. He could provide a good life for your mother without having to work very hard. What your father did not realize was that my father was scheming all along to take advantage of your mother. Plus, he had knowledge of some of your father's struggles, which he used later to blackmail him to keep quiet when my father forced himself on your mother and created you. A child born from what was very close to rape could not be considered a legitimate member of the Lawson bloodline, so your father was paid well to accept things as they were, and your mother was promised a large compensation for what my father had forced her to do. All of this came out when my father died and I was left with a huge fortune and an even larger attack of guilty conscience. I had to make things right."

Will paused and looked hard at Phyllis. There was no denying that she was a Lawson. He just had to convince her to not be the one to deny him the right to do what he knew he must before he left town that day. "Phyllis, even though our great-grandfather lived modestly, he left us – you and me – an extremely large fortune. Millions. He had made investments, owned property all over the world, and had a portfolio full of valuable possessions. This is more money than either of us will spend in our lifetimes. But, there is no way I can rest comfortably knowing that you do not have your share. So, I came to town to find you and make things right. I hope you will allow me to complete my mission."

Phyllis studied hard the brother she never knew she had. The story was hard to believe, but it was believable. She could see in herself the resemblance to the Lawson family, and she had always known that there was an extremely close affinity with Arthur Lawson. She now knew why she loved giraffes. They were the epitome of her great-grandfather's appearance and character. They were her one connection to her family that she never really knew.

"Millions? We, I, have millions of dollars? Why, I can hardly believe any of this! And, you want to share it? You would come all the way here to give me money?"

"Yes," said Will, "it is hard to believe. But, what would it profit me to have all of this money and lose my soul due to my selfishness? Besides, it doesn't mean anything if I can't have a relationship with the only other blood relative I have left in this world." He extended his hand again to Phyllis. "I would rather know that you respect and one day hopefully love me than to sit in a room full of money every day for the rest of my life."

This time, Phyllis took his extended hand. "I want you to know that right now, I am in a state of utter shock. I really think that I am still asleep and will wake up at some point with a smile on my face, happy to know that I at least dreamed that I had a brother and millions of dollars." Phyllis laughed and Will smiled and squeezed her hand. "But, if this is not a dream and I really am your sister, plus a millionaire, I just want to say right now that I don't have to ever again buy another giraffe!"

Will looked at her with a questioning face, and Phyllis began to laugh out loud. Soon, he joined in, even though he was not sure why. Her laughter was so contagious, though, that he couldn't help it. "Why? Why? Why?" he asked, in between his puzzled bouts of laughter.

"Why?" she replied. "Well, because I will never be depressed again!" Phyllis lifted herself from her chair and walked to Will and embraced him. "Come on, Big Brother, let's go. If you want this property, I'll buy it for you. I just came into a little money," she winked at him with a smile, "and I'd like to do something nice for someone with it. Plus," she continued, "I'm ready for something more than coffee. I'm ready for life!"

As Phyllis locked the door of the house, she turned sideways to where Will was standing behind her. "Say, Brother, do you think you have a few minutes to visit the zoo with me? I'd like for you to see where they will build the Lawson Giraffe Habitat. It might cost a few million, but I think I have that to spare." She smiled as she took his arm.

"I'd love to," Will said. "They are beautiful animals." He stepped back to look at her. "In fact, you remind me of a giraffe."

Phyllis hugged him hard and then whispered, "Thank you, Brother. That is the most wonderful compliment I have ever received in my whole life!" She wiped a tear as she released him, and breathed a prayer of thanks for the miracle that God had shown to her. A generational giant of a fight won without breaking a sweat! Walking to her car, arm in arm with her brother, she felt ten feet tall!

Jordan River is Muddy and Cold

"A word fitly spoken is like apples of gold in pictures of silver." Proverbs 25:11

*

"Roy! Come in, Roy!"

"I don't want to come in!" Roy thought, but he said, "Yeah, go ahead, Joe."

"Roy, we have a couple who had a flight scheduled for 1400 hours. You coming?"

"On my way, Joe!" Roy's voice had a sharp edge to it. He hoped it sounded more professional than irritated. He had started this business to be his own boss, not to have private bookers and old couples with helicopter rides on their bucket list bossing him around. The sky was clear, hardly a cloud in sight. This was the kind of day he loved, one that made him remember why he chose to be a pilot in the first place. Now, these demanding old people with a time-stamped ticket were ruining it all for him. Making a sharp left turn, he headed back toward the copter pad.

Roy had spent the last seven years of his life trying to literally get his helicopter business off of the ground. He had started by providing delivery services for businesses that wanted their products to move faster than they would with ground service. That went well for a while, but he did miss a few time deadlines. So, when that business slowed, he decided to advertise to give flight training in his helicopter. He figured he could charge enough to pay his fuel bill and his hangar fee. He got a few calls, fielded some questions, but no one ever followed through on the lessons. He had tried to be cordial and patient, but answering questions like, "How soon can I get behind the wheel?" made him want to hang up the phone. So, he did.

Six months ago he decided to give helicopter rides. Up to two people could pay fifty dollars to get a thirty-minute ride over the city and the ocean. That business took off immediately. He contracted with the ferry boat attendant to book his flights. He had a pad down by the main dock where he picked up his riders. They paid the attendant, who scheduled the rides and kept the riders entertained until their turn came along. Roy collected the proceeds at the end of the day and then gave the attendant his share, plus a tip. Before long, Roy realized that he was building a pretty profitable business.

Some of his favorite rides occurred after the sun went down. The sky was black velvet, studded with rhinestone stars. The city lights looked like flickering candles on a birthday cake. The water was calm and shimmered under the rush of air that came from the downdraft of the propellers. He felt like the king of the world. Everything was under his feet.

Roy needed to feel like he was in control all of the time. That had been a problem in his life. He had a hard time in relationships. Give and take was not a function that worked well for him. He was a kind man, and extremely intellectual. He had a powerful mind. He saw multiple perspectives within his own reasoning. Often, he would outthink himself. But, his own conclusions were the last word for him. It was difficult to sway him when he made up his mind, and that was a challenge for any woman who needed to feel like she could be his intellectual match, if only for the length of a conversation.

Roy found it very difficult to allow himself to be approachable for any woman. He was very attractive and exuded pheromones like a cloudburst releases a midday shower. Tall, beautifully brown-skinned and muscular, he could have easily had a successful career as a model. But, he was just a former high school and college athlete who had earned a degree playing basketball on scholarship, then joined the Air Force to complete his career as a commissioned officer and hopefully retire from the military in about twenty years.

But, as often happens, things did not go as planned. Two major battle injuries in the Gulf War left him disabled. What didn't show up on the outside had left plenty of evidence on the inside. He lost his nerve for battle. Try as he might, he could not gear himself up to get back in the air for a fight. On the day that he looked like he might harm others by aborting a flight, he applied for a furlough. A merciful doctor examined his knees where he had four steel plates and dozens of screws from the crash that had broken both of his legs in multiple places. The same doctor then examined his brain which had suffered traumatic stress. The doctor wrote a recommendation that he should receive a medical discharge and exit the military honorably with full benefits.

Transitioning to civilian life was quite a challenge for him. Losing his nerve affected him in every area. He had little confidence and therefore had a hard time devising a concrete plan for supporting himself. He had very little success in his first few jobs because he didn't want anyone telling him what to do. He preferred to walk away rather than yield to the direction of someone less intelligent than him. That was an insult.

Later, he realized that it was easier to eat insults than it was to eat nothing. So, he vowed to do what he needed to in order to survive. Menial jobs became a means to stability. Once he realized that intellect had little to do with a paycheck, he began to apply for, and be hired to do, jobs that matched his skill level. He got a real break when the airport hired him to service the small cargo planes. Financially, this was a breakthrough. He was earning good income and compiled a nice nest egg. He started to dream. He wanted to buy his own helicopter and beat the fear that threatened to control his life. That was something he couldn't allow to happen. He had to be in control.

So, that is why he had a hard time allowing a relationship to start. Women were attracted to him, but they wanted to be the ones to control how the conversation started, how they approached him, how they summed up his value. He was selective and exclusionary, but he looked out for himself first. He was a survivalist. He hid his vulnerability underneath a scowl and a slouch. He couldn't stand the thought of losing his nerve, or himself, ever again.

He dropped the copter on the pad and shifted his hat bill from the back to the front. He liked to look professional, even though his job was more pleasure than business. Turning off the ignition, he stepped out of the door and headed to the office. As his eyes shifted to focus in the dimness of the shaded inside, he saw Joe talking to two women who were seated at the bar sipping an afternoon drink. One looked like she was enamored with Joe's stale jokes. She was smiling up at him with her mouth hanging open, awaiting the delivery of his next well-practiced punch line. The other one looked mad and bored. She glared at Roy as he approached.

"Is he the pilot?" she asked Joe in a disgusted tone. Roy was surprised that she would be so insulting toward the man who was about to take her fifteen thousand feet into the air. He walked toward her with his hand extended.

"Good afternoon," he said bowing slightly. "I'm Roy. Ready to ride a grasshopper?" He smiled a big, corny smile. He wanted her to know that she couldn't shake him with her rotten mood.

"Umph!" she responded and stood up, placing her hand on her hip.

"Okay…" Roy continued as he turned to extend his unaccepted hand to her friend. She stood up tall and smiled, admiring Roy's warm smile and shaking his hand.

"Hi, Roy! I'm Shirleen! We are so excited about going up with you today! We wanted to get in some sightseeing and figured that a helicopter flight would be the best way to do it…" Turning to the other lady, Shirleen asked, "Carrie, are you ready to go?"

"Been ready!" Carrie exclaimed, scowling at Roy. Her frustration at the inconvenience of waiting a few minutes for him to arrive was obvious.

"Then, let's go! Joe, did you take care of the business?" Roy usually didn't discuss the fee in front of clients, but this lady was really getting on his nerves. He wanted her to know that he didn't think too much of her right now, either.

Joe looked at him with a puzzled look. Roy immediately wished that he hadn't said that. It made him seem unprofessional. But, Carrie acted as if she hadn't heard a thing and Shirleen was still gazing at Joe with puppy dog eyes. Roy jiggled his keys and nodded his head at Joe to signal that everything was okay. He decided to be a gentleman.

"Let's go, ladies," he continued in a softer voice. He opened the office door and waited for them to exit before he followed.

As the three of them loaded into the copter, Carrie in the back and Shirleen and Roy occupying the front seats, Roy noticed that a few clouds were drifting into the once clear blue skies. He looked at his watch and figured that they had at least an hour before more clouds would begin to form. In his experience, storms did not blow up quickly when you watched the sky. Experienced flyers knew how to judge the strength of the wind against the moisture in the air and determine when and if any storm was forming. Plus, his instrument panel would give him the digital information he needed to monitor their safety.

"Fasten your seatbelts down tight, ladies. It might feel as if we are wobbling from time to time, but just relax. That is part of the fun of the ride. If you begin to feel uncomfortable or ill, just let me know. We won't be so high up that we can't come right down if we need to. The only thing we'll have to worry about is having to come right down when we don't want to! That's when the seatbelts come in handy!" Roy smiled at the women as if he had just told them his best joke, and Shirleen seemed to get it. Carrie was looking at Roy with an icy glare.

"Just kidding, ma'am!" He looked at Carrie with a sincere smile. He felt a little sorry for her. How could anyone choose to be that mean, especially with a bubbly friend like Shirleen? Still, he didn't know what she might have on her mind, so he shouldn't be trying to make her scared or angry. He was beginning to feel a little ashamed of himself.

"I know," she responded, drily. "I've just had a rough few days. But, business is business, so let's get going."

"All right!" Roy said and turned on the motor, engaging the large propellers and lifting the copter slowly off of the pad and into the blue-gray sky. He veered smoothly to the right and began to carry them over the water toward the deeper ocean. Looking down, the women could see the waves cresting and moving rhythmically toward the shores. This was a sight that never ceased to amaze Roy. The power of nature was unparalleled. These waters could never be controlled by any man or woman. They had to be respected.

Shirleen was fascinated with the stories Roy was telling them about the area – all of the coves, islands, caves, and keys where pirates would hide or ships had wrecked. Much of what he told them was community folklore, but some stories were steeped in history, especially those related to Civil War battles. In between Shirleen's questions, Roy kept a sharp eye on the sky. He was concerned about a stream of clouds slowly moving their way that was still at least twenty miles out, but thickening enough over time to keep his attention.

Suddenly, Carrie sat forward and pointed, "Over there! Over there! That's where we want to go! We need to see what is on the other side of that clump of trees!"

Roy was puzzled. He understood they just wanted a tour of the area highlights. What was Carrie talking about? Carrie sat up close between Roy and Shirleen, grabbing Shirleen's shoulder and shaking it. Shirleen had a very serious look on her face. Maybe she wasn't such an airhead, after all. But, what was their real agenda? Why hadn't they told him they wanted to view a specific spot in the first place? As he was trying to sort all of this out, Shirleen spoke in a serious tone.

"Roy, would you mind terribly taking us around on the south side of that grove? Carrie and I have been trying to reach it by land, but it was challenging to navigate. We thought we might catch a glimpse of what we needed to see if we took the air tour. But, it looks like we're right here, and we'd appreciate it so much if you'd accommodate our wishes." Her voice was syrupy sweet. All she left out was the batting of her eyes and calling him Honey. Roy really didn't want to do it because they could have been up front and told him what they wanted in the first place. But, they were up here now, so he might as well go ahead. However, once he flew them around that way, he was going to head right back to the pad and blame it on the incoming cloud cover.

Roy took a deep breath, then nodded. Shirleen smiled widely, patted Carrie's hand, and sat back, looking out of her window. He navigated the copter around the outside edge of the area the ladies had identified. He couldn't see anything that would be so intriguing as to make them insist on adding that to their flight agenda. Just a bunch of trees with a small beach front and patchy grass. This was not even a prime building area unless you were going to erect a shack and dig a hole in the ground for your personal processes. This was hardly worth his time or gas, and Roy was just about to turn the copter around and head on in.

"There it is!" Carrie screamed in his right ear. She began pulling his arm. "Go down! Go down! Please, sir!"

"What are you doing, lady? Are you crazy?" Roy snatched his arm away and turned to Carrie, hollering at her. She was about to make him wreck! Suddenly, his neck began to get hot and he was sweating. Large clouds were moving in and Carrie's actions had caused him to jerk the controls. The helicopter bounced a little. "That crazy lady is about to make me crash this thing!" he thought. All of a sudden, he thought about the last crash he had experienced. The memory flashed before his eyes. The feel of the copter falling in spite of his best efforts to right it, the helplessness he experienced as the ground rose to meet his machine, the grip of fear and the attack on his manhood. He was impotent, a failure, weak, incompetent. He couldn't keep himself, let alone a machine, in the air. He crashed. He was broken. He was worthless.

Carrie's voice brought him out of his reverie. He realized he was now flying low and could hit the tree tops if he didn't do something quickly. "Roy, I'm sorry! Please, this is so important to me. You can't understand now, but I'll explain it later. I need you to help me, please. I can't do this by myself. If you don't help me, I don't know what I'll do." Her voice began to crack. The vulnerability and emotion that was so raw in her words shook him back to reality. He had a choice. He needed to do the right thing.

"What do you expect me to do?" he demanded, righting the copter. He noticed that the wind had picked up and the resistance was increasing. He really needed to think about getting these ladies back on the ground as soon as possible. He wished that he could have foreseen this craziness before now. They had looked so harmless sitting in the office. He never imagined that both of them were nuts.

"Roy, this is very important to us. It's about our Dad. We think part of his plane was spotted on that piece of land. It would mean a lot for us to find out for sure." Shirleen's voice was firm and held a quiet plea. She placed her hand on his arm. She looked him in the eye. "I'm sorry for my sister's behavior. It's just that we have waited for so long…" she ended her sentence with a sob.

Women crying and hysterical. Roy knew he wasn't prepared emotionally for this. How could he feel sorry for two women who had tricked him, then assaulted him, then begged him? Somehow, he felt violated and compassionate at the same time. He wanted to help but he was afraid of what would happen to him if he did. But, now he was curious. What was the story behind their father? Was he still out there?

"All right," Roy growled. "But, why didn't you ask for this in the first place? We could have gone straight out there before touring the whole town." Neither of the women responded. When Roy finally threw a glare their way, they both had their heads down and wouldn't make eye contact. They looked like small children who had just received a scolding. Roy made one pass over the area and then began to slowly lower the helicopter.

As they went down, Carrie began to get more and more animated. She was focused on whatever she could see through the window. Treetops turned to thick foliage, which then became soft ground. Thank goodness there was a half acre where the copter could land without any trouble. Roy had barely hit the ground before Carrie was trying to open the door and climb out. "Sit down!" he hollered at her. What was wrong with her? "You have to wait until I have completely shut the copter down before you can take off your seatbelt." Once again, she sat back like a child who had been disciplined. Roy took his time unlatching his seatbelt and then unlocked the doors.

Immediately, both ladies jumped out of the copter and began to run toward a high ridge of rocks. Looking out toward the ocean, there was almost a mirror image of a line of rocks jutting up from the water. Roy kicked dirt around the copter until he heard Carrie scream. Looking her way, he saw her dropping on her knees toward the ground. Impulsively, he ran toward them, thinking maybe a snake had bitten her. They could be pretty populous on these deserted islets. He realized that he had left the first aid kit in the copter, and was about to turn back to grab it when Shirleen dropped to her knees too and began to dig with her hands.

"What's wrong?" he called as he ran toward them.

"We found it!" Shirleen said through short breaths, digging furiously.

"What is it? Some kind of buried treasure?" He wasn't sure if these ladies were crazy or playing some kind of prank on him. What would be out on this remote space that would make them so excited? His curiosity got the best of him and his pace picked up. As he neared them, he could see Shirleen scraping sand and dirt off of a rusty piece of metal sticking out of the ground. It looked like an old bike fender, thin with a slight curve. He walked over to where she was frantically trying to pull it up while digging into the ground with her hands to loosen it.

"What do you think this is?" He sank down beside her on his knees. She looked at him quickly, trying to figure out if he was taking her seriously or faking condescension. She must have figured that he really did want to know.

Still digging and pulling, she explained between labored breaths, "Twelve years ago, my father took a hopper from the airport and headed back up east. The weather turned bad and the pilot lost contact with the air traffic controller. They later said they thought the pilot may have turned around to get back to the airport. They never made it. No one knows for sure what happened to them, but they think the little plane went down in the ocean. It must not have wrecked, because no debris was ever spotted. They think it just submerged and the pilot and my Dad drowned. They hunted for a long time and never found anything, so he was declared dead."

"But, he's not dead to us!" Carrie cried. "He won't be dead until I see him dead. Bones, clothes, part of the plane, something! Anything! I just need to know that it's over. I need closure." Carrie had come to join them and now was helping Shirleen dig.

"Well, why would you think he or his plane were here? If they went down in the ocean, how could they end up here?" Roy was having a hard time believing their story, even though he did feel sincerely sorry for them. Apparently, something had happened to drive them to be here doing this. Plus, the clouds were gathering and they were losing some sunlight. He really did not want to be stuck out here in the middle of a thunderstorm. But, he also wanted to help them if he could.

"After the tsunami last spring, some ocean debris washed in and was deposited up and down the shore line. A shore patroller thought he saw some airplane debris. They contacted us so that we could hire somebody to check it out. The night we got the call, Carrie had a dream. She dreamed that Dad's plane had washed up on the shore. In her dream, she saw the mirror rocky ridges." Shirleen pointed to the ridge on the land to their left and the ridge on their right in the ocean. Roy noticed, and thought how unusual it was to see what appeared to be an identical set of ridges. Shirleen continued, "That same day, Carrie saw a picture of the twin rock ridges in a travel brochure. She was hysterically excited. She saw that as a sign and immediately coerced me into accompanying her on this trip." Shirleen looked at Carrie and tears began to fill her eyes. She turned again to Roy. "I know this sounds like a crazy story, but we love our Dad." Reaching out to hug Carrie, she finished, "We just had to know."

Looking up at the sky, Roy could see that he had to make a decision very quickly. Either they would ride the storm out unsheltered right where they were, or attempt to beat it back to the dock office and try this again another day. "Ladies," he said, "I'm going to go against everything my screaming brain is telling me to do and help you two. But, we're going to have to do it tomorrow." Anticipating their disappointment, he pointed up to the sky. "If we load up really quick, we will get back to the dock before the storm starts. If we don't, we may wish we would have very soon. Trust me. I will dedicate my entire day to you tomorrow. Pack a lunch. We'll start out bright and early. I'll bring some digging tools and we'll get to the bottom of this before the sun goes down. Does that sound like a plan?"

Carrie looked up at him with hope draining from her eyes. She wanted to believe that he was not intent on aborting the plan she had dreamed of for the past nine years. She needed to trust him to not emerge as the monster in her nightmares. Sensing her need for assurance, Roy reached out his hand to her. She took it and stood up. He felt the sand transfer from her palm to his, almost like a pact. It was a kindred exchange, as if they had chosen to become blood brother and blood sister. She squeezed his hand hard in a statement of trust. He felt as if he had just walked on water.

The sun rose to greet them early the next morning as they headed back out on their mission. Bright, showing off in an intense glow of red and yellow, making strong orange streaks across the eastern sky, it was empowering. Each of these three seekers knew their mission. Roy was seeking an opportunity to revive his trust in himself. Shirleen needed to know that emotional balance was ready to awaken from a decade of hibernation. Carrie. Carrie was on a search for personal survival. This was it. Now or never.

Roy had done some research of his own after they landed right before the storm rolled in. It was good that they had decided to leave the islet when they did, because the thunderstorm lasted all night long. While the lightning was flashing and the thunder was rolling deep into the late evening hours, Roy was reading old flight logs in the airport records room, scouring them for information on a flight that departed and then likely crashed on June 28 a decade ago. He found an Adam King who was a passenger on an old Cessna 152, Galair, B-JRRB, piloted by a Jake Booth. The flight was scheduled to depart at 19:48 hours but was delayed by half an hour due to inclement weather. Actual takeoff was logged as 20:19 hours. Adam King was Carrie and Shirleen's father, so they weren't making that up. With that evidence in hand, Roy headed home to gather tools that would help them in their quest.

Shirleen seemed very quiet that morning. She had packed a lunch and smiled wanly as she handed him two large grocery bags to load into the helicopter. He was about to tell her that she would need to try to get everything into one bag, but he decided to let it go. She looked as if she had not had much sleep the night before. Carrie, on the other hand, looked rested and ready for a day of hard work. She had pulled back her hair and had no makeup on. Still, Roy noticed, she looked very pretty and acted unusually nice. Before they took off, she handed him an envelope. Enclosed, she told him, was more than enough to cover his daily rate. He had not discussed any fee with them the day before, but he was glad to know they hadn't planned to take advantage of his curiosity and goodwill.

The first few hours of digging passed quickly. Unfortunately, the storm and high waves had washed a load of new sand on top of what the ladies had tried to dig up yesterday. But, Roy had come prepared. Each of them had a shovel and a pick. Roy had a plan. If they stepped out ten feet from each other heading east, north, and west, they could cover more ground as they worked back toward where Shirleen remembered as the spot where they had seen the rusty white object buried yesterday.

They started with the picks, hitting the sand deep and hoping to feel or hear something. Mid-morning, no signs of anything made Shirleen appear to wilt. Every stroke of the pick seemed to drain her energy. She sat under a bush, lifted her knees to her chest, dropped her head, and fell asleep. Roy wanted to wake her. This was their mission, not his. If anyone should be taking breaks while others worked, it was him. But, this had become a personal mission for him. He wanted to solve this mystery of the missing airplane. He wanted to feel an involvement in something productive and positive. Plus, he wanted to figure out who was the real Carrie.

She was muttering something that he couldn't understand, so he called out to her. "Did you find something?"

"Yes," she replied. "Sleeping Beauty." She pointed at Shirleen.

"I'm not sleep," Shirleen murmured.

"Did you say something?" This time, Roy directed his comment toward Shirleen. It was time for her to get up and get back to work.

"I need something to eat. I think my blood sugar is too low."

Immediately, Roy dropped his pick. He ran back to the copter and pulled out the grocery bags. One had sandwiches and chips. The other had fruit and cookies. He grabbed an orange and the package of cookies and rushed back to Shirleen.

"Why didn't you say something earlier? Did you think we'd appreciate you having a stroke out here while we're playing in the sand?" His hands were shaking as he twisted the orange in half and pushed one of the halves into her hand. He lifted her arm at the elbow and guided it to her lips. She began to suck the juice out of the orange and then he squeezed the rest into her open mouth. He took the rind bowl and gave her the other half. She sat up, looked at him, and then started to laugh lightly.

"Why are you shaking? I'm not going to die. I just should have taken time to eat breakfast. I've got to take better care of myself!" She sat back and slowly opened the package of cookies, taking two and nibbling on both at the same time. Roy looked at her and shook his head. She smiled.

He turned to Carrie and pointed at Shirleen. "You deal with this all the time?" he asked.

Carrie laughed. "It takes a special kind of man to ride Shirleen's merry-go-round. Check her pockets. She had three mints in each pocket. She knows what to do. She's just lazy. But, we're all we have left." The smile that was on her face slowly faded. "I'm tired, too, and it's only ten o'clock. I almost wish we hadn't seen anything yesterday. That way, I could still be without hope. Hope hurts."

Roy knew what she meant. When life starts shifting things and making you think that it is about to change and a dream is about to come true, then you have to deal with a new set of realities. New isn't always comfortable. Old house shoes, old friends, old t-shirts, those are comfortable. New stuff has to be broken in. New stuff is tight. New leather gloves don't fit well until they are at least a year old. New is uncomfortable, and Roy wasn't sure if he himself was ready for anything new; so he couldn't get frustrated with Carrie and Shirleen right now, because he figured that they weren't, either.

"Here's our plan, ladies. Let's break for a snack. While we are eating, we will devise a new plan of attack. We know we saw something yesterday. It could have come off of a plane. I did some checking last night. What little I saw in the sand yesterday could – and remember I said could – have come from a twenty-year-old Cessna 152 Galair."

Shirleen stood up quickly. "Are you serious, Roy? Do you think that really could have been a part from the plane that Dad was on? It would be a miracle if we found anything, but do you really believe that it could have been part of the plane?"

Roy felt himself becoming very excited. Actually, he hadn't thought about that. It really could be part of the plane. He could possibly be instrumental in solving a mystery and helping these two sisters close a difficult chapter in their life. He glanced at Carrie. She had been very quiet. He noticed that she was standing with her palm resting on the handle of the pick. Its head was planted firmly on the ground. She looked as if she had laid claim to that plat of ground and was posing for a picture which would confirm her ownership. He suddenly saw a strength in her that he had not noticed before. He looked in her eyes for direction, for confirmation to his plan. Knowing what he was asking, she nodded.

He continued with a confident tone, "So, we are going to stop for fifteen minutes to eat and to scout out this area. If the waters rushed in during the storm, they could have lifted and moved anything that was close to the shore. Maybe we aren't looking far enough up shore. We will move back fifteen to twenty feet, the length of a wash of waves, and resume our search after we eat. Does that sound like a plan?"

Carrie extended her hand for him to shake. "That's a plan, Captain!" she said with an air of trust and shook his hand firmly. "Let's eat!"

Shirleen began to walk off fifteen feet. She had new energy and seemed to have zoned out Carrie and Roy. In the way that a diviner follows a rod, she moved in the direction of the pick handle extended from her right shoulder. Carrie had taken two sandwiches from the bag. She gave one to Roy and sat down in the sand to eat. He stood as he unwrapped his sandwich and watched Shirleen, lost in his own thoughts. In the middle of a bite, he froze. He knew now what they should have been doing! The debris would not have been pushed higher up on the shore. It weighed too much. It would have been pulled back toward the sea. They needed to check on the shore line, not higher up!

Carrie sensed that something had changed with Roy. She stood up, looking at him for direction. "Shirleen," he called, "come back this way!" Roy rushed over to grab his pick, Carrie right on his heels. "Look, let's go down by the water line. I'm thinking that the strong storm tide may have carried it out toward the water instead of further up on the shore. Start hitting the ground around the shore line."

Carrie went to his right. She began attacking the wet sand with a vicious fervor. It was as if her entire life was being invested in her work, as if she was digging her own final resting place. Suddenly, she cried out, "I've hit something! It feels big!" She dropped the pick and headed back toward the copter where the shovels were laying. Grabbing one by the handle, she dragged it back to where the pick lay and began to dig.

Roy and Shirleen dropped their picks in the sand and rushed to get shovels themselves. Hurrying back to help Carrie, they sensed that destiny and opportunity had collided. Surely, this had to be that for which they all had searched for so long!

Almost an hour later, they had uncovered two large white rusted pieces of metal which could have come from a small plane. But, they could have also come from a salvage yard or an old tin tub. There were no identifiable markings on either of them to signify that they were part of that ill-fated plane. They were nearing a point of desperation once again, but continued to dig deeper and deeper. Roy imagined the structure of the plane. He looked again at the pieces they had uncovered lying in the sand. What if they were part of the rear, light enough to move easily in the water? What if the front part of that panel would have washed up, as well? How many feet long would a panel be? Maybe if he walked up ten or twelve feet and started to dig, he might uncover the part that was still intact, the full side panel with the identification letters still there. Maybe if he just stopped thinking and followed the intense leading in his inner self he might begin to see what he thought was true.

Roy picked up his shovel and stepped off twelve feet with careful precision. He began to dig, slowly. With every shovel-full of sand, he looked deep in the hole left behind before a thin coat of new sand could sift back in. He was looking for something white, or red, or blue. Some letters in some color, or a vague remnant of a letter that would look like a B or an R or a J. Something, anything. He just needed a sign.

"Roy, look!" Carrie was standing beside him, looking down into the extremely deep cavern he had dug in what seemed to him like minutes. Adrenaline was a powerful thing. He hadn't felt it in a long time. She pointed to a rusty tip, twisted and threatening in an ugly way. It looked like one of those gargoyles set to guard a cemetery. Roy paused, wondering for a moment if he should continue. What might happen if they disturbed the dead? Carrie looked at him. The trust he saw in her eyes was unparalleled by any sight he had ever seen so far in his life. She stared at him with raw need, dependence, and complete trust. He knew what he had to do.

"I've got it," he told her, resolutely. "Go sit down, you and

Shirleen. I'll take care of it from here." He wasn't sure how he knew, but the sight of a "B" on the panel he was able to uncover after digging four more feet into the deep pit was not a surprise. It became extremely difficult to uncover much else. It was as if someone or something had thrust the long panel deep into the earth as the frame for a foundation that had to be planted forty feet into the ground to hold up a high structure. He knew that it was there to stay. But, they had seen what they needed to see. And, they were all satisfied with this glimpse of finality.

Carrie and Shirleen stood on either side of him at the face of the hole. They embraced one another around the waist and bowed their heads. Carrie led them in a prayer of gratitude for providing closure to their quest. She prayed that their father had not suffered and had known that they would one day know that he rested in peace. She prayed that God would give them strength to leave the past behind and move forward in their lives. Finally, she prayed for Roy and thanked God that He had allowed them to meet him, and blessed him to be a blessing to them.

Roy could not remember ever hearing anyone pray for him. He had prayed himself a number of times, and had prayed for himself a few times. Hearing someone pray for him burst a boil in his spirit. He could feel poisons washing through his system and out of his eyes. He did not realize he was crying until he opened his eyes and looked at Carrie. She was crying too, but reached up to wipe his face with her sandy, dirty hand. "Thank you," she mouthed to him. Then, both she and Shirleen hugged him and their corporate tears fell to the ground as an offering of repentance and gratitude for forgiveness and love.

Up in the sky, a tiny two-seater passed across the sun. It threw a long shadow on the sand where the three of them stood. Shirleen looked up, laughed, and began to jump up and down, waving. Carrie looked puzzled, and then began to laugh, too. Soon, all three were dancing in the sand and waving at the Angel who had come to still the troubled waters and signal glad tidings to those who remained, "All is well, children. All is well. It's time to cross over. All is well."

And Sinners Plunged Beneath the Flood Lose All Their Guilty Stain

"As a mad man who casteth firebrands, arrows, and death, so is the man that deceiveth his neighbor, and saith, 'Am not I in sport?'" – Proverbs 26:18 & 19

*

Abby sat at the back of the church. She had made eye contact a few times throughout the service with her friend, the one who had invited her. She was sort of glad that she had come. It had given her at least an hour to forget about the craziness of her life.

After service, many of the attendees had said hello to her and some of the older ones had shaken her hand. She smiled the first few times this happened. It seemed so old-fashioned and sweet, like a scene from a corny black and white movie. Could people really be this happy all the time? Abby wasn't sure. Still, they were sincere and very nice; and being around them made her feel good for the first time in a long time.

She dreaded going home. Her stepfather had lit into her again last night about the same old things. She knew he just wanted her out of the house. He picked a fight over anything, nothing. Her mom acted like she didn't even know her anymore. All she wanted was peace and quiet for a few more weeks. Then, she would be gone away to college and would never come back to this hell hole.

Walking up to the house, she prayed that she could at least have a quiet Sunday afternoon. Usually, he would have a few beers while he watched whatever game was on television, then he would go to sleep unless something made him mad. That could be anything. The outcome of the game. The meal her mother fixed for dinner. How loud he thought Abby was being in her bedroom. Whether it was raining when he wanted the sun to shine, or whether it was hot and sunny when he was hoping for a cool, refreshing rain. With him, you never knew what to expect.

She thought about last Friday night when she had come home from her shift as a lifeguard. It had been a nice day for sitting on the beach. She felt warm and safe all day long. Her mind hadn't drifted once to the decisions that were facing her. She was able to get in a few relaxing swims and had played with the children on the beach during her breaks, helping them build sand castles and learn a new swim stroke. She had felt like a regular teenager, fresh out of high school and looking forward to college in the fall.

Coming home that Friday night had ruined everything. Her mother was on the porch, crying. Her step-father was inside ranting. When her mother looked up at her, Abby could see the beginnings of a bruise under her right eye. "Oh, God," Abby thought, "not again. Not tonight." She had gone to sit down beside her mother on the splintery porch step, trying to figure out what she could do. Usually, she would already be in her room when they would begin to fight. She would put a pillow over her ears and scream into another pillow as she lay face down in her bed. That way, she could zero out their noise with her own and go to sleep knowing that, true to form, they would do the same within an hour or so.

After a while, she decided to go into the house and see if she could circumvent her step-father and get to her room. Stepping in the door, she could see him sprawled on the couch, one hand around the neck of a bottle of beer that sat on the floor. It sounded like he was snoring, but she couldn't be sure. She was wary, nervous that he might do something like throw the bottle at her as she walked by. She tiptoed toward the bedroom.

"Abby," he growled, "come here!"

She hesitated, afraid of what might happen next. He may not have been as drunk as she had supposed, and he was more cruel to her sober than he was to her mom when he was drunk. She thought about turning and running out of the door, then realized that would just make things worse later on.

"Yes sir?" Abby's voice trembled as she took a step toward him. Her legs were shaking. Her eyes shifted to the beer bottle. His hand was even more tightly gripped around its neck. She was afraid he was getting ready to throw it at her head. She kept an eye on his hand as she walked toward the couch with pretentious resolve.

"Abby, cook me something and don't burn it! I don't care what it is. I'm hungry. Your mama is drunk. She's been burning up food all day!" He rolled over on the couch with his back to her, mumbled a few things, and then got quiet. Abby stood there for a few minutes, making sure he was really asleep. She wasn't going to cook him anything. She couldn't stand him. Her mother could have prepared a four-star meal and he would have spit in it. He was crazy. Besides, he had beat her before for less things than fixing something he didn't think was fit to eat.

After the last beating, she vowed she would kill him if he ever touched her again. He seemed to sense that she was different. He stopped hollering at her and began to watch her with a mistrustful eye. What he didn't know was that she had let the sea do for her what years of therapy would have been unable to do. Sitting on the beach the day after that beating, she had watched how the waters would rush up on to shore; tall, bouncing white caps that jumped at the opportunity to wash away old debris. They would flow in on top of one another, each competing for a higher mark on the shore. Then, they would drag whatever was unsettled back out to the sea before starting the next race. "Take me!" she cried out to them.

Abby realized that she did not really want to die. Her whole life was ahead of her. So, she changed her request on the spot and asked the waves to take her pains instead. She laid herself out on the sand. Others were swimming and playing on the beach, but Abby didn't care. With her arms and legs extended, she looked like a sand angel. Yet, in what felt like an out of body experience, she saw herself as a sacrifice. She was giving up everything that could hold her back in life to the sea. She just prayed that the sea would take it.

One of the new seasonal hires, Chris, had come down the shore to check on her. He had seen her sprawled and talking to herself while the water continued to wash over her. She looked distressed. Typically, Abby was serious but funny. Worried that she had swum out too far and swallowed some water or something, he had trotted down the beach.

"Abby! Abby, are you all right?" Chris looked sincerely concerned. Abby opened her eyes to see his face a few inches away from hers. She sat up quickly.

"Chris, hi!" She brushed the sand off of her thighs. "Sure, I'm fine! Are you okay?" She wondered why he looked so questioning.

"Yea, I'm fine. I thought something was wrong with you!" Chris started to laugh. "I guess this is just how you meditate! I thought maybe you had swallowed some water or something." He sat down on the beach beside her. "I guess I over-reacted!" He seemed a little embarrassed. "I'm sorry for bothering you, Abby! I'll let you get back to your meditation." Chris rose to his feet.

Abby reached up for his hand, shielding her eyes from the bright sunshine. He took her hand and helped to pull her to her feet. "Aw, thank you, Chris! I appreciate you just being concerned." She looked down and began to brush more sand off of her long brown legs. "I'm not used to that."

Chris took a moment before he let her hand go. "Maybe you should get used to it," he said. When she looked back up at him, she realized that he had a serious expression that said he meant it.

A few days later, it occurred to her that she had lost her fear of her step-father. She wasn't sure if it was because of the seaside experience or if she had just decided that he would never hold power over her again. This night, though, had tried to bring it all back. Still, her refusal to cook him anything confirmed to her that he could not intimidate her like he had in the past.

Abby headed into her bedroom and shut the door. She knew that her step-father would be out until morning and her mother would eventually come into the house and go to bed. She had seen this play out the same way too many times before. She had lost all hope of her mother divorcing her abusive husband and she and Abby going back to being the happy twosome they had been before her senseless marriage. She decided that her mother was dependent on him for things that Abby couldn't provide or figure out, so there was no point in Abby trying. She had to live her own life.

As Abby undressed for bed, she thought about her first date with Chris. It had been two months ago, about a week after he had rescued her on the beach. She called it a rescue because he had allowed her to experience a healthy emotional exchange with someone who really seemed to care about her as a girl. He made her feel special, beautiful, funny, and valued. They had just gone out for ice cream after their shift ended. They sat at a table outside of the shop and watched the people pass by. They laughed and talked for hours. The night was warm and the passersby were friendly. They recognized a few from the beach. A couple of little kids looked at them as if they thought they were going to tattle on them to their parents. They seemed so funny to them that Abby and Chris began to make faces at them and point between them and their parents. The kids looked scared, then started jumping up and down and pulling on their parents to walk faster. Abby and Chris laughed about that for the rest of the evening.

After that night, they began to find something fun to do every day at the end of their shift. Soon, they had an understanding with each other that they were "steady" friends. Chris was getting ready for his second year of college. He was going to major in business. He hoped to own his own CPA firm once he completed his masters in business administration.

Abby was very impressed with his maturity and straight focus on his future. He knew what he was going to do with his life, how long it would take him to achieve his goals, and what new goals he would set when he got there. She loved to hear him talk about himself and his future plans. She wished she could be the same. She knew she wanted to be a nurse, but not much more. Abby thought it was because she had just looked forward to getting out of the house and going to college. That was her main goal. After that, she figured, everything else would fall into place. Now, she wasn't sure.

She had been unsure about why Chris would want to spend time with her when he was older and mature, a college man. Surely, he had been dating college girls. Abby imagined them to be smart and funny, cultured, socially savvy. She felt like a country bumpkin compared to what she imagined they would be like. Was he spending time with her because he was bored, or because he just saw her as some little girl who would listen to him talk about himself and not give him any trouble?

Guys usually didn't approach her in a mature and respectful way. That's why she had not had any boyfriends in high school. Another reason was that her step-father had threatened to beat her to death if he ever saw her talking to a boy. She had been more afraid for the embarrassment he would cause with the boy than she was with being beaten to death, knowing that he was likely exaggerating but still would probably beat her to some extent. Anyway, it wasn't worth the potential trouble; so she had just smiled and nodded a "no" to any boy who asked for her phone number.

Chris, on the other hand, really did like spending time with Abby. She was refreshing. She could stand on her own two feet. She was funny and a good listener. She helped him think through his ideas and gave him good insight. She asked just the right questions but never sounded stupid or bored. She wasn't clingy or whiny. She never asked him to buy her anything. Besides, she didn't know that his parents were wealthy and he was set to inherit a fortune that would leave him set for the rest of his life. She just thought that he was a typical student working his way through college as a lifeguard, and that suited him fine. At home, he always suspected that the girls he dated wanted him for his money, even though they always insisted that they didn't. Still, if they knew he had lots of money coming to him, how could he be sure that they were being truthful? Plus, he always had a good time with Abby.

Just once, they had a better time than usual. They had gone to the movies on a Saturday night. It was a romantic comedy. Even though they had many laughs, they held hands and also kissed after the romantic scenes. Abby had never been happier. Riding home that night, Abby had snuggled close to Chris. When he asked if they could park down on the beach for a few minutes before he took her home, she agreed quickly. She had enjoyed kissing him in the movies. She hoped he would want to kiss some more.

One thing led to another. Abby wasn't sure what was going on, but she trusted Chris. He asked her a couple of times if she wanted him to stop. He told her that he respected her and he cared about her a lot. She seemed to be half-asleep to him. She would just moan softly and kiss him again. He realized that he had crossed the line a few times too many, but she didn't tell him to stop. When she finally stepped out of the car in front of her house, both knew they had escalated to a level of intimacy in their relationship that left them questioning it, each other, and themselves.

Their evening routine did not change after that episode. However, they developed an unspoken pact to not add the element of full intimacy to their relationship again. They had moved too fast and gone too far, and both knew it. They needed to stop and reassess their relationship before adding in adult activities that would muddy their respect for one another.

So, they set their relationship back an evening and started all over again.

Abby was happier than she was before until she missed her cycle. At first, she wasn't worried because she had been irregular before, many times. However, there was the possibility that she could be pregnant this time, due to that one-time incident on the beach with Chris. It had nagged the back of her mind for a while. Would God use this to punish them, to expose their youthful mistake? For the first time, she admitted to herself that she cared about what God thought about her actions. For years, she had assumed that God didn't care about her or her mother. If He did, why would He let her step-father treat them the way he did? After that day on the beach when she had asked the sea to wash away her pain, she really had felt relief. She wondered if God was the One who used the sea to cleanse her, if He had actually acknowledged her sacrifice and helped her when she needed it most. Her agony had been lifted, and except for the worries she was experiencing now, her life had been filled with hope and joy.

Abby had vacillated for a few days over whether or not she should let Chris know that she had not had a menstrual cycle yet. She didn't want him to panic for no reason, because she had been late in the past. Still, she also didn't want to walk through this alone. Even though her mother had her issues, Abby knew she would be very disappointed in her. Her step-father would put her right of the house, she was sure about that. He would know that he would face legal charges if he put a finger on her, and for him that would be hard not to do. He'd be incensed if he found out that she was pregnant! When he got that mad, it was impossible to handle him. Plus, she didn't even know Chris' parents! What would they say? Would they assume she was a tramp trying to entrap their son? He was working his way through college. He didn't need added burdens. Yet, they both had equal responsibility in this situation. She wasn't going to be like her mother and let him get off the hook. She didn't want to have to face the same decisions in the future that her mother had – to settle with any man that had a job so that she and her child could survive.

By chance, Abby had run into a friend from high school at the store. Stephanie was a few years younger than her, but they had quite a few interests in common and had taken some elective classes together. Abby felt like a big sister to Stephanie and had been a mature friend at school. She had met Stephanie's mom and sister a couple of times at choir concerts and at the honor roll assembly. Stephanie had invited her to visit her church a few times, but after that first visit, Abby began to come up with excuses. She was not used to going to church, and she was frankly afraid.

This day, though, she was looking for help with her problem. She felt that God caused her to see Stephanie at the store. So, instead of waiting for Stephanie to invite her again, she told Stephanie that she would be there again the next Sunday. Stephanie was ecstatic! She was going to be singing a solo with the choir, so she was glad that Abby was coming. She asked Abby if she needed a ride, because her mother would be glad to pick Abby up. However, Abby had already decided that she would ask her mother to use the car so that she could leave if she got too uncomfortable. She wasn't sure what to expect.

As it turned out, the service was nice. The pastor talked like he was having a conversation with you, not like he was preaching at you. At the end of the service, he asked for anyone who wanted prayer to come up to the front. The music was soothing, beautiful. The people had been so friendly. Abby felt like she should go up front because of all of the things she was facing, but she was terrified. She didn't know these people. What would they think of her? She could see Stephanie sitting in the choir stand. She tried to make eye contact, but Stephanie kept her eyes closed while she was singing.

"God!" Abby cried out in her spirit. "Who is going to help me?" She could hear a soft voice reply, "I am!" She was startled for a moment. Was she hearing voices or was it really God telling her that He cared about her? She had decided to take a chance. If she didn't have to be afraid of her step-father any more, she didn't have to be afraid of people she didn't even know. Walking up to the front of the church, she felt like she was hidden in a cloud and no one was watching her. She saw the pastor right in front of her. He looked so kind. He looked at her like he knew she was going to come to him so that he could pray with her. He looked welcoming.

"I wonder if he knows I sinned and I might be pregnant?" she thought. "God, if You really do care, please help me get out of this mess!"

She had walked up to him and stood still in front of him. He had placed his hand on her shoulder and began to pray softly. She couldn't hear everything he said, but she felt strength from his touch. She also felt unusually warm and comforted. Was this what God's love felt like? She wondered if God was showing her how much He cared for her, even though she had sinned. She didn't mean to, though. She had just been overcome, looking for love. She was sorry for what she had done. She asked God to forgive her as the pastor prayed for her. When he finished, she felt better than she had in a long time.

Stephanie and her mom had come right up to hug her after the pastor prayed for her. He had smiled at her, a big toothy smile, and told her he was so glad she had come to church. He said that he hoped she would come back again. She remembered nodding and then turning around so Stephanie and her mom could walk her back to her seat. All of the people they passed smiled warmly at her, too. She wished her mother could have come to church with her. She really needed this, too. It might help her get up the nerve to leave her step-father.

Driving up to the house after service, she determined that if God did love her, He would show her beyond the shadow of a doubt today. Her step-father would be calm. Her mother would be calm. That would be enough of a sign. Still dreading what she might encounter, she locked the car door and walked up to the porch. Climbing each step carefully, she opened the screen door slowly and stepped into the house. She glanced at the couch and didn't see anyone. She could smell roast beef coming from the kitchen, so she knew her mom was okay. But, where were they? Heading toward her bedroom, she heard soft voices. The sound was coming from her mother's room.

As Abby walked toward the door, trying to hear the conversation, she realized that no one was arguing, just talking. She decided not to knock. She walked to her bedroom and opened the door. Her mother must have heard it creak, because she called her name. Abby waited in her open door.

"Abby, you're home! How was the church service?" Her mother looked very tired. Abby wondered if she would ever get a rest.

"Hi, mom! How are you feeling? Yes, it was very nice. Stephanie sings in the choir and she sang a solo. It was really good. The message was good, too. I think I'll go back again. Maybe you'll come too?" Abby stood in the doorway, rushing through her response, unsure what would come next. Her step-father was being unusually quiet. Maybe the calm before the storm?

"We'll see." Her mother followed her into her bedroom. Abby sat down on the bed and slid off her shoes. Her mother sat beside her. "Abby, Fred had a bad fall today. He hurt his back again."

Abby tried to look concerned, but she struggled. She knew her mother loved him, but she couldn't figure out why. She just shook her head at her mother.

"I called his doctor's answering service to see if we should bring him in to the hospital. But, they said to wait until morning and see how he felt if nothing was sprained or broken. I gave him some of his strong pain medicine. He should sleep well until morning." She looked nervous and worried, but also a little relieved.

"Aw Mom, he'll be okay, especially if he has a chance to rest. Dinner smells great!" Abby wanted her mother to not worry, about Fred or about her. She wanted her to feel good about herself, too. "Roast beef?"

Her mother smiled. "And mashed potatoes, peas and carrots, and tossed salad. I even made fresh dinner rolls since I had some quiet time!"

"Yum! I'm ready to eat!" Abby exclaimed. It felt good to be just her and her mom, both being happy again. She hadn't felt that way in a long time. She felt like a little girl again. But, how could she still be a little girl if she was possibly having a little girl or little boy herself? She pushed the thought away. She didn't want to have to deal with that right now. Abby hugged her mother tightly. Her mother laid her head on Abby's shoulder. They needed each other so much.

Abby decided to say her prayers that night. It had been years since she had done that! When she was a very small girl, she could remember kneeling beside the bed with her mother, praying a rhyme and then asking God to bless a long list of people. Most often she started with her mother and grandparents, but then would add anybody who came to mind. She had stopped doing it after her mother married Fred. She vaguely remembered having refused to pray for Fred, so her mother had stopped making her pray at all.

Tonight, she did pray for both her mother and Fred. He needed prayer. When he woke up in the early evening hours, she could see he was in real pain. She wondered if that was why he had drank so much in the past, to deaden the pain. Still, that was no excuse for his meanness. Maybe if he was off his feet for a while, he would dry out. Maybe if he didn't drink for a while, he would become nicer. Who knows? Maybe if she prayed for him, God would help him. Abby went to sleep that night thinking about Chris and feeling a little bit of hope fluttering in her stomach.

Stomach cramps woke her up in the middle of the night. She had eaten a roast beef sandwich right before she went to bed. Halfway between waking and sleeping, she recalled rolling over and wrapping her arms around her stomach. She had been dreaming about being in a rowboat during a bad storm. She had lost the oars and the boat kept rocking back and forth violently. She kept trying to see the lost oar in the murky water. Every time she thought she saw it and tried to grab it, it just disappeared. She was frustrated and angry, but she could see the shore dimly so she kept trying to find the oar so that she could get back home safely. Feeling helpless, she began to cry. Her own voice woke her up, moaning loudly. She felt a strong urge to go to the bathroom.

She wasn't sure whether to stop at the sink or head straight for the toilet. She felt like she was going to throw up, but the cramps were terrible and she could feel a bout of diarrhea coming on. Opting for the toilet, she sat down hard and dropped her hot head into her shivering hands. For a moment, she thought she was about to faint. Abby leaned against the cool wall. She hoped that whatever was going to happen would happen soon. She hated being sick.

Abby realized quickly that her life was changing. Signs of a merciful God met her eyes. She had been given another chance to make a fresh start at life. She did not have to fear premature motherhood. She vowed that she would never again look for love in a physical package until she was committed to a permanent partner, be it Chris or whoever God had for her. He had shown her that He could take care of her from Day

One, which was yesterday. Everything she had asked for during and after the prayer at church, He had done. Wasn't Fred quiet when she came in from church? Didn't she start her period? Only God could have done those two things!

Crawling back into bed, Abby pulled the covers up high around her nose. She breathed in the coolness of the room. Her thoughts were clear, but simple. She needed to make a plan. Not everyone got a second chance. She didn't want to blow it. Then, she recalled that the pastor's prayer had helped her think about God, that He might be willing to help her. He had! So, she thought she should back up and start there. With God.

"God, I really don't know a lot about praying," she started. "I know that You did help me today, though. Thank You! It was quiet when I came home. My mother seemed to feel better than she has in a long time. Thank You. I don't know if I was pregnant or not, but You allowed me to have a new start and not just with that, but with my life, too. Would you please help me learn about how I'm supposed to talk to You and how I am supposed to live? What I'm supposed to do? Wow! For the first time in my life that I can remember, I'm not afraid of what could happen to me or Mom. I believe that You really will take care of me! Us! Thank You, Lord!"

Her blanket felt like the arms of God, holding her tightly and making her feel warm and secure. "So, if I do this every night and then go to church on Sunday, will things keep getting better?" she thought. They had to! It just made sense. She resisted the urge to call Chris and tell him what had happened. There would be time tomorrow evening. Somehow, she knew he would be happy for her. Maybe he would come to church with her and Mom next Sunday. She could see him smiling during the message and shaking hands with the pastor. She knew Chris would like the pastor. They seemed a lot alike. Both made her feel special. "But, God, You have done that best of all!" She hugged her blanket tight and smiled. "Good night!"

Deep River, My Home is Over Jordan!

"Wrath is cruel, and anger is outrageous; but who is able to stand before envy?" Proverbs 27:4

*

Ivy Lee Babcock had been a feisty little thing all her life. What she lacked in size she made up for in attitude. Not many women, or men, wanted to take her on in an argument during her prime. She had hopes of becoming an attorney in her youth, but life and lack of resources thwarted that plan early on. Still, she took what she had and made the most of it. She also made a lot of enemies along the way.

Ivy Lee was a brilliant student. She made straight A's all through school! Her third grade teacher had impeccable penmanship, and the sight of earning that very first "A" in "Vocabulary" had made Ivy Lee crave more and more of these beautiful letters written and awarded by her teacher. She loved to review her grade card at the end of each school year. All "A's" all year, every year, from third grade through twelfth grade. Her mother had kept every grade card and Ivy Lee would often open the gilded box that held the collection of treasured grade records. Separating each card from the others to organize them chronologically, she would open them ceremoniously, glancing at each grade, line by line, page by page. She was so proud of herself!

Ivy Lee had been born on the other "poor" side of the tracks, literally. Her family's home was right on the railroad tracks. In fact, it was an old rail car. Someone had set it down there, maybe right off of the track, back in the 1940's. Then, they had put it on a foundation, remodeled it on the inside, added electricity and plumbing, and called it a house. It was terrible. Raggedy and rusting, it looked like the centerpiece of a dump. But, that is where she had been born, raised, and loved. "Jus' because we poor, don't mean we can't live." That is what her mother always said. It took Ivy Lee years before she really understood what her mother was teaching her.

Ivy Lee's father was the hardest working man she ever knew. He loved to work. He got up before the sun came up every day. He got home long after the moon was high in the sky. Ivy Lee didn't know when he slept. She had only seen him asleep a few times during her adolescent years. Later, she learned he worked all but six hours of every day the Lord sent, and he slept when and where he could during those six hours. Still, he barely made enough doing manual labor to do more than keep the railcar roof over the family's head and put humble meals on the table.

Ivy Lee's mother was disabled. She had contracted polio when she was a small child. Her uncle had come back from the war and stayed with the family for a short time while he got on his feet. He brought the virus into the house. Sadly, six months after she was infected, the vaccine was released to be administered all across the country. By then, it was too late for Mother. Ivy Lee's grandmother used to cry and say her poor baby was born out of time. Had her life calendar been six months delayed, she would not have been a cripple. Still, with all of the challenges that befell her mother's family, if it wasn't polio, it would have been something else.

Since her mother could not stand or walk well, Ivy Lee's father had to carry the weight of full household financial responsibility. However, that was his joy. He loved his wife and his daughter, a gift that the doctor thought would surely not survive gestation or birth. He was glad to work as much as he needed in order to keep them in his family homestead and make sure Ivy Lee got a good education so that she would not have to do common labor as he had done all of his life, since he only attended school to the fourth grade. He was proud that he could read, write, and do basic math. But, he wished above everything that he could have earned a high school diploma. Before he died, he told Ivy Lee how proud he was that she had been a good student. For her, though, that wasn't enough.

The experience of seeing and hearing about all of her parents' struggles was the impetus Ivy Lee needed to set high goals for her own life. She vowed that she would use her good looks and her good grades to take her somewhere in life. Like her mother said, she didn't have to give up on life just because she was poor. So, she took advantage of every open door and each open hand to make good of any and all resources that came her way.

College was a dream come true. She had gotten a job as a companion for an older woman in town. The lady turned out to be one of her greatest supporters. She was an alumni of the state college. A call to the admissions office got Ivy Lee a few scholarships so that she could attend in the fall. Back then, classes were small and coursework was challenging. Ivy Lee soon saw that she did not fit in well. Her clothes were outdated. Her confidence in class discussions wavered. The bubbly, outgoing girl that her parents had sent off to school with their prayers and tears was now the poor girl that the other girls shunned and the boys found amusing. Her grades suffered, as did her ego. By November, she was ready to go home.

Her father had gotten ill and was diagnosed with pneumonia that fall. Her mother was struggling to care for him and for herself. Ivy Lee decided that she would come home and take care of them herself. Actually, it was her excuse to leave school. There was no way she could continue to stay there, given the emotional struggles she was experiencing. Yet, she would never say that her circumstances had beaten her. So, she stepped away from her dreams and back into the nightmare of a consuming poverty.

Ivy Lee's mother died in early January. She was shocked and devastated. She had gotten up that morning and made the coffee. She had planned to go into town and look for an office job because the pay for professional jobs was higher than it was for other menial jobs. Plus, she didn't want to work herself to death like her father. He had been coughing all night and she had gone in to check on him a few times. Around five o'clock, she had given him a dose of his antibiotics and his pain medication. She hadn't noticed anything unusual about her mother. But, when she brought a cup of hot coffee into her bedroom and then walked over to open the curtains and lift the window shades, she noticed her mother's hand dangling off of the side of the bed. Her fingers looked bluish-gray. They appeared to be very stiff. Right away, Ivy Lee knew something was wrong. She didn't even go to check on her. She walked right out of the room to the kitchen, lifted the receiver off of the wall phone, and dialed the operator. She noticed that her voice was very calm as she asked for an ambulance to come to the house, but thought it unusual that tears were streaming steadily down her cheeks.

By Memorial Day, Ivy Lee was placing flowers on two fresh graves. Her whole life had shifted within a matter of months. She was an orphan. She was penniless. She had to sell their railroad car house to pay off the hospital bills and burial costs. Thank goodness that Mrs. Griffin, the lady she had helped before she went to college, was willing to let her stay in a room of her home until she could find a job and get on her feet. Ivy Lee was determined that would happen within just a few weeks. As it turned out, she was right.

Mrs. Griffin was one of the few white people who faithfully attended Metropolitan Community Church. It wasn't as if people at the church made a big deal about whether someone was of a certain race. There was a Hawaiian family that attended the church. Many families from some of the Caribbean islands attended. It was just a big family and the pastor welcomed everyone. Ivy Lee needed a family. She wasn't that particular about whether the family members were white or brown. She needed love and acceptance. So, she joined the church the very first Sunday she attended with Mrs. Griffin. She was aggressive and decisive, and she knew that could get her in trouble at some point. But, it had always worked for her and she was low on options for making connections to get herself settled. She actually hoped that someone in the church might help her get a lead on a job. She was right.

A man who came to church every now and then happened to be

there the Sunday Ivy Lee joined the church. He overheard Mrs. Griffin introducing her to the pastor. He overheard the story about her losing her parents back to back. He heard Mrs. Griffin say that Ivy Lee was staying with her until she could get a job and get herself on her feet. That was when he stepped into the conversation.

'Excuse me, Pastor," he interrupted. "I couldn't help but overhear this young lady's predicament." He looked at Ivy Lee and extended his hand to Mrs. Griffin. "I'm sorry, I didn't even introduce myself to you ladies." He smiled. "I'm Charles Curry. I have a small law firm downtown." Charles looked specifically at Ivy Lee. "I heard you need a job. I can use a summer clerk. Eight hours a day, five days a week. Typing and filing. Answering the phone, too. Do you think you can do that?"

"How much does it pay?" Ivy Lee wasn't going to look easy, even if she was desperate. She remembered what her mother used to say. Just because she was poor, she didn't have to act like it.

Mrs. Griffin looked at her sharply. Ivy Lee hoped she hadn't sounded insulting. She just needed to know he wasn't going to take advantage of her predicament. Ivy Lee looked at her new pastor. He smiled at her and nodded. Ivy Lee thought that she was going to like this man. Turning to stare at Mr. Curry as she awaited his response, she noticed that his ears were beginning to turn red. "Well," she thought to herself, "it's a good thing I asked. He hadn't even thought about that. Now, he's trying to come up with an amount. What he doesn't know is that I'll take just about anything. But, that's exactly what I didn't want him to know." She smiled at him and waited for him to answer.

Mr. Curry cleared his throat and then responded. "Well, do you think one hundred and fifty dollars a week is fair?"

A hundred and fifty dollars a week! Ivy Lee was ecstatic, but she maintained her poker face. "That sounds like a fair wage," she responded. "What is the address? I will be there early tomorrow morning."

Early she was. She was waiting at the front doors at 7:30 a.m. Mr. Curry arrived at 7:50. He looked surprised to see that she had gotten there before him. She had gone right in and made coffee, then began to tackle the piles of papers that were on the small table that became her first desk. Soon, she had the papers sorted alphabetically, the reception area sparkling clean and smelling fresh, and three sets of briefs transcribed with no errors. Mr. Curry was impressed, but worried. Was this girl going to burn out fast and move on?

As it turned out, Ivy Lee repeated her routine every day for two weeks. So, Mr. Curry gave her a key to the front doors so that she could get the office open and the coffee going before he got to work each day. At the end of three months, she had received two raises and was in her own efficiency apartment not far from the law office. Every Sunday, she would ride to church with Mrs. Griffin and then go home with her and fix a nice dinner for the two of them. They would catch up on Ivy Lee's week and share a few good laughs. The time flew by.

Mr. Curry was a busy man. He was also a very private man. That aspect of his personality had surprised Ivy Lee. For someone who listened in on others' conversations, even if it was so that he could give them a job, it was ironic that he was unwilling to share much of anything about himself with her. Ivy Lee was determined to not appear nosy or probing, so she never initiated conversations with him about his personal life. Still, if he brought up something, she was quick to follow up with a question. At times, he seemed a lot like her – orphaned or without family. Yet, he never revealed where he had come from or what family ties he had. Ivy Lee felt sorry for him.

One Sunday, she was surprised to see him at church when she and Mrs. Griffin arrived. He had not told her on Friday that he planned to attend. Not that he had to, but she thought they were comfortable enough with each other now that he may have shared that when they said goodbye on Friday evening. Her feelings for him were much like those she would have for an uncle. She did her best to take care of his professional needs, but also felt the need to care for his emotional needs as she did for her parents and Mrs. Griffin. He was at least twenty years her senior; but in her mind, he needed her attention in order for him to survive.

Glancing his way a few times during the service, Ivy Lee thought that Mr. Curry looked a little sad, somewhat lonely. She asked Mrs. Griffin if he could join them for dinner, if he wanted. Mrs. Griffin was excited to have him come over. After church, Ivy Lee approached him.

"Hi, Charles! It's good to see you."

"Why? You see me every day?" Mr. Curry scowled, trying to convey an attitude of irritation.

Ivy Lee saw right through it. "True! But, Sunday is a brand new day to see you. Where have you been the past few weeks?"

"Well, if you just must know," he said, looking like she was getting on his nerves, "I hired this new office aide who has created more work for me than what she has done for me. She gets in early, cleans things up, piles papers on my desk for me to sign, and makes me look so proficient that my business has increased more than ten percent of what it was before I hired her. I tried to bribe her with two raises so that she would slow down her production, but it hasn't worked. That is why I have had to work on Sundays. I'm trying to stay a step ahead of her."

"Won't work!" Ivy Lee exclaimed with a laugh. "Mrs. Griffin wants you to come over today for lunch so that she can drill holes in your defense. Will you come, or are you afraid that you can't hold your own against her?" Ivy Lee smiled at him and then turned to Mrs. Griffin for back up. As she glanced away from his eyes, she noticed a child-like bashfulness about him. He seemed uncomfortable, but hopeful. She wondered if he had ever experienced embarrassment and rejection like she had her first semester of college. So, she didn't force him to answer. She just grabbed his left arm and Mrs. Griffin's right arm and maneuvered both of them out to the parking lot.

That Sunday was the first of hundreds. Over the fifteen years that the three of them celebrated Sunday dinners, Ivy Lee and Charles got married at Metropolitan Community Church, bought their own home, purchased beach front real estate property to rent to seasonal tourists, and established themselves as one of the premiere business couples in town. Theirs was a small family, but a strong one. Mrs. Griffin took three cruises with them, one to Alaska and two through the Caribbean Islands. A few days after they returned from their last Caribbean cruise, Mrs. Griffin died with a smile on her face.

Ivy Lee had never met any of Mrs. Griffin's relatives until her funeral. Because Mrs. Griffin had symbolically adopted Ivy Lee as her daughter, she just assumed she should handle all of the arrangements. She had helped Mrs. Griffin plan her end-of-life wishes many years ago. Mrs. Griffin had given her a copy of her will, and Ivy Lee knew that she was the primary beneficiary. She and Charles were very wealthy, so she had no interest in any of Mrs. Griffin's property. Still, she had wanted her to know that when she passed, everything would be taken care of by Ivy Lee and Charles. The funeral had been paid for early, along with the cemetery plot and headstone. Mrs. Griffin wanted to be buried beside her husband who had died when he was thirty-four. He was a savvy businessman himself, carrying on the family printing business. His investments had left her debt-free and set for the rest of her life. She sold the business and divested those funds. Ivy Lee knew that she and Charles would likely set up an endowment at the university in Mrs. Griffin's name for young ladies who came from impoverished households, yet had the potential to be successful students. She wanted to be sure each recipient would receive enough to cover a college wardrobe purchase.

They say the funeral spray brings the family pests out of the woodwork. Ivy Lee chuckled as she thought of this maxim her mother would repeat when she and her father would talk about the antics of greedy family members when some neighbor died. It reminded her of what happened whenever her father would spray to repel the gigantic palmetto roaches. Instead of driving the bugs away, the spray would make the ones that were hiding in the cracks come pouring out. You would hate to disturb them, because their aggressive confidence was more frightening than the few you would see scatter across the floor when you would turn on the lights at night.

Mrs. Griffin's human roaches were disgusting. Ivy Lee expected to see someone she didn't know at the funeral, as she had never met or even heard about a single relative from Mrs. Griffin. However, she realized why when she met these people. The Bradshaws. They were the opposite of what her mother used to talk about. They were supposedly rich people who acted poor. They showed up on Friday night for the wake in a long dark blue Cadillac. It almost looked like a limousine, but it wasn't quite that long. They had made no hotel reservations, so they wanted to stay at the house.

Ivy Lee wasn't sure how to respond. She wanted to be hospitable, but the house was legally her property and she did not know these people. They looked shady. She didn't trust their motives. Quite a few of Mrs. Griffin's household goods of value were still out in their traditional places throughout the home. Ivy Lee offered to pay for a hotel room for them. She smiled warmly and shared that the meals in the hotel restaurant were five-star quality, and they would be her guests. She expected that offer would pacify them.

Mr. Bradshaw was sullen. Mrs. Bradshaw was furious. Their son, Junior, began to berate his mother loudly, saying something about what she had promised him, enough to buy a car. Mrs. Bradshaw began to scream at him to shut up, and Mr. Bradshaw stood up with his hat in his hand and then went out the front door.

Ivy Lee assumed that he was preparing to go to the hotel and that his wife and son would follow. She stood, picked up her purse, and walked toward the front door. However, Mr. Bradshaw met her there with two suitcases in his hands.

"Why, you could have left those in the car. I will drive ahead of you all to show you the way to the hotel. I really think you will like the rooms. All have a sea view, and the food is delicious. Fresh seafood every night!" Ivy Lee tried to keep her voice up, and hoped she sounded genuinely excited. They all looked like such angry people.

"We are going to stay here tonight!" said Mrs. Bradshaw, emphatically. "Teddy, take these suitcases upstairs to an empty bedroom."

Ivy Lee could feel her face flush. She now knew that she was dealing with people who would take her to the next line of defense. How dare they try to push past her into the house? Where had they been all these years? They didn't know who they were messing with!

Ivy Lee tried to maintain a calm demeanor. She spoke slowly. "Mrs. Bradshaw, the house is not prepared for guests. I am afraid you and your family will not be staying here tonight. If you do not want to accept my offer of complimentary rooms and meals, that is up to you. I will assume you are going to arrange your own overnight lodging. But, that lodging will not be in this house." Ivy Lee paused, hoping that they would see she was not playing.

Mrs. Bradshaw turned to face her. Ivy Lee thought she was about to argue. Instead, she began to cry. "My aunt! My aunt! She was my favorite, and now she is dead! Oh my God, why? We have driven so far to come to this funeral! We just want to rest a few minutes in her home, the last place she rested before she left this earth! Won't you please give us that small pleasure? Please?"

Mrs. Bradshaw looked so sincere. Ivy Lee knew what it was like to lose someone very close to you suddenly. It had happened to her three times now. Her mother, then her father, then Mrs. Griffin. She stepped away from the door. Would it really hurt anything for them to stay one night? What if they did take a keepsake or two? Ivy Lee and Charles had so much, it wasn't as if they needed any of Mrs. Griffin's personal property. She was watching over it more for the sake of Mrs. Griffin, because she knew that is what had been expected of her.

Ivy Lee glanced at the son. His mouth was hanging open. He looked like he was confused about what his options might be, and kept one eye on his father. Mr. Bradshaw was still standing in the door, holding a suitcase in each hand. Ivy Lee made a decision.

She walked toward Mr. Bradshaw. "Here, let me take one of these. You all are welcome to stay." Mr. Bradshaw stumbled back a bit as Ivy Lee grabbed the handle of one suitcase and turned to head toward the stairway. The suitcase felt very light, almost as if it were empty. A puzzled air came over Ivy Lee, and she turned to Mrs. Bradshaw who was looking at her husband in a panic and shaking her head quickly from side to side. When she saw Ivy Lee looking at her, she began to smile and nod up and down, but her eyes betrayed her fake response. The suitcase was empty! These fools were going to stuff everything they could into two empty suitcases and then probably beat it out of town before the funeral.

By the time Ivy Lee finished reading them up one side and down the other, Junior had picked up both suitcases and run to the car as fast as he could, hoping to escape before the police arrived. Ivy Lee had insinuated that she thought she had heard of a family of crooks who pretended to be relatives and came into the home of a deceased individual to steal their valuables. Noticing their discomfort, she continued along this line of accusation as Mr. and Mrs. Bradshaw hurriedly collected their belongings and headed to the car. She told them that she thought they were the ones, and she was calling the police immediately. She had a description of their vehicle, which she suspected was borrowed or rented. She had a description of them. If they didn't get out of here right now, she would have the state police on them before they could blink twice!

As they sped off down the street, Ivy Lee began to laugh uncontrollably. She couldn't wait to tell Charles! She didn't know if she was laughing because of how funny they looked with Junior in the back seat crying like a big old baby, or laughing out of relief that they had not called her bluff and tried to overtake her, or worse. "I'll bet they aren't even related to Mrs. Griffin! Just a bunch of crooks trying to steal the remains of an old lady they heard died! That is a shame!"

Ivy Lee sat down on the couch to gather herself. She decided to not call the police. They didn't take anything. Maybe this had scared them enough to not try this prank again. Tomorrow was the funeral. She prayed that Mrs. Griffin rested in peace, knowing that she would do her best to fulfill her wishes. She would close down her home and her assets. She would provide for other lonely young people who needed a push to get to their next step in life. People like her and Charles, Mrs. Griffin, and her parents. People who may not have been born with entitlement at their fingertips, but who weren't afraid to work their fingers to the bone to continue a cycle of giving. Giving didn't have to always be money. It could be love, companionship, friendship. It could be Sunday dinners and church services. It could be a wise word that would carry you through life. It could be a fussing out with a chance to make a change. It could be living a life that you know will please God and those who have had a hand in your character development.

"Just because you're poor, you don't have to stop living! Amen, Mama! Poor is just an opportunity to take what God has given you and pinch off a piece for somebody else. That's what living is all about!" Ivy Lee laughed loudly, and the whole house rang with the sound. In the echoes, she thought she could also hear the laughter of her mother, her father, and Mrs. Griffin. "Amen, you all! I think I've got it!" she said, laughing until she cried.

I Stood on the Banks of Jordan

"He that covereth his sins shall not prosper; but whoso confesseth and forsaketh them shall have mercy." Proverbs 28:13

*

As soon as Emily woke up, she knew that something was wrong. All night long, she had been dreaming about random physical activities. She was trying to ride a bike through the woods but she couldn't push the pedals because her stomach was hurting. She was walking and eating ice cream that kept melting and then coming back, but every now and then she would find herself sitting on something because her stomach would start hurting. She would start to talk and then couldn't understand what she was saying, or her mouth would be moving with no words coming out. Then, she would hear the sound of a horn in a tunnel and realize she was walking behind a stranger trying to talk to them, trying to grab them, but as she reached forward in slow motion they would always elude her grasp. Then, she felt herself floating in shallow water. Lily pads and reeds surrounded her. Her hair was floating like a limp crown and she could only see dimly out of her right eye. She was having a hard time breathing. It felt like the water was seeping into her nostrils. On the verge of smothering, she fought to gain consciousness. Emerging from the dim clouds of her sleep, she realized that she needed to have a bowel movement – fast!

Emily sat straight up in bed and then almost doubled over from the crashing pain. She lay down on her left side. "What is wrong with me?" She felt the urge to defecate return. As she swung her legs over the bed, she felt a lot of wetness underneath her. "Oh no! Did I pee on myself in the middle of the night? Why didn't that wake me up?" Then, she wondered if she had pushed it out when she felt the need to have a bowel movement. She slid off of the bed and looked back at the spot where she had been laying. There was a light pink puddle there. "Blood and pee?" she wondered. "Whoa! Did my water break in the middle of the night?"

Emily realized the cramps that woke her up were very strong and painful. She was almost afraid to go to the bathroom, but she felt like she needed to empty her bladder and her bowels at the same time. "What if the baby comes out?" she thought. "Should I call somebody?" Emily couldn't think of who to call. Her mom lived three states over. Randy had left her for the girl who worked in the tavern months ago. Her neighbor lady had been helpful in the past, but she was old. Plus, she didn't have a car, so she couldn't get Emily to a hospital.

When Emily wiped herself, she noticed that there was more blood and something that looked like snot on the toilet paper. The sight of the blood made her nervous. Her hands began to shake and she started to feel hot. "Oh God! I don't know what I should do! Please help me think of something. I don't want this baby to come while I'm home all by myself." She got up slowly, but that didn't keep another cramp from starting. Holding on to the sink, she bent her knees and waited until it passed. Now she was really scared. "Am I really about to have this baby? Oh my, I am not ready! And, how am I going to get to the hospital? Come on, girl! Get yourself together. You have to do something and quick!"

Emily grabbed a towel from the rack and put it in the sink. She let the water run until it got warm. It felt good on her trembling hands. She took the bar of soap and wrapped it in the towel, then ran more warm water over the towel. Unfolding it, she washed her face and arms, then her underarms. She pulled off her nightshirt and began to wash her upper body. When she rubbed the warm towel across her abdomen, the baby rolled toward her hand as if to say, "Good morning, Mama!"

"Don't get too happy in there," she gritted through closed teeth as the wave of pain began to radiate from her groin toward her back. She moved the towel around to prop her lower belly, lifting it slightly as if that would relieve the pain. It seemed to make it worse. "God, is it going to be more than this? I don't think I can stand it!" She wanted to cry. She felt so helpless. But, she knew that she had to get herself together and out of the house, to the hospital, before she went into more labor. She could imagine that it could get so bad that she wouldn't be able to move. Then, what would she do?

She finished washing herself off and was leaning over to wipe the tops of her feet when she heard something pop. She straightened herself up slowly. As she did, a stream of water began to course its way down her right thigh. Panic began to overtake her once again. She just wanted to lie down on the bathroom floor and let whatever was going to happen just happen. But, something seemed to rise up inside of her and control her as if she were now a robot. She grabbed a bath towel and wrapped it around her waist. Shuffling into the bedroom, she went to her dresser and took out a set of underclothes. She could feel another cramp coming on, but she pushed through it to get herself dressed. She opened a second drawer and took out a large, loose sundress. She slipped that over her head, slid her feet into the sandals that were beside the bedroom door, picked up her purse and the small sack she had packed for the hospital, and headed toward the door.

As she walked, the pain seemed to lessen. "Good," Emily thought. "Maybe I can get to the sidewalk. Maybe someone will see me and give me a ride." Before stepping outside the door, she looked around the small apartment. She had meant to change the sheets on the bed, but it was too late now. The bathroom was still a bit of a mess. She should have cleaned that up. She wondered if she had left anything plugged in. Then, she remembered that she hadn't even combed her hair. "Oh well, too late for that." She figured she would smooth it with her hand when she got a chance.

Emily stepped out of the door onto the porch. She could feel another cramp coming, but she thought she might do like she did last time and keep on walking through it. Pulling herself up tall, she moved her left leg then her right leg forward. The cramp wasn't quite as bad as she thought it would be, but she could feel more of that fluid coming out. "I should have put on a pad," she thought.

Mr. Whitaker, the guy who managed her apartments, was taking out the trash just as she was heading for the sidewalk. "Hi, Emily! How are you doing this morning? You're up a little early today. Have a doctor's appointment?" He was really a nice guy, not weird or anything. Even though she had only said "hi" to him, he always seemed to have a smile and to be sincere about asking her how she was doing.

Emily tried to manage a smile, but the last pain was just dying down. Her face must have looked a little twisted, because he walked over to her quickly and grabbed her under her right arm. Maybe it was also because she was starting to have another pain and had stopped for a moment to tense up until the pain passed. Whatever it was, it caught his attention; so, he came to catch her.

Immediately, Emily started to cry. She didn't know what to tell him, but she did know that she felt horrible. She was scared and she was hurting. Mr. Whitaker seemed to know what to do right away.

"Emily, are you about to have the baby?" Emily nodded in the midst of her tears. Mr. Whitaker grabbed her purse and her bag. "Sit right here." He lowered her gently onto the step. "I'm going to get my car. I'll put your things in it. You just sit right here and I'll be back in less than a minute." Emily looked at him. He noticed how she looked like a little girl, afraid but yet trusting. He stopped long enough to pat her on the head, then trotted to the back drive. Tossing her things into the back seat, he quickly stepped into the car and started the engine. He didn't put on his seatbelt. He would be getting out in a few seconds.

When he came around the corner and pulled up to the sidewalk, Emily was leaning sideways. It was obvious that she was having a pain. He wondered how long she had been in labor. He hoped that they would be able to get to the hospital in time. In his estimation, it would take them about seven or eight minutes if the traffic on the freeway wasn't bad. He prayed that it would not be.

Gingerly helping her down the sidewalk, he thought about the last time he had done this. His wife was young, pretty like Emily. She was really short and small built. Too small to carry the big baby, the doctor told him later. Too small to survive the long labor. Mercifully, when she died, his son did, too. He hadn't thought about that day in a long time. Even now, tears rose up in his throat like a bitter drink. They tried to force the tear ducts in his eyes to open once again, but he denied them that privilege. He had not cried since that day, and he had vowed that he would never cry again. He couldn't cry. If he did, he might lose more than his mind. He might lose his own will to live.

Emily groaned just a little. That snapped him back to the present and his task at hand. "Sorry, little girl! I didn't mean to rush you! Take your time. That's it. Take it easy." Mr. Whitaker spoke softly to Emily, coaching her into the front seat. Rushing around to his door, he worried that they might not make it, that something might happen and cause him to be part of another tragedy. No! He couldn't let himself think about anything like that. Emily was going to be okay. They were going to make it!

The drive to the hospital seemed to take hours, even though he noticed only three minutes had elapsed by the time he entered the freeway. The hospital exit was just two exits down the road, which meant they only had two miles to travel. He could do that in a minute. After that, he would just go down three, no four, blocks and he would be at the emergency entrance. If all of the lights were green...please God, please let them all be green...they could make it. "Send an angel before us, God! Let that angel make all of the lights be green!" He prayed anything he could think to pray as he watched his mirrors for police and other cars. He just had to get her there in time.

Emily groaned again. He could tell she was trying to mask her pain. How long had it been since he had heard her last groan? He looked at her. Her eyes were closed. She looked like she was sleep but having a bad dream. His palms began to sweat. Where is the baby's father? Is he a military man? Why isn't he here taking care of this situation he helped to create? Why wasn't he driving his wife and baby to the hospital? Was she even married? He realized how little he knew about her. But, he did know that she needed his help, and he had to stay focused if he was going to be able to do anything for her.

Carol had been his college sweetheart. They had met the first week of their freshman year at the frosh sock hop. It was a get-together for new students so that they could make new friends. It worked. He asked her to dance and she said yes. After that first dance, they never stopped dancing until the day she died. In all of her goodness and pureness, he never imagined that anything bad could ever happen to her.

They were chaste in their relationship and saved themselves for each other. Both were virgins when they married the day after their college graduation. It wasn't easy, but it was worth it. That act of acknowledging God and preserving their intimacy for the sanctity of marriage caused each of them to value the other highly, and their every interaction was one of true love and respect. He had majored in business, and she in accounting. She immediately landed a job as a fiduciary with a local bank and was content every day to balance books and manipulate numbers. After two months of competitive interviewing, he was hired by a marketing firm. They were soon able to purchase a cute little cottage near the hospital. All was well until the night the baby didn't come.

Ron Whitaker tried hard to think about Emily as he maneuvered the car carefully in front of the sliding glass doors. Putting the gear into "Park", he couldn't help but think of the last time he had hurried to this entrance, looking for a wheelchair to transport his precious cargo. He took her in, but couldn't bring them back out. He lost that race.

Ron shook himself as he hurried to Emily's door. He looked frantically for someone to help. He saw a wheelchair just inside the sliding glass door. As he stepped toward the door, it opened automatically. Rushing inside, he grabbed the handle of the wheelchair, swung the chair around, and headed right back out to the car. He could see Emily trying to lift herself to come and meet him.

"Hold it, I'm coming for you," he said to her. She staggered slightly toward the chair and put her hand on the arm rest. He grabbed her other arm and helped her to sit. The car was still running and the door was open, but he turned and pushed her into the lobby. There was a receptionist sitting there. She looked at both of them quizzically.

"She's having a baby!" Ron spoke quickly and wheeled Emily toward her. The receptionist stood and came around her desk to meet them.

"How long has she been in labor?" She looked at Ron.

"I don't know! She lives in my building. I saw her outside. I just gave her a ride to the hospital." He was talking quickly as he handed Emily off to the receptionist. He stepped back, not knowing what he should do next. The receptionist had wheeled Emily back over to her desk.

"Ma'am, how long have you been having labor pains?"

Emily opened her mouth to begin to answer, but began to cry instead.

"Are you in a lot of pain?" the receptionist asked as she lifted Emily's wrist. Emily nodded. "On a scale of one to ten, how bad would you describe the pain to be?"

Emily held up all ten fingers. They were shaking badly.

"Okay, we'll get you right up to the maternity ward and ask questions later." She turned to Ron. "Sir, you can park your car and then come back in these doors. Take the elevator at the end of this hallway and come up to

Floor Three. When you get off, walk straight ahead. Let the nurse know that you are here to see…what's your name?" She paused while she was taking Emily's pulse.

"Emily Johnson," she responded weakly.

"Tell the nurse you're there to see Ms. Johnson." She looked Ron sternly in the eye. "You got that?"

If Ron ever thought of just dropping Emily off and going back home, that thought was eliminated by this nurse/receptionist. She expected him to follow this mission through and be there when Emily had the baby. He nodded emotionlessly and turned to head back to the car. Before he left, he walked back to pat Emily's hand. "It'll be all right, little girl!" She grimaced and nodded, then rolled her head back and moaned. The nurse whisked her on down the hallway.

Ron stood still for a moment. He had not expected his day to follow this path. He had just gotten to the place where he could drive in this part of town again. Now, he was right back at the same hospital where he had last seen his wife alive so many years ago. Back in the same place in the same predicament – trying to support a woman who was having a baby. "Lord, please don't let Emily's baby die. Please don't let Emily die. Help me, please!"

Ron could feel the tears trying to rise again as he walked from his parked car back to the hospital doors. Who did that nurse think she was, telling him what to do? She didn't know what he had been through before. How could she assume that he could just drop everything he had to do that day to come and sit with some young girl who had chosen to get pregnant without having a husband to walk through this with her? If she would have done like he and Carol had done, she wouldn't be in this situation. If she would have waited to be married to have sex, she wouldn't be in this spot. But, what difference did that make to God? He took his precious love and their child anyway.

Ron's steps down the hallway to the elevator felt mechanical. Each one seemed to shake his core. He felt nauseous. He really did not want to enter the elevator and go to the third floor. Too many memories were rushing back into his consciousness. He wasn't ready for them yet. He didn't appreciate being forced into facing these feelings. He needed more time. Yet, he saw himself on the elevator, pushing the "3". The rise of the elevator increased the feeling of nausea. His knees were weak. His mouth was beginning to dry. When the doors of the elevator opened, he started to stay on and let it take him back to the first floor. But, before the doors could close, the receptionist/nurse came rushing through the maternity wing entrance doors. She saw him and called quickly to him. "Sir! Hurry up! She's already dilated to eight. It won't be long! She needs you!"

Ron placed his foot in the elevator door and it reopened. She grabbed his hand. "Come on," she said. "I'll take you right to her room. You have to hurry, though!"

They stopped at the cleanser station and pumped a couple of squirts of disinfectant foam into their palms. While he was briskly rubbing his hands together, she went into a room and then came back out with some shoe covers, a paper gown, and a hat.

"What's all this about?" Ron asked gruffly.

"Put it on!" she commanded. "We're about to have a baby!"

We? Ron didn't know how he had been included in this little situation, but he did want to check on Emily. As the receptionist/nurse led him into her room, he could see that things were lighted up and there was another nurse there monitoring a printout from the computer. She smiled at him as he walked in, then nodded at Emily.

"She's coming along real well! Her pains are about two minutes apart and lasting about thirty seconds. The baby will be here before you know it. Have a seat. You won't have to work too hard. She's doing it all by herself!"

Ron walked over to the side of the bed where Emily's head was turned. He wanted to see her face and make sure she was okay. For a moment, he thought she looked like Carol. But, they were totally different. Emily's face was strong and well-chiseled. Carol had been delicate, pale, pink like a peony. He patted her arm so she would know he was there. She opened her eyes and smiled weakly. Her lips looked dry. He felt sorry for her.

"How you doing, Emily? I guess you'll be a mama soon." He smiled back at her. "Do you want me to go or stay? That bossy nurse made me come up here, but she didn't ask you if you wanted company. What do you say?"

Emily reached for his hand. "Please stay. I need somebody here with me. I'm scared." She looked like she was about to cry again.

Ron squeezed her hand. "I'm here for you. Don't be afraid. You are going to be fine. You are going to have a beautiful, healthy baby. In just a few minutes, all of this pain will be a memory. You'll be holding your baby and you will be happy. And, I'll stay until it's all over, okay?"

"Okay. Thanks." As Emily returned the squeeze he could feel her grip become more intense. Ron thought she was having another contraction. She opened her eyes and stared at the wall, opened her mouth slightly, and breathed slow, measured breaths.

"Wow! That's a good one!" said the nurse, watching a needle make zigzags on the paper printout. "I think I'd better check you after that one." She squeezed past Ron and pulled the curtain. He sat down in a chair beside the door. He was sweaty and nervous. He needed some water. As he was turning to walk out into the hall to find a fountain, the nurse came from behind the curtain.

"Show's on!" she exclaimed as she rushed past him. What did that mean? The receptionist/nurse came into the room immediately and headed straight for Emily. She began to move some things around on the bed and unhooked a rail at the end of the bed.

"What's going on?" Ron asked, still standing beside the door.

"She's about to have this baby. It's crowned and she has dilated to ten. Connie had gone to get the doctor. Are you ready?"

Ron wondered if he even wanted to stay in there. He might get in the way. He didn't want to watch this birth, anyway. He just wanted to be sure Emily was fine.

"Okay, come on over here," said the bossy nurse. "I need for you to stand here and make sure she keeps her eyes open. Talk to her. Help her count her breathing. She can't push until the doctor comes. Thanks!" She moved to prep the birthing station, leaving him to talk to Emily. He could see she was about to have another contraction.

"Well, I guess we have to do this and we have no choice," he joked. "Okay, Emily, open your eyes. That's good!" She began to breathe hard. "Okay, look at my nose and try to blow on it. That's good, take a deep breath and breathe it out slowly, slowly, that's good. Don't push! Blow out the candle! Good! Good!"

He hadn't seen the doctor enter the room. When he looked away from Emily's face, he saw a lady leaning over Emily's lifted knees. One of her silicone-gloved hands was under the sheet and the other was on Emily's left knee. She looked at the nurses on both sides of her and nodded. Then, she spoke to Emily.

"Okay, you are ready and the baby is, too. You can push the next time you have a contraction." She looked at Ron, nodded, and smiled. "We'll have a baby soon!"

"There goes that 'we' again!" Ron thought. "I'll never have a baby again. But, if I can help Emily get through this, I'm willing to do that." He noticed Emily's lip begin to quiver. Boy, was she brave. He had expected her to get hysterical when the actual birth process started, but she had stayed focused and kept her cool. Strong kid! She squeezed his hand hard. He went into coaching action. "Okay, Emily, she said you can push on this one. You can do it. That's good. Push. Push." He really wasn't sure what he was supposed to tell her, but he wanted her to get through this okay. If she was supposed to push, he wanted her to do that. She squeezed his hand harder. It felt like she was crushing his bones. She began to moan loudly.

"Good job!" the doctor said. "Come on, keep pushing. It's coming." The doctor kept pulling something under the sheet. Ron kept his eyes on Emily's forehead. Sweat was popping, but he was nervous about looking down. He didn't even know her that well. Why was he here? He had just gone to take out the trash and ended up at the hospital. Having a baby. Again. Not his, but a life, hopefully. Why?

"Here she is!" The doctor lifted a blood-smeared, greasy creature. Arms and legs were waving. Ron was afraid to look at its face. It wasn't crying. Weren't they supposed to cry? Was something wrong with her? Panic gripped his belly. Would this baby die, too? The nurse took her and wrapped her quickly in a blanket, then laid her on Emily's stomach. Emily hadn't turned to look at her yet. Was something wrong with Emily? Ron stepped close to Emily's face. Her eyes were closed.

"Emily! Emily! You have a baby girl!" He waited for her to open her eyes and respond. She didn't. "Oh no," he thought, "she can't be dead!" Ron realized that his mind was reeling out into a ridiculous space. If something was wrong with her, the monitors would have told them. Looking closely at her, he realized that she was crying. "Emily, you have a beautiful baby. Open your eyes and see her!"

Emily nodded her head no. "I'm scared! Is she okay? I spent most of my pregnancy praying that she would go away, that this would all be a dream! I figured God would punish me by killing her or making her deformed. I'm afraid to look at her!" She began to sob softly. "Please, Mr. Whitaker, check her for me. I can't open my eyes until I know she's okay!"

Ron hated that his day had turned out like this. He didn't want to see her, either. He thought she might be dead, or die if he looked at her. Before he could decide what he was going to do, the receptionist/nurse touched his arm. She was holding a small bundle. It was the baby.

"Here she is, Miss America! And, she's adorable. Congratulations!" She handed Ron the baby and stepped away to begin to press on Emily's stomach. Emily kept her eyes closed and tears flowed from under her lids. Ron looked down at the baby. Her face was rosy and round. Her little lips were slightly pouted, but smoothed out when he focused on her face. She opened her eyes and looked at him. She didn't cry or make any expression. She just stared. He stared back.

"Hello, my friend!" he said softly. She closed her eyes. He lifted the blanket slightly and looked at her tiny pink fingers. She looked fine. He wrapped her back up tightly and held her more closely. "My friend." She sucked her lips together, but didn't cry. She seemed very comfortable and content in his arms. He looked at her innocent face. He hoped that she would never be disappointed by anyone she loved. He thought that she would be a blessing to Emily. Why didn't Emily open her eyes and meet her new child?

"Emily," he said softly, "she's beautiful! She's fine! All of her fingers and all of her toes are in place." He chuckled. "She is a doll. I'm so glad that you forced me to make a new friend today. I think we'll be friends for a long, long time." He walked her to Emily's side of the bed. "Mama, meet your baby girl!" He stood still, waiting for Emily's eyes to open.

"I can't. I'm scared."

"Scared of what?" Ron asked quietly.

"Scared that I won't be a good mom, that I won't love her, that I won't be able to take care of her like she deserves!"

Ron waited a couple of seconds. He remembered those panicked feelings the last time he stood in a delivery room. But, she had a living, breathing baby! Her baby lived! Her love was not cut short like his had been. She had no reason to be fearful.

"Emily, please open your eyes and behold your blessing. The last time I was in this hospital was to say goodbye to my wife and our stillborn son. My wife died in childbirth. My son died because he couldn't survive the labor. My wife was in hard labor for hours and her body wouldn't recover from it. You have a beautiful daughter who is living and will be able to take your love and love you back. I will never again have that opportunity. I don't know what you did or why you are here today but I do know that I am holding one of the most beautiful babies I have ever seen, and if you don't open up your eyes and appreciate this miracle from God then I don't know what I'm going to do!" Ron could hear his own voice shaking uncontrollably. He was mad, but he was also amazed at all he was seeing and feeling. Who could reject such a beautiful gift? How could Emily be so selfish? He looked at the baby. She yawned and opened her eyes again, then began to make the sucking noises like she had before. "She needs Emily. She needs me. She needs somebody to love her," he said to himself. Then aloud, he told her, "Don't worry, little princess! Old Ron is here for you. I'm here for you!" He didn't realize it, but tears were coursing down his cheeks. One bounced onto Emily's face, then two and more. She opened her eyes. Seeing Ron crying, she began to cry.

"I'm sorry!" she said. "I'm just scared!"

"I know. I am too. But, I'm not stupid. Love your baby. She's worth it!"

Emily reached up her arms. Ron laid the baby gently in them, and held on to both of them as Emily rested her arm back on the bed. She pulled back the blanket to look at her daughter. She was beautiful, so delicate and sweet. They could be okay. She would be all right. She kissed her forehead.

Ron stepped back and then realized that he had cried so much that the front of his paper gown was wet with his tears. He had hardly noticed it, but somehow felt better for it.

The nurse came back into the room. She had to take the baby. Neither Emily nor Ron wanted to see her leave, but she promised to bring her back once they took her vitals and got her all cleaned up. She was a fine baby, and she would be back with her in a few minutes.

After the nurse left with the baby, Ron stood beside Emily's side of the bed and thought about the events of the day. "God, I think you did this for me," he thought. "I needed this healing. But, Emily needed me, too. Thanks for helping me to be in place and giving me the strength to walk this through."

As if reading his thoughts, Emily said, "Mr. Whitaker, thank you so much for helping me today. You helped in more ways that you will ever realize. I may not have made it through this if you wouldn't have been there to help me. Thank you so much!"

Ron waited for a moment and then said, "I think you helped me more than I helped you. Honestly, I think God set us up from early this morning to help each other. What do you think about that?"

"I think that's great, Mr. Whitaker! So does my brand new daughter! I don't know what would have happened to us if you would not have been there for us."

"Well, it seems like Someone much wiser and more Ancient than you or I recruited me for a special ops mission, Miss Emily! So far, it has been my pleasure! And from the looks of things, both the mission and the pleasure are destined to last a long, long time. So, enough of this 'Mr. Whitaker' stuff. From now on, just call me Uncle Ron."

Roll Jordan, Roll

"The rod and reproof give wisdom; but a child left to himself bringeth his mother to shame." Proverbs 29:15

*

"Hey, Tock!" Tom turned to see who called him by his old nickname. He hadn't expected to run into anyone else out this early in the morning on the beach. Squinting into the rising sun, he saw an old school friend approaching him from about 500 feet.

"Hey, Brice!" Tom waited until they were just a few feet apart and then opened his arms wide for a hug. "Good to see you, man! Been a long time! How you doing?" Tom stepped back to check out his old friend. They had been best buddies all throughout junior high and high school. Even though both still lived in town, he hadn't seen Brice for a couple of years.

"Ah, man, I'm doing okay. How about you?" Brice raised his hand sideways over his brow as if to shade himself from the sun. Tom thought that was a little strange, since the sun was coming up behind his back.

"Doing good, real good! Thought I'd get my early walk in before it got too warm. I remember when that early walk used to be an early run, though!" He slapped Brice lightly on the back with his left hand, half-hugging him again. He remembered all of the fun the two of them used to have.

"Man, I know what you're talking about!" Brice agreed. "Those were the days!" He laughed heartily.

"They sure were," said Tom. "Boy, you know nobody calls me 'Tock' anymore! I outgrew that one a long time ago!" Tom laughed, too. It felt good to be talking to his good friend once again. He tried to remember why they had stopped talking so often.

"You mean nobody calls you Taco Tommy anymore?" Brice nudged Tom in the ribs. It reminded him of when they used to roll around in the grassy lot between his house and the vacant, dilapidated fish-cleaning shack. Old local fishermen used to stop there with their fresh catch, clean it, and then either build a fire on the shore and cook it right there, or take it home ready for the pan. But, no one had used it in decades. The boys would pretend that the shack was a pirate hideout and they were looking for the buried treasure that the pirates left a hundred years ago. One might pick up a rusty slug and jump up and down, screaming that he had found a gold coin. The other would chase him out the door to get it, catch him, wrestle him to the ground, and roll around trying to get his hands on the "gold coin".

Tom remembered how Brice and some other boys had started calling him "Taco Tommy". His mother was from Mexico. She cooked traditional Mexican food all the time. One day they had tacos for dinner and Brice came to get him to come out and play. He had stood in the doorway with half a taco in his hand, waving to Brice and saying he was coming. Brice had waited until he got impatient, and then went on off with the other boys to play. When Tom finally joined them, Brice teased him that he was late because he had to stay home and finish his taco. He kept up the teasing, calling him "Taco Tommy" over and over until all the other boys were doing it and laughing. At first, Tom had joined the laughter. Then, he got angry. He knocked Brice down and made his nose bleed.

Immediately, he was sorry. There was something about seeing Brice's dirt-smeared face and bloody nose that made him sick to the stomach. He was mad at himself for doing that to his friend. Still, he didn't like it that Brice had teased him and made the other boys laugh at him. The two made up the next day, but that didn't stop the other kids from calling him "Taco Tommy" when they saw him again. The name stuck all through junior high, but they quit when he became the running back on the high school football team. No more "Taco Tommy". He was "Tom" to everyone except Brice. From the day of the fight until now, Brice had called him "Tock". Tom didn't mind.

He realized that they were long overdue for some conversation, but he also knew he had to get back home to get ready for work. How time flew! He wished that he had the leisure they enjoyed as youth, plenty of time to swim and play around all day. Room for imagination and pirate ships. Time to play football and baseball. Moms who cooked your favorite foods every day and let you sleep in until you were ready to get up. Those were the good old days.

"So, where have you been, man?" Tom questioned. "I haven't seen you in over a year."

Brice looked out toward the water before he answered him. Tom noticed that Brice's eyes were watering, but he didn't know if it was from the wind or if it was something else. He wanted to ask, but just waited for Brice to answer.

Brice cleared his throat and looked at his watch. Tom figured he might not think he had time to talk much, and that was okay. He was about to let him know that it was good to see him and they could pick another time to have a bite to eat and catch up on old times, when Brice answered.

"Uh, two years ago, right about this time, my five-year old little girl drowned right over there." He pointed to the huge rock that was jutting out of the water to their left. It was what the kids called "Dinosaur Rock", like the kids' show that used to come on television. It kind of looked like the humps you would imagine on a dinosaur, and there was an extension on each end that an imaginative child could claim was a head and then a tail. Tom remembered hearing about a drowning, but he was on vacation when it happened. He just read a few late details about it when he got back home a couple of weeks after the incident.

Reaching out to Brice, Tom said, "Oh man, I am so sorry to hear that! I remember hearing about it, but I was out of town at the time. I had no idea that was your daughter! Whoa, that is terrible! How are you doing?"

Brice dropped his head. It was evident that he was still grieving. She must have been very precious to him; and even after two years, the pain was still fresh. Tom couldn't imagine what Brice was going through. Brice continued, "Yeah, it's been rough. But, the one hurting most is her twin sister. She's seven years old. She misses her a lot. She feels responsible for her sister drowning, even though there was nothing she could have done. They were just playing together on the beach. When she looked up, her sister was gone. She never saw her go into the water." Brice wiped his eyes with the back of his hand.

"Has she been able to talk to anybody? A counselor or something? I know that has to be hard for her." Tom put his hand on Brice's shoulder. "You, too."

"Yeah, man," Brice said. "It's hard. She's been, well we all have been going to a psychiatrist. He's a nice guy. He listens more than he talks. He told me that it will help me take power over my self-blame if I come out here and see this place as what it is – an opportunity for loss if no one is there to stop it. I wasn't there. Nothing I can do now but accept what happened. The sea won this one. I have to give it up. I can't blame myself for something that I could not prevent. Coming out here in the mornings helps me put that into perspective, so I've been doing this for about three weeks now." Brice chuckled, then wiped his eyes. "I guess that makes it a habit."

"Wow! I admire your strength, man! I don't know what I would do if I lost my child, if I even had one." Tom didn't know what to say. Brice didn't look very impressed with his compliment, if that even was one. Tom wanted to hug him again, but didn't feel like Brice was expecting pity. Affirmation, maybe?

Brice leaned over and began brushing sand off of his ankles. Tom took that as a signal that Brice was ready to move on down the beach. Tom knew that he, too, had to get home and get ready for work before long. Yet, he didn't want to leave his old friend like this.

"Tell you what," Tom said. "Let's get together again, maybe this

Friday night. We can catch up on old times, and maybe share a tray of tacos!" They both laughed. "What do you think?"

Brice paused for just a moment, then replied, "That sounds like a plan. Where shall we go? Sal's?" Sal's was a spot where the teenagers used to hang out. They had a little bit of everything there, though Tom couldn't remember whether or not they served tacos. Still, there would be good food and good music. Tom hoped that he could count on good company, too.

"Sal's it is," said Tom, shaking Brice's hand hard. He stepped up to his friend and gave him a big hug. "So good to see you, man," he said into Brice's shoulder. "It's been a long time. Too long."

"Yep," said Brice, patting Tom on the back. The two stepped apart. "But," he continued, "we're about to make up for lost time. And, it's none too soon."

The two parted and continued to walk in their different directions. Tom thought about trotting to redeem the time, but he just wanted to walk it out. He was glad he had seen Brice, but the story of his daughter's drowning really brought him down. That was a tough thing to deal with, and Tom didn't want to think about anything so depressing this early in the morning. Still, Brice had been his friend and he wanted to be there to support him, no matter what. Death. There never had been anything pretty about it.

An orange tabby cat ran from the brush and across his path when he was a few steps from his car. It startled him. He never had liked cats, and seeing this one brought up an image he had tried hard to forget. Even though he hated cats, he had never felt quite right about what he had done to those kittens when he was thirteen. Brice had tried to talk him out of it, and had cried when Tom smashed the gunny sack with the six small mewling kittens into the stump of the old oak tree in the field where the boys used to play baseball. They had found them and thought they were motherless. A couple of the guys wanted to each take one home. Brice wanted them to wait and look for the mother.

But, Tom had another idea. He hated kittens and he hated cats. Remembering the incident, Tom was trying to recall what had created that extreme and vicious dislike for cats. Then, he remembered that big tom cat that had scratched his baby sister. His mother whipped him because he was supposed to be watching her while she was hanging the clothes out on the line. He was mad at the cat for making him get a whipping with that long, stinging switch. It cut his legs and made them bleed. The more he wiped the lines of blood, the madder he got at that tom cat. A few days later, he trapped it with some chicken livers, hit it in the head with a big rock, put it in a paper bag, and burnt it up out in the baseball field.

After the day he killed the kittens, Brice and a few of the guys stopped hanging around with him. It wasn't until they got to high school and he became a star football player that they started to talk to him again. Nobody ever brought up the kittens, but sometimes they looked at him as if they didn't trust him, as if they thought he was a little crazy. Maybe he was. He did dream about cats from time to time, usually when he was anxious about an upcoming challenge.

Some of the women that he dated reminded him of cats. The way they moved, the looks they gave, how they cried. He had found it difficult to maintain healthy relationships with women. He never argued with them or put his hands on them in an aggressive manner, but he would break up with them quickly when he began to notice feline tendencies in their behaviors.

He moved out of his parents' house during the summer when he was seventeen. He got hired at the fishery right away and stayed with Alex, one of his friends from school, until he could get enough to rent a tiny apartment week by week. When his senior year started in the fall, he worked the afternoon shift from three until eleven, and then went to school during the day. The football coach needed him so badly that he let him play on Friday nights without practicing at all during the week. Tom had let him know early on that it would have to be that way if he wanted him on the team. The coach was too happy to accommodate him. His tenacity on the job was admirable. His boss was impressed with his hard work and promoted him to supervisory levels while he was still in high school. By the time he graduated, he was making a good salary and saw his placement as permanent. Now, he was an upper manager and a homeowner. But, he had severed ties with his own family when his sister had started to get on his nerves, and he had no wife or children of his own. Hope of a family in the future was dim, too, because he didn't even have a girlfriend.

Tom hadn't minded solitude. In fact, he preferred it. That was why he began coming to the beach very early in the morning. He could avoid the crowds and not have to worry about running into anyone. He didn't consider himself anti-social. He just preferred his own company to anyone else's. He could see himself being a lifetime bachelor, but not a hermit. He did like working and supervising people. It gave him a sense of purpose and he enjoyed exercising his authority over others. He needed to be in control.

Even though he knew he had come a long way in his emotional healing, he was still somewhat surprised at himself for suggesting that he and Brice meet at Sal's on Friday. Brice had touched him at his core, and he felt at the time that was the right thing to do. Maybe the therapy sessions were helping. He realized that he had an appointment tomorrow evening after work. Doc Fannister would be glad to know that he was reaching out to others in a healthy way. Tom smiled to himself as he pulled into his garage and turned off the engine. Maybe he really was making progress in his quest to kill those old dragons.

Tom knew that his meetings with Doc had begun to change his life. He was able to talk about why he was disappointed in his father, a weak man who had turned to alcohol and succumbed to depression rather than stand up to his abusive wife. The switchings he got from his mother weren't the worst of her abuses. She seemed angry all the time. Later in life, he realized that it was because of her undiagnosed cancer. She must have been in constant pain, the doctor told the family, all those years that the melon-sized tumor was growing in her uterus. Before she died, she apologized to them for not going to see a doctor. She didn't think the family could afford to spend money on any treatments that might be recommended. Plus, she had hoped and prayed that it would go away.

Prayer. That was something he had been trying lately. His friend, Greeley, had invited him to a church called Metropolitan. He had told him that the pastor was cool and only preached for about twenty minutes. Tom had promised to come and watch Greeley's kid sing one Sunday. He sat in the very back, waiting for an opportunity to slip out once he saw the boy sing. But, then the pastor started talking. It would be the first of many Sundays that he would come, sit in the back for the message, and then slip out. No one would ever try to stop him or even look as if he was doing anything wrong. In fact, most people smiled at him and made him feel welcome. The real reason he stayed and kept coming back, though, was that the pastor talked as if he was Tom's friend and knew everything there was to know about him. He read his mind, he knew his fears, he spoke to his hopes. Tom fed on those messages.

One Sunday morning, the pastor talked about Jesus being like a friend who loved to hear from you and spend time with you, but never got angry with you for anything wrong you might do. He loved you in ways that challenged your own logic. He loved you when you didn't think you deserved to be loved. All He asked from you was an apology, and it was more for your own good than it was for Him. The pastor said, "Mastering the art of saying, 'I'm sorry', can turn a rock head into a rock star!" The teenagers all thought that was funny. Some of the older people frowned, some laughed. Tom had sat straight up, as if a bolt of lightning had struck him on the top of his head.

For most of his life, he thought others had owed him an apology – his father for not being physically and emotionally present, his mother for taking her pain out on him, his sister for being a burden of responsibility for him, the women in his life who could not tolerate his idiosyncrasies, his friends who only cared about him when he could do something for them. All of these people had used him and then left him alone. But now, the pastor was suggesting that he should practice apologizing to them! For what?

All that Sunday afternoon, Tom had mulled over that challenge. The more he thought about it, the more he could highlight instances in his life that he had hurt others and felt justified for doing it. Turning off the impulse to be the victim who then turned into the victimizer was going to be hard. They deserved to feel badly for the things they had done to him. Wasn't that what "turn about is fair play" was all about?

But, what had that gotten him? Here he was, alone and unloved. How could he start again? The answer came that next day when he visited Dr. Fannister. Tom told him about seeing Brice on the beach and the message on asking forgiveness that the pastor had preached on Sunday. He felt like he was ready to make things right with his family, but he didn't know how to start the process. Would they be angry with him? Would that set him back in his process of self-healing? How could he help his friend deal with the loss of his daughter if he couldn't help himself? As Tom struggled with his conflicting emotions, Doc asked him what he thought he should do. Tom already knew the answer. He had two people to visit before he could move on with his own healing.

Tom's father and sister still lived in the old family home. He hadn't seen them since his mother's funeral, and that was four years ago now. He had called them early the next Saturday morning, hands sweating as he held his cell phone, afraid it was going to slip out of his hands. His sister's voice was soft and warm, and when she said his name it sounded like she was smiling. Of course, she had answered, Dad would love to see him. He hadn't been able to get around well after his last stroke, but seeing Tom would cheer him up.

Stroke? Tom hadn't even known his father had been sick at all! What must they think of him? He had not been around for them when they obviously needed him so much. He was angry with himself for how he had allowed unforgiveness to damage his life. Could it be too late to change course? "God, please help me to do this!" Tom prayed as he pulled up in front of his old home.

Walking up the sidewalk to the house felt to him like he was moving in slow motion. He wanted to hurry and get this over with, but he also wanted to prolong the time before he had to face his father and his sister and explain to them why he hadn't come to visit until now. By the time he reached the bottom step, though, his sister had run out onto the porch and then down the steps. Nearly knocking him off of his feet, she embraced him tightly.

"Tommy! Tommy!" She buried her face in his chest and kept repeating his name. It was as if she was ten again, instead of twenty-seven. He felt his chest shaking and realized that he was crying into her hair.

"Angeline, baby girl, it's so good to see you. I'm sorry I haven't come over sooner." His tears were now flowing and he was not ashamed.

"It's okay, Tommy! Come on in! Daddy has been waiting to see you!"

Tom was witnessing, firsthand, a miraculous demonstration of unconditional love! His sister had acted as if he had never before harmed her spirit. His father had embraced him, shaking, trying to talk but only able to manage a series of long moans punctuated with flailing hands that continued to try to rub Tom's forearms. He cried and cried the entire time that Tom was there.

Tom stayed for dinner and dessert, impressed with his sister's wit and amazed that some man had not yet come along to sweep her off of her feet. She was beautiful! Her hair was long and straight, her eyes were smoky and exotic, and she was built like a model. She had been content to go to nursing school for two years until her mother's death, and then she had dropped out to care for her father. Tom determined on the spot that he would hire an in-home health aide to care for their father full time so that Angeline could go back to school and begin to live her own life and achieve her own dreams.

"I'm sorry!" had changed his life. Those two words had reopened a door to relationships with his remaining family members. They had also healed his spirit and allowed him to release anger that had threatened to destroy his soul. His apologies to his father, sister, and God had given him a fresh start.

Tom had lost count of the number of times he had apologized to God. He probably had done it every day since the Sunday Pastor preached that message on asking for forgiveness. He knew he had offended God by his treatment of the cats, other people, and his own family. Most of all, though, he knew that in order to treat others right, he had to cultivate a real relationship with God. Realizing that he probably did something wrong every day, or maybe had forgotten to ask forgiveness for something he had done to someone in the past, he just kept apologizing to God. Lately, he felt like he could see God smiling each time he said, "Oh yeah God, I'm sorry about that, too!"

Tom also apologized to Brice when they met on that Friday night at Sal's. Brice needed a friend he could trust to help him walk through this difficult time in his life. Tom planned to introduce Brice to his pastor. From personal experience, he knew that conversations with a counselor could only take you so far. But, if you were able to practice having conversations with God in prayer, permanent changes would occur in your life. Tom knew that he had to be accountable for his adolescent actions if Brice was going to trust anything he had to share with him. It wasn't just about him anymore. He had to be there for others in any way they needed him, whenever they needed him. Others had done it for him, and he had to pass it on.

Tom picked up his cell phone and scrolled until he found Brice's number. "Hey man, how are you doing?" he said when Brice answered. "What are you up to today? Nothing much? Well, in that case, I was wondering if you, your wife, and your little girl want to hook up with me for dinner this evening, my treat! You would? That's cool! I had a sudden craving for another big plate of tacos!" Sharing a hearty laugh with Brice, Tom continued, "Yeah, man, so I thought you might want to join me in knocking those off. Figured we could show your little girl how we used to do it back in the day. Okay, I'll meet you guys there in an hour. Love you, man!"

Tom rubbed his hands together and then clapped them hard. He stood up, talking as he walked into his bedroom to get dressed for dinner. "Thank You, God, for helping me so that I can help somebody else. Thank You for healing me and healing my family. I know I'm not all the way there yet, but I'm a lot farther along than I used to be, and I know that is because of You. So, I can tell Brice and his wife about You and invite them to come to church with me, even if we just sit in the back and dip out after the message!" Tom chuckled and imagined he could hear God laughing, too.

He continued, "But, I know that You can do for him what You did for me. I know you can! As his friend, I have to make sure I do everything I can to give him a chance to get to know You so that You can help him like you helped me. Who knows, maybe his daughter will start singing in the choir!" Tom laughed out loud, and then finished his prayer with, "Who would have ever thought that a cat killer could become a missionary? Move over, Apostle Paul! There is hope for me yet! Amen!"

On Jordan's Stormy Banks I Stand

"Every word of God is pure: He is a shield unto them that trust His name." Proverbs 30:5

*

"One man's trash is another man's treasure. One man's poison is another man's pleasure." Trash. That is basically what he had called her. She felt her cheeks begin to flush as the memory of that last court date crept once again into her consciousness. How could he have been so cruel?

"Your Honor, I ask that my client be allowed to lower his alimony to $50.00 a week. Mrs. Wall has been a leech and a milksop for the past fifteen years. She has not worked a day in all that time. She is able-bodied and can support herself. My client has supported her for fifteen years. It is time for her to support herself."

Milksop? Who even used that word anymore? What was that supposed to mean? That she couldn't work because of his insecurities, not wanting her to have friends or talk to anyone socially? That he would rant like a madman if breakfast wasn't fixed by 7:30 a.m. and dinner by 5:30 every evening? And that he wouldn't allow a cleaning lady to come in because he didn't trust anyone in the house other than the two of them? How could she work and do all of the duties that he demanded she perform? And, wasn't he the one who told her that she could not work, ever, and he would pay the bills so he could have her stay home and watch the house?

She had realized not long after the honeymoon that he was insane. Oh, he could be a nice guy and he did take care of his business, but he had little idiosyncrasies that looped out to major mental disabilities as their years together progressed. It's a good thing that they never had any children, even though she had wanted a baby early in their marriage. Now, she couldn't imagine how dysfunctional that child would probably have been due to living in their unstable household.

She was grateful that the judge was not swayed by his silver-tongued attorney and had reviewed his portfolio before they appeared in court. She had wanted to laugh out loud when the judge had glared over his reading glasses at Sheldon and his attorney and then shook his head. The judge cleared his throat and then proceeded to tell those two that their proposal was not only unfair, but utterly ridiculous. If anything, he planned to increase the alimony to $5,000 a week. Due to the value of his business, his investments, their home, and the salary Mrs. Wall could have earned in fifteen years, it was evident to the judge that Sheldon owed her fifty percent of his total assets and $5,000 a week until her demise, whether she chose to remarry or not.

Geena had been completely shocked, though she fought hard to register no emotion when she heard the judge's words. For one reason, she was physically and emotionally tired. The divorce process had drained her spirit. She had little motivation to do anything in the six months since Sheldon had announced that he wanted to divorce her because he had fallen out of love with her. She doubted that he ever loved her and figured that he must have met someone else but wasn't man enough to disclose that, and she didn't care enough about the loss to force him to tell her the truth. The second reason that she maintained a passive face was that she didn't want him to see that she was happy or hurt by him. She was tired of him knowing that he could manipulate her every emotion, good or bad. She was just tired.

Sheldon, on the other hand, was furious! Neither he nor his lawyer had seen this coming. Both were fumbling on the table for papers and trying to stand up to address the judge, but he had already banged the gavel and was on his feet, turning to leave the courtroom. Both men kept calling, "Your Honor, Your Honor, Your Honor…" as he exited to his chambers.

Sheldon had turned to her, red and sweating bullets, and pointed his shaking index finger in her direction. His last words to her were, "You think you're getting half of my money? Never! You don't deserve it! You didn't earn a penny of it! All you did was sit around the house like a piece of dirt, a piece of trash! I won't stand for it! I won't!" At that point, his lawyer had grabbed his arm and pulled him from the courtroom.

As it turned out, he didn't know what he was talking about. Within a month, she and her lawyer had set up her financial business to accommodate her three million dollar windfall, and she was figuring how she would spend another five thousand every week. So, she had decided to take a vacation to clear her mind and heal her spirit.

Her parents used to bring her to this little seaside town every summer when she was a child. Those were some of the best memories of her life. They stopped coming when her father's railroad job caused the family to relocate to the West Coast and their beachside vacations were now in California. Still, it she found nothing to compare with the feelings of exhilaration she enjoyed in this setting. So, she had shut everything down for a month, rented a small cottage, and decided to get a grip on herself and her life before doing anything else.

She felt very sorry for Sheldon and was determined to not be bitter. She knew that would hurt her more than it would ever hurt him. But, she was hurt and not sure how she was going to get over that. Maybe if she had been unfaithful, or ungrateful, or messy, or negligent she could understand his displeasure with her. But, she had done everything he ever asked, she was always complimented by others for being a good wife, and he had never had a reason to distrust her in any way. She didn't deserve to be treated like this.

"I can sit around feeling sorry for myself, or I can get out and begin to discover myself and my life once again," she had told herself as she boarded the plane. Her head was hurting a little and she felt a cold coming on. She didn't want to be sick, though, so she tried to keep her mind flowing in a positive direction. It seemed she was always in a state of limbo lately, somewhere between depression and daily management. She wasn't ever happy, but she fought to not succumb to sadness. She kept telling herself that two or three months down the road, things would be different and she would feel different. But, there had been too many days of things not getting better at all.

She looked out the window when the plane climbed high enough to be over the clouds. Looking down, she wished she could jump out of the windows and bounce onto the bed of cotton ball clouds, have them cradle her to sleep softly, let her rest gently on them until she felt refreshed and whole. Rationality convinced her that she would just fall straight through and then splatter on top of someone's driveway, making the news and scaring someone's children to death when she dropped from the sky and landed at their feet while they were riding their Big Wheels up and down the driveway. At that thought, she had begun to quiver with inner laughter. Did kids even have Big Wheels anymore? The young Asian man sitting next to her had looked up from his magazine to give her a sideways glance. She knew her shoulders were hunching up and down from stifled laughter, but she couldn't help herself. Dead or alive, she had some issues.

Not wanting to make him uncomfortable too, Geena took a deep breath and quelled the laughter. She had felt hysteria creeping into her system and didn't want to alarm anyone if she were to have a breakdown. She pulled the complimentary airline magazine from the back of the seat in front of her and decided to read herself to sleep. "Time, I just need a little time to get myself together," she said to herself. Hopefully, that is just what she would have over the next four weeks. If not, she wasn't sure what would happen to her.

The cottage seemed like the perfect vacation spot; right on the water, the ocean a few steps from her front door. Secluded within a comfortable resort complex, she felt isolated and safe at the same time. "This is just what I need," she thought. There was a pool and weight room in the common facility that was two doors over. She didn't plan to visit either amenity, but it was nice to know that if she did want to see others while she was here, she could do so with very little effort.

Since no one knew her or Sheldon, she could be whoever she wanted for the next four weeks. That would have been impossible at home. Their divorce became a high profile community news item due to all of the money that was involved and Sheldon's angry outburst in the courtroom. After that, everywhere she went people were either whispering or looking at her with pity. She hadn't been sure of how she should react to either of these responses. She resolved that it really didn't matter. None of them were her friends, anyway. Sad to say, she really didn't have any friends.

Geena had never planned for her life to turn out this way. With lots of friend throughout public school and college, she had been very popular and socially involved. She met Sheldon in the fall of her senior year. He had transferred to the university to begin his MBA program. At that time, the university had offered a five-year graduate degree program, so he was accepted as a junior to begin his masters degree in his senior year. He was brilliant and charming.

He had been sitting in the courtyard in front of the bookstore one day. He looked lost. When she walked out of the bookstore, he called to her. He wondered if she could tell him the way to the cafeteria. She happened to be going in that direction, so she offered to walk him there. The rest became history. She was his only acquaintance on campus and soon became his only friend.

She should have wondered back then why he wanted to monopolize her time, why he complained when she spent time with her friends, why he acted so rude toward them when she tried to include him in the circle that they soon began to disassociate themselves from her, as well. Looking back, it seemed that he had a systematic plot to isolate her so that he could control her. It had worked for a decade and a half. Finally, she was free.

Geena wasn't sure how she would even assimilate back into normal society and build new friendships. She knew that she used to enjoy just listening to others share their stories about what was going on in their lives. She recalled enjoying the times when she and her friends would get together and laugh and talk into the wee hours of the morning. Sometimes, they would play board games or card games. The competition was hilarious and they would often not even worry about the score because the real fun was in the comical interchanges among the friends.

She wondered about some of her old college buddies. Where were they? Did they have families of their own now? What might they say if she reached back out to them after all of these years? Geena wasn't sure if she even knew how to contact any of them, it had been so long.

Geena had packed five books in her suitcase. She had planned to read each one of them during her vacation. They were all self-help books. One was about co-dependency. The jacket looked interesting: Cut the Cord and Let the Child Live. Who was the child? Her or Sheldon? So, that is why she wanted to read it, but it seemed kind of serious. She wanted something a little lighter to start off her vacation reading. The others looked equally engaging, but also just as therapeutic. She wanted something more entertaining.

Grabbing the Gideon Bible from the desk drawer in the cottage, she headed down to the beach, a large bathing towel slung over her shoulder. She remembered that the Old Testament had some exciting battle stories in it, plus characters that had gone through experiences that made for entertaining reading. People like Noah, David, Ruth, Abraham, and Absalom were characters whose lives had caused her imagination to soar as a child. She remembered spending hours reading a volume of Bible character stories, especially during her teen years. She used to wonder about the people who would say that all they read in their Bible was the 23rd Psalm. Why, when there was so much more? Maybe this was the kind of excitement that would get her blood flowing again.

Geena had committed her life to Christ during a summer youth camp when she was thirteen. It was a hot and hazy night, and the group had just sung a series of Christian camp songs in a large open covered space set on a raised concrete slab. They called it The Pavilion. With a soft wind gently blowing the warm evening air, the atmosphere was charged and the youth pastor had just shared a stirring testimony. He talked about God's love and how it had saved him from trouble. She wanted to be saved. They sang, "I Have Decided to Follow Jesus" as she walked up front with quite a few of the other teens. She was sincere when she repeated "The Sinners' Prayer" and she felt changed when she walked back to her seat on a wooden slat set up on four cinder blocks.

It did seem that God had been with her ever since, even though there were times when she may not have totally been with Him. Still, she had always felt blessed and she prayed a lot, though maybe not every day. But, it had been a long time since she had read her Bible, and even longer since she had attended a church. Sheldon did not want her to go to church and he refused to go himself, so she had soon settled into the routine of sleeping in late on Sundays and cooking him brunch instead of the usual 7:30 a.m. morning breakfast.

Something had been missing from her life for a long time. She couldn't, in all fairness, blame Sheldon. She could have insisted on going to church. God would have protected her. She had just given in, and now she wished she would have taken better spiritual care of herself.

Geena found a spot near the water where a patch of long, thick grass made a comfortable beachfront carpet. Looking out, she could see the shimmering overlay that was the reflection of the sun on the moving blue-green waters. Iridescence had always fascinated her. She loved seeing rainbows in things such as prisms, chandeliers, and diamonds. The colors were mesmerizing. They reminded her of Noah's story, so she decided to read that first. She was surprised by some elements of the story that she had forgotten, like what happened when he got drunk. But, what stood out to her most was the covenant God made with him and his descendants. He would never destroy them or their world again with water. The rainbow was the sign of that promise.

Looking out on the water, she saw both the tool of the world's destruction and the promise to Noah. "Nothing can harm you again," God seemed to be showing her. "My promise is on top of anything that could destroy you." Geena thought about Sheldon and wondered what had destroyed him. She thought about how she could have been destroyed by what she had gone through. Water supports life; but it can also destroy life. Life's experiences can make you or break you. "What makes the difference?" Geena questioned.

She closed the Bible and smoothed out the large towel, then lay back flat, facing the sun. She closed her eyes and willed the warmth to bake her brain, bake out all of the pressure and fogginess that had plagued her for so long. She wanted to be covered again by the promise, but she first needed to be rescued from drowning. She realized that she had been swirling for years, struggling to keep from spiraling downward to her destruction. For the first time in a long time, she felt like a lifeline had been thrown to her; and if she just grasped it and held on tight, she would come out of this whirlpool of helplessness and be saved.

"Save me," she whispered. "Save me, Lord," she spoke aloud. Something stirred in her spirit. The sun was warming her body and her forehead felt its pressure most. Not uncomfortable, but much like a massage, it seemed that clearer thoughts were rising to the crown of her head. She didn't want to open her eyes. She was afraid that the process would be aborted and she would not be able to get back to this place again.

She wanted to go through this process of rehabilitation, even through the fire if she must, in order to be restored. Money and all of the comforts it could afford were not going to help her. She needed for her spirit to be revived, to come alive again, to feel and to care, to open up to others and to be available to help them when needed, to rejoin the human family, to move forward from the past and press toward her own fulfillment. She needed to be saved from eminent death. She needed God and all of His promises.

When Geena finally opened her eyes, she realized that she must have fallen asleep for at least a couple of hours. A shower cloud was gathering. Stretching, she felt refreshed and clear-headed. Could it be that God had undone in a few hours the damage that had been created over the past fifteen years? That was impossible! Wasn't it? Geena heard a rumble of thunder and realized that she had better gather her towel and the Bible and head back to her cottage. Rising to her feet, she looked deep into the sky to see how far away the storm appeared.

There, high in the azure sky was a single black cloud. Trimming its edges was a silver frame, probably created by the reflection of the sun. But, streaking through the cloud was a shimmering array of blue, purple, pink, green, violet, orange, and yellow. Rainbow colors in her sky! Confirmation of God's promise that nothing could destroy her ever again. Just that sight was more affirming for her than any number of self-help books. It was a personal message to her from God.

Geena wanted to stop there on the shore line and cry. She was humbled, yet also relieved by just the sign of the rainbow. A gentle, cleansing, refreshing rain began to fall. Geena's tears mingled with the raindrops that struck her face. Thunder applauded, shaking the ground. The sound and the feel made her panic for a moment, and she was tempted to run toward the cottage, but she felt bold and safe. "Nothing can harm me!" she spoke loudly. "Nothing!" As if the storm cloud could hear her and respond, the rain stopped immediately.

Geena began to laugh, amazed at herself standing boldly in the midst of a thunderstorm. She then realized that these brief showers were common in this region. They would come and go within minutes, so this was no great miracle. "But it is a miracle," she said to herself. "God is showing me that He is in control of my life, not Sheldon or even me. If I trust Him, He will direct my life from here on. I don't have to worry. I am safe. I have been saved. Nothing will harm me ever again. I have a rainbow covering me!" Geena laughed loudly, tossed her towel around her shoulders like a cape, and strode confidently back up the walk to her cottage. Drying her face before ducking into the door, she noticed her beach towel was rainbow-patterned! "God, I love You!" she cried through her laughter and tears. "You're not just more than enough, You are too much!"

Love Lifted Me

"She will do him good and not evil all the days of her life." Proverbs 31:12

*

Lois emerged from a deep sleep with a smile on her face. "Turner..." she thought. "He's home." She had just been dreaming about him. They were riding down a beach front road in the yellow convertible roadster. The wind was blowing her hair straight back and she was looking straight ahead. Turner took her hand and held it securely, their fingers intertwined, as he skillfully guided the car with his left hand on the steering wheel. She felt warm and safe.

The next thing she knew, he was kissing her passionately. He smelled so good! Some earthy sweet European scent was soaked densely into his skin. She buried her nose in his neck and breathed in deeply. Oh, how much she loved him, she thought. She touched his face lightly, tracing his sculpted lips and working her index finger down to rest in the dip of his cleft chin. "My Turner..." she mumbled, cupping his face with her hand. "Turner!"

Lois woke herself up with her own voice saying, "Turner!" Her eyes flew wide open, and she looked around her room. She sat up quickly and turned her head from side to side. He was here! She could smell him! He had to be here! Panicking, she gripped her chest; then, she sank slowly back onto the pillows. Why? Why couldn't her dream have been reality and this reality of loss just a dream? Why did her precious Turner have to leave her after all of these years, after all that they had been through?

"God, why did you take him?" Making two hard fists, Lois pounded the soft fleece blanket on her lap until her upper arms felt fatigued. She was crying quietly, limitlessly, futilely. No amount of frustration and tears would ever bring him back. Turner was dead. "But he was so alive in my dream," she said quietly. "Turner, I need you!" Fresh tears began to flow. Lois hated that she had awakened from that beautiful respite. She wished that she could lie back down and force herself back into the dream, picking up where she left off. She wanted to say his name over and over until she fell asleep. She wanted to call him back. She wanted to smell his neck again.

Tears rolled from the sides of her face into her ears. Draining down into her ear canal, the moisture began to tickle. Lois sat up and turned her head from one side to another, then inserted her pinky finger into each ear and shook it quickly, loosening the clogged fluid and causing it to run back out. She felt ridiculously helpless. She knew that Turner would not want her to be acting like this. It was just so hard.

Her cell phone rang. She looked at the clock under the television. Seven-forty. Who would call her this time of the morning? Nobody but her sister. Lois loved her, but she irritated Lois to no end. She was so nosy, so intrusive. Lois had told her that she was going to be very busy for the next few days. She figured she would take the hint. Apparently not. Lois debated whether or not to answer the phone, but she knew her sister Rhonda. If she didn't answer it now, Rhonda would call back in ten minutes and then every ten minutes after that until Lois finally answered. She may as well get it over with.

Blowing her nose and wiping her cheeks, she picked up her phone and then slid the arrow to answer it. "Hello?" She hoped she sounded tired so that Rhonda would cut the conversation short. Lois wasn't feeling much like talking.

"Girl, what took you so long? I know you woke up at least fifteen minutes ago! Were you still in the bathroom? I can't believe you let this phone ring five times. I almost hung up! What you doing? You got some man up in there? Girl, you move fast! Turner just been gone a year next week." Rhonda began to laugh some raw, raucous laugh that was making Lois sick to her stomach. How dare she call with this mess first thing in the morning? Didn't she have any sympathy for her grieving sister? A man? How could she even form her mouth to say such a thing?

"Rhonda! Why are you calling me at this time in the morning? I really need to be getting ready for the day. I'll call you back later." She was about to hang up when Rhonda responded.

"All right, all right. I'm just trying to cheer you up, Girl! You've been in the dumps too long." Rhonda's voice softened. "I know you miss Turner, but he wouldn't want you walking around looking and acting like you are. He would want you to be happy for him! He's feeling no pain no more! He would want you to move on with your life, and that's why I'm calling."

"Oh no," Lois thought. "My sister the therapist. And she needs one more than anybody!" Lois could feel a headache coming on.

"Listen, Sis, my job is sending me to a conference in Florida next month. Everybody else was invited to take a spouse or friend since we met our sales quota for the last three quarters. Because I have neither, I'm taking you."

That was it! The last straw! Sputtering angrily, Lois asked, "Don't I have anything to say about that?"

"Nope," Rhonda replied. "I won't let you look a gift vacation in the mouth. Listen, there is no cost for the trip, plus they give us each one thousand dollars in spending cash. Look, you can treat me like a stranger once we get there, but I'm not going to let you say no. You are not the girl I grew up with. You are turning into some old withering widow who will die of a broken heart." Rhonda's voice began to quaver. She continued, "That's why I'm calling you. I have to turn in your name today. I'd rather kidnap you than lose you. I love you, Sis!"

Rhonda went silent. Lois hated this moment and the decision she knew she would make. How could she be happy without Turner, let alone go on a vacation? The thought of that felt like a betrayal of his memory. Why did Rhonda do this to her, especially on a morning when she had just relished in a dream of him that was so true-to-life that she had really smelled him!

"All right, Rhonda," Lois said with a sigh. "But, don't expect me to be good company. I don't even know why I'm agreeing."

"I do!" Rhonda exclaimed. "It's because you love your little sister and you have learned to listen to me because I always know what I'm talking about!" Lois could hear the smile in Rhonda's voice. She wondered what Rhonda was really up to this time. "Lo, I love you, Sis! I really do. I'm glad you said yes. Look, I'll call you later and give you more details, okay? Okay! Take care, love, and have a good day." Rhonda's voice took on a genuine tone. "You won't regret it, Sis. Promise!" She hung up the phone.

Lois sat holding the phone to her cheek for a few seconds. As her hand dropped, she thought about how their relationship had always been reversed. She was the older sister, but Rhonda had always bossed her around, taken care of her. "Oh, well, no point in trying to fix what's not broken," she said to herself. A week in Florida with Rhonda and her co-workers? What had she been thinking about when she agreed? Maybe a change.

Rhonda was fifteen and she was eighteen when she and Turner got married. Fresh out of high school, him heading into the military, she was looking forward to getting out of the house, out of the town, and into her own world. She was ready to travel and see new places. She loved Turner and Turner loved her. He and his love were all she needed. They had all grown up in this little town. They had all gone to Metropolitan all of their youth. Both sets of grandparents had been some of the first pastor's first members. Looking back, she realized that some of her life's finest memories had been made right there at Metropolitan. Good people who would love the death out of you. That is what she really needed right now, a whole lot of good Christian love.

But, a lot had changed at the church when she and Turner moved back to town a few years ago. The old pastor was dead. His nephew was the new pastor. He was a nice person and his sermons were good, but his wife was strange and there were many new people that they didn't know, making things awkward. The place looked the same, but the people were all different. She and Turner hadn't attended services enough times to decide whether or not they could adjust to the new Metropolitan, so they had just stopped going.

Then, all of a sudden, her world had bottomed out. Turner had gone to the VA hospital for his annual physical. His stomach had been giving him a little trouble and he figured he just needed a good laxative to clean out his plumbing, as he called it. When he got back home, he was quiet. He told her that she would have to drive him back tomorrow, because they were going to do a colonoscopy and he couldn't drive after it. She didn't ask too many questions because Turner always took care of himself, so she just said okay. That next day turned out to be the first of the worst days in her life.

The technician told her that they had seen something in Turner's colon that they wanted to check further. She asked right away if it was cancer. He had laid his hand on her arm and said that the doctor would talk to her soon. As a response to her distressed look, he added that colon cancer in men was usually treatable when it could be caught early. After weeks of trips back to the hospital every few days, they found out that Turner had terminal cancer. Not only was it in his colon, but in his liver, his gall bladder, his stomach, and his intestines. It had spread like wildfire, burning up his life and his insides all at the same time. Before she could gather her wits and realize that this was really happening to her and Turner, he was in hospice and then in the ground. Turner was snatched away from her before she could even get a fingerhold on him. So unfair, it was a nightmare that left her in limbo.

Rhonda had been with her every step of the way. She had taken off of work for three straight weeks, walking Lois through the last two weeks in the hospital and then hospice, and finally helping her through the small funeral service and burial. Turner had been his parents' only child, and she and Rhonda were their parents' only children.

Both sets of parents had died a few years back, each within a couple of months of the others. They were only in their seventies. Lois had expected that at least her mother would have lived a long time. She was a trim, muscular woman who stayed busy constantly until she died in her sleep of a heart attack. Their father died exactly six months later in his armchair. Rhonda had found him when he hadn't answered his phone all day.

Now, her precious Turner was with them. The thought of joining them all had become a preoccupation over the past few months, but what always pulled her back was her sadness at leaving Rhonda behind all by herself. Even though her baby sister knew how to get on her nerves, Lois really did love and appreciate her. Rhonda knew just how to pull her from her low moods, too. What meant even more to Lois was that Rhonda had always been right by her side, all of her life.

After she and Turner married, Rhonda figured out a way to spend every summer with them no matter what state they were living in from the time she was sixteen until she turned twenty-four. Somehow, she always convinced their parents that she deserved that summer trip, so they would pay the plane fare and all of her summer expenses. She would spend the time entertaining Lois and Turner, cleaning the house, coercing Lois into taking her to every mall in the area, researching tourist sites for her and Lois to visit on quick day trips while Turner was at work, and making Lois enjoy her so much that she would miss her for a month after she left.

As Lois slipped her sundress over her head and slid her feet into her sandals, she decided that time spent with Rhonda had never been disappointing. She would trust her again. God knew she needed to take a step toward restoration. Maybe Florida was the place to make that happen.

Her first stop was the lawyer's office to sign some papers that would transfer Turner's parents' house into her name. He had kept it to rent it out during vacation season, but she wasn't sure if she felt up to managing it on top of taking care of their own business. She had time to decide, though, before the property taxes were due.

Lois decided to stop by the store on her way home. She noticed this morning that the coffee tin was low and she didn't want to run out one morning when she could have some on hand if she planned ahead. It had been a while since she had been to town. Rhonda had done a great job of stocking her pantry on a regular basis. Lois realized that she was going to have to pick up the slack and take care of herself.

She parked in front of the grocery store. She had been going to "Bobby's" all of her life, at least since she was a little girl. "Bobby's" was a local fixture, and she liked Linc, the young guy that some people now called, "Bobby, Jr." He wasn't Bobby's son, but he was so much like him that he could have been. He knew how to treat customers, how to stock the favorites, and how to keep the store clean and well-organized.

She had actually known Linc's mother. It was tragic how she had died in a car accident coming home from the hospital when Linc was a newborn. Every time Lois saw him, she thought of his mother and felt very sorry for him. A motherless child. Still, he had to be one of the most caring people she had ever met. He seemed to be focused on dedicating himself to making sure others felt special.

Linc spotted Lois as soon as she walked into the door. He moved from behind the counter, came over to her, and gave her a big hug. She felt herself melting in his arms. It felt like Turner was hugging her. She wanted to cry.

"Good to see you, Miss Lois! I've been thinking about you." He squeezed her tight and then stepped back. "Uh, huh, you came in just in time. I was just getting ready to get in the truck with a box of Twinkies and come by the house to check on you!" He winked at her with a smile.

"Well, it's a good thing you didn't," she laughed, "cause I would have sent you right back for a gallon of milk to go with those Twinkies!" They laughed heartily. Boy, that felt good to Lois. She had needed that for a long time. She selected a cart from the group of three at the front of the store and then began perusing the aisles for a few staples. She browsed through a bin of cosmetics that were on display, choosing a few she thought she might use in Florida. "What? Am I really making plans to travel? I don't know if I'm ready for that yet." She started to put them back, but changed her mind. They might not be on sale if she waited until later.

Ribeye steaks were also on sale. She hadn't had a good steak in a long time. Charcoal-grilled with a tossed salad, rolls and iced tea, the thought was making her mouth water. Maybe she would cook a couple tonight for them to eat when Rhonda came by to tell her about the trip. "There you go, thinking about Florida again!" She rebuked herself. It was too soon to begin focusing on her own pleasures. Turner would be disappointed! Or, would he?

Wheeling up and down each aisle, Lois realized that she hadn't thought much about what Turner would think about anything she was doing with her life these days. Most of her thoughts had been on herself. Would Turner have approved of that? He was always one to think of others, to put them first. He wasn't very patient with selfish people. Even though he had been an only child, he had never been spoiled. His parents had gone overboard in teaching him to share. That training had carried over to his adult life. He was always giving to others, and that is what seemed to make him most happy. Even in his last days before death, he had told her a joke every day, most of them terribly corny, but all of them designed to make her laugh. He would push past his inner torment and pain to laugh with her. That was Turner. It was always about the ones he loved and never about himself.

It hit her like a ton of bricks. If he had taught her anything, he had taught her that. What was she doing moping around looking like Old Mother Hubbard? So focused on her pain that she had lost touch with life? Turner would have wanted her to live and to connect with others, to laugh with Linc and to travel with Rhonda. To meet the people who rented his parents' house for the summer and to bring little gifts to their children, if they had any. To volunteer at the girls' school and to cook for the elderly that came to the community center every Wednesday. To get busy doing something for someone else and not pine her life away. Why, if she sat around until she died of boredom and mental exhaustion, she could imagine what he would say when he met her at the Pearly Gates. And, it might include some choice words that would cause him to lose his seat in the heavenly choir! Lois smiled to herself as she picked out some fresh fruit. The thought of Turner blessing her out tickled her!

Life after death seemed much more attractive the way she thought about it now. And, Linc seemed to be in partnership with Turner, pointing people's attention to planning for the afterlife. She had noticed a basket of gold fishing hooks on the store's checkout counter a few weeks ago.

Linc had explained, "This crazy old guy came in about a year ago, ranting and raving about this girl I used to date. If anybody needed Jesus, he sure did! When he left, there was a gold fish hook lying on the floor where he had been standing. I picked it up and wondered what it could mean. Why did he drop it? Was he leaving me some kind of masked threat, or was God leaving me a message? Maybe. Jesus was a fisherman. He went all out for souls! Walked on water and everything!"

Linc paused to laugh, but then continued. " Was that what I was supposed to be doing? I knew I wasn't a preacher like Rev. Patterson. I'm still trying to memorize 'The Lord's Prayer'!" He chuckled again and Lois had smiled and gave him a pitying nod. Then, he became very serious. "But Miss Lois, I have some friends who are struggling to get their lives on track, like I was. And, the guy who dropped the gold fish hook looked like he was headed straight to Hell. So, I decided to assume it was a challenge from God. I decided to use it to witness as best I could. I decided to give them away free."

He pointed to the little "Free" sign in a basket of gold fish hooks. "Some people might use them to fish. Some may think they are just cute little collectibles. But, everyone who asks gets a lesson on the love of God and what He has done for me in the past year." With a big smile, he added, "Every time someone takes one, I pray that they will be the one to lead that crazy guy to Christ!"

Lois had taken a gold fish hook and hung it on a small string that dangled from her rearview mirror. Each time she looked at it, she thought about Linc's testimony. And about Turner.

Linc walked toward her. "Miss Lois, you sure look pretty today! I think you just came in here to make me smile!"

"It's the other way around, Linc! I came in here today because I knew you would make _me_ smile!" She parked her cart at the register.

"Well, either way, it worked! Say, Miss Lois, I was just talking about you a couple of days ago. You know, we have this new ministry at church that I think you would be perfect for! You know that nobody makes stew and cornbread like you! I remember you brought me some when you heard I had been sick. I got well overnight! Well, they are starting to feed the homeless every day at noon. They need a good cook who doesn't have a day job." Linc looked down, and then continued, "I thought about you. I know you might want to be busy these days. What do you think?"

Lois wondered what she really did think. She hadn't planned on this avalanche of decision-making today. First Turner, then Rhonda, and then Linc. Turner. What would he expect her to say in response? She could almost hear his voice. 'Do it, Lo! You know you need to get busy! Don't make me fuss at you!'

"How many days a week, Linc?" She held her breath, now unsure if this was really something she was ready for.

"How many days, Miss Lois? Every day! Folks got to eat every day the Lord sends. And, they'll live to eat another day if they are eating your good cooking! Tell you what, all you have to do is set your menus. I will bring all of the ingredients every Monday, fresh and ready for your gifted hands. Then, I'll show up every day for lunch to do my taste tests!" Linc laughed loudly. It was infectious. Suddenly, Lois was laughing, too. "How does that sound, Miss Lois?"

Truly, the Lord works in mysterious ways. She wanted to say no, but her mouth was so contorted with laughter from looking at Linc make all those crazy faces that all she could do was nod her head and say, "Haaa, haaaa, yaaaa!" That made her laugh even more, and soon tears were running down Linc's face. Lois was holding her stomach now. It had been so long since she had laughed like that, her muscles were hurting. She wanted to stop, but couldn't. The more she laughed, the more he laughed. It's a good thing no one came into the store. They would have thought that Miss Lois and Linc had been sampling the cooking sherry from Aisle Seven. What they wouldn't have known was that they were drunk with the promise of life, that joy that flows when you know that worry is left in yesterday and hope is the substance of your tomorrows.

Back to church, helping people, conquering the pain of loss, comforted by Turner, embraced by Rhonda, rescued by Linc, so much had happened in just a few hours. Driving home with the top down on her memory-rich yellow roadster, Lois began to sing a song she hadn't thought of in decades. From somewhere, it had just dropped into her spirit suddenly. The lilting timbre of her strong soprano carried the heart-felt tune out of the car and into the heavenly realm on a wave of conviction, blown by gentle sea winds to ears that had been yearning a long time to hear that voice bear a song of praise. Had God opened Lois' eyes to see the great cloud of witnesses hovering over the balustrade in Glory cheering her on to victory, she would have known that Turner stood in the forefront, a smile as big as the sun shining on her as she registered her recognition of the route that was leading her to finally being prepared to live until the moment she would meet him again one day ~

"Love lifted me! Love lifted me! When nothing else could help, love ~ lifted ~ me!"

ABOUT THE AUTHOR

Dr. Beryl Ann New is living proof of God's amazing grace. A career educational leader in Topeka, Kansas, she is also an avid writer, composer, playwright, and poet. She is married, has eight grown children, and thirteen grandchildren. Loving them is her passion. God is her eternal inspiration. "I have trusted in Him with all of my heart since 1972 and chosen to obey Him rather than lean to my own understanding. I have acknowledged Him in all of my ways, and He has faithfully directed my path!"